EMPLOYMENT without
INFLATION

EMPLOYMENT without
INFLATION

BENJAMIN HIGGINS

TRANSACTION PUBLISHERS

NEW BRUNSWICK (U.S.A.) AND LONDON (U.K.)

Copyright © 1998 by Transaction Publishers, New Brunswick, New Jersey 08903.

All rights reserved under International and Pan-American Copyright Conventions. No part of this book may be reproduced or transmitted in any form or by any means, electronic or mechanical, including photocopy, recording, or any information storage and retrieval system, without prior permission in writing from the publisher. All inquiries should be addressed to Transaction Publishers, Rutgers—The State University, New Brunswick, New Jersey 08903.

This book is printed on acid-free paper that meets the American National Standard for Permanence of Paper for Printed Library Materials.

Library of Congress Catalog Number: 97-16702
ISBN: 1-56000-259-X
Printed in the United States of America

Library of Congress Cataloging-in-Publication Data

Higgins, Benjamin Howard, 1912–
    Employment without inflation. / Benjamin Higgins.
        p.   cm.
    Includes bibliographical references and index.
    ISBN 1-56000-259-X (alk. paper)
    1. Unemployment—Effect of inflation on.   2. Employment (Economic theory).   3. Inflation (Finnance)   4. Fiscal policy.   5. Full employment policies. I. Title.
HD5710.H54   1997
331.13'72—dc20   97-16702
                                                                     CIP

Contents

Part V: Policy

Preface

This book has been long in the making. I actually began writing it in 1978, when I was at the University of Ottawa, and Consultant to Public Works Canada, under a brilliant, imaginative, but controversial Assistant Deputy Minister for Corporate Planning, Douglas Hartt. In 1979 PWC published my monograph *Growth and Stability in Construction,* dealing with unemployment and inflation in Canada. It showed that in recent decades the government had acted as a destabilizer of the Canadian economy, by pursuing a *cyclical* pattern of public spending instead of a *counter-cyclical* policy. It argued that by an appropriate policy of timing *and placing* public works expenditure, the public works program could eliminate about half the country's unemployment, and reduce inflationary pressure as well (and, incidentally, reduce regional disparities). Later that year I had the opportunity to defend my thesis before the Senate Finance Committee. My report caused a considerable stir in the media, but elicited howls of rage from the Treasury, the Ministry of Finance, the Privy Council, and the Bank of Canada. ("What does *Public Works* think it is doing meddling in monetary and fiscal policy?")

It was at this time that I first met Gaston Haddad Luthi, who has had more influence on this book than any other single person. In 1978 he was a member of the same "brain trust" in PWC as I was, and he was simultaneously writing a Ph.D. dissertation under my direction at the University of Ottowa, on *Business Cycle Theory and Stabilization in a World of Shifting Trade-Off Curves*. Luthi and I have continued working together on unemployment and inflation ever since, at PWC, the University of Ottawa, the Canadian Institute for Research on Regional Development, L'Université de Sainte Anne, and the Australian National University. As I say in chapter 11 of the present volume, it is becoming difficult to say which of us had what idea first, but certainly the idea of the "topocross," which I use in that chapter, is his and his alone. He has also carried the idea of "hysteresis," in the form of cyclical loops, further than I have yet dared to do.

A third factor in shaping this book has been growing dissatisfaction with simple Keynesian macroeconomics as an explanation of what was really going on in the world, especially with respect to economic fluctuations, unemployment, and inflation. Policy prescriptions based on the hypothesis that most countries faced *either* inflation *or* unemployment at any time, which could be cured by either budget surpluses *or* deficits, were obviously wide of the mark. I became convinced that in order to deal with the various combinations of inflation and unemployment that existed in reality it would be necessary to disaggregate national economies into smaller regional units, and to differentiate policies among regions according to whether they were generators of inflation or pools of protracted unemployment.

As Luthi and I looked longer and harder at relations between unemployment and inflation in various countries since 1950, we found that, far from the stability of the famous "Phillips Curve" (relating wage increases to unemployment in the United Kingdom from 1862 to 1957), the Phillips Curves or trade-off curves since 1950 displayed a high degree of instability. If we are to explain the relationship between unemployment and inflation since 1950, we must explain the *shifts* of Phillips or trade-off curves, as well as their existence, their positions, and their configuration.

It has always puzzled me that on the whole, the economics profession has paid so little attention to trade-off curves. True, during the years following the publication of Phillips's seminal article, a number of quantitatively minded economists showed an interest in producing econometrically derived Phillips or trade-off curves for countries other than the United Kingdom. But when it became clear that these curves did not follow any long-run empirical law after 1950, most of these economists lost interest in them. Some of them sought refuge in the "nonaccelerating-inflation rate of unemployment" (NAIRU), arguing in effect that no truly involuntary unemployment exists anyhow. Some maintained that the only way to reduce the NAIRU is to fight inflation and eliminate inflationary expectations.

Fortunately, there was another group of economists, and theirs was the line of thought that I followed. This group was primarily interested in development of underdeveloped countries, and in regional development planning as an instrument of national economic development. The 1970s and early 1980s could be considered the "golden age" of regional development planning. This was the period when the United Nations established the United Nations Centre for Regional Development in Nagoya, Japan, and the program of research on regional development, under the direction of Antoni Kuklinski, at the United Nations Research Institute for Social Development in Geneva. It was also a period when a growing number of less developed countries embarked on programs of regional development as part of their national planning exercise, and a growing number of bilateral aid agencies evinced interest in providing assistance for regional development.

Around the two United Nations institutions there grew up a "community of scholars" from both underdeveloped and industrialized countries, who met frequently at various seminars, conferences, and training programs. We soon learned that those of us who came from industrialized countries were learning more from than we were teaching to our colleagues from the third world. The latter had the same kind of formal training and read the same literature as we did, but whereas the profession of regional planning in advanced countries stood a bit apart from those who were engaged in policymaking at the national level, in the LCDs regional planning became an integral part of national planning.

And so was born the concept of planning national and regional economies *together,* in such a way as to assure the stabilisation and growth of *both.* Such an approach requires thorough knowledge of national and regional economies, and of *differences* among the latter; differences that would permit the cooling off of regional economies that were overheating and generating inflationary pressure, at the same time that regions with chronic unemployment were speeded up. In this fashion, unemployment and inflation can be tackled together, and regional disparities as well.

Hence the title of this book: *Employment Without Inflation.* I considered first the more prosaic title, *Unemployment and Inflation;* but that title does not convey accurately the true objective of the book, which is to convey the message that by disaggregating national economies into the widely differing regional economies that compose them, it *is* possible to reduce unemployment without adding to inflationary pressures. True, *Employment Without Inflation* may sound a bit too much like a "How-To" book, given the limitations on the current state of our knowledge when confronting such an enormous and complicated task. But *Unemployment and Inflation* may sound a bit too much like the books already published under that or a similar title, a bit humdrum if not "ho-hum."

This book seeks to marry macro-economics with regional economics, in a fruitful union, even if we cannot at this moment foretell precisely what the progeny will be with complete certainty. But at least the suggestions made in this book, if acted upon, would carry us closer to the ideal of "full employment without inflation: than we have ever been since World War II.

Part I

Introduction

1

From "Business Cycles" to Shifting Trade-Off Curves and Loops

In the period between the two world wars, few matters concerned the economics profession, and those involved in making economic policy, more than *business cycles* (or in the United Kingdom, the *trade cycle*). Some preferred the term *economic fluctuations,* on the grounds that the alternations of inflation and unemployment were not regular or uniform enough to justify the term *cycle.* In any case, however, it was recognized that in industrialized capitalist countries (ICCs) or "advanced market economies," there had been, at least since the end of the Napoleonic wars, fairly regular, or at least intermittent, periods when prices, output, incomes, and employment rose together, and other periods when all these things fell and unemployment increased. Apart from the suffering that either inflation or unemployment may bring, these fluctuations bothered economists because they weren't supposed to happen. According to the dominant neoclassical economic theory of that era, the *natural* tendency of the economies of ICCs was toward equilibrium with full employment and without inflation; and if some outside shock to the economic system dislodged it temporarily from equilibrium—a war or revolution, a natural disaster, a major technological innovation or resource discovery—the *natural* tendency was for the economic system to move automatically, rapidly, and smoothly back to equilibrium.

Nonetheless, the cycles or fluctuations were there, and in the interwar period seemed to be getting worse. They were consequently an intriguing but irritating puzzle to the economics profession. Since they ought not to exist, *somebody* or *something* must be preventing the economy from functioning as it should. But who or what? A vast literature accumulated, attempting to provide answers to these questions, as we shall see below.

3

Toward the end of the Great Depression of the 1930s, a startling new concept was introduced into the economic literature, notably by John Maynard Keynes in the United Kingdom and Alvin Hansen in the United States: equilibrium with full employment and without inflation was not "natural" at all in ICCs. On the contrary, equilibrium could be established with large-scale unemployment, and the natural tendency at full employment levels of income was for people to try to save more than private entrepreneurs were willing to invest, so that total spending, incomes, and employment would fall, and unemployment rise, until enough saving was squeezed out so that investment would once again equal savings. That was the bad news. But the new theories brought good news as well: the unemployment natural to mature capitalist economies could be prevented, or at least offset, by a combination of an easy money policy and—more importantly—a fiscal policy that would raise incomes by cutting taxes, increasing government expenditures, or both.

Just after World War II, Roy Harrod in the United Kingdom, Evsey Domar in the United States, and others, elaborated these new ideas into the *knife-edge theory*. This theory stated requirements for steady growth, with full employment and no inflation, so stringent as to make it appear not just unnatural, but extremely unlikely, unless monetary, fiscal, and other economic policies were remarkably astute and flexible. But there was good news with the knife-edge theory too. Such a constellation of policy was difficult, but not impossible. In fact, something like it had been pursued during World War II and during the postwar reconstruction period. The war had been fought with full employment and almost no inflation, and the transition to peacetime economies was achieved without much unemployment. It appeared that advanced and "mature" economies could be so managed that the cycle of alternating inflation and unemployment could be largely ironed out. Thus, it could behave *almost* as though equilibrium with full employment and without inflation were a natural state of affairs.

Alas, after the war came a series of rude shocks. First, as wartime controls were abandoned and monetary policy continued to aim at low interest rates to speed reconstruction, several of the former Allied Nations experienced severe inflation. Then, in the mid- to late 1950s came a still more shocking observation: the inflation was not reducing unemployment. On the contrary, in a good many countries, inflation and increasing unemployment were taking place together.

In 1958, A. W. Phillips of the London School of Economics published a seminal article on the long-run relationship between changes in wage rates and unemployment in the United Kingdom. (Phillips, 1958) This relationship was immediately labelled "the Phillips curve." Similar relationships were found for other countries. Then, since it was well-known that wages and prices tend to move closely together, several people began looking into the relationship of unemployment to increases in the price level (Lipsey, 1960; Phelps, 1970, 1967; Friedman, 1977; Okun, 1975; Bodkin et al., 1966). This relationship was labelled the *trade-off curve,* or TOC. Interest shifted from the Phillips curve to the trade-off curve, because the latter seemed to represent a genuine policy option. Wage increases are not a bad thing in themselves, but rather, something devoutly to be wished. Inflation and unemployment, however, are both bad things; and the concept of a trade-off curve seemed to suggest that governments could choose between a bit more inflation and less unemployment, or a bit more unemployment and less inflation. It even seemed to offer them an excuse for not tackling both at once.

The trade-off curve, however, still treats more inflation or more unemployment as alternatives. Behind it lurks still a concept of a *cycle* of alternating periods of rising prices with falling unemployment, and periods of falling prices with rising unemployment. The TOC concept cannot deal with periods when both move together. By the same token, it cannot offer any ideas as to policies that would tackle both together. No government, capitalist or socialist, has yet found a means of tackling simultaneous inflation and unemployment, let alone simultaneously increasing inflation and unemployment. By and large, most governments have not even tried. They have limited themselves instead to trying to find the best possible point on the TOC confronting them at each point of time. The essentially conservative governments that have prevailed in ICCs in recent decades—like the Reagan-Bush administrations in the United States, the Thatcher government in the United Kingdom, the Mulroney administration in Canada, the Hawke-Keating administration in Australia, and the Lange government in New Zealand—in determining what is the "best" position on the TOC at each point of time, have given considerably more weight to containing inflation than to fighting unemployment.

Moreover, professional economists have devoted very little time and effort to the discovery of the *causes* of simultaneous, and simultaneously increasing, unemployment and inflation. Not having ideas about the causes, they have, as a consequence, had no clear policy recommendations for curing both maladies at the same time. Some have taken refuge in the concept of "the natural rate of unemployment," including the Economic Council of Canada (Economic Council of Canada, 1990; Miller, 1987) At first, the natural rate of unemployment was defined as the level consistent with stable price levels; but efforts to quantify this concept led to estimated natural rates of unemployment so horrifyingly high that many economists retreated to a definition of the natural rate as the level of unemployment consistent with no *acceleration* of the rate of inflation. Even this concept leads to estimates that are disturbingly high, especially in the relatively retarded regions of countries like Canada. F. C. Miller calculates a natural rate of unemployment for Canada as a whole, in 1983, of 9.2 percent, as compared to an actual rate of 11.9 percent, and calls the difference of 2.7 percent "cyclical." For the Atlantic provinces in the same year, however, his estimated natural rate is 10.5 percent, compared to an actual rate of 15.0 percent, giving a "cyclical" rate of 4.5 percent. Obviously, the term *natural* (invented by Milton Friedman) is designed to suggest that it is really alright, just the way that a free market works in a democratic society; or at least that there is little to be done about it. Only the relatively small "cyclical" portion can be treated by monetary and fiscal policy (Miller, 1987).

Miller, to his credit, doesn't say *quite* that. He does say:

> Given this high amount of structural unemployment, a policy of stimulating aggregate demand to combat unemployment would have served only to drive up prices without doing very much to reduce unemployment. (73)

He goes on, however, to make a case for tackling structural unemployment and lowering the "equilibrium rate of unemployment" by measures other than monetary and fiscal policy, such as market-oriented manpower retraining programs, improving labor mobility, and "tightening up the Unemployment Insurance Act," lowering benefits and making them harder to get.

It will be a major conclusion of this book that while not much can be done through regionally differentiated *monetary* policy, a great deal can be done by regionally differentiated *fiscal* policy, to reduce unemployment, inflation, and regional disparities all at once. Reaching this conclusion, however, will require pursuing a long and somewhat tortuous route. First we must have a look at prewar business cycles, the major theories that were evolved to explain them, and the kind of policy recommendations that emerged from these theories. We will find that nearly all these theories made some sense in a world of recurring alternations between unemployment and inflation. We will find, moreover, that these theories are not totally wrong, even in today's world of shifting trade-off curves and loops. They are only incomplete and, consequently, an inadequate base for policy prescriptions. Then we shall look at the postwar world to determine precisely how and why it has changed. We shall take a particularly hard and long look at the manner in which regional disparities of all kinds, and differences in degree of regional integration and disintegration among various countries, and among regions of the same country, affect the height, position, slopes, configuration, and shifts of trade-off curves. We shall find that these regional differences have much to do with the nature, scope, and intensity of the problem of simultaneous inflation and unemployment and that, consequently, this problem can be tackled adequately only if at least part of the policy is cast in regional terms.

The main thesis of this book, then, is that when the causes of simultaneous unemployment and inflation, and of fluctuations of both of these, are properly understood, regional policy, rather than being at the periphery of efforts to achieve steady growth of the national economy, is at their very core. The unsatisfactory macroeconomic performance since 1950, with respect to growth of Gross Domestic Product, inflation, and unemployment, is to be explained in large measure in terms of the regional disintegration of the economy. At the same time, however, the regional differences afford opportunities, through policies differentiated in space as well as in time, to accelerate growth, reduce unemployment and inflationary pressure, and to diminish regional disparities, all at once.

Business Cycles in Theory and Reality, 1815–1950

Economists like to think of themselves as pure, positive scientists, plugging away in their laboratories like physicists or biologists, and gradually adding to the store of knowledge. The reality is different. In the first place, in contrast to the natural sciences, where new discoveries are usually additions to old ones, in economics "new knowledge" frequently displaces and replaces "old knowledge."

In the second place, in economics much more than in natural sciences, the direction of "scientific" investigation is determined by what is going on *outside* the laboratory. Nowhere is this fact more glaringly apparent than in the field of economic fluctuations and growth. The Classical School, writing in a period that saw the height of the industrial revolution, the settlement of the new world, and the first wave of imperial expansion, were primarily interested in growth, or more broadly in "development," in the sense of "the wealth of nations," or general improvement in human welfare. Indeed, they virtually identified "political economy" with the economics of development in this broad sense. Yet the "business cycle," in the form in which it was to persevere until World War II, appeared immediately after the Napoleonic Wars. Indeed, there are striking similarities between the economic history of western Europe and the United States from 1812 to 1860 and from 1913 to 1940: inflation during the war; a sharp drop in prices and recession after it; a rapid though incomplete recovery; then a boom lasting several years led by the stock market; and finally the stock market crash, collapse of the financial system, widespread bank failures, bankruptcies and massive unemployment; leading to deep and prolonged depression. Yet, the classical economists, except to some extent Malthus and Marx, paid little attention to all that. "Panics" were regarded as aberrations, somehow centered in a faulty financial system and to be cured by reforms of that system (such as the Bank Charter Act of 1844 with its "100 percent reserve system"). Little effort was made to provide a systematic theory of recurrent unemployment and inflation, or business cycles, or to relate such theory to the general body of received economic doctrine.

Except for Jevons, with his "sunspot" theory of the trade cycle, tracing economic fluctuations to sunspots and the rainfall cycle, the first generation of neoclassical economists, following the "marginal revolution" of the 1870s, hadn't much to say about unemployment and inflation either. They were, to be sure, interested in the determinants of the general price level, as well as individual values and prices, but little of their time and energy was devoted to explaining recurrent economic fluctuations. Jevons's theory was not quite so "way out" as it seemed at first blush, as we shall see below. (At certain stages of economic development the rainfall cycle can indeed generate general fluctuations in economic activity). But it gained little credence at the time, or since. For the most part, except for some Marxists, the economists of the last quarter of the nineteenth century continued to talk of "panics" and "crises," which were considered abnormal deviations from the expected smooth operation of a market economy.

They can be forgiven. The western European, North American, and Australasian economies at the time were working rather well. It was a period of global expansion, relatively steady growth with high levels of employment and fairly stable prices, rapid technological progress and rising living standards. The low rates of interest and profits that led to references to a "great depression" reflected a rapid rate of capital accumulation, growth of output, and a gently sagging price level. Economists could indulge their fascination with marginal utility, cost curves, demand and supply, value and price, with a clear conscience, confident that their world was getting better and better without their help.

World War I had a cataclysmic effect on many aspects of western civilization and culture, and economics was no exception. The war put an end to the comfortable confidence in steady economic progress. The inflation during the war was disruptive enough to cause deep concern. In postwar Germany, hyperinflation was catastrophic, and paved the way for Hitler. Great Britain never really recovered from the primary postwar recession. Unemployment continued high right through the 1920s, and balance of payments pressures were chronic. Even in the United States, the so-called boom was largely confined to the stock market. The 1920s were actually a period of rather slow growth, and in the southeast and southwest regions of the United States, per capita incomes actually fell. After the 1921–1923 recovery, the price level fell slightly. The stock market boom ended in the Great Crash of 1929, ushering in the Great Depression of the 1930s.

The economics profession responded to the disturbances of the 1920s by directing a much larger share of its energies to problems of unemployment, inflation, and economic fluctuations. Major works appeared in the United Kingdom, the United States, and Germany devoted entirely and systematically to this set of problems: R. G. Hawtrey, Arthur Spiethoff, Irving Fisher, Gustav Cassel, J. M. Keynes, D. H. Robertson, Warren and Pearson, Adolph Lowe, and Emil Lederer, were among the contributors. These works constituted the platform from which the more complete and refined analyses of the 1930s were launched.

And then, of course, came the Great Depression in which the capitalist world was so badly shaken that it seemed for a while as though it must disappear. The economics profession was quite unprepared for it. None of the works of the 1920s were complete enough, clear enough, or convincing enough to serve as a basis for policy. They seemed, moreover, to contradict each other. The author arrived at the London School of Economics as a graduate student in September 1933, in the depths of depression. The London School of Economics was one of the great centers of business cycle theory at the time, with Friedrich von Hayek, J. R. Hicks, Nicholus Kaldor, Abba Lerner, and Lionel Robbins. To me, as to countless others, what was thought and taught about the Great Depression at the time seemed like hopeless confusion. When I arrived three years later at the University of Minnesota, another leading center of business cycle theory, (Alvin Hansen, Arthur Marget, Oskar Morgenstern, Eugen Altschul), it was little better. We had not yet absorbed the implications of Keynes's *General Theory*. It had just been published, and at Minnesota the economists were still busy attacking Keynes's *Treatise on Money,* which had been published four years earlier. It was hard to assess the conflicting claims of the London School, the Cambridge School, the Stockholm School, the German School, the Harvard School, and the Yale School to have the right solution. As graduate students we had a sneaking, disquieting suspicion that all of them could be wrong. It never occurred to us that they might all be right.

One of the major troubles with the economics profession of the 1930s, a difficulty still with us fifty years later, was that economists, in their passionate desire to emulate the physicists, hoped and even expected to find uniformities in the universe of the global economic system, "laws" true always and everywhere. A second difficulty, related to the first, but fortunately relegated to the background since Keynes's *General Theory,* was that economists expected the economic system to move always toward equilibrium; and believed that at the macro-level equilibrium would bring full employment without inflation. The two beliefs together led quite naturally to the conclusion that, considering the massive unemployment of the Great Depression, there must be some *one* reason why the machine was not working properly, some *one* impediment to the equilibrating forces, just as there is usually some *one* reason when an expensive and well-kept car won't start or when a healthy person has a fever. Thus, there could be only *one* among the several rival theories of economic fluctuations that could be correct.

We understand better today that full employment without inflation is a rare and accidental happening, a condition likely to be achieved for any length of time only by the most astute and thorough management of the economy. There are many things that can go wrong with an economy, just as there are with a car or a person, no matter how new and expensive, or basically healthy, they are. The leading business cycle theorists of the 1930s were both brilliant analysts and keen observers of the real world. As we shall see in chapter 2, all of them were essentially right, in the sense that all of them explained *one* of the ways in which an unregulated market system can go wrong; if the system doesn't get stuck on a sandbar it can hit a submerged rock or go over a waterfall. But in the mid 1930s, we were not ready for such heretical ideas. We were determined to find *the* theory of economic fluctuations that provided *the* explanation that was *both* necessary *and* sufficient. Once we had *the* theory, we would know exactly what to do to remove the roadblock to full employment without inflation.

And then, in 1936, came Keynes's *General Theory* and the storm of controversy that followed. At the time the *General Theory* seemed to many of us—young as well as old—to be difficult, strange, iconoclastic, probably wrong, hard to accept. But our conversion was quick. By the time World War II came along, the Keynesian theory had been accepted, elaborated, refined, improved. It had been applied in many countries to overcome continuing unemployment and it became the basis in all the Allied Nations of policies for fighting World War II without inflation and getting through the postwar transition period without another great depression.

Once understood, the Keynesian system turned out to be elegantly simple, and its major policy implications even simpler: treat unemployment with budget deficits and easy money at low interest rates; treat inflation with budget surpluses and tight money at high interest rates. The prescription seemed to work very well. By the time the war began, deficit spending and cheap money in the Allied Nations—and Germany, too—had drastically cut unemployment. War time spending and continued low interest rates soon changed the remaining unemployment into a labor shortage. With a combination of Keynesian policies and direct controls, World War II *was* fought without inflation; for six years the goal of full employment without inflation was attained, and other goals too, such as improved distribution of income among regions and social groups. There was a brief spurt of inflation as controls were lifted after the war and monetary policy was directed toward keeping interest rates low to speed the transition; but there was no postwar recession. The 1950s and 1960s were the longest period of *nearly* steady growth since the late nineteenth century, and growth was much more rapid than anything seen before. One economist wrote a whole book on the "puzzle": given the knife-edge theory, how come the economy is actually so stable (Cornwall, 1972)?

But then in the mid 1950s, we gradually became aware of a new and different problem: despite the good performance of the western economies both inflation and unemployment refused to go away. Worse, both seemed to be becoming more severe; unheard of, unimagined, there were periods when *both increased together,* and the trend was toward aggravation of both. This phenomenon was something completely outside the Keynesian book. The Keynesian system and the policies derived from it is designed to combat unemployment *or* inflation. It cannot fight both together. Thus, just as we thought we had the economic system pinned down and the problem of assuring "steady growth" solved, we were presented with a system that behaved in a totally new way; and, moreover, a way for which we were totally unprepared.

Plan of this Book

The principal aim of this book is to discover, explain, and recommend policies that are capable of dealing adequately with the problems of unemployment and inflation in the real world of today. These are horrendous monsters, and it is advisable to approach them slowly and cautiously. We reserve the discussion of actual policies for the last three chapters but one. In the next chapter we present some of the most important business cycle theories that prevailed before World War II. These theories still contain large chunks of truth, and the knowledge contained in them, and the tools of analysis utilized, are necessary for a complete understanding of the basic mechanism of the economies of the industrialized capitalist countries (ICCs) today, and still underlie their functioning. In chapters 3 and 4, we present the consolidation of "post-Keynesian economics" that took place between the late 1930s and the early 1950s. This consolidation was more a matter of tackling the problems of the period, with more sophisticated tools and a better sense of reality, than it was of tackling the new problems of the late 1950s on. These tools are also essential for the attack on today's problems, but they do not constitute a complete toolkit for dealing with them.

With part II and chapter 5 we enter today's world; and a strange new world it is. We find ourselves confronted not only with simultaneous unemployment and inflation, but with simultaneously increasing unemployment and inflation. Most ICCs have experienced periods when unemployment and inflation rose together, other periods where they fell together, and still others when unemployment and inflation moved in opposite directions. The last of these three types of conjuncture suggest the presence of a trade-off curve (TOC) between unemployment and inflation. The first of these situations suggests a TOC that is shifting upward and outward, the second suggests a TOC that is shifting downwards and inward toward the origin. If these shifts take place in a regular sequence, as they seem to do in some countries, they suggest at least the *possibility* of cyclical loops as well. Chapter 5 discusses the concepts of trade-off curve, shifting trade-off curves and cyclical loops. Chapter 6, 7, and 8 turn to a detailed examination of the experience with unemployment and inflation since World War II, both at the national and the regional levels in three countries: Canada, Australia, and the United States. Chapter 9 points out some similarities and differences in that experience, and discusses the implications for analysis and policy of both the similarities and the differences. Chapter 10 analyses the new long-term unemployment that is virtually a worldwide phenomenon, but is especially marked in the industrialized countries.

On the basis of these observations of the facts, some of them contradictory, part IV attempts a systematic analysis. Several plausible hypotheses and theories are suggested in chapter 11. Chapter 12 presents our own theory of shifting trade-off curves and loops. A major conclusion is that there is no reason to expect patterns of unemployment and inflation, and of fluctuations in both, to be identical in all countries and all regions within them. Too much depends on government policy, and on *expectations* of businessmen, financiers, trade union leaders, and other major actors on the economic scene, with regard to policy, prices, wages, employment, interest rates, and profits, for that. There is no reason for Wall Street and Lombard Street to expect the same policies, or to react in the same way to policies actually undertaken; or for trade union leaders to behave in exactly the same way in the United States and the United Kingdom. To design policy to fight unemployment, inflation, and regional disparities all at once, policy must be both flexible and fine-tuned, take full advantage of regional differences, and be based on thorough knowledge of the behavior of the leading actors in *the Game,* discussed in chapter 12, together with *the Machine* and *the Structure.*

With these lessons in mind, we deal in part V—at last—with policy, given our new—though incomplete—knowledge of this "strange new world" of unemployment and inflation sometimes increasing together, sometimes decreasing together, sometimes moving in opposite directions. The knowledge gleaned in part II is still useful, especially in understanding the mechanism of the Machine, but totally inadequate for designing policies for economic stabilization in today's world. The Keynesian analytical framework is also helpful; but essentially, it recommends a universal policy for all countries suffering from unemployment *or* inflation. We know now that such a simple, aggregative approach will not do. Instead of a uniform macroeconomic monetary and fiscal policy throughout the land, we need today a carefully differentiated regional policy, buttressed by appropriated meso- and microeconomic policies of other sorts. Policy cannot be the same for every country in the world, nor even for every region within the same country. With the approach to policy that arises out of the analysis in this volume, regional development policy, instead of being on the periphery of monetary, fiscal, and foreign trade policy, becomes an integral and major part of all three. When national economies are regarded as bundles of regional economies, sometimes only loosely tied together, the whole approach to regional policy and regional development changes. It is not merely a matter of reducing regional disparities, but of improving the performance of the national economy as a whole.

Thus when we come to chapter 14 on "Designing Policy for the Late 1990s and Beyond," the reader should not expect a single, general, grand formula for dealing with unemployment, inflation, and related ills of the same style as the Keynesian formula. The aim of this chapter is at once more ambitious and more modest than that. It provides rules for formulating effective policy, rather than outlining specific policies as such. The first rule is that the policy makers themselves must be wise, knowledgeable, and astute. They cannot hope to find a reliable textbook that will tell them precisely what to do in every situation. Sound monetary and fiscal policy is the foundation of all policy; but it must be buttressed by tailor-made wage and price policy, manpower planning, education and training, and other policies at the meso- and microeconomic levels. Above all, it must be buttressed by selective fiscal policy, designed to fit the circumstances of particular regions and sectors of the country.

Given this kind of approach to and implementation of policy, virtually every country can reasonably accept as a target nothing less than full employment without inflation. Chapter 15 indicates how this target might be attained. Although our knowledge of just how a particular economy behaves is limited, our knowledge is at least as good as it was during World War II, when the Allied Nations achieved full employment without inflation, and a good many other of today's economic policy targets as well, for almost six years. In peacetime, the targets could be attained with much less government intervention in the economy than was needed during World War II. The chapter explains how full employment without inflation, or a close approximation to it, can be achieved, if the people "really want it."

The final chapter of the book presents a "conclusions and summary," instead of the usual "summary and conclusions." It first presents conclusions, showing where we ended up; and then it goes backward through the book chapter by chapter, explaining how we got there. In this manner, the chapter provides a review of the logical structure of the entire volume.

Throughout the book, we have avoided the high level of abstraction that characterizes much of the recent literature in the field of economics. We have tried to describe the phenomena of unemployment and inflation as they actually appear in various countries, and to suggest explanations for them. We have given due weight to the differences that exist among different countries, and even among regions in the same country—differences in policy, and in behavior of strategic groups like trade unions, employers, the media, and others who affect the course of economic events. Accordingly, we have not attempted to present *the* theory of postwar economic fluctuations. And when finally we come to policy, we have not suggested *the* solution to unemployment and inflation. We are of the opinion that appropriate policies can reduce the levels of both unemployment and inflation in any country. In the penultimate chapter, we make a case for striving for full employment without inflation, and suggest ways of approaching this ideal. But the "optimal blend" of management of the economy and letting the market do its job will differ for every country, and to some extent for every region within each country.

References

Bodkin, Ronald G., Elizabeth L. Bond, Grant L. Reuber, and T. Russel Robinson. *Price Stability and High Employment: The Options for Canadian Economic Policy.* Ottawa: Economic Council of Canada Special Study 5, Queen's Printer, 1966.

Cornwall, John. *Growth and Stability in a Mature Economy.* London: Martin Robinson, 1972.

Economic Council of Canada. *Transitions for the 90s: Twenty-Seventh Annual Review.* Ottawa: 1990, 43.

Friedman, Milton. "Nobel Lecture: Inflation and Unemployment." *Journal of Political Economy* 85, 3 (June 1977): 451–72.

Lipsey, Richard. "The Relationship Between Unemployment and the Rate of Change in Money Wages in the United Kingdom, 1862–1957: A Further Analysis." *Economica* (new series) 27 (February 1960): 1–21.

Miller, F. M. "The Natural Rate of Unemployment: Region Estimates and Policy Implications." *Canadian Journal of Regional Science* (Spring 1987): 63–70.

Okun, Arthur M. "Inflation: Its Mechanics and Welfare Cost." Brookings Papers on Economic Activity, vol. 2. Washington, D.C.: The Brookings Institution, 1975.

Phelps, Edmund S. "Money Wage Dynamics and Labor Market Equilibrium." In E. S. Phelps (ed.), *Microeconomic Foundations of Employment and Inflation Theory.* New York: W. W. Norton, 1970, 124–66.

———. "Phillips Curves, Expectations of Inflation, and Optimum Unemployment Over Time." *Economica* XXXIV (new series) 135 (August 1967): 254–81.

Phillips, A. W. "The Relation Between Unemployment and Rate of Change of Money Wages in the United Kingdom, 1862–1957." *Economica* XXV, 102 (November 1958).

Part II

Business Cycles and Theories to Explain Them: 1825–1960

2

Unemployment *or* Inflation:
Experience, Theory, and Policy 1825–1960

We noted in chapter 1 that economists lead a double life. As "scientists," trying to behave like physicists, economists seek universal laws, true always and everywhere. As theorists, however, they must start with observation, and there they are handicapped by the fact that the universe they are studying is subject to constant change, not just in the sense that the events are different, but in the sense that the fundamental way in which economies function seems to change through time. Economists have responded to this situation–albeit slowly and reluctantly, as a rule–by changing their perceptions of how the machinery (or organism) works, and altering their theoretical models accordingly. As policymakers, their situation is even worse. They have been compelled to deal with the problems of the moment, whether or not their perception of what was going on was accurate and complete, and whether or not they had ready at hand a theory that explained perfectly what they did see, or thought they saw. It follows that one cannot understand the history of thought regarding unemployment and inflation without knowing something of the economic history that lies behind it.

We start with the year 1825 because this was the year of the first "modern" crash. There is general agreement that the *business cycle,* as it was known from the Napoleonic Wars until World War II, did not exist before the Napoleonic Wars. In one of the standard textbooks of the early post-World War II era, Professor James Arthur Estey of Purdue University wrote:

> The records of business fluctuations, at least in the recognized pattern of recurrent ebb and flow of activity, do not in all probability extend back of the Napoleonic Wars. It is true that all economic life in the past, as far as records go, has been

subject to many vicissitudes and changes, but the kind of fluctuation to which the term business cycle applies seems to be a characteristic of relatively recent industrial history, more particularly of that modern industrialism which has developed since about the time of the Napoleonic Wars.... For example, Tugan Baranowski (*Les crises industrielles en Angleterre*) holds that what we would call "business cycles" began with the English crises of 1825. He regards the crises that marked the close of the Napoleonic Wars, 1811, 1815, and 1818, as non-periodical, suitable to the war, and properly to be grouped with the "non-business" crises of the eighteenth century. (Estey 1946)

Probably the arrival of business cycles cannot be precisely dated, but "it is certain that their first definite and undeniable appearance occurs in England in that modern period ushered in by the end of the Napoleonic Wars.... England...by that time, was beginning to display the essential characteristics of modern industrialism" (45–47).

Before this period, there were bad times arising from bad harvests, "panics," disturbances, and "bubbles," periods of frenzied speculation in particular development projects followed by collapse, such as the infamous South Sea Bubble of 1720. (For an excellent description and discussion of eighteenth-century bubbles see Cyril James, 1940, chapter 8.) The *cycle*—more or less regular fluctuations consisting of alternating periods of inflation with falling unemployment, and deflation with increasing unemployment—was generated by the machine or organism, of modern industrial and financial capitalism. By 1825 that machine or organism was in place, at least in the United Kingdom.

We choose 1960 as the cut-off date because it was about then that economists began taking notice of the fact that the nature of the capitalist organism (design of the machine) had fundamentally changed, and that the old patterns of alternating unemployment *or* inflation had given way to something quite different, shifting TOCs or cyclical loops. The 1958 edition of Gottfried Haberler's classic work, *Prosperity and Depression,* and the 1961 edition of Robert Gordon's widely used text, *Business Fluctuations,* contain no references to either Trade-Off curves or Phillips curves (Haberler, 1958; Gordon, 1961).

As already noted in chapter 1, the Great Depression of the 1930s was perceived by at least some economists (Hansen, Harris, Harrod, and Keynes to name but a few) as a fundamental structural change in the economies of the more advanced capitalist countries. In addition to cycles of varying durations, they argued that "mature" capitalist countries were subject to "underemployment equilibrium" or "secular stagnation." As always, the new perceptions gave rise to new theories, quite different from the previous business cycle theories, and with quite new policy implications. Accordingly, we shall treat this body of thought separately to test its usefulness in treating today's ICCs, in the light of the further structural change that has evidently taken place.

But while the "modern" business cycles began with the 1825 crash, that doesn't mean that economists devoted a great deal of attention to the explanation of cycles before 1870. There were exceptions, like Malthus and Marx, who anticipated not only much of later business cycle theory, but the theory of secular stagnation as well. The great majority of economists, however, in this period, ignored the phenomenon of cycles completely. Robert Gordon, writing in 1961, goes so far as to say, "Systematic study of business cycles, is, surprisingly, a relatively recent phenomenon. Most of the important contributions in this field have been made in the last 60 years or so" (Gordon, 1961, 339). Certainly the period from the turn of the century until the appearance of Keynes's *General Theory* in 1936 was the "Golden Age" of business cycle theory proper, when distinguished economists in the United Kingdom, the United States, France, Sweden, Norway, Germany, Holland, and Australia turned their attention to the problem.

Why was the phenomenon, which in retrospect was clearly visible after 1825, generally neglected until three generations later? From 1790 until 1825 the economies of Europe, North America, and even to some extent of the colonies, were dominated by the wars, which were a substantial monkey wrench thrown into the works of the capitalist machine. It was easy to blame whatever happened to these economies at the time on the disturbances created by the war. Financing it brought inflation, and shortages created by the war continued the inflation for two or three years after the war was over. Then in 1818 through 1819 came the crash, with falling prices and increasing unemployment—a "primary postwar recession." Recovery came quickly, and the boom of 1823 through 1825 set in, with rapid monetary expansion, steeply rising prices, diminishing unemployment, and, above all, a runaway stock market boom, ending in the great panic of 1825. This time recovery did not come quickly. The crash was followed instead by twenty-five years of "secondary postwar depression," which could also be attributed to the fundamental disturbances created by the war.

There was, however, another reason why most nineteenth-century economists did not make the effort to look for systematic causes of alternating inflation and unemployment: they believed that the nature of the free market economic system was such as to make regular departures from equilibrium impossible, and to assure a rapid return to equilibrium (implicitly with full employment and stable prices) if a disturbance less jarring than the extraordinary shocks generated by major wars, revolutions, or natural disasters, occurred. The basis of this belief was *Say's Law*. Basically, this law states that supply creates its own demand; the entrepreneur's costs are other people's incomes, and the differences between costs and prices are profits, which are also incomes. Thus, the very process of production always generates just enough income to buy the total product, and any imbalance must be temporary and minor. This argument is traced back to the French economist Jean-Baptiste Say, and his *Traité d'économie politique,* published in Paris in 1803. There is obviously a large chunk of truth in the law, and later we shall have to show why it is not quite right. But it fitted into nineteenth-century liberal thought very well, and exercised enormous influence during that century. Alvin Hansen takes note of the fact that even Alfred Marshall "quotes approvingly Mill's classic statement of Say's Law—that the means of payment for commodities is simply commodities; all sellers are buyers; double the supply of commodities and you double the purchasing power." Hansen also notes that Marshall, despite his general approval of the principle, was aware of the basic flaw in it (Hansen, 1951, 271–72). But many nineteenth-century economists, and even some later ones, were not fully aware of it; and since regular, cyclical alternations of unemployment are impossible in a capitalistic economy, why look for causes of a figment of imagination that cannot possibly exist in the real world?

But just how regular were the cycles that took place in the nineteenth and early twentieth centuries? Before endeavoring to answer this question, two observations must be made. The first is that the literature refers to several kinds of cycle of varying duration. The shortest is the seasonal cycle, most obvious in economic activities directly affected by the weather, such as farming, forestry, fishing, and construction. Since the causes of this cycle are obvious, it has not aroused a great deal of interest, except for its repercussions on other cycles. Next is the "forty months cycle," often called the Kitchin cycle after its discoverer. The National Bureau of Economic Research, founded by Wesley Mitchell, which has concentrated for two thirds of a century on the study of economic fluctuations, calls this one "*the* business cycle." Probably the cycle that has caused most concern and received most attention is the one of about ten years—give or take a few years in either direction—and identified with Clément Juglar. Some economists, including Hansen, Kuznets, and Schumpeter have identified a construction cycle of about twenty years. Finally, there is the "long wave," or Kondratieff cycle of about fifty years. As may be expected, the degree of regularity claimed for each of these cycles varies somewhat.

The second point is that no one ever claimed complete regularity for any of these cycles. The economy is too much affected by random shocks for that. What is maintained is that the capitalist economic system contains mechanisms which incline it to fluctuations of varying durations in a more or less regular pattern. Tugan-Baranowsky, for example, in his pioneering work of 1894, spoke of (Juglar) downturns at intervals of seven to eleven years. Hansen, summarizing Tugan Baranowsky, says: "The cycle is not a phenomenon regulated by mathematical laws. The movement is periodic in the sense that there occur successive phases of prosperity and depression which rise and fall like a cycle. The industrial cycle may be conceived of as a law inherent in the very core of the capitalist economy." Hansen also makes the point that the great contribution of Juglar, writing in 1860, was that he "was one of the first to see that the problem is not one of crises but of cycles" (Hansen, 1951, 280–82). But do these cycles have enough regularity to justify the intensity of the search for a theory that would explain them? Burns and Mitchell, for example, maintain that if we are speaking of observed behavior of economic systems, and not about theoretical models, Schumpeter for one claimed too much regularity for his cycles (Burns and Mitchell, 1946, 440–42). But the National Bureau has frequently been criticized for its reluctance to develop theoretical models of its own, insisting on the need for more and more facts before such models can be built, and its implication that people who build models until all the facts are collected are wasting their time (Koopmans, 1947; Burns and Mitchell, 1946). The reader can make up his or her own mind on this question, perhaps after consulting more of the literature and looking at more of the facts. My own view, however, is that there is too much repetitiveness, too much regularity, in the nineteenth- and early twentieth-century experience to attribute it entirely to a series of random and unrelated shocks, and the search for a systematic theory that would provide explanations in terms of the intrinsic nature of industrial and financial system itself was fully justified.

We shall, therefore, turn next to the major theories that emerged as a response to observation of the kind of economic fluctuations we have briefly described. Let me be clear, however, that it is not my intention to provide either a thorough economic history of the period 1825 through 1960 in terms of unemployment and inflation, nor a complete history of thought about unemployment and inflation for that period. Rather, we are sifting the sands of the past to see if we can find flecks of gold which will help us in our search for explanations of today's problems. Accordingly, rather than trace the evolution of ideas about inflation and unemployment, and alternating cycles of first one then the other, we will go straight to business cycle theory in its heyday, between 1920 and 1936. (After 1936, knowledge of the functioning of the capitalist system improved a good deal, and for some two decades very rapidly; but the focus shifted from fluctuations as such to long-run trends, secular stagnation and under-employment equilibrium, conditions for steady growth, the knife-edge theory and the like; the literature took on a somewhat different character, in which questions of periodicity and timing of cycles lost much of their interest.) Obviously, if the theories and policies of the past apply only to a world that has *totally* disappeared, they are of little use in tackling today's problems. But if the functioning of today's organism (or machine) can still be explained to a significant extent in terms of components that were important yesterday, then some of yesterday's theories, and even some of yesterday's policies, are still valid. Our next task is to discover which of these theories and policies are still valid, and how.

Business Cycle Theory

Reading the literature on business cycles, or listening to debates on the subject, during the mid 1930s, gave the impression of violent disagreements, if not total confusion, among economists. The diametrically opposed views of, for example, Robbins and Hayek on the one hand and Hawtrey and Keynes on the other, as to what had caused the Great Depression and how to get out of it, left no choice but to throw up one's hands in despair, or to swear allegiance to one school of champions, as I did to my mentors, Robbins and Hayek. Each school felt that it was on the only track leading to the truth. Today, with the benefit of hindsight, one can see that they were in fact on tracks converging toward a common view. What seemed then violent differences of opinion appear today as differences in emphasis. As Haberler puts it:

> Normally, a complex phenomenon such as the business cycle is caused and conditioned by a large number of factors and circumstances. Even if the same theory holds for all cycles, there is still room for a multitude of "different" explanations which need not all be logically exclusive or contradictory. Each of them stresses one or other of the relevant factors and conditions and calls it the "dominant" or "causally relevant" one. (Haberler, 1958, 6–7)

At the time, however, the debates were bitter enough. I recall listening to a lecture by Hawtrey, in 1934, in the big lecture hall at the London School of Economics; Robbins and Hayek sat on the platform behind him and, as he spoke, made gestures to the audience clearly indicating that Hawtrey was a dangerous lunatic. The truth is that from the beginning of the concern for unemployment and inflation, crises, panics, fluctuations, departures from equilibrium, or however we want to term the phenomenon once called business cycles, there was an understanding that it arose from interactions among investment, savings, and consumption, decisions concerning these major factors in the economy, and the relationship of monetary expansion and contraction to all of these. Some thought that variations in the flow of money were the cause, some the result, of fluctuations in the other variables; others thought that there was a feedback mechanism amongst all of them. Virtually everyone who studied the phenomenon, however, focused on the same set of variables. The fact that so much shared understanding was accompanied by diametrically opposed policy recommendations reflects once again the view, widespread outside Marxist circles, that the capitalist system ought to work smoothly, and if it didn't, the task was to find out the defect and fix it. It was almost as though the world had many brilliant theoretical physicists who understood perfectly the various principles governing the manner in which an automobile functions, but no engineers to predict when it might break down, and no technicians to fix it when it did.

There are several possible ways of classifying business cycle theories, but a fairly common taxonomy goes something like this (ranked from simplest to most complex concept of the functioning of the "economic machine" itself):

1. *Natural causes*: harvests, rainfall cycles, etc.
2. *Psychology, expectations, errors in foresight*: Panics and crises occur because people expect them.

3. *Purely monetary theories*: Cycles occur because the banking system operates in such a way as to generate periods of monetary expansion followed by periods of monetary contraction.

4. *Random, "exogenous" shocks and reactions restrained by the mechanism of the economic system*: Events occur that are not generated by the economic system itself, but which have an impact on the functioning of the system: wars, revolutions, natural disasters, gold discoveries, other resource discoveries. Such theories require sophisticated analysis of the functioning of the economic system to show how random shocks can generate more or less regular cycles.

5. *Over-investment theories*: A capital structure is built up which cannot be maintained because there is insufficient demand for its products, because there is an inadequate flow of savings and credit to finance its completion and maintenance, because costs rise to a point where it is unprofitable, because the equilibrium or "natural" rate of interest is too high to justify such a capital-intensive technique of production. Haberler divides these theories in two: monetary, with the initial cause of the imbalances in the capital structure located in the behavior of the monetary system; and non-monetary, in which the mechanism of the capitalist economic system itself generates, more or less automatically, overproduction of capital goods, and the money supply adjusts to these "real" factors in the economic system, but inadequately.

6. *Under-consumption theories*: The economic system operates in such a way that the rate of increase in production, savings, and consumption are not in balance. As a boom (or upswing) progresses, the capital structure expands, and output increases; but as incomes rise, the proportion of incomes spent falls and the proportion saved increases. As a consequence, investment, both what has already taken place and that planned for the future, becomes unprofitable. As a consequence, investment falls, a crisis results, and pushes the system into recession and depression. Recovery takes place as interest rates and other costs fall, the ratio of savings to incomes falls and the proportion of income spent for consumption rises, and new investment opportunities appear.

7. *Structural maladjustments*: Gottfried Haberler included in his classic work, *Prosperity and Depression,* a separate chapter on "Changes in Cost, Horizontal Maladjustments and Overindebtedness." In a sense, of course, all theories of business cycles are concerned with structural maladjustments within the economy. Similarly, changes in cost play a role in virtually all theories of economic fluctuations, and over-indebtedness plays a role in several of them, especially those laying emphasis on the monetary system. However, Haberler included this chapter in order to have a heading for the contributions of several important writers on business cycles that do not seem to fall neatly under any of the other headings, and we shall do to same.

Good and Bad Harvests

Of all business cycle theories, the ones that are most "real," in the sense of associating economic fluctuations with basic causal factors that lie entirely outside the economic system as such, are those that attribute business cycles to periodic changes in weather patterns. The remoteness of causation from the mechanics of the economic system is especially clear in the case of the "sunspot theories" of W. S. Jevons, H. S. Jevons, and H. L. Moore (W. S. Jevons, 1909; H. S. Jevons, 1909, 1910; H. L. Moore, 1923). Here the argument is that the periodic appearance of sunspots explain the rainfall cycles, which cause cycles of good and bad harvests, which in turn cause business cycles through their repercussions on the economy as a whole.

There are hundreds of millions of people in the world whose incomes depend primarily on the amount of rainfall in the growing season. In the arid zone, the rainfall cycle can be the major factor in fluctuations in output, income, and employment.

The similarity of the configuration of rainfall cycles to that of the "Juglar," seven- to eleven-year cycle in advanced countries has long since been noted by economists. W. Stanley Jevons drew attention to this correlation in his paper for the British Association in 1875, and elaborated on it in his *Investigations in Currency and Finance* some decades later. A more refined presentation of the rainfall cycle theory of economic fluctuations was presented by Henry Ludwell Moore.

Jevons seemed to feel that his theory stood or fell according to the closeness of the correlation between sunspot cycles and economic fluctuations. Thus, in his *Investigations in Currency and Finance*, he wrote:

While writing my 1875 paper for the British Association I was much embarrassed by the fact that the commercial fluctuations could with difficulty be reconciled with a period of 11.1 years. If, indeed, we start from 1825, and add 11.1 years time after time, we get 1836.1, 1847.2, 1858.3, 1869.4, 1880.5, which shows a gradually increasing discrepancy from 1837, 1847, 1857, 1866 (and now 1878), the true dates of the crises. To explain this discrepancy I went so far as to form the rather fanciful hypothesis that the commercial world might be a body so mentally constituted, as Mr. John Mill must hold, as to be capable of vibrating in a period of ten years, so that it would every now and then be thrown into oscillation by physical causes having a period of eleven years. The subsequent publication, however, of Mr. J. A. Brown's inquiries, tending to show that the solar period is 10.45 years, not 11.1 (*Nature* xvi: 63), placed the matter in a very different light, and removed the difficulties. Thus, if we take Mr. John Mill's "Synopsis of Six Commercial

Panics in the Present Century," and rejecting 1866 as an instance of a premature panic, count from 1815 to 1857, we find that four credit cycles, occupying forty-two years, give an average duration of 10.5 years, which is a remarkably close approximation to Mr. Broun's solar period. (1909)

As economists, we need not be concerned about possible association between rainfall cycles and sunspots. We may take rainfall cycles as given and ask whether and how fluctuations in rainfall generate fluctuations in income and employment. Jevons's own theoretical framework was very simple. Concerned as he was with fluctuations in his own country, he argued that drought in the colonies led to famine there and consequent reduction of imports of British manufactured goods, especially textiles, with repercussions on the economy of the mother country:

Probably, however, we ought not to attribute the decennial fluctuation wholly to Indian trade. It is quite possible that tropical Africa, America, the West Indies, and even the Levant are affected by the same meteorological influences which occasion the famines in India. Thus it is the nations which trade most largely to those parts of the world, and which give long credits to their customers which suffer most from these crises. Holland was most easily affected a century ago; England is most deeply affected now; France usually participates, together with some of the German trading towns. But I am not aware that these decennial crises extend in equal severity to such countries as Austria, Hungary, Switzerland, Italy and Russia, which have comparatively little foreign trade. Even when they are affected, it may be indirectly through sympathy with the great commercial nations.

Here again some may jest at the folly of those who theorize about such incongruous things as the cotton-mills of Manchester and the paddy-fields of Hindostan. But to those who look a little below the surface, the connection is obvious. Cheapness of food leaves the poor Hindu ryot a small margin of earnings, which he can spend on new clothes; and a small margin multiplied by the vast population of British India, not to mention China, produces a marked change in the demand for Lancashire goods. (1909)

Although Moore's analysis was somewhat more sophisticated, he, too, attached primary importance to statistical correlations; his elaboration of Jevons's theory was mainly on the statistical side. Moore's main argument was that rainfall cycles bring fluctuations in yields of raw materials, which in turn bring fluctuations in their prices. Bad rainfall means high raw materials prices, which in turn squeeze profits of manufacturers and lead to a decline in industrial investment and a general downswing. Bad harvests may also result in an increase in real wages (given great flexibility of money wages) and a consequent drop in profits and investment. Moore was satisfied that, with the introduction of appropriate leads and lags, this explanation of fluctuations fitted the facts.

Much more study should be devoted to the process by which such fluctuations are generated; nevertheless, there can be no doubt of the violence of fluctuations in income and employment in arid zone countries nor of their relation to rainfall cycles. The impact effect is clear and direct: no harvest, no work for the rural population, and perhaps even no seed for them to plant for the next harvest. In the pastoral sector of the Libyan and similar economies, drought means that the animals die, leaving pastoralists with no source of income.

However inadequate a "rainfall theory" of economic fluctuations may be for advanced countries, there can be no doubt of its importance in underdeveloped arid zone countries, especially those without petroleum. We may note, for example, the importance of the monsoon in India, not only for agricultural output, but for industrial investment. Most important, of course, is rainfall during the growing season; it was in this form that Moore cast his theory. However, cycles of total annual rainfall are closely related to cycles in rainfall during the growing season, in countries that count on more than one crop per year or on grazing.

Figure 2.1 illustrates fluctuations caused by rainfall cycles. We shall assume that this is a poor country, caught in the low-income trap. We shall ignore the upper, high per capita income portions of the curves. We start with equilibrium at Y1. There is little technological progress and also little diminishing returns, because population growth is small; high fertility rates are offset by high death rates. Thus, the investment curve will be affected mainly by the stock of capital and will have a negative slope like I1.

Now assume that a drought occurs. The immediate impact is a shift of the capital requirements curve to the left; more capital would be required than before to maintain the same low level of per capita income. Per capita incomes drop. But with lower per capita incomes, savings also fall; the new capital requirements exceed savings at the lower level of income, and income falls further. Moreover, with a rise in the costs of food and raw materials, industrial investment shifts downward to I2-I2. The new equilibrium is established at Y2. If this income is below the subsistence level, income may return to Y1, through starvation, which reduces the rate of population growth and so reduces capital requirements.

When cycles are generated from the supply side, a different kind of stabilization policy is required from that suggested by orthodox fiscal policy. In these cases, the downswing does not start because of an excess of effective supply over effective demand. Hence, monetary and fiscal

FIGURE 2.1
The Rainfall Cycle

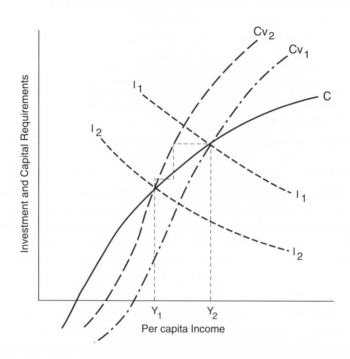

measures designed to maintain effective demand are irrelevant; a different kind of stabilization policy is required. Under drought conditions, no amount of internal spending will maintain the output of the private sector of the economy. A major problem in a drought period in such countries is simply to maintain the physical supplies of foodstuffs. For aggregate demand may exceed aggregate supply, and if supplies are not made good by imports or sales from stocks, unemployment and inflation can occur side by side.

On the whole, writers on business cycles have taken the harvest theories seriously, in the sense that they consider alternations of good and bad harvests to be a significant factor in the behavior of the economy as a whole, even in highly industrialized countries. They have not associated themselves with sunspots, and they do not assign to crop cycles sole or even major responsibility for fluctuations of unemployment and inflation in the entire economy. They have tended to show more interest in how the economic "machine" propagates a disturbance—good or bad— to the rest of the economy than in the initial impulse itself. For example, Aaron Gordon begins his section on "Agriculture, the Weather, and Business Cycles" as follows:

> Even in a country as industrialized as the United States, the behaviour of agricultural production, prices, and incomes has important effects on other types of economic activity. In many countries, agriculture dominates the domestic economy; and the role played by agriculture in the United States 50 or 100 years ago was, of course, much more important than it is now. In view of this, it is not surprising that a number of writers have looked into the relations between agriculture and the rest of the economy over the course of the cycle. (Gordon, 1961, 385)

On the basis of the available evidence, he concludes that "it is unlikely that regular cycles in crop production play an important role in business fluctuations," but then he quotes J. M. Clark to the effect that "this does not mean that agriculture has no effect on the business cycle.... It simply means that agriculture is not a regularly acting force, tending typically and regularly to help initiate the recovery, or stimulate the revival, or in any other way to play habitually the same role in at least a predominant number of cycles" (386).

Gottfried Haberler devotes a whole chapter of his *Prosperity and Depression* to "Harvest Theories: Agriculture and the Business Cycle" (Haberler, 1958, 151–68). In it he goes systematically through the various ways that good or bad harvests can affect the economy: through their impact on demand for nonagricultural goods and services; through their effects on expectations; through their influence on monetary contraction or expansion; through their effects on wages and raw materials costs; through their impact on rural-urban or urban-rural migration; by changing patterns of savings and investment; and by inducing optimism or pessimism. These interactions sound like quite a lot. But then Haberler summarizes by saying that "the channels through which...good and bad harvests exercise their effect upon the economic system in general and industrial activity in particular are not other than those with which we have become familiar in the perusal of the various theories discussed in this work" (265). In his concluding remarks to this chapter, Haberler confesses: "The above review of the possible interactions of agriculture and industry on one another cannot be said to yield a clear picture.... Spontaneous agricultural fluctuations may have a positive or a negative effect on the general business cycle and on monetary demand and may react back on agriculture through this channel. Lastly, variations, however caused in the demand for and cost of agricultural produce may, after a time, give rise to variations in agricultural output which will act on industry like spontaneous disturbances, and set up a vicious circle of expansion or contraction" (167).

Estey also has a chapter in his textbook entitled "Real Causes: Agriculture and the Business Cycle." It begins:

> That the national welfare depends upon agricultural prosperity is a common opinion in this country. Businessmen have taken it for granted that changes in the volume of the principal crops are an important factor in business prosperity or depression. They accept good crops as a sign of good business and poor crops as a potent cause of depression. Always they have looked to agriculture to lift them out of slumps, and they are ready to attribute the prolonged depression of the 1930's to the inability of agriculture to stage a recovery of its own. They tend to regard good crops as a spontaneous source of new demand that fills the pockets of the farmer with money, and, at least in the past, they have commonly adjusted their plans to the state of the harvest and the general prospects of the rural districts.

> This belief in the importance of the crops has been shared by economists, at least to the extent that they include agricultural changes among the contributing causes of cyclical variation in industry. A few only accept agricultural factors as important, but also regard them as the chief generating cause of cycles. Among them are those who trace cycles to meteorological causes (such as are associated with sunspots) operating through the medium of crop variations. (Estey 1946)

After a few pages of analysis of interactions between industry and agriculture, Estey answers his own question: "It seems fair to conclude that an increased volume of agricultural output is definitely stimulating to industry, save when it comes at peaks of expansion when further stimulus is useless and likely to be dangerous" (184).

Alvin Hansen, in his discussion of harvest cycles, reminds us that Jevons was fully aware of the importance of psychological factors in booms and crises; but Jevons added, "but it seems very probable that the moods of the commercial mind, while constituting the principal part of the phenomenon, may be controlled by outward events, especially the condition of the harvests" (Hansen, 1951, 220). He also reminds us of something else that is more surprising: "Keynes fits the Jevons explanation into his own pattern of analysis in a most interesting manner." Exceptionally large harvests, says Keynes, lead to investment in stocks (inventories) of agricultural products, contributing to the boom. While agriculture plays a lesser role today than it did in earlier generations, Hansen adds, "even today changes in the stocks of raw materials, agricultural and mineral, play a considerable part in determining the volume of current investment" (1951, 345). Haberler cites an early article of Hansen's to show that Hansen attached little importance to the impact of industrial fluctuations on agriculture, which Hansen regarded as the "football of business." As a man brought up in the agricultural Midwest, Hansen no doubt shared the suspicions of, and resentment toward, the machinations of eastern industry and finance, and their evil effects on the midwestern farmer; but his later writings also show that he was well aware of the impact of agricultural fluctuations on industry and finance as well.

So where do we end up on good and bad harvests? Obviously we cannot relax in confidence that they are the sole explanation of unemployment and inflation. But equally obviously, we cannot drop the "real" factors causing variations in harvests out of the picture altogether.

Psychological Theories

Everyone knows that if everyone who is trading in the stock market expects a crash, there will be one. When everyone wants to sell and no one wants to buy, share prices must fall. If on the other hand all traders expect share prices to rise, and so are eager to buy, and no one is eager to sell, prices will surely rise. The same principle holds in the market for any good or service. Decisions to buy, sell, save, invest, hoard, dishoard are based on the current situation and expectations regarding the future; and the decisions are essentially psychological responses to individual evaluations of present and future. What happens in any market is the outcome of these individual decisions. In this sense, all business cycles are "psychological." All writers on business cycles recognize this fact.

Economists have differed widely, however, on the degree to which these psychological factors are exogenous "impulses" coming from outside the economic system, and the degree to which they are merely propagating forces, amplifying the impact of impulses generated within the economic system. It is hard to believe that waves of optimism and pessimism, moods, and "business climate" are generated within human beings themselves, quite independently of any outside influence. Something must happen to trigger the changes in mood, the transformations of business climate, the shifts from optimism to pessimism. H. S. Jevons thought that sunspots, apart from their effect on rainfall, might contribute to cycles through their effect on moods, causing shifts from optimism to pessimism. If this interesting idea were true, the psychological factors in business cycles could be regarded as exogenous; but the idea remains unsubstantiated. Economists, on the whole, have said "yes, there are psychological factors, and they are of some importance; but they cannot be regarded as the sole, or even the major, initiating factor in economic fluctuations." Haberler says, cautiously:

> The real difference (between "economic" and "psychological" theories) is this. The "psychological" theories introduce certain assumptions about typical reactions, mainly on the part of the entrepreneur and the saver, in certain situations; and these reactions are conventionally called psychological because of their (in a sense) indeterminate character. But the distinction between the writers who give prominence to these "psychological" factors and (the others) is, taken as a whole, a distinction of emphasis rather than one of kind. (Haberler 1958, 145)

Haberler also points out, however, that consideration of psychological factors introduces a certain degree of irrationality into decision-making, and accordingly a certain degree of uncertainty, and even some degree of indeterminacy:

> With the introduction of the element of expectation, uncertainty enters the field. Future events cannot be forecast with precision; and the farther they are distant in the future, the greater the uncertainty, and the greater the possibility of unforeseen and unforeseeable disturbances...but the introduction of optimism and pessimism signifies more than this. It implies that the connection between a fall in the rate of interest and a change in the other objective factors, on the one hand, and the decision of the entrepreneur to invest more, on the other hand, is not so rigid as the "economic" theories sometimes maintain.... The response of total investment to changes in the objective factors becomes stronger than the "rational" economic considerations would suggest. (Haberler, 1958, 145–47)

Haberler quotes Pigou regarding "errors of optimism," and also Keynes, who, as a speculator in the foreign exchange and stock markets (and a highly successful one), bursar of King's College (which he made embarrassingly rich), and Director of an insurance company, knew a good deal about market moods and speculation: "It is an essential characteristic of the boom that investments which will in fact yield, say 2 percent in conditions of full employment are made in the expectation of a yield of, say, 6 percent, and are valued accordingly." Haberler then adds, "the theorists who stress the psychological factor, and especially Professor Pigou and Mr. Keynes, point out, furthermore, that the discovery of errors of optimism gives birth to the opposite errors of pessimism," which aggravate the downswing (148). In general, Haberler accepts the view that psychological factors make reactions of investors stronger than purely economic factors would dictate, and thus increase the amplitude of business cycles.

Estey underlines the point that the contribution of psychological factors to the aggravation of economic fluctuations is not just a matter of expectations, or waves of optimism and pessimism, but of *mistaken* expectations:

> Fundamentally, therefore, psychological causes arise from mistakes or errors of judgement. We get a wrong view of the facts. We are misled. We change our view of the facts, although the facts have not changed; and when the facts do change, our frame of mind is somehow so influenced that we cannot make correct judgements as to the significance of the change. (Estey 1946)

Estey lays particular stress on the role of irrational pessimism in deepening and prolonging depressions. He speaks of "despairing attempts to keep things going" which "must be futile in the end" (209). One is reminded of President Franklin D. Roosevelt's great speech during the Great Depression of the 1930s, in which he said, "we have nothing to fear but fear itself." In conclusion, Estey remarks that "psychological explanation of cycles can hardly claim to be more than elucidations of one important factor in the process of expansion and contraction." But then he adds, "one must admit the existence of these changes of confidence, of business 'tone,' of the general mental atmosphere or 'climate.' The annals of business history confirm this at every point" (210–11).

Daniel Hamberg also stresses the importance of error, and of the interactions of errors in each direction: "Errors of optimism and pessimism are not independent of each other. Rather, they tend to provide the basis for each other. The larger the error in one direction, the larger tends to be the error in the other" (Hamberg, 1951, 303). Hamberg, however, introduces an extremely important point, sometimes overlooked by other writers, which he calls "the proximity of businessmen to each other":

> Because of the various relationships which businessmen have with each other, it becomes a fairly simple thing for optimistic or pessimistic outlooks to spread quickly throughout the business community, taking the form of "waves" of opti-

mism and pessimism. Firms of the same industry...tend to concentrate in the same geographical areas, making it possible to exchange views fairly easily. The same is true in the big cities where giant office buildings containing hundreds of offices abound. Similarly in most cities, a variety of businessmen's clubs and trade associations exist which also afford an easy and convivial exchange or views and opinions.... The widespread use of trade journals and business report sheets, too, facilitates no end the spread of the prevailing state of mind in the business community. (Hamberg, 1951, 301)

Today, businessmen share a "proximity" that is much more than physical; there is an ideological and informational proximity as well. There is an ever-increasing sophistication on matters of economics within the business, industrial, and financial community, and an ever-growing effort to be well informed as to what is going on in the domestic and world economies, and as to what current economic policies are and what policies are likely to be pursued in the future. Consequently, businessmen subscribe to the same economic intelligence services, the same financial newsletters, listen to the same speeches by politicians, economists, and bankers, watch the same economic analysis programs on television. As a consequence, they share the same hopes and fears at the same time. This high degree of unanimity of outlook ought in itself to amplify the magnitude of economic fluctuations. Offsetting this tendency, however, is another: the growing confidence that governments will manage the domestic and world economies so as to avoid disaster. Thus, the 1987 stock market crash did not push the world economy into deep depression, as did the comparable 1929 crash. We shall return to this important point below.

Aaron Gordon's treatment of psychological factors is much like those we have already discussed. "Businessmen," he says, "stand at the centre of the productive process, and the level of economic activity depends on their evaluation of profit possibilities. Because they act in response to anticipations, human psychology inevitably plays an important role in the course that the business cycle takes" (Gordon, 1961, 206). He continues: "The marginal efficiency of capital (expected profits discounted for uncertainty and illiquidity)—which, with the interest rate, determines the volume of investment—rises and falls with the state of business psychology" (349).

The role of psychological factors in economic fluctuations seems clear enough. They are extremely important, but there is no reason to believe that changes in "mood," or swings in optimism and pessimism, totally unrelated to any apparent and objective factors, forces, and events in the real world, can explain the economic fluctuations that we observe in the real world. We still have to pin down these real factors, and determine the mechanism through which they interact to generate fluctuations, unemployment, and inflation. There is no reason either to imagine that the psychological factor has disappeared in the real world of the 1990s. It may be that the transformation of the behavior of the world economy since the 1950s is due in part to some change in the way human psychology affects it. That is a question to which we shall have to return below. But we can be sure that the psychological factor is still there.

Purely Monetary Theories

Strictly speaking, there is no such thing as a *purely* monetary theory of economic fluctuations. The supply of money (M) and the flow of money (MV, where "V" is the velocity of circulation of money) do not expand and contract spontaneously. Variations in M and V take place in response to human decisions, and these decisions always have some reason behind them. Except for the rare occasions when governments have literally taken to printing money to finance extraordinary expenditures, as the United States did during the Civil War, the industrialized countries during the period under consideration have increased M through bank lending to individuals, enterprises, and governments; and have reduced M when repayments of, or defaults of, bank loans have exceeded new credits. These fluctuations may be initiated either by the banks or by the borrowers. "V" is, if anything, an even more complex concept than "M." It depends on a host of decisions by individuals, enterprises, and governments as to how much money they want to hold in cash balances, rather than spending it for consumption or investing it. Usually individuals, enterprises, and governments will increase their cash balances more or less proportionately to increases in income and spending, on what is called the "transactions motive." The ratio of cash balances to income and spending goes up when people are nervous about the future; they are afraid to spend much for consumption lest their incomes fall and they are unable to maintain routine expenditures; and they are afraid to invest lest the value of assets drops. They therefore hold more cash on the "liquidity motive." Thus, the level of "V" reflects all the expectations regarding the future of the economy of all the individuals, enterprises, governments, and institutions in it. A "monetary" theory of the business cycle involves a lot more than money.

What is called a "purely monetary" theory, however, is characterized by two features. First, it is argued that the basic decisions leading to alterations in M or MV are made within the banking system itself. Second, changes in V are assumed to be the consequence of changes in M, or are formally assumed to be zero (V is treated as a constant), or are simply neglected.

Haberler has a chapter in his *Prosperity and Depression* entitled "The Purely Monetary Theory," and since our purpose here is to outline thought on business cycles during the period under review, we shall follow more or less his treatment of this category of theory. Like most writers on this topic, he concentrates his discussion on the works of R. G. Hawtrey, economist for the Bank of England, who wrote several books on the subject between 1913 and 1937, which attracted a good deal of attention (Hawtrey, 1913; 1919; 1923; 1928; 1931; 1932; 1933; 1937). Haberler begins his discussion of Hawtrey's theory thusly:

> The purely monetary explanation of the business cycle has been most fully and most uncompromisingly set out by Mr. R. G. Hawtrey. For him the trade cycle is "a purely monetary phenomenon," in the sense that changes in "the flow of money" are the sole and sufficient cause of changes in economic activity, of the alternation of prosperity and depression, of good and bad trade. When the demand for goods in terms of money (that is, the flow of money) grows, trade becomes brisk, production rises and prices go up. When the demand falls off, trade slackens, production shrinks and prices sag. (Haberler, 1958, 15)

Shocks to the economic system such as wars, crop failures, or natural disasters may reduce national income and spending, but a trade cycle depression, with widespread unemployment and excess capacity, cannot occur without a fall in consumer spending and, thus, in money flow. Changes in consumer spending, however, are due mainly to changes in the supply of money in the first place. "The upswing of the trade cycle is brought about by expansion of credit and lasts so long as the credit expansion goes on, or at least, is not followed by a credit contraction. A credit expansion is brought about by the banks through the easing of conditions under which loans are granted to the customer" (Haberler, 1958, 18). Merchants, or traders, are particularly sensitive to small changes in interest rates, and vary their inventories (stocks) accordingly.

Irving Fisher introduced a famous equation, $PT=MV$, where P is the general price level and T is the volume of transactions, or flow of goods and services. Arthur Marget made a major contribution to monetary theory with his concept of "the velocity of circulation of goods." He broke up Fisher's T into G, the quantity of goods, and v, the velocity of circulation of goods. Fisher's equation thus becomes P.Gv=MV, or P=$\frac{MV}{Gv}$. Hoarding of goods in anticipation of a price rise reduces v, and thus Gv makes prices rise faster. Dishoarding (dumping) of goods in the expectation of a price fall makes prices fall faster. Cast in these terms, Hawtrey maintained that v is very sensitive to changes in interest rates; when the banks raise their interest rates by even a modest amount, v rises and prices fall. When the banks reduce their interest rates, even a little bit, v falls and prices rise—thus inducing merchants to borrow more and to hold bigger inventories, reducing v and raising prices once again, in a cumulative expansion process.

According to Hawtrey, in Haberler's words, "prosperity comes to an end when credit expansion is discontinued" (1958, 20). The boom could go on forever, provided credit expansion continued; but once the economy hits the ceiling where all resources are fully employed, production can expand only so fast as the labor force grows, new resources are discovered, and techniques improved, which in most economies is not very fast. Consequently, any significant expansion of credit will bring inflation and—a matter of great importance to Hawtrey, a Bank of England economist, at the time when he was writing—the abandonment of the gold standard. Here the human, or psychological factor comes in. If the commercial banks continued to exercise restraint on the basis of their own good judgement, the central bank will step in, refuse to expand bank reserves further, or even reduce them, through open market sales of securities, recalling or refusing to renew loans to the banks, or, if the banking legislation permits, raising reserve requirements. The downturn, in other words, is man made. When it comes, it leads to a cumulative contraction, or downswing. Revival comes only after wages and other costs have fallen enough, bank loans have been liquidated, interest rates have fallen to a very low level, and bank reserves have increased, and the banks are eager to lend again.

It is interesting to note that in some of his writings after the onslaught of the Great Depression, Hawtrey anticipated Keynes's concept of the "liquidity trap"; in a deep depression the outlook may become so gloomy that people are reluctant to borrow and invest no matter how low the interest rates or how easy the terms of lending. He also anticipated the Harrod-Domar concept of the knife edge, to be analyzed below: equilibrium is such a delicate state of balance that the slightest disturbance may launch a cumulative movement away from equilibrium, in one direction or another. It is also interesting that Hawtrey thought of his theory of cycles, at least in the sense of periodic and regular fluctuations, as being tied to the gold standard and central bank management under it. With the disappearance of the gold standard Hawtrey thought the cycles were replaced by more or less random disturbances. Haberler points out, however, that periodicity is not essential to the validity of Hawtrey's theory. To the degree that it is correct, it can also explain fluctuations that are more irregular than his own concept of "cycles." Haberler also thought that Hawtrey's concept of the inventory cycle responding to bank policy was a unique and valuable contribution to the literature on business cycles.

Estey's summary appraisal of the "pure" monetary theory of the trade cycle would probably be accepted by most specialists in the field:

> How acceptable the monetary theory of the cycle will be depends on what it is taken to mean. If it means that the cycles that actually occur, and in the shape in which they occur, cannot be explained in the absence of monetary factors, probably everyone would accept it. It is an indispensable contributing cause, a *sine qua non* of cycles as we know them. Whatever else happens, the compliance of the banks must be assumed.

> (The evaluation depends on what is included in the term "monetary.") Thus, for example, is velocity of circulation a monetary factor? There is no doubt that it has important variations which spring from non-monetary sources. If one chooses, with Hawtrey, to regard velocity as a monetary factor, it is undeniably easier to think of the cycle as "a purely monetary phenomenon," but it might be more illuminating to regard velocity as the expression of many non-monetary factors, changes in real demand, changes in cost, inventions, and so on which, too, may be powerful contributors to cyclical fluctuations. (Estey, 1946, 233–34)

Random Shocks Constrained by the Machine

We have characterized the "pure monetary theory" as a relatively simple explanation—as far as it goes—of economic fluctuations. It is not quite a matter of "business cycles are all the fault of the bankers," but the main generating force is the banking system operating in accordance with fairly simple rules, and reactions of others in the economy, also acting in a fairly simple, straightforward, and easily understood way. At first blush the set of theories we are now about to consider may seem even simpler, indeed almost a "cop-out." It starts by saying in effect, "all kinds of things may dislodge the economy from equilibrium, and it need never be the same thing twice in a row. And the nature of the economy is such that once disturbed, it tends to move cumulatively away from equilibrium, until something happens to push it toward equilibrium again." But the theory is not as simple as all that. It is saying that the economic "machine" is a highly complex one, so that erratic and irregular shocks produce a result that appears like a regular cycle. This theory requires a more sophisticated concept of the functioning of the economic machine than the purely monetary theory. Ultimately the concept embraces the multiplier, the accelerator (or the relation) and their interactions, as we shall see below. It also includes the idea of a "ceiling" on expansion during upswings and a "floor" under contractions during the downswing, also to be discussed below.

The early presentations of the theory that cycles consist of random shocks to an economic machine with built-in constraints on the amplitude and duration of its fluctuations—a sort of thermostat, regulator, or servo-mechanism—did not spell out the specifications of these components of the machine in total detail or complete clarity, although they were implicit in them. Often economists embracing this theory made use of analogies. For example, Ragnar Frisch, one of the grandfathers of econometrics and one of the first winners of the Nobel Prize in economics, in a famous paper, began by quoting Knut Wicksell. "Knut Wicksell," he wrote, "seems to be the first who has been definitely aware of the two types of problems in economic cycle analysis—the propagation problem and the impulse problem—and also the first who has formulated explicitly the theory that the sources of energy which maintain the economic cycles are erratic shocks." Shocks in the form of major innovations and resource discoveries, establishment of new enterprises, and the like may come irregularly, even "jerkingly"; but the mechanism of the economic system is such that "these irregular jerks may cause more or less regular cyclical movements." Wicksell then provides an analogy. You may hit a wooden rocking horse with a club, with more or less force, from different angles, in different parts of the horse, and at irregular intervals; and the movements of the rocking horse will be very different from, and much more regular than, that of the club.

Frisch himself provided a much more sophisticated mechanical model as an analogy to the operation of the economic system. Here the economic system is presented as a system of articulated pendulums, related to each other in the manner illustrated in figure 2.2. The big pendulum is the "Kondratieff" cycle, the intermediate one the "Juglar" cycle, and the smallest one the "Kitchin" cycle. Only the smallest one is actually visible to the observer. If a shock is transmitted to any one of these pendulums, however, all three will start swinging. The course of the smallest one, which is the equivalent to the course of observed economic events, will be the product of three distinct but articulated movements.

Moreover, because of the "restraints" imposed on the amplitude of swings by forces within the "system," the course of the smallest pendulum will not vary proportionately to the strength of the initial shock. Consequently, a series of intermittent shocks to the economic system— such as wars, revolutions, elections, innovations, and so forth—might give the appearance of a fairly regular cycle, because the mechanism of the economic system itself imposes limitations on the violence of reactions to the shocks. This point is important because it means that we do not need to demonstrate regularity of the initial "shocks," to explain cyclical movements with the limited degree of regularity demonstrated by the economic fluctuations of the real world (Frisch, 1933).

An "impulse-propagation" model that attracted a good deal of attention was the "cobweb theorem," in which the impulse consisted of random shocks in the form of shifts in aggregate effective demand, however caused, and the propagation took place through the reactions of entrepreneurs with imperfect foresight. (The cobweb theorem, like most business cycle theorems, is thus in part "psychological.") This theorem is illustrated in figures 2.3 through 2.6. The theorem derives its name from the appearance of the diagrams. The curve $D_1 D_1$ represents the initial demand for goods and services in general, $S_1 S_1$ the initial supply of goods and services. The initial price level is therefore P_1, and the initial level of output is G_{v1}. Now suppose an unforeseen increase in effective demand to come about, so that the general price level rises to P_2. Output cannot be immediately increased, and entrepreneurs make a windfall profit, amounting to $[P_1 P_2 . G_{v1}]$.

If entrepreneurs expect the prevailing price level to continue, they will expand their plant capacity enough to supply the volume of goods and services that is considered appropriate to the new price level, as indicated by the supply curve $S_1 S_1$. This amount will be G_{v2}. When the new plant is put into operation, and the increased supply of final products reaches the market, the demand price will fall to P_8. If entrepreneurs now expect this lower price level to prevail, they will contract their supply to

FIGURE 2.2
The Cobweb Theorem

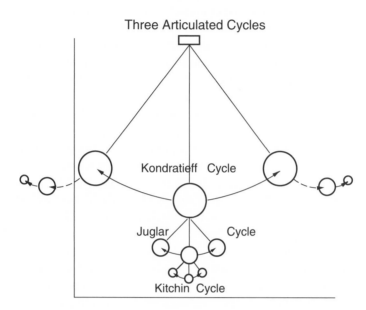

Three Articulated Cycles

Kondratieff Cycle

Juglar   Cycle

Kitchin Cycle

G_{vs}. But then the price rises to P_4, supply will be expanded to G_{v4}, and so on. Plotted as a time series, the course of prices and output would have the contours demonstrated in figure 2.4. Thus, the "cobweb theorem" provides a "sufficient" explanation of economic fluctuations.

There are some obvious defects in this model. What causes the initial increase in effective demand? Why should businessmen be so naïve as to always expect current prices to prevail? How can we be sure that business will survive the first mistake, and the windfall losses that result? With the contraction of output, and the unemployment that accompanies it, will not effective demand fall again? May not the slopes of the demand and supply curves be such as to produce a "diverging" cobweb, of the sort shown in figure 2.5, leading to an "explosive" movement of prices and output of the kind illustrated in figure 2.6?

FIGURE 2.3
The Cobweb Theorem

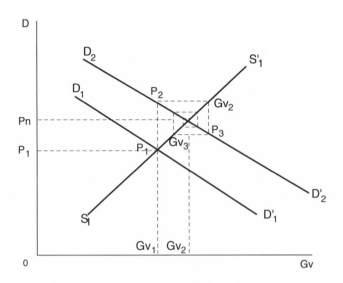

FIGURE 2.4
The Cobweb Theorem

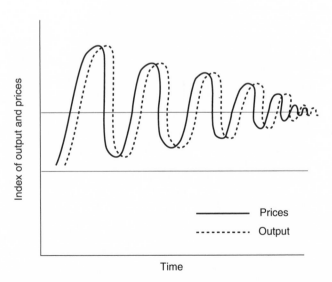

FIGURE 2.5
The Cobweb Theorem

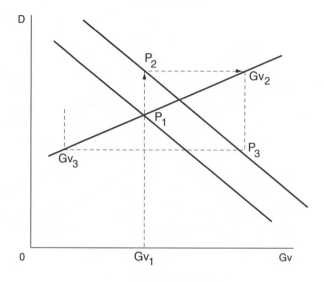

FIGURE 2.6
The Cobweb Theorem

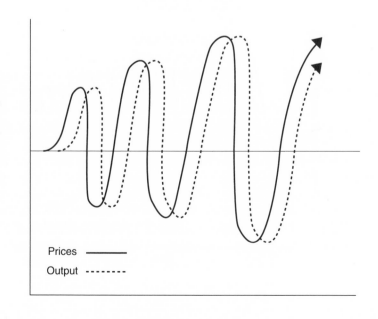

It is clear that the cobweb theorem is a very inadequate theory of economic fluctuations. Nevertheless, a process not unlike the one described is involved in actual economic fluctuations. While businessmen are not unaware of the effects on prices of increases in their production, current prices weigh very heavily in their considerations, and each individual entrepreneur is apt to underestimate the effect on prices of similar action by his rivals. This sort of behavior is particularly prevalent in highly competitive industries, such as agriculture, where each firm provides only a tiny fraction of total supply; and it is to such industries that the theorem has usually been applied. The theorem fits agriculture better than other competitive industries, because in agriculture there is often a considerable time lag between decisions to expand output and the marketing of the increased final product.

Perhaps the greatest value of the theorem is that it can be combined with the relation-multiplier analysis to show how a fairly regular cycle can be produced by a series of irregular "random shocks." What we see in the real world, in other words, may be successions of "cobwebs," converging or diverging, first moving toward higher levels of income and employment and then toward lower levels. An initial increase in investment may start an expansion process of the "cobweb" type, which may even be "diverging" while it lasts, and which is complicated and amplified by multiplier and relation effects; but then an adverse "shock" comes along, or the initial impetus may be withdrawn, and a movement toward lower levels of income and employment sets in, also following a "cobweb" pattern complicated by multiplier and relation effects. If nothing else happens to stop an expansion, the failure of consumption to go on expanding indefinitely at the same rate will ultimately bring a negative "relation" effect into play, investment will fall off, and a contraction will set in. The end results of this intricate process may very well give the appearance of a fairly regular cyclical movement—at least as regular as the economic fluctuations of the real world.

One of the best statements of the random shock theory of business cycle came from an economist who was not a specialist in business cycle theory at all, and was never published. Frederic B. Garver was professor of economics at the University of Minnesota when the present writer was there in the late 1930s. Minnesota had at the time a number of brilliant business cycle theorists, but Garver, who was best known for his microeconomic sections of the famous Garver and Hansen *Principles* textbook (the "Samuelson" of the time), had little empathy for their model building. To graduate students he knew well, he divulged his "Garver Garden Theory of Economic Fluctuations":

> Every year I plant my garden in the same way, but the results are never identical two years in a row. Sometimes there is an early frost, sometimes a late frost. Sometimes insects attack the roses, sometimes the tulips. Sometimes there is drought so severe as to preclude watering the garden properly. Sometimes there is too much rain. In exceptional years everything goes well, and I have a "boom." I could keep statistics, plot them, and make it appear that a "cycle" is operating. Actually, while there are certain constants of soil, climate, and human behaviour that limit the range of outcomes, the specific outcomes in each period are the result of causes specific to that period. It is the same with economic fluctuations. The mechanism of the economic system imposes some restraints on the range of possibilities, but to explain events in particular countries at particular times it is necessary to analyze the specific economic history of that country at that time. The appearance of approximation to regular cycles is largely illusory.

I have a good deal of sympathy for the "Garver Garden Theory." Explaining what has happened in the real world requires a good deal of economic history as well as economic theory. Still, it is not enough to describe the impulses. A complete explanation of business cycles requires also detailed analysis of the mechanism of propagation, including an explanation of why the system keeps going at all. Here the "constants" are of extreme importance. The capitalist economic system does not behave in a totally random fashion, and the task of the economist is to unravel the mystery of the degree of regularity and stability that it displays.

Over-Investment Theories

It is easy to understand how, in this world of uncertainty, individual entrepreneurs might get themselves into trouble by investing too much, either by overestimating the demand for their final product, or by underestimating rises in costs, especially wages and interest rates, in the near future. But why should so many entrepreneurs make the same mistakes, in the same direction and at the same time, that the entire economy gets into trouble? The "overinvestment theories" of the business cycle are designed to show why and how that can happen. There are two broad categories of overinvestment theories; those that explain the downturn and depression in terms of investment that is excessive relative to the amount of consumer spending and those that explain them in terms of investment that is excessive relative to the amount of voluntary saving. The first of these argues in effect that the boom breaks down because consumption is too low (savings are too high) and the second maintains that the downturn comes because savings are too low. (consumption is too high)

Hayek and the "Structure of Production"

Of all the "over-consumption" theories, the one that was at once the most intriguing and the most abstruse, and the one that brought the most passionate counter-attacks because of its policy implications, was that of Professor Friedrich von Hayek, then of the London School of Economics and later of the University of Chicago. Hayek's policy recommendations were described in capsule form as "bigger and better bankruptcies." Once the downturn comes—preferably even before it comes—the excessively capitalistic structure of production must be scrapped, wages must fall more than prices, and on no account must any money or credit be pumped into the system, or any government spending be undertaken, in a vain attempt to get the economy going again.

Hayek concentrated on one special feature of the functioning of the capitalist machine: the relationship between the "structure of production" and the rate of interest. He envisioned an economy with virtually complete flexibility regarding the choice of technology for producing the entire range of goods and services. If interest rates are low relative to wage rates, entrepreneurs will choose capital-intensive techniques, with high ratios of capital to labor and to output, roundabout methods of production involving many different stages in the production process, and with long time intervals between the beginning of the production process and the sale of the final product. If interest rates are high relative to wage rates, they will do just the opposite; and, moreover, according to Hayek, they will do so even if a capital-intensive structure of production is already in place. If at some point of time and for some reason interest rates are too low, and accordingly an excessively capital-intensive, multistage, roundabout technique of production is installed, and then later the interest rate is raised to its true equilibrium or "natural" rate, the existing structure of production becomes unprofitable. It must be scrapped, and replaced with a less capital-intensive, more labor-intensive, less roundabout, fewer-stages, less time-consuming structure. Only then can healthy expansion be resumed.

Following the fashion of the times, Hayek begins his analysis with the economy in a state of equilibrium, with full employment of all resources, and the price level stable, or, if productivity is increasing at a significant rate, gently falling. (For Hayek, maintenance of equilibrium required a constant MV, with the monetary authorities astutely varying M to offset changes in V.) Unemployment and inflation were for Hayek, as for most neoclassical economists of his day, aberrations to be explained; to start an analysis of economic fluctuations with unemployment or inflation already existing would be cheating. He takes Wesley Mitchell to task for not following suit:

> The existence of such unused resources is itself a fact that needs explanation. It is not explained by static analysis and, accordingly, we cannot take it for granted. For this reason I cannot agree that Professor Wesley Mitchell is justified when he states that he considers it no part of his task "to determine how the fact of cyclical oscillations in economic activity can be reconciled with the general theory of equilibrium, or how that theory can be reconciled with the facts." To start from the assumption of equilibrium has a further advantage. For in this way we are compelled to pay more attention to causes of changes in the industrial output whose importance might otherwise be underestimated. I refer to changes in the method of using existing resources.... What I have here in mind are not changes in the method of production made possible by the progress of technical knowledge, but the increase in output made possible by a transition to more capitalistic methods of production. (Hayek, 1935, 34, 35)

Nonetheless, the assumption of full employment of resources is vital to Hayek's analysis, for it validates his concept of the production of consumer's goods being in competition with production of capital goods for the same bundle of resources, rather than being mutually supportive, and even his concept of competition for resources among the various "stages" of the production process.

In elaborating his concepts of "structure of production," stages, roundabouts, and "the period of investment" Hayek utilized, and made famous among economists, the "triangle" introduced into the economics literature earlier by W. W. Jevons and Knut Wickwell. This concept is illustrated in figure 2.7. Here value of output is measured on the horizontal axis and time (in the downward direction) on the vertical axis. The production process is divided into stages, beginning at the top of the triangle, and proceeds, downward, through time, stage by stage, value being added to the total output with each stage, until we come to the bottom bar, which represents the final output of consumers' goods, the end result of the whole process. For example, the production of automobiles may be thought of as starting with the mining of iron and coal, and the planting of rubber trees; proceeding to the manufacture of steel and the tapping of rubber; then the making of steel shapes and latex; and finally the assembly of parts into automobiles and the manufacture of tires. The area of the triangle is the total amount of capital in use; the lowest bar can be thought of as the inventory of unsold consumers' goods at any point of time. The distance from top to bottom along the vertical axis is the period of investment.

It is essential to Hayek's theory that "by lengthening the production process we are able to obtain a greater quantity of consumers' goods out of a given quantity of original means of production...within practical limits we may increase the output of consumer goods from a given quantity of original means of production indefinitely, provided we are willing to wait long enough for the product. The thing which is of main interest to us is that any such change from a method of production of any given duration to a method that takes more or less time implies quite definite changes in the organization of production, or...in the structure of production" (Hayek, 1935, 37–38). He adds that, "as the average time interval between the application of the original means of production and the completion of the consumers' goods increases, production becomes more capitalistic, and *vice versa*" (42). ("Capitalistic" in this context means capital-using or capital-intensive, and does not refer to the "capitalist system".) In a stationary state (an economy in static equilibrium) the value of final consumers' goods produced will just equal the incomes paid to factors of production. The stock of capital (the shaded areas of figure 2.7) will not last forever independently of human decisions; it needs to be constantly renewed, and it will not be renewed unless it appears profitable to do so.

Hayek introduces at this point savings; consumers voluntarily decide to save and invest one fourth of their income for one period. The ratio of demand for final products to demand for intermediate goods changes from 40:80 to 30:90, or from 1:2 to 1:3. The average period of production and the number of stages must be increased in the same proportion as the increased demand for intermediate goods, as shown in figure 2.8. The amount of money spent in the later stages of production, as well as the amount spent on final consumers' goods, falls. The amount spent in

FIGURE 2.7
Hayek's Triangle

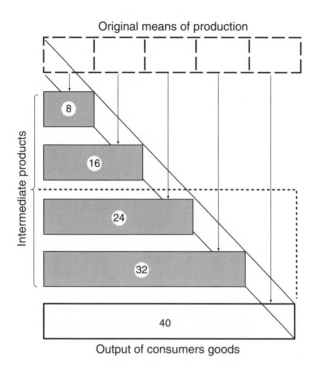

Original means of production

Intermediate products

Output of consumers goods

Source: F.A. von Hayek, *Prices and Production,* figures 2–6: 44, 52, 56, 59, and 61.

the earlier stages increases. The actual output of consumers' goods, however, will actually increase, because of the more capitalistic (roundabout) method of production. Since the amount of money and its velocity of circulation remain unchanged, prices of consumers' goods fall, and also the prices of factors of production; but prices of factors fall less than prices of consumers' goods, real incomes rise, and a new equilibrium is established with everyone better off.

The story is very different—according to Hayek—if the lengthening of the period of production comes about, not through voluntary saving, but through extension of credits and an increase in the money supply. Let us suppose that the producers receive forty units of extra money. As shown in figure 2.9, the changes in structure of production that will be

FIGURE 2.8
Hayek's Triangle

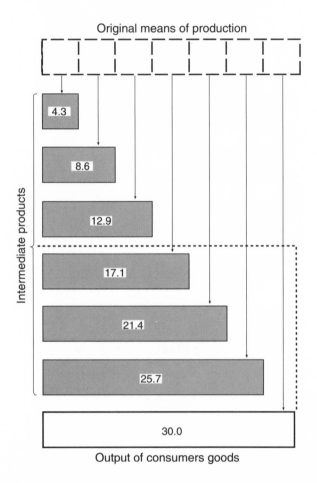

Output of consumers goods

Source: F. A. von Hayek, *Prices and Production*, figures 2–6: 44, 52, 56, 59, and 61.

needed to absorb this extra money will be the same as if the funds had been provided by saving. Now, however, because of the increase in money supply, prices must rise, to a level one third higher than in figure 2.9; but this is not the only difference between the figures 2.8 and 2.9.

There is, however, another and far more important difference which will become apparent only with a lapse of time. When a change in structure was brought about

FIGURE 2.9
Hayek's Triangle

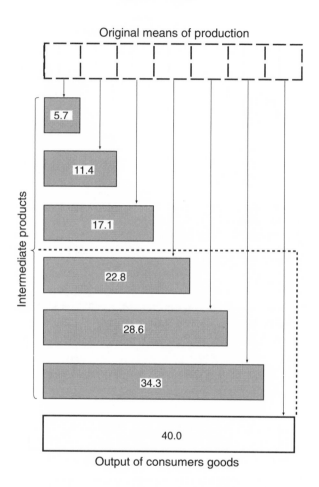

Source: F.A. von Hayek, *Prices and Production,* figures 2–6: 44, 52, 56, 59, and 61.

by saving, we were justified in assuming that the changed distribution of demand between consumers' goods and producers' goods would remain permanent, since it was the effect of voluntary decisions on the part of individuals.... There would accordingly exist no inherent cause for a return to the old proportions.

In the same way, in the case we are now considering, the use of a larger proportion of the original means of production for the manufacture of intermediate products can only be brought about by a retrenchment of consumption. But now this sacri-

fice is not voluntary, and it is not made by those who will reap the benefit from the
new investments. It is made by consumers...who are forced to forego part of what
they used to consume. It comes about not because they want to consume less, but
they get less goods for their money income. There can be no doubt that, if their
money receipts should rise again, they would immediately attempt to expand consumption to the usual proportion. (Hayek, 1935, 55–57)

Thus, a lengthening of the period of production that is based on "forced
savings" is inherently unstable. Hayek argues that the behavior of the
economic system, and especially of its banking component, is such that
the consumers will get more income in the course of the boom, they will
bid up prices and profits of the consumers' goods industries; they, in
turn, will bid resources away from the producers' goods industries, and
the latter will be in trouble.

If we assume that the old proportions are adhered to, then the structure of production will have to return to the old proportion, as shown in Figure 2.10. That is to
say production will become less capitalistic, and that part of the new capital which
was sunk in equipment adapted only to the more capitalistic processes will be
lost. We shall see...that such a transition to less capitalistic methods of production necessarily takes the form of an economic crisis. (Hayek 1935, 58)

If Hayek were right about the nature, causes, and effects of such
changes in the structure of production, all we would need to complete
Hayek's theory of economic fluctuations is some reason for the initial
expansion of credit at interest rates below the "natural" rate that limits
investment to the level of voluntary savings, and some process by which
the consequent boom and lengthening of the period of production puts
income into the hands of consumers, enabling them to bring about the
necessary but disruptive shortening that will ultimately restore equilibrium. Here Hayek joins the other monetary theorists. Banks with excess
reserves do not immediately raise interest rates when some favorable
development—an important innovation, for example—bring about an
increase in demand for credit. Investment based on bank lending brings a
cumulative expansion, which cannot continue indefinitely, and when consumers exercise their newly increased purchasing power and the banks,
finding their reserves exhausted, will expand credits no further, the capital goods industries collapse, generating a cumulative downswing.

Hayek's description of the operation of the banking system is not very
different from Hawtrey's, except for two features: Hayek makes the point
that the higher the stage of production—the further from sale of final

FIGURE 2.10
Hayek's Triangle

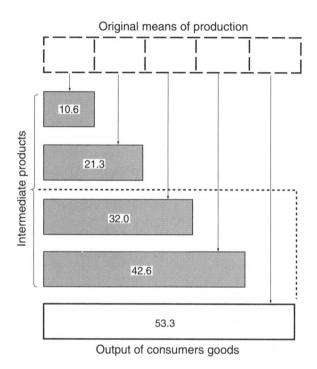

Original means of production

Intermediate products

10.6

21.3

32.0

42.6

53.3

Output of consumers goods

Source: F.A. von Hayek, *Prices and Production,* figures 2–6: 44, 52, 56, 59, and 61.

consumers' goods—the more potent the impact of an interest rate below the natural rate. Low interest rates are more influential on people who want a twenty-five-year mortgage to buy a house than those who want to borrow for a week to finance a holiday. Thus, interest rates below the equilibrium lengthen the period of production. Conversely, when interest rates rise at the end of the boom, it is the higher stages of production that are most adversely affected. Thus, where Hawtrey stressed the impact of changes in interest rates on the holding of inventories, Hayek stressed their impact on roundaboutness of production. Secondly, Hayek emphasized his argument that the longer a boom is kept going by further injections of bank credit, the worse will be the crash when it comes.

[W]e are forced to recognize the fundamental truth, so frequently neglected nowadays, that the machinery of capitalistic production will function smoothly only so long as we are satisfied to consume no more than that part of our total wealth which under the existing organization of production is destined for current consumption. Every increase in consumption, if it is not to disturb production, requires previous saving, even if the existing equipment with durable instruments of production should be sufficient for such an increase of output.... If the foregoing analysis is correct, it should be fairly clear that the granting of credit to consumers, which has recently been so strongly advocated as a cure for depression, would in fact have quite the contrary effect; a relative increase in the demand for consumers' goods could only make matters worse. (Hayek, 1935, 95, 97)

While Hayek's theory commanded a great deal of attention and prompted much discussion and criticism, it cannot be said that it led to prompt and widespread acceptance. With the "Keynesian Revolution" and the clarification of macroeconomics that followed, Hayek's ideas were increasingly rejected. One of the most sweeping dismissals of the Hayek theory came from Aaron Gordon:

There is no need to criticize this type of theory in detail. Although credit tightness and a shortage of loanable funds played some role in many of the American downturns before 1914, there is little evidence in the business-cycle history of the last 40 years to support this...capital-shortage theory. The theory is unrealistic to an extreme degree, particularly in its analysis of the investment process. It ignores nearly the whole range of factors that influence business expectations and the evaluation of investment opportunities by businessmen. It grossly exaggerates the importance of the interest rate in influencing the volume of investment. It largely ignores the role of technological change.... No attention is paid to the ways in which investment is linked to consumers' demand. (Gordon, 1952, 1961, 360)

A theory leading to policy recommendations so contrary to the current trend in economic thought, and so harsh and unpopular, was bound to run into fierce opposition.

Estey devotes a whole chapter to Hayek's theory, and his treatment is balanced and fair. In conclusion he says, "Hayek's theory of the cycle is an ingenious solution of the problem posed by the disproportionate production of capital goods" (1946, 253). But he goes on to state, "There are serious obstacles, however, to the acceptance of this theory" (253). First, if lengthening and shortening the period of production means increasing and decreasing the number of stages, then the theory does not fit the facts, especially as regards the "shortening" in the downswing. The contrast between "voluntary" and forced saving is overdrawn. Violent fluctuations in voluntary saving could cause cycles, and steady forced savings need not be disturbing. Estey's main objection, however, is to Hayek's assumption of equilibrium with full employment of all resources as a starting point:

> There is still further objection to Hayek's theory arising from his assumption that cycles are disturbances of an equilibrium where resources are fully employed, and the necessary consequence that expansion of production goods can be only at the expense of consumers' goods, and vice versa.
>
> This theory is paradoxical. Not only is it belied by the evidence of fact, but it seems to mistake completely the relation of the demand for producers' goods to the demand for consumers' goods. As to the facts, far from there being at any time a complete employment of resources, what actually occurs is unemployment of both capital and labor even at the peaks of activity. One of the principal characteristics of industrial fluctuations is the simultaneous expansion and contraction in the output of both producers' and consumers' goods. In fact, the latter outcome is what would be expected because of the nature of the demand for producers' goods. This demand is a derived demand, dependent upon and reflecting the demand for consumers' goods. When the demand for consumers' goods rises or falls, so will the demand for the producers' goods which go to their making.

Gottfried von Haberler gives his fellow Austrian's theory a respectful analysis. "The most valuable and original contributions of the monetary over-investment theory," he says, "are (1) the analysis of the maladjustment in the structure of production brought about by credit expansion during the prosperity phase of the cycle and (2) the explanation of the breakdown as a consequence of that maladjustment" (Haberler 1958, 71). But, he adds, "the theory is not in all respects complete," and its "claim to exclusive validity is open to doubt." He is skeptical of von Hayek's asymmetrical treatment of lengthening and shortening the period of production, and asks, why shouldn't the initial inflationary expansion of investment cause as much trouble for consumers' goods industries as the later expansion of the consumers' goods industries causes for the capital goods industries? He finds the assumption of full employment too restrictive, and concludes that the theory provides "no simple formula" that could explain "why one cycle follows another without interruption" (67).

Alvin Hansen dissects the Hayek theory into ten theses and then proceeds to show why none of them is wholly satisfactory. Several of them just don't seem to fit the facts, such as the basic "Thesis No. 1" that depression is brought about by a shortening of the period of production, that is, by a shrinkage in the stock of capital goods. Hansen maintains that depression is brought about simply by a decline in net investment, and that it is only rarely that depressions are so severe as to bring net investment below zero. He complains that "Hayek's analysis not only overlooks the real factors which cause spurts in capital formation, but it also overplays, to a degree that is not defensible, monetary causes of disturbance" (Hansen 1951, 390).

Hayek gave a sturdy defense of his theory, and through the years following the publication of his *Prices and Production* provided several restatements of it. Finally, in 1939, he wrote a new book presenting a radically different version, in which the breakdown comes, not as a result of a rise in the rate of interest, but a consequence of a rise in profits in the lower stages of production, due to a fall in real wage rates. Even if interest rates are stable, in this new version, the rise in profits will bring a shortening of the period of production, downswing, and depression (Hayek 1939).

This restatement pleased Hayek's colleagues even less than the original one. The idea that the economy collapses because profits are too high seemed bizarre. But there was no mistaking Hayek's meaning:

> Once the cumulative process has been entered upon the end must always come through a rise in profits in the late stages and can never come through a fall in profits or an exhaustion of investment opportunities. (Hayek, 1939, 33)

In 1942, Nicholas Kaldor published in *Economica* a brilliant if unkind article, under the somewhat disrespectful title, "Professor Hayek and the Concertina Effect," likening Hayek's lengthening and shortening periods of production to a musician playing a concertina. The article was republished in his *Essays on Economic Stability and Growth* (Kaldor, 1942, 1960). He begins:

> It was more than ten years ago that Professor Hayek first fascinated the academic world of economists by a new theory of industrial fluctuations which in theoretical conception, and perhaps even more in its practical implications, was diametrically opposed to the current trend of monetary thought.... In comparison to Professor Hayek's "triangles," "distorted price-margins," and unduly-elongated production periods, the prevailing concern with price levels, and with the banks doing this and that, must have appeared facile and superficial. (Kaldor, 1960, 148)

But, says Kaldor, this was only the first impact. On second thoughts, the theory was "by no means so intellectually satisfying as it appeared at first" (148). Hayek's *Prices and Production,* says Kaldor, "produced a remarkable crop of critics...which could rarely have been equalled in the economic controversies of the past." His article is concerned with the "new version of his theory, which in many ways radically departed from, and contradicted, the first" (148–49). Kaldor was not impressed by the new version:

> In my view, the "concertina-effect" as a phenomenon of the trade cycle is non-existent or insignificant, while the supposition that a scarcity of savings causes booms to collapse is fallacious. The first is one of those blind alleys of economic speculation which appear very suggestive for a time, but whose significance evaporates as soon as one tries to fit the theoretical conclusions more closely to the observed phenomena. The second, I am now convinced, must be altogether abandoned as a supposition before any reasonably consistent explanation of the trade cycle can be reached. (153)

Hayek's main thesis, Kaldor reminds us, "is that a rise in demand for consumers' goods leads to a fall in investment expenditure, thereby causing unemployment and general depression." Hayek asserts that this reversal must inevitably happen, because the fall in real wages will lead to a substitution of labor for capital and thus a fall in demand for capital goods, and a shift of capital from earlier to later stages of production. Kaldor asks, "Can it (this reversal) happen at all?" (169). Kaldor thinks not:

> However hard we try, we cannot construct a case where as a result of a rise in profit the capital intensity falls and as a result of this fall in capital intensity, investment expenditure will be less than it was before...the reduction in capital intensity will make the rise in investment less than it would have been if capital intensity had remained constant. But it cannot eliminate it altogether because capital intensity would not have fallen if investment expenditure had not risen.
>
> This is the fundamental point, which knocks the bottom out of Professor Hayek's new theory of the trade cycle, quite apart from any arbitrariness or unreality of the assumption on which it was based. (169–70)

Other trade cycle theorists were scarcely more enthusiastic about Hayek's revised theory than was Kaldor. Hansen says of it, "There are several things in this analysis which on closer scrutiny appear more than doubtful. It is not clearly established that real wages do in fact fall in the last half of the boom. Moreover, it is not the relations of the money wage rate to the index of cost of living (real wage rate) which determines the substitution of machinery for labor, or vice versa; rather it is the wage rate in relation to the price of machinery, assuming no change in technology or the personal efficiency of the worker" (Hansen, 1951, 392). Gordon, after a brief outline of the new version, dismisses it with the remark, "Neither version is of sufficient importance to warrant further discussion here" (Gordon, 1960, 365).

Can we, then, forget about monetary overinvestment theories, or at least Hayek's version of them? I think not. Hayek was certainly wrong in presenting his theory as *the* explanation of economic fluctuations, to the exclusion of all others. But, despite the flaws in his theory, there remains an important element of truth in it. There *is* a relationship between the structure of production and the structure of interest rates, the structure of prices, the structure of profits, and the structure of wages. Structures of production that are compatible with some of these structures will be incompatible with others. One of the ways in which an economy can go wrong is if entrepreneurs make investments on the expectation of certain of these structures, and then these structures turn out to be different, requiring adaptation of structures of production that may be troublesome—and if they give rise to panic, or even to a deflationary monetary policy, to downswing and depression.

Nonmonetary Overinvestment Theories

We shall say little about nonmonetary overinvestment theories because, as stated above, our aim here is not to present a comprehensive survey of the history of thought in the field of business cycles, but to pour earlier theories through a sort of analytical sieve, to see what remains of them that is still valuable in improving our understanding of what goes on in the world's economies (and the world economy) today. It is obvious that nonmonetary factors play an important role in economic fluctuations, and our understanding is enhanced more by theories that include them than by ones that don't. Nonetheless, it is important to recognize that economies can get into trouble even if monetary policy is immaculate, so we shall say a word or two about these theories.

In a complex industrial society, it is not difficult to imagine that from time to time supplies and demands, both for factors of production and for final products, can get out of balance. Both foresight and the spread of information are imperfect. The market and the price system are supposed to take care of these excesses and deficiencies of demand or supply, and to some extent they certainly do so. But how quickly and how thoroughly? Shocks as severe as the increases in oil prices of the 1970s and 1980s can take years to overcome, and meanwhile some enterprises may not survive. The supply of raw materials or types of capital equipment important for particular industries may prove to be less than anticipated, and prices higher, causing difficulties. Most industrialized capitalist countries allow individuals (or their parents) considerable leeway in their choice of education and training programs; shortages of some types of technical, scientific, and professional skills and surpluses of others are inevitable, leading to educated unemployed in some fields and excessively high labor costs in others. The question is, however, why should such imbalances lead to general unemployment or inflation throughout the entire economy, and why should unemployment or inflation appear periodically, in more or less cyclical patterns?

Perhaps the economist most cited in connection with nonmonetary overinvestment theories is Arthur Spiethoff; and of all the arguments and illustrations provided by Spiethoff, probably the favorite has been his example of the pair of gloves. If one of a pair of gloves is lost, Spiethoff says, the other becomes an unsaleable surplus stock. One can easily imagine that if the glove industry were divided into two branches with little contact between them, one producing left-hand gloves and the other right-hand gloves, the industry could be frequently in trouble. Spiethoff thought that a capitalist economy is something like that; it is divided into sectors with little coordination between them. The principal sectors are current consumption goods, durable consumers' goods, durable capital (producers') goods, and raw materials needed to build up these capital goods. The upswing is initiated when investment is stimulated by a favorable "shock" like an innovation, resource discovery, or opening up of new territory. The investment may result in expansion of credit and the money supply, but this expansion is the result, not the cause, of the upswing. The expansion generates a cumulative, but unbalanced, growth of the economy. The nature of the economy is such that the capital goods industries always expand more rapidly than the others. Yet the four categories of goods are complementary to each other; the shortage one category means overproduction of another. Gottfried Haberler describes well how this situation leads to a downturn:

> Thus there develops an over-production of producers' goods and durable consumers' goods. These are the remaining glove. But where is the missing one? Is not the missing one a purely monetary phenomenon—namely, investible funds which could be supplied by the printing press? No, answers Professor Spiethoff. The

lack of monetary funds available for investment represents a shortage of physical goods of a certain kind.... A lack of investable funds simply means that these complementary goods (labor and means of subsistence) are not available. There we have the missing glove. It consists of labor and consumers' goods. (Haberler, 1958, 77)

This theory is valid as far as it goes; but since we know that the functioning of the banking system plays a vital role in economic fluctuations, why not include them in our theory? As Haberler says of Spiethoff, "his diagnosis of the disequilibrium at the end of the boom is substantially the same as that given by the monetary over-investment school. The allocation of factors of production to the various stages of production does not correspond to the flow of money, the lower stages in the structure of production are under-developed" (77–78). Cast in terms such as these, there is an obvious similarity between Spiethoff's theory and Hayek's, and there can be little doubt that Hayek was influenced by Spiethoff. Also, in Spiethoff's theory it is not altogether clear why the capital goods industry must always expand disproportionately to the rest of the economy during a boom, and contract disproportionately during the downswing. There is in Spiethoff an implication of the acceleration principle, but it is not clearly spelled out. The acceleration principle does explain why fluctuations are particularly violent in the capital goods industry, and will be discussed below.

Underconsumption Theories

Among the categories of trade cycle theories commonly identified, there remain the underconsumption (or oversavings) theories. It is easy enough to see that trouble will occur if a number of major industries expand their capacities together beyond the point where consumers will buy their total output at profitable prices. But once again, the trick is to explain why that should happen, and why it should happen more or less regularly, in a cyclical pattern.

Because the basic ideas are relatively simple, the concept of underconsumption as the cause of downturns and depressions is one of the earliest to appear in the economics literature, dating back at least to Lauderdale and Malthus in the early nineteenth century. Lord Lauderdale's book, *An Inquiry into the Nature and Origin of Public Wealth,* was published in 1804. He was concerned by the inequality of income distribution. He recognized that unequal income distribution promoted saving, which could finance investment and the accumulation of wealth; but he also saw clearly that saving is basically nonconsuming, and that investment cannot be profitable unless its product is sold at a price that will more than cover costs. Unlike most economists of the period, he did not accept Say's law as established truth; nonconsuming (saving) is not automatically offset by increased investment: "What is affirmed, and what we have attempted to establish by argument, is 1st, that the old maxim, `a penny saved is a penny gained,' is not applicable to public wealth," that is, to what we would now call national income. He also sensed that as national income rises, the proportion of it that is saved (not spent for consumption) tends to rise, and that the same is not always true of investment. Hansen states, "Lauderdale had, in a vague way, as was true of many early economists, a conception of the multiplier; i.e. he saw that the changes in national income and consumption can be a multiple of changes in investment, and that this principle applies in both directions. Thus, being only a little bit charitable, we can say that Lauderdale understood that an initial increase in investment can generate a cumulative expansion, but that the very expansion will eventually bring an increase in savings not offset by an increase in investment, so that national income must eventually fall, bringing a decrease in investment, bringing the multiplier into action in a negative direction and generating a cumulative downswing. That statement is the essence of the underconsumption theory."

Lauderdale was primarily concerned with the increasing burden of public debt, and his statements about that are of great interest today, when so many countries, less developed and industrialized, share the same concern. He argued that the servicing of the national debt could withdraw so much income that it would diminish both investment and consumer spending, and thus cause unemployment. It is interesting to compare this statement with the 1990 Budget Message of Harold Wilson, then Finance Minister of Canada, one of the countries worried about its increasing national debt today:

A public debt growing faster than national income does more than feed on itself. It consumes more and more of the dollars we need to maintain existing programs, meet new priorities and keep taxes down.... The prospects for lower inflation and interest rates depend crucially on keeping costs under control. If we try to take out of the economy more than it is capable of producing, our inflation problems will worsen and the economy will suffer.... This will be a testing year for the Canadian economy.... Employment is expected to continue growing, but not as quickly as the labor force, and the unemployment rate will rise. (Wilson, 1990, 16–17)

Thus, a modern industrial nation, with all of the most sophisticated instruments of monetary and fiscal policy at its disposal, finds itself incapable of containing inflation, reducing its debt, and avoiding higher unemployment. Lauderdale was a good prophet.

Thomas Malthus

Malthus was not much interested in economic fluctuations. He was more interested in economic development, and particularly in the depression, poverty and unemployment that followed the Napoleonic Wars. As Alvin Hansen put it,

Malthus did not have the concept of a "cycle" of trade or employment. He was concerned with a condition—that of inadequate demand and unemployment. The problem of inadequate demand is related to the process of saving. Inadequate demand could not in any fundamental way arise in a society that consumed all its income. (Hansen, 1951, 242)

In many ways Malthus foreshadowed the concepts of secular stagnation, economic maturity, and underemployment equilibrium that were introduced into the economic literature a century later by writers such as Hansen, Kalecki, and Keynes.

Twentieth-Century Underconsumption Theories

It is easy enough to see how underconsumption and oversavings could lead to stagnation and chronic unemployment; but why should they take a cyclical pattern? Several economists of our own day have sought to answer that question. Haberler says: "In its best-reasoned form (e.g., in the writings of Messrs. J. A. Hobson and Foster and Catchings) the under-consumption theory uses under-consumption to mean over-saving. Depressions are caused by the fact that too large a proportion of current income is being saved and too small a proportion is spent on consumers' goods" (Haberler, 1938, 122). Hobson—and a good many other economists—thought that this oversaving was related to the unequal distribution of income. This relationship could explain cyclical downturns if booms made the maldistribution of income worse, as they well might. There have been many booms in which prices rose faster than wages, so that real wages fell and profits rose, reducing consumption and raising savings. Alternatively, regular downturns could occur if there were a general tendency for the propensity to save to rise as incomes increased during booms, as some economists have claimed. Haberler is skeptical regarding this claim, stating bluntly that "there is no evidence for the claim that the rate of saving rises at the end of the boom and so creates serious difficulties. On the contrary...it would seem rather that the rate of saving falls in the later phase of the boom" (Haberler, 1938, 126–27).

Haberler also considers the argument that during a boom resources are diverted for a time from consumers' goods industries to producers' goods industries; incomes and demand rise, consumers' goods become scarce, and prices rise; then the new plant and equipment comes into use; "consumers' goods begin to be poured out; the markets for consumers' goods are glutted; and this reacts with increasing intensity on the higher stages of production" (Haberler, 1938, 128). He does not deny this possibility, merely reminding his readers that other economists have argued the exact opposite, too much consumption and a consequent lack of savings to finance the completion of the new investment undertaken in the boom.

We are confronted here with a question of fact, which cannot be settled by "pure reason." We shall not devote more space to this question in this chapter, because it was largely resolved by the developments in economic thought that took place in the late 1930s and in the 1940s, when attention turned from the question, "Why are there cycles?" to the questions: "Why is the great depression of the 1930s so deep and so prolonged? What could cause secular stagnation, and why should the economy get stuck in what seems like an equilibrium position with large-scale unemployment? Could the capitalist economic system actually tend to move cumulatively *away* from equilibrium, once disturbed? Are there *many* factors in the normal functioning of the economic system that could cause a disturbance, so that the economy is continually poised on a knife edge (or a tightrope) between unemployment and inflation?"

To these questions we shall turn in the next chapter. In this chapter we have already seen various ways in which the economic system could go wrong. None of the theories we have reviewed can be dismissed out of hand, as totally irrelevant. The trouble with the classic literature on business cycles was that all the authors (excluding the Marxist) basically expected the capitalist system to perform well, were puzzled when it didn't, and looked for *the* cause of the misbehavior, to the exclusion of all others. Once economists got around to the twin ideas that (a) the capitalist system is naturally prone to disturbances, with many possible causes, and (b) most of these causes can be eliminated, or at least moderated and modified, by astute economic policy, the stage was set for a great leap forward in the understanding and the management of capitalist economies.

Schumpeter's Theory of Innovations

We have seen that an economic system with built-in restraints on the violence of movements in either direction, and subject to random shocks, can produce cyclical movements as regular as those observed in the real world. We have seen, too, that in a capitalistic economy the "shocks" are most likely to be reflected initially in increases or decreases in private investment. But why should private investment be subject to more or less regular fluctuations? Among prewar theories of business cycles, the best explanation of why capitalistic economies should experience occasional spurts in private investment, leading to economic fluctuations, is the theory of "innovations" developed by Professor Joseph Schumpeter of Harvard University. An innovation is the introduction into use of a new product or new technique, the development of a new territory or a new natural resource, an improvement in organization—indeed, "any `doing things differently.'" Technically, an innovation is defined as a reduction in the total unit costs of producing a given sort of good or service without a drop in the price of any factor of production used. Innovations must be sharply distinguished from inventions; the patent office is full of applications for patents on inventions that never see the light of day. Only inventions that are actually developed, and so have an impact on the economy, are considered innovations.

An innovation entails the construction of new plant and equipment. It may do so in any of three different ways. First, it may hasten the replacement of existing plant and equipment by rendering it obsolete. Second, it may create an expectation of high monopoly profits for the first firm in the new field, and thus raise the "marginal efficiency" of capital in general, leading to an increase in total net investment. Third, it may produce a new product that seems so attractive that people are willing to cut into their savings to have it, thus raising the propensity to consume and making additional plant and equipment profitable and necessary. Professor Schumpeter himself stresses the second of these types of expansionary processes. He also argues "as if" the construction of new plant and equipment was undertaken by new firms, and points out that historically there is no lack of realism in such an argument; most of the major innovations—such as the railways and steamships of the nineteenth century and the automobiles, chemicals, and electric power of the twentieth—have in fact been developed mainly by new firms. Schumpeter also argues that the development of the new firms is usually associated with the rise to business leadership of new men, and here too he points to history to substantiate his argument.

This part of Schumpeter's theory is very important, for it means that unless business leadership is forthcoming to build up new firms for the exploitation of innovations, capitalist economies may suffer more or less chronic depression. Enterprise of the sort basic to economic expansion, Schumpeter insists, is something different from the genius of the inventor, or the efficiency of the executive of a going concern, or even the willingness to risk one's own capital in new enterprises. It consists mainly of seeing and seizing the *opportunity* for development of a new firm; historically, it has been this kind of special skill that has been most handsomely rewarded in capitalistic economies.

Once the innovator has demonstrated the profitability of his venture, followers will enter the field in "clusters." The original innovator will of course try to maintain his monopoly position, but in the past he has seldom had complete success in this regard. Today, with more and more of the inventions coming forth as the product of research departments of existing firms, the chances of protecting monopoly positions and preventing the "cluster" of would-be followers from entering the new field are better. By the same token, the expansionary force of innovations is diminishing.

The development of the new industry is followed by the adaptation of old industries to the changed pattern of demand. The development of railroads entailed the construction of new towns, relocation of old industries, expansion of the iron and steel industry, and so forth. The development of the automobile industry brought with it the move to the suburbs, the construction of highways, the development of new recreation centers, the development of the petroleum and rubber industries, and so on. A "big" innovation like railroads or automobiles can generate an enormous wave of new investment through its direct and indirect effects on the economy.

Schumpeter, like most other analysts of economic fluctuations, assumes that the wave of new investment is financed largely by new credit created by the banks. This assumption is, of course, perfectly realistic. In other words, the investment is financed by monetary expansion rather than by an increase in current (*ex ante*) savings, a spread between investment and *ex ante* savings develops, and the upswing is under way.

In the models of the cycle presented above, all that is needed for a complete explanation of the cycle is the initial increase in investment; from there on, the various phases of the cycle can be explained in terms of the interactions of the strategic variables—investment, savings, multiplier, relation, expectations, and so on. Thus, our theory is really complete at this stage. However, Schumpeter has his own explanation of the down turn, which can be readily superimposed on explanations cast in terms of multiplier and relation, or in terms of disappointed expectations. When the "gestation" period is over, and the new plants are completed, the rate of investment drops to the level necessary for replacement only; net investment ceases. Obviously, the operation of a railway involves less current investment than its construction.

Moreover, once the new plants are in operation, there will be a new and increased flow of consumers' goods onto the market; this factor in itself would tend to reduce prices. The tendency for prices to fall is enhanced by contraction of the money supply; as the new firms begin to sell their product, they come into possession of a "stream of receipts," which enables them to reduce their indebtedness to the banks. Reducing debt means simply the cancellation of deposits, and consequently the money supply contracts. With increasing supplies of goods on the market and a decreasing supply of money to buy them, prices naturally tend to fall. Some firms make windfall losses as a result of this unforeseen drop in prices: commercial failures increase, aggregate profits decline, expectations become gloomy, and the impulse for innovation itself dries up; depression ensues.

A significant conclusion to be derived from Schumpeter's theory is that continued economic expansion requires a steady stream of innovations, each more capital-absorbing in its aggregate effects than the last. Unless a new innovation is reaching its peak effects when the last one is completed, total investment, and so income and employment, will tend to fall. Clearly, this is a tall order. Having once had an innovation that absorbed such huge quantities of capital as railways, it became very difficult to develop other innovations, or even "bundles" of innovations, that were even more capital absorbing.

Unemployment, Inflation, and the Keynesian System

The Keynesian economic system is an integral part of contemporary economics, as quantum mechanics or Newtonian physics is an integral part of contemporary physics. That is, it no longer makes sense to speak of Keynesian economics *versus* some other kind of economics; one may as well speak of "2+2=4" arithmetic *versus* other schools of arithmetic thought. Thus, the explanation of unemployment and inflation, and the search for solutions, inevitably involve elements of Keynesian economics. However, we cannot here provide a thorough exposition of Keynesian and neo-Keynesian economics; there are plenty of good textbooks on macroeconomics, and this book is not designed to be one of them. Since we want this book to be understandable to noneconomists as well as interesting to professional economists and students of economics, we provide a very brief section presenting the bare bones of the Keynesian system; those who want more, but not more than one book, might read Alvin Hansen's *Guide to Keynes* or any contemporary text on macroeconomics (Kenneth Boulding's, for example).

There are other reasons for keeping our discussion of the Keynesian system to a bare minimum in the present volume. Keynes's great work *The General Theory of Employment, Interest and Money,* which revolutionized economic thought at the time of its publication in 1936 and is now thoroughly incorporated into the received doctrine, *was general.* Although written at a time when interest and concern were focused on unemployment, it is equally applicable to an explanation of inflation, and is equally valid as a basis for policy prescription for either. (As such, it does not explain simultaneous inflation and unemployment, nor does it provide policy solutions to this phenomenon.) Moreover—and curiously enough—Keynes had relatively little interest in "the trade cycle," or economic fluctuations. In comparison to Alvin Hansen, for example, Keynes even had little to say about the particular reasons for the extraordinary depth and duration of the Great Depression, during which he wrote his

General Theory. What he did do was to show the possibility of equilibrium being established with a large volume of unemployment, thus shattering the myth so long held by so many economists, that true "equilibrium" meant full employment, and stable (or perhaps gently falling) prices.

The *General Theory* does include a chapter entitled "Notes on the Trade Cycle," but it tends to confirm his lack of concern with discovering specific causes of trade cycles in general, or of the Great Depression in particular. Sydney Merlin says of these notes:

> These comments do not constitute anything like a systematic theory of the cycle and are in the nature of penetrating conjectures rather than hypotheses reasoned from empirical evidence.... A theory of the business cycle based on Keynes' work has been developed by Harrod and stated in more rigorous form by Hansen and Samuelson. (Merlin, 1949, 105–9)

Keynes's Notes on the Trade Cycle

Keynes begins his comments on the trade cycle with a well-nigh impeccable statement of the futility of searching for *the* cause of economic fluctuations, and of expecting every downturn or upturn to have precisely the same causes:

> Since we claim to have shown in the preceding chapters what determines the volume of employment at any time, it follows, if we are right, that our theory must be capable of explaining the phenomenon of the Trade Cycle.

> If we examine the details of any actual existence of the Trade Cycle, we shall find that it is highly complex and that every element in our analysis will be required for its complete explanation.... The Trade Cycle is best regarded, I think, as being occasioned by a cyclical change in the marginal efficiency of capital, though complicated and often aggravated by associated changes in the other short-period variables of the economic system. (Keynes, 1936, 313)

He does not really endeavor to pin down the precise reasons for the cyclical behavior of the marginal efficiency of capital, but he has some wise words to say about the meaning of the term cycle and about periodicity:

> By a cyclical movement we mean that as the system progresses in, e.g. the upward direction, the forces propelling it upwards at first gather force and have a cumulative effect on one another but gradually lose their strength until at a certain point they tend to be replaced by forces operating in the opposite direction; which in turn gather force for a time and accentuate one another, until they too, having

reached their maximum development, wane and give place to their opposite. We do not, however, merely mean by a cyclical movement that upward and downward tendencies, once started, do not persist forever in the same direction but are ultimately reversed. We mean also that there is some recognizable degree of regularity in the time sequence and duration of the upward and downward movements. (313–14)

Keynes then notes the asymmetry between upper and lower turning points; the former is sharp, sudden, and violent, taking the form of a crisis ; the latter is a more gradual substitution of an upward for a downward tendency. He goes on to say that "any fluctuation in investment not offset by a corresponding change in the propensity to consume will, of course, result in a fluctuation in employment" (214). The typical crisis is caused, not by a rise in the rate of interest, but by "a sudden collapse in the marginal efficiency of capital." The later stages of a boom bring excessively optimistic expectations regarding future yields on capital goods, which more than offset the rises in costs of production and interest rates (315). Keynes's skeletal theory of the trade cycle certainly has many of the features of a "psychological theory." When disillusion comes, he says, it falls "with sudden and even catastrophic force, bringing "a sharp increase in liquidity preference—and hence a rise in the rate of interest" (316). The time element in the trade cycle is explained by the life span of durable assets and the carrying costs of surplus stocks [inventories (317)]. With a "stock-minded public," such as is found in the United States, a rising stock market is "almost an essential condition of a satisfactory propensity to consume," and a stock market crash aggravates the crisis (319).

> Moreover, the corresponding movements in the stock market may, as we have shown above, depress the propensity to consume just when it is most needed. In conditions of *laissez-faire* the avoidance of wide fluctuations in employment may, therefore, prove impossible without a far-reaching change in the psychology of investment markets such as there is no reason to expect. I conclude that the duty of ordering the current volume of investment cannot be safely left in private hands. (320)

Keynes dismisses Hayek's overinvestment theory, and maintains that "the remedy for the boom is not higher interest rates but lower interest rates!" (322). "Thus an increase in the rate of interest, as a remedy for the state of affairs arising out of a prolonged period of abnormally heavy new investment, belongs to the species of remedy which cures the disease by killing the patient."

Keynes concludes that the best way to prolong prosperity is to encourage *both* investment and consumers spending:

> Whilst aiming at a socially controlled rate of investment with a view to a progressive decline in the marginal efficiency of capital, I should support at the same time all sorts of policies for increasing the propensity to consume. (325)

As mentioned above, Keynes's "Notes on the Trade Cycle" is reminiscent of the "psychological theories of the business cycle"; the chapter is highly descriptive and more than a little impressionistic. It must be remembered, however, that Keynes was himself a highly successful speculator and investor for himself, for King's College Cambridge (of which he was Bursar), and for the insurance company of which he was a director. When he talks about "the psychology of the investment market" we can be sure that he knows what he is talking about.

The Kaldor Model

While Keynes himself never tried to develop a complete theory of business cycles based on the analytical system of his *General Theory,* there were plenty of other economists who did. One of the best illustrations of the kind of models that arose from the application of the Keynesian system to business cycles is the one produced by Nicholas Kaldor; it is clear, simple, and remains faithfully close to the framework of Keynesian economics (Kaldor, 1960).

It is essentially an oversavings/underconsumption model. In figure 2.11, the curve Ig(Y)g is a "static" investment function; it shows the volume of investment that would be forthcoming at various levels of gross national income at a particular point of time, with given techniques, given expectation, a given demand for cash balances and for less liquid assets, and a given stock of capital. If at a certain point of time national income is at a very low level, gross investment is also apt to be very low, consisting of minimal outlays for replacement purposes. Indeed, in the depths of depression, replacement may be insufficient to maintain the existing stock of capital goods, net investment may be negative, and capital may be consumed, as it was in the United States during the 1930s.

If the level of income were somewhat higher, gross investment would not be very different, since the higher level of consumption that would be forthcoming at the higher level of income could be met out of the excess

FIGURE 2.11
The Kaldor Model

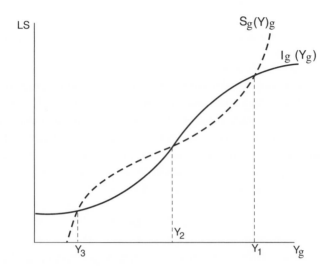

inventories or by utilizing the excess plant capacity that is apt to exist at such intermediate levels of income. At higher levels of income, however, such excess inventories and excess plant capacity are unlikely to exist, and the higher level of consumption would require net investment. Accordingly, gross investment would be at considerably higher levels. At very high levels of income, consumption would not be proportionately higher, and gross investment would also be less than proportionately higher. Thus, the investment curve rises slowly over low levels of income, rises steeply over intermediate levels of income, and then flattens out again.

The curve Sg(Y)g is a "static" *ex ante* savings function, showing gross *ex ante* savings as a function of gross national income. Gross savings cannot be less than zero, but might be zero at some very low but positive level of income. At higher but still low levels of income, savings are apt to be considerably higher than at very low income levels, since firms will be endeavoring to replenish reserves, and households will be trying to reduce debts, catch up on mortgage and insurance payments, and so forth. At prosperity levels of income, however, such debts are not apt to exist, and savings will not be proportionately higher. At extremely high levels of income, however, more families will be in income brackets where the average propensity to save is high and gross savings of the whole economy will rise more than proportionately to income.

It is apparent that curves with the shape and position of those in figure 2.11 give three possible equilibrium levels of income: Y1, Y2, and Y3. An income of Y2, however, would be unstable; any disturbance resulting in the slightest increase in income would mean that investment would exceed *ex ante* savings, and income would rise to Y1. The slightest contraction of income would mean that *ex ante* savings would exceed investment, and income would contract to Y3. Thus, only Y1 and Y3 are stable equilibrium positions; any disturbance resulting in temporary change in income would cause such a divergence between *ex ante* savings and investment as to bring income back to Y1, or Y3 as the case may be.

Following Mr. Kaldor, let us assume that the economy is in a prosperous phase of the cycle to begin with, with income at Y1. We must now consider the "dynamic" aspects of the operation of a capitalist economy; as time passes, various things happen to change the *positions* of the "static" savings and investment functions. For one thing, as time goes by techniques of production improve, and a given level of money income, or a given level of employment, yields an increasing flow of goods and services. As the standard of living rises in this manner, most people will want to use part of their higher real income for savings; they will take out more insurance, buy more securities, hold larger cash balances, and so forth. Thus as time goes by with a *given* level of employment, the savings curve tends to shift upward.

The investment curve, on the other hand, tends to shift down. As the stock of capital accumulates, its "marginal efficiency," or expected yield or further net additions to capital, tends to fall. The failure of consumer spending to continue rising at the same rate also has unfavorable effects on investment decisions, especially regarding inventory accumulation. Moreover, as businessmen get more and more money tied up in illiquid assets like plant and equipment, their "marginal liquidity preference" increases; that is, liquid assets become relatively more desirable in their eyes, and a smaller share of their savings will flow into real investment, in plant, equipment, inventories, and new housing, which alone creates income and jobs. Perhaps also interest rates rise as a result of growing pressure on bank reserves, so that inventories become more costly to

FIGURE 2.12
The Kaldor Model

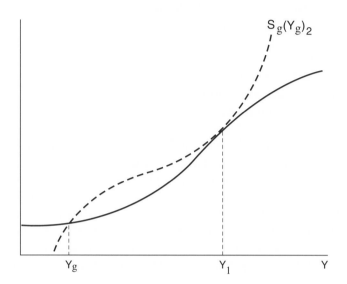

hold. Finally, in a society which is business-cycle conscious, the very prolongation of prosperity develops expectations of a downturn, making businessmen increasingly cautious in their investment policy.

As the savings curve rises and the investment curve falls, they eventually assume the positions of Ig(Yg)2 and Sg(Yg)2 in figure 2.12. The equilibrium is then unstable in the downward direction; the slightest disturbance—an election result unwanted by the business community, a bad harvest, a drop in the stock market, completion of a large-scale investment project, failure of a well-known firm—or anything else bringing a slight temporary decline in investment and income, will mean the *ex ante* savings exceeds investment, and income will go plunging down to the depression equilibrium level, Y3.

In depression, the curves eventually begin moving in the opposite direction. Savings are gradually squeezed out in the effort to maintain a minimal standard of living for households, while firms reduce savings in order to make some dividend payments and retain some public confidence. Since consumption does not fall to zero, the time comes when excess inventories have disappeared, and the stock of capital has been

FIGURE 2.13
The Kaldor Model

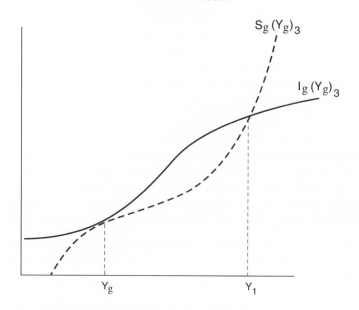

depleted so much, that net investment is needed just to meet existing demand. The reduction of the stock of capital tends to raise its marginal efficiency, and some businessmen at least begin thinking that "prosperity is just around the corner." Perhaps interest rates fall enough to make inventory accumulation seem desirable when expectations improve. Eventually, the curves attain the position shown in figure 2.13. Now the equilibrium is unstable in the upward direction. Any accident producing a slight rise in investment—a tax cut, a favorable rumor, an innovation—makes investment exceed savings and will start income and employment on their way up again.

Conclusion

In sum, the efforts to provide a complete and accurate business cycle theory during the period between World War I and World War II were not entirely successful. Not one of the theories that emerged provided a satisfactory foundation for prescribing policies that would have ironed out the fluctuations that actually took place in that period. Still less did they provide an adequate basis for prescribing policy today. However, in the aggregate, they increased our knowledge of how a capitalist economic system works a great deal. They also paved the way, once the Great Depression came along and forced economists to rethink their basic concepts of equilibrium, fluctuations, cycles, and growth, for the Keynesian Revolution—which, like most revolutions, had its seeds planted deep in the past. The Keynesian Revolution led in turn to acceptance of the possibility that capitalist economic systems might remain in a state of "underemployment equilibrium" for a long time, and alternatively, might suffer from chronic inflation; it led too to the concept of secular stagnation, and by implication to recognition that under certain circumstances there could be a long-run boom; and finally, to the concept of the knife edge, the reluctant acceptance of the idea that all kinds of things can go wrong with a capitalist economic system, and Hicks's idea of an explosive cycle constrained by a floor and a ceiling. The scope of thought about performance of the economic system was enormously broadened; approaches to policy became at once more complex and more flexible. Altogether the period from the late 1930s to the late 1940s was one of rapid advance in economic thought. Let us now, therefore, turn to this literature.

References

Burns, Arthur F. Economic Research and the Keynesian Thinking of Our Time. 26th Annual Report of the National Bureau of Economic Research. New York, 1946.

Burns, Arthur F., and Wesley C. Mitchell. *Measuring Business Cycles.* New York: National Bureau of Economic Research, 1946.

Domar, Evsey D. *Essays in the Theory of Economic Growth.* New York: Oxford University Press, 1957.

Estey, James Arthur. *Business Cycles: Their Nature, Cause, and Control.* New York: Prentice Hall, 1946.

Frisch, Ragnar. "Propagation Problems and Impulse Problems in Dynamic Economics." In *Economic Essays in Honour of Gustav Cassel.* London: George Allen and Unwin, 1933.

Gordon, Robert Aaron. *Business Fluctuations.* New York: Harper and Row, 1952.

Haberler, Gottfried von. *Prosperity and Depression.* Cambridge, Mass.: Harvard University Press, 1938.

Hansen, Alvin H. 1951.

———. *Business Cycles and National Income.* New York: W. W. Norton, 1957.

Hamberg, Daniel. *Business Cycles.* New York: Macmillan, 1951.

Hawtrey, R. G. *Monetary Reconstruction.* London: Longman Green, 1923, 1926.

———. *Currency and Credit.* London: Longman Green, 1927.

———. *Trade Depression and the Way Out.* London: Longman Green, 1933.

———. *Economic Destiny.* London and New York: Longman Green, 1938, 1944.

78   **Employment Without Inflation**

———. *The Gold Standard*. London: Longman Green, 1947.
———. *Income and Money*. New York: Barnes and Noble, 1967.
———. *Good and Bad Trade*. New York: A. M. Kelley, 1970.
Hayek, Friedrich A., von. *Prices and Production*. London: George Routledge & Sons, 1931–1935.
———. *Monetary Theory and the Trade Cycle*. New York: Macmillan, 1933.
———. *Profits, Interest, and Investment*. London: George Routledge & Sons, 1939.
Hicks, John R. *A Contribution to the Theory of the Trade Cycle*. Oxford: The Clarendon Press, 1950.
James, Cyril. *The Economics of Money and Banking*. New York: Ronald Press, 1940.
Jevons, H. S. *The Causes of Unemployment: The Sun's Heat and Trade Activity*. London: Macmillan, 1910.
———. "Trade Fluctuations and Solar Activity." *The Contemporary Review* (August 1909).
Jevons, W. Stanley. "The Solar Period and the Price of Corn" (1875). Reprinted in *Investigations in Currency and Finance*. London: Macmillan, 1884 and 1909.
———. "The Periodicity of Commercial Crises: Its Physical Explanation" (1878). Reprinted in *Investigations in Currency and Finance*. London: Macmillan, 1884 and 1909.
———. "Commercial Crises and Sunspots" (1879). Reprinted in *Investigations in Currency and Finance*. London: Macmillan, 1884 and 1909.
Kaldor, Nicholas. *Essays on Economic Stability and Growth*. Glencoe, Ill.: The Free Press, 1960.
Keynes, John Maynard. *The General Theory of Employment, Interest and Money*. London: Macmillan, 1936.
Klein, Lawrence. *The Keynesian Revolution*. New York: Macmillan, 1947).
Koopmans, Tjalling. "Measurement Without Theory" *Econometrica* (August, 1947).
Mathews, Robert. *The Trade Cycle*. Cambridge: Nisbet and the Cambridge University Press, 1959.
Merlin, Sidney D. *The Theory of Fluctuations in Contemporary Economic Thought*. New York: Columbia University Press, 1949.
Moore, Henry Ludwell. *Economic Cycles: Their Law and Cause*. New York: Macmillan, 1914.
———. *Generating Economic Cycles*. New York: Macmillan, 1923.
Schumpeter, Joseph. *Business Cycles*. New York: Macmillan, 1939.
Wilson, Harold. *Budget Message 1990*. Ottawa: Queen's Printer, 1990.

3

Underemployment Equilibrium, Secular Stagnation, and the "Knife Edge"

A glance at figure 3.1 will suffice to realize that the Great Depression of the 1930s was one of extraordinary depth and duration. As the depression wore on, the attention of economists, politicians, and the general public was diverted from the question, "What causes economic fluctuations?" to the question, "What is wrong with the capitalist economic system that it should generate a depression with such crushing unemployment, and such an appalling number of business and financial failures, with no sign of a genuine and complete recovery in which one could have any confidence?" What Schumpeter called "the disappointing Juglar"—the sharp downturn of 1937 after less than four years of limited recovery—was particularly devastating. When World War II began in 1939, despite massive government expenditures for rearmament, unemployment in most of the industrialized countries was still running at around 15 percent.

The concentrated effort to explain the great depression yielded results before it was even over. In his *General Theory,* published in 1936, Keynes demonstrated that because of the "liquidity trap," an economy could get stuck in a position where there is large-scale unemployment. When the outlook is gloomy, when uncertainty and even fear prevail, when scarcely anyone expects to make a profit, interest rates even as low as zero may not stimulate enough investment to restore full employment. Under such conditions most people may prefer to hang on to their money, in a safe and liquid form, rather than invest in anything. It is not enough for entrepreneurs to be willing to invest on a scale sufficient to absorb the savings forthcoming from a full-employment level of national income, in order to have full employment and stable prices. People must also be willing to hold precisely the amount of money in existence, at a level of interest

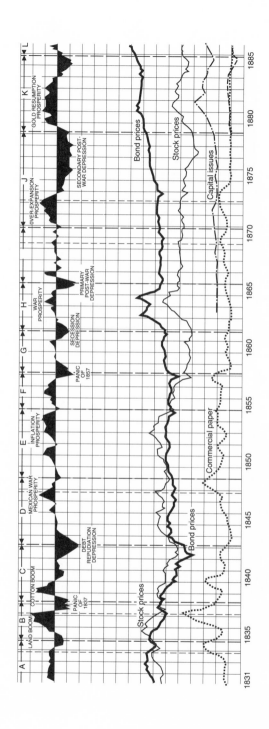

CHART 3.1
Business Cycles 1831–1940

CHART 3.1 (continued)
Business Cycles 1831–1940

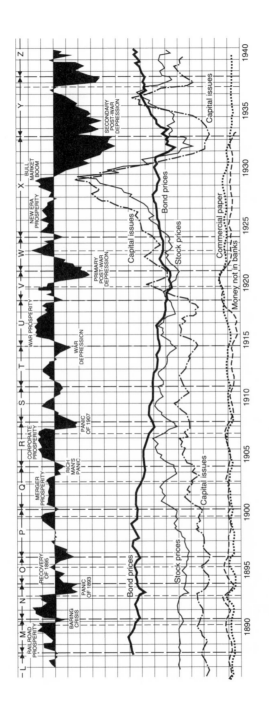

rates compatible with full employment without inflation no more and no less. If people are frightened and want to convert everything into cash, prices of everything will fall, assets will be liquidated, and no one will want to invest. If, on the contrary, there is a scramble to get rid of cash and buy goods or assets, prices of both will rise and eventually serious inflation will ensue.

In the discussion following the publication of the *General Theory,* this sort of argument was finally summarized in the fashion presented in figure 3.1. Here national income is measured on the horizontal axis, interest rates on the left-hand vertical axis, and savings and investment on the right-hand vertical axis. The LM curve is a "liquidity-preference" or "demand for money" curve. "L" stands for liquidity and "M" for (supply of and demand for) money. The curve shows combinations of interest rates and national income that are consistent with equilibrium, in the sense that the demand for money equals the supply of money. The IS (investment-savings) curve shows levels of (*ex post*) savings and investment consistent with equilibrium at the corresponding level of national income and interest rates. People have two reasons for holding money: (1) to have enough cash on hand to make their usual purchases of goods and services (the transactions motive); and (2) to have cash, as a safe and liquid asset in case prices of other assets fall, and to be in a position to take advantage of good investment opportunities as they arise (the liquidity-preference motive). Demand for money on the transactions motive increases with income. Demand for money on the liquidity preference motive decreases as interest rates rise; but when uncertainty, and hence liquidity-preference, is high, it may take very high interest rates to persuade people to part with their cash. In figure 3.1 full employment would be established with national income at Yf, which would require the LM curve to be at LM' and the IS curve at IS'. However, in a deep depression, with interest rates at (say) 4 percent (which would encourage IS' investment if circumstances were more favorable), people may want to hold so much money, and spending would accordingly be so low, that savings and investment would only be the amount shown by IS. Consequently equilibrium is established with a national income of only Yu, at which there is substantial unemployment. There is no *automatic* tendency to move away from this equilibrium. Something else has to happen if the economy is to move toward an equilibrium at full employment.

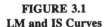

FIGURE 3.1
LM and IS Curves

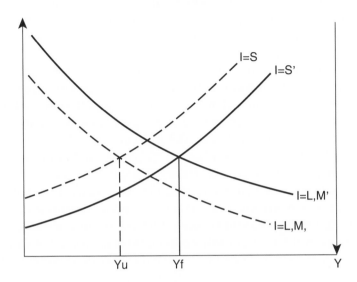

Secular Stagnation

In comparison with Keynes's general theory of underemployment equilibrium, Alvin Hansen's secular stagnation thesis was much more directed toward explaining the extraordinary length and depth of the great depression, particularly in the United States. It was founded on economic history of the late nineteenth and early twentieth centuries, rather than on any purely theoretical model of the functioning of the capitalist economic system. He found his explanation of the great depression in the declining rate of population growth, the disappearance of the frontier, and the absence of "great new industries"—all long-run forces belonging to a particular period of American history.

Alvin Hansen was an advisor to President Franklin Roosevelt, and economists and members of the business and financial community who hated Roosevelt's New Deal policies, especially increased public spending to fight unemployment, hated Hansen and his stagnation thesis too. What they hated most was the implication that "mature" capitalist countries would need continuous government intervention and management in order to avoid chronic unemployment. When Hansen introduced the concept, the great depression had lasted long enough for many financiers, businessmen, and Republican politicians in the U.S.A. to have accepted the idea of "pump-priming" as a means of promoting recovery: that is, the government would intervene with a judicious dose of public spending to get the private enterprise economy going again, and then withdraw while the private entrepreneurs took over and the recovery continued automatically through natural forces, until "equilibrium" was re-established with full employment and no inflation. Even this degree of departure from principles of balanced budget and laissez-faire still scandalized many; but Hansen's idea of *permanent* management of the economy was a good deal more shocking, and led to outraged counterattack.

Actually, as Professor Hansen himself pointed out, the literature of economics has almost always contained a doctrine of economic maturity. Indeed, any theory of economic expansion has implicit in it a theory of economic stagnation, and a theory of economic decline. Unfortunately, few economists have stated clearly their concepts of economic trend and its causes, and the interpretations suggested in the present essay may well be subject to error. However, it is hoped that they will serve to facilitate the isolation of the special features of Hansen's secular stagnation concept of trend.

The classical concept of the stationary state, which for the classical school was an historical phase and not just an analytical model, was essentially a concept of a mature economy. In Adam Smith, the stationary state was even recognized to be one in which wealth might be very great, but nevertheless one in which "there would be a constant scarcity of employment." In the stagnation theories of Ricardo and Mill, however, unemployment plays no significant role; stagnation in Ricardo's analysis referred to what Mill called gross annual produce, and what we would now call gross national product at full employment. The stagnation resulted from the natural tendency of profits to fall and the consequent choking of capital accumulation. Ultimately, stagnation would result in a constant population, but capital accumulation might cease, in Ricardo's view, long before population reached its highest point. In Mill's stationary state, there would be no increase in either population or stock of capital, profit having reached the minimum necessary to prevent net dissaving by the economy as a whole. However, there might still be a rising standard of living, due to improvements in the art of living and increased leisure through technological progress.

The classical economists regarded economic development as a race between technological progress on the one hand, and diminishing returns to labor (population) on the other. The rate of capital accumulation affected the level of production, but capital accumulation was itself a dependant variable; it was a function of the rate of profit, and profits depended on the outcome of the race. Much the same was true of population in the classical system. So long as production increased sufficiently, population would grow; but as production reached stability, population would do likewise.

The ideas of Karl Marx about the trend of gross national product at full employment were not markedly dissimilar from those of the classical school. As a result of the tendency of profits to fall, capital accumulation in Marx's view is checked, and the rate of economic expansion declines. However, Marx added two new theories regarding the actual trend of production and employment in a capitalist society. First of all, the increasing ratio of fixed to circulating capital, the concentration of industry, and the tendency toward monopolization, would in themselves result in increasing excess capacity, and perhaps also in unemployment. Second—and on the whole more important in Marxian analysis—economic fluctuations of increasing intensity lead to a growing gap between potential and actual gross national product. Moreover, full employment may not be established even at the peak of the boom. The general pattern, so far as the actual and potential trend of gross national product is concerned, is not greatly different, whether full employment is reached at the top of the boom or not. Employment cannot exceed full employment by very much or for very long, unless full employment is curiously defined. Consequently, "increasing intensity of cycles" of *employment* means deeper and longer depressions. The resulting trend of gross national product, in the sense of average level over the cycle as a whole, must therefore fall further and further below the trend at full employment.

Hansen's own treatment of the theory, which never pulled together his ideas in a systematic exposition in one place, left the door open to two interpretations. One was that "secular" in this context meant a very long period of a century or more, like Walter Prescott Webb's "three hundred year boom" in Europe due to the opening of the frontier in the New World (Webb certainly had an influence on Hansen). In this version the doctrine of economic maturity was a theory of history, an argument that with increasing affluence savings out of full employment income tend to reach ever higher levels, while investment opportunities dwindle, resulting in chronic excess savings and, in the absence of appropriate government action, in ever-increasing unemployment. In this version the theory bears some relationship to that of Marx, except that where Marx expected capitalism to break down altogether, Hansen was saying that breakdown could be avoided by astute government policy, particularly by secularly increasing public spending. In the other version, the secular stagnation thesis was a special form of the theory of long waves, applied specifically to the Great Depression of the 1930s. Its purpose in this version was to explain the peculiar length and depth of that depression, rather than to make a longer run prognosis regarding the future of capitalism. I once asked Hansen very pointedly which of these two concepts he had in mind; he replied unequivocally that he was thinking of long waves. It is in this form, therefore, that I present it.

It is convenient to treat the theory as explaining why, over a period of two decades or more, and always excluding government action to prevent it, there is an increasing gap between potential GNP and actual GNP. Let us designate potential GNP as 0_p (potential total output) and actual GNP as 0_a (actual total output). We shall use in addition the following symbols:

L = Size of the labor force or total population, treated for convenience as varying proportionately.

K = The stock of known resources. We shall regard Hansen's concept of "the moving frontier" as identical to a high rate of resource discovery and utilization (including agricultural land).

Q = Stock of capital ($\Delta Q = I$, investment).

S = Savings; τ = Tax payments; I_i = Induced investment; I_d = Developmental investment; I_g = Governmental investment; T = Level of technology.

We shall assume the economy to be closed, as Hansen did for much of his analysis, and ignore foreign trade and foreign investment.

Potential output is determined by a production function:

$$0_p = f(L,K,T,Q) \dotfill (1)$$

The level of actual GNP, or "0_a" depends on the multiplier and the level of total investment:

$$0_p = \frac{1}{dS/dY + d\tau/dY}\, [I_i\,(O) + I_d\,(L,K,T) + I_g] \quad\dots\dots\dots\dots\dots \text{(2)}$$

The growth of "0_p" through time (t) will be:

$$\frac{dOp}{dt} = \frac{\partial Op}{\partial L}\cdot\frac{dL}{dt} + \frac{\partial Op}{\partial K}\cdot\frac{dK}{dt} + \frac{\partial Op}{\partial T}\cdot\frac{dT}{dt} + \frac{\partial Op}{\partial Q}\cdot I \quad\dots\dots\dots\dots \text{(1a)}$$

Treating the multiplier and its components as constants, the growth of "0_a" through time will be:

$$\frac{dOa}{dt} = \frac{1}{dS/dY + d\tau/dY}\cdot\left[\frac{\partial Ii}{\partial O}\cdot\frac{d^2O}{dt^2} + \frac{Id}{\partial L}\cdot\frac{d^2L}{dt^2} + \frac{\partial Id}{\partial K}\cdot\frac{d^2K}{dt^2} + \frac{\partial Id}{\partial T}\cdot\frac{d^2T}{dt^2} + \frac{dIg}{dt}\right]$$

The level of long-run developmental investment is a function of population growth, rate of resource discovery, and rate of technological progress.[1] Induced investment depends only on the rate of change in consumption or sales. It will be seen at once that growth of O_p depends on growth of L,K,T, and Q; but the growth of O_a depends on the *second* deratives, that is, the *acceleration* of these same variables. In a situation where population growth, resource discovery, and technological progress are all taking place, but at a decelerating rate (second derivatives are negative), "O_p" will continue to rise but O_a will fall, unless the drop in "I_d" is offset by a rise in I_g. "I_i" cannot long continue to be positive when "I_d" is negative, as we shall see more fully below. "dO_a" is not *sui generis*; for the accelerator to come into action and induced investment to take place, there must be some growth in the first place. To *launch* a process of growth I_d (or I_g) must be positive. And of course, $S_a = S(O_a)$. If investment falls off as income rises there will be a tendency toward excess savings and falling income. Thus, under the conditions postulated a growing gap between "O_p" and "O_a" will appear, with increasing underemployment.

Much of Hansen's effort was devoted to providing empirical support for his contention that a declining rate of population growth, a declining rate of resource discovery ("disappearance of the frontier"), and a declining rate of technological progress ("lack of great new industries") were in fact a characteristic of the inter-war period, and that these phenomena went far to explain the great depression. I have dealt with these matters at length elsewhere, and do not wish to repeat myself at length here; let me say that I still consider Hansen to have been right on these matters, and deal with them briefly.

The Rising Propensity to Save

With regard to the savings side of the argument, it is necessary to decide first of all whether the discussion relates to the *volume* of savings, the savings *function,* or to the average *propensity* to save. Hansen himself has pointed to the downward historical drift of the savings function; the stagnation thesis obviously does not rest on any tendency for the savings function to rise. A rising trend of total savings, with a constant or falling average propensity to save, requires only a rising trend of total offsets to saving, while a rising trend of the average propensity to save requires a rising trend of the ratio of offsets-to-savings to national income. While the discussion has not been clear at all points, it appears that what Hansen had in mind was the average propensity to save rather than the volume of savings.

The savings relevant to the Hansen thesis are, of course, *ex ante* savings, and attempts to test the validity of this part of the thesis by measuring *ex post* savings, which are necessarily equal to investment, are therefore irrelevant. While *ex ante* or intended savings are difficult to measure, an approach to their volume might be made through figures of income and employment. With balanced trade and balanced budgets, an excess of *ex ante* savings over *ex ante* investment appears as a decline in income. Failure of income to rise enough to attain full employment in an upswing indicates an excess of *ex ante* savings relative to *ex ante* investment at high levels of employment.

Declining Rate of Population Growth

Least difficult to test of the four main pillars of the Hansen thesis is the argument concerning the effect of the declining rate of population growth upon investment. For one thing, the main facts are beyond dispute. The percentage increase in the American population began to fall about 1850, although it did not fall much until the 1920s, and the absolute increase began to fall about 1925. For another, population growth is a secular trend if any economic quantum is. And finally, no one has really denied that other things being equal, a rapidly growing population will call forth more investment than a slowly growing one.

There are two main ways in which population growth affects investment. First, a growing population provides a growing labor force. So long as population growth keeps pace with capital accumulation, the marginal productivity of capital will, in the absence of other influences, remain constant. But when population growth falls off, capital accumulation must also fall off, if, apart from other influences, the marginal productivity of capital is not to decline. Second, a growing population provides an increasing demand for goods and services. The correlation between long-run increases of population and of consumption is so high that one can be more or less substituted for the other, and consequently the "acceleration principle" argument, which states that a mere drop in the rate of increase in consumption may cause an absolute decline in investment, can be applied with minor modifications to population. In addition, of course, a declining rate of population growth involves changes in the composition of population that may be of great importance.

Capital-Saving Innovations

The third argument in support of the stagnation thesis is that inventions have increasingly become capital saving rather than capital absorbing, because of the absence of "great new industries." This tendency has usually been tested by comparing the growth of capital formation with the growth of production of final products. The Kuznets data of ten-year averages, with a five-year overlap to reduce the effects of cycles, show a rising trend in the ratio of output of capital goods to output of final products from 1869 through 1878 to 1914 through 1923, followed by a sharp drop for the decades 1919 to 1928, 1924 to 1933, and 1929 to 1938. However, these data do not, in themselves, demonstrate that inventions are becoming increasingly capital saving.

There can be little doubt that many of the significant twentieth-century inventions have been capital saving, in the sense that output per dollar of investment is greater with the newer techniques than with the older ones. Indeed, it is hard to believe that inventions have not always been capital saving in the technical sense. The ton-miles of freight carried per dollar of investment are greater for a steamship or steam train than for a sailing ship or stage coach. What matters, however, is not whether inventions are labor saving or capital saving or both, once they are in place, but whether the process of installing them absorbs or releases capital on balance. This part of the discussion of Hansen's thesis would therefore gain from a shift of attention from capital-saving *inventions* to capital-saving *innovations*. The introduction of a new commodity or new technique may result in net absorption of capital, whether the invention itself is capital saving or not, in one of three ways:

1. It may give rise to an expectation of windfall profits arising from a temporary monopoly position for the first firms in the new field, to a wave of "followers" when the success of the venture has been demonstrated, and to further innovations in related industries, according to the well-known Schumpeter model. The "great new industry" innovations seem to have been of this type.
2. Even with pure competition existing and expected to continue, an innovation, by accelerating the rate of replacement through obsolescence, may result in a temporary increase in the rate of capital absorption.
3. An innovation may provide a new product so attractive that the propensity to consume is raised. This kind of expansionary effect of innovation has received less attention than it deserves.

It seems probable that the development of the automobile, and the accompanying development of consumers' credit, had this kind of effect.

There is no *a priori* reason, and little empirical evidence, to support the thesis that a new trend for innovations to be capital saving made its appearance in the inter-war decades. However, as any country adds to its stock of plant and equipment, it tends to accumulate replacement funds at a rate roughly proportional to the value of the stock of capital, or even at an increasing rate if the rate of obsolescence increases. While these funds are normally used for replacing worn-out equipment and consequently represent a demand for investment goods, if capital-saving inventions are continuously being introduced the replacement funds may be more than adequate to replace worn-out capacity with more modern machines. If this is true, the replacement process will have a net deflationary effect. If this deflationary effect is to be avoided, *new* investment must rise at an increasing rate. The more highly developed a country is, the more difficult it is to add to capital at a rate even faster than in the past. In this connection, the "trend" regarding innovations is extremely important. The investment generated by any one innovation increases at an increasing rate over a certain range, tapers off, and finally declines. In order to have a rising trend of net additions to capital, each successive innovation (or group of innovations) must be *more* capital absorbing than the last. This is rather a tall order. Having once had a railway age, it became almost impossible to develop innovations—or groups of innovations—even more capital absorbing than railways and contemporaneous innovations were. The real truth of the "capital-savings inventions" argument may be simply that in recent decades innovations have not been sufficiently capital-absorbing to maintain the rate of increase in additions to capital of earlier decades. There seems to be no simple way of finding out whether or not such is the case. Figures are available only for *ex post* investment, which is the product of the whole nexus of economic forces.

The Disappearance of the Frontier

In support of the stagnation thesis, it has been said that the presence of undeveloped land and other national resources in the United States offered extraordinary opportunities for investment, and that the disappearance of the frontier is therefore likely to retard the rate of capital accumulation. In order to test empirically whether the frontier "has disappeared" or "is disappearing," or when it "started to disappear," it is necessary to have a more precise, objective definition of geographic frontier than Hansen's "discovery and development of new territory and new resources." Moreover, in order to determine what contribution the existence of a geographic frontier makes to a high level of investment, it is necessary to distinguish the opening of a frontier from the growth of population and from innovations.

When is a territory "new"? When it is entirely unpopulated, or when population per square mile is below a certain figure, or when production techniques lag behind other regions or countries, or when its natural resources are as yet unknown? The mere presence of unoccupied territory, that is, land upon which no one is employed, clearly does not constitute a frontier in the economic sense, if it is worth no one's while to employ someone to do something with it or on it. Yet growth of population in one part of a country may at some stage make it worth while to exploit previously unoccupied territory. Similarly, an innovation may make some previously worthless resource highly useful—witness atomic energy and known but untouched uranium deposits—and so make it worth while to move people into a region formerly unoccupied.

A reduction in transportation costs, or cheaper power, may also result in development of known resources formerly left idle. Development of new territory is clearly one of the incidental effects of population growth and of some kinds of innovation. A shift in demand may also open up new territory.

Many tenable concepts of the frontier suggest themselves, but it seems most useful to define a *geographic* frontier as an area within which there are increasing returns to both labor and capital with existing technical knowledge, population, and tastes. An area within which increasing returns would appear only with a change in techniques, population, or tastes might be called an *economic* frontier. Thus, economic frontiers become geographic frontiers as a result of dynamic changes. The frontier might be said to have disappeared when the point of diminishing *average* returns to labor and/or capital has been reached, and might be said to begin disappearing when the point of diminishing *marginal* returns to labor and/or capital has been reached.

A less tangible factor, which may nevertheless play some role, is frontier psychology. In economic terms, this factor would consist of a relatively low level or liquidity—and safety—preference, or a relatively high marginal efficiency of capital, for any given set of objective conditions.

Additive Effects of the Four Factors

There are good reasons for supposing that the effects of the four factors taken together will be considerably greater than the sum of the effects of each taken by itself, and much of the force of the Hansen thesis derives from the contention that the four factors have coincided historically. One of the most obvious of such combined effects arises in connection with the argument concerning the production function. Returns to capital will tend to diminish more rapidly if both the supply of labor (population growth) and the supply of natural resources (opening and development of frontiers) fail to keep pace with capital accumulation, than they would if either labor supply or available material resources increased with the supply of capital. It is also obvious that the dwindling of investment opportunities in general will be more serious if the *ex ante* average propensity to save is rising than if it is falling. Similarly, a rapidly growing population will tend to enhance the expansionary effects of technological progress by virtually guaranteeing a net increase in demand for the product if a new technique is introduced; and conversely, technological progress of the sort that raises the propensity to consume will help to offset any long-run tendency toward a rising average propensity to save, and will help to avoid adverse effects of a declining rate of population growth.

Interactions of Cycles and Trends

Hansen was certainly well aware of interactions of Kondratieff and Juglar cycles, and believed that downswings in the Juglar would tend to be more violent during periods of Kondratieff recession. However, this was one of the many aspects of his concept that he never spelled out in systematic fashion. (Hansen was accustomed to throwing out ideas right and left to his graduate students, and since he was surrounded by a remarkably brilliant group, including Samuelson, Musgrave, Tobin, Fellner, Metzler, Reynolds, Duesenberry, Domar, and many others, many of his ideas were elaborated by others.) Nonetheless, it is clear that his concept of potential GNP bears a relationship to Hicks's concept of the ceiling, and by bringing together Hansen's basic ideas and the Hicks model of the trade cycle, further insights can be gained.

An essential feature of the Hicks model is that induced investment depends partly on changes in consumption (sales, output) over very recent income periods, but partly on changes that took place in periods further in the past. Presumably the parameter linking induced investment to changes in consumption declines as we go further into the past, although, because of the "shadow effect" on replacement of capital, we cannot be sure that the decline is continuous. Once a boom starts, according to Hicks, income will rise to the ceiling (determined by $\dot{L}$, $\dot{K}$, $\dot{T}$ in my own reformulation) because the cycle is inherently explosive (the accelerator is large relative to the multiplier). But once the ceiling is hit growth slows down. As time goes by and the economy "creeps along the ceiling," periods of high growth are dropped from the "tail" of the induced investment function while periods of relatively low growth are added at the head. Eventually the whole expression representing the aggregate effect of past changes in consumption becomes negative, induced investment falls, the multiplier effect brings even greater reductions in national income, and recession ensues. It continues until the economy hits the floor (a somewhat fuzzy concept in Hicks's presentation, but let us define it as the income generated by whatever developmental investment remains, less maximum possible capital consumption as replacement falls to zero in the induced-investment sector). If the floor is upward sloping, periods of declining consumption in the "tail" are replaced by periods of rising consumption at the "head" as time goes by; eventually the whole expression governing induced investment becomes positive, and recovery sets in.

Once arrived at this point, it is an easy step to recognizing that the amplitude and configuration of Juglar cycles, based on induced investment, depend on the slope of the ceiling (and floor); these are determined by the phase of the Kondratieff cycle, that is, the level of developmental investment. During a Kondratieff upswing, when $I_d = I_d(\dot{L}, \dot{K}, \dot{T})$ is high, the slope of the ceiling is steep. Hitting the ceiling has a limited effect on the rate of growth. The economy can "creep along the ceiling" for a long time before the expression governing induced investment becomes negative. The boom can last a long time. Moreover, when "I_d" is vigorous the floor also tends to be at a high level and steeply upward sloping. (This tendency is partially offset by the fact that a rapid rate of capital accumulation increases the maximum rate of subsequent capital consumption, in itself tending to lower and flatten the floor.) Thus, the floor is soon hit. When it is, periods of rising consumption quickly replace earlier periods of falling consumption. The accelerator soon becomes positive and recovery ensues after a short, shallow recession. But in a Kondratieff downswing, even if defined only as stagnation of developmental investment, the ceiling is flat. When a Juglar upswing takes place the ceiling is soon hit, bringing a drastic reduction in rates of growth. Periods of rapid growth in the past are replaced by periods of zero growth. The accelerator effect soon becomes negative, the boom is short lived, and a sharp downswing soon appears. Moreover, the floor is also flat. Strictly speaking, if it is really flat, hitting it does no good at all; negative growth is replaced by zero growth, which cannot bring induced investment into play. The depression could go on forever, without government intervention or a new Kondratieff upswing.

In figure 3.2, we show a growing economy that goes first through a Kondratieff trough, then a Kondratieff upswing, then a new Kondratieff trough. The Juglar cycle is violent in the first period, with short periods of prosperity and sharp, deep, and prolonged depressions. In the second period booms are prolonged, depressions shallow and short. The third period reverts to the pattern of the first.

FIGURE 3.2
Juglar and Kondratieff Cycle

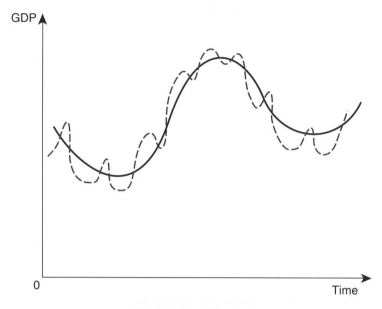

The Postwar Period

The first period conforms to Hansen's description of the inter-war period. Given the description, the model of interactions of Juglar and Kondratieff cycles explains what happened during the great depression.

Some people have been inclined to dismiss the stagnation thesis because stagnation, with mass unemployment, has not reappeared since World War II. But there are three reasons why the postwar experience does not disprove the Hansen thesis. First, deep depression has been avoided, in large measure because the sort of policy Hansen recommended to avoid it has in fact been pursued in the ICCs. Government management of, and intervention in the economy *has* been continuous; the money supply *has* been continuously expanded; the role of government in the economy *has* increased. Second, and in some ways more important, when Hansen's theory of secular stagnation is interpreted as a theory of interactions of Juglar and Kondratieff cycles, it works both ways; a period of rapid expansion of "I_d" should be one with relatively little unemployment and with mild fluctuations. There is a good deal of evidence that the period 1946–1972 was such a period. Population growth accelerated in

ACCs as the "baby boom" worked its way through the schools, the universities, and into the labor force, creating swelling demand for housing, public utilities, transport, schools and hospitals, and so on. The rate of resource discovery picked up, with important new finds of petroleum, uranium, bauxite, copper, forest reserves, and the like, and with LDCs as well as ICCs playing an important role. The rate of technological progress is always difficult to measure, but it could certainly be argued that the 1950s and 1960s brought accelerated technological progress as well, with electronics, computerization, jet travel, nuclear energy, scientific instruments, synthetics, and petrochemicals. If so, the relatively steady growth of the 1946–1972 period is explained.

This brings us to the 1970s and 1980s. Were we then in a Kondratieff downswing, which (unfortunately) began at about the same time as the energy crisis of 1972? An increasing number of economists think that we were.[2] If so, the tendency toward increasing unemployment in that period could be explained in terms of the model. Are we now in a Kondratieff upswing, which explains the drop in unemployment in the United States since 1982?

What cannot be explained by this model alone, obviously, is the appearance of simultaneous—and during the 1970s and early 1980s, simultaneously increasing—inflation and unemployment. The period since 1946—and particularly the period since about 1967—does not look like figure 3.2. We have not had sharp declines in GNP. Least of all have we had periods of increasing unemployment accompanied by falling prices. To be sure, the failure of prewar patterns of economic fluctuations to appear, with *alternating* periods of inflation and unemployment, can be attributed partly to improvements in policy. In part, the recent tendency of inflation and unemployment to move up together (trade-off curves shifting upward to the right) could be explained by the need for governments to expand money supply more than ever to prevent the violent downswings associated with Kondratieff troughs from appearing. I believe this relationship is part of the picture. There is no reason to believe that the fundamental interactions of multiplier and accelerator, and interactions of Juglar and Kondratieff cycles, should have disappeared. But these interactions, which I label "the Machine," clearly do not explain the whole of the postwar experience. If it did, we would be better off than we are; for the Machine is what economists understand and know how to manage, and what has in fact been managed with reasonable competence. Unfortunately, there are two other forces at work in the postwar economy that aggravate the problem of moving back toward full employment without inflation. One of these I call the Structure, the other I call the Game; we will deal with them in part II.

The Knife-Edge Theory

Returning to figure 3.1, from a purely theoretical point of view it is possible to think of the economy getting stuck in a position of "overfull employment," that is, a situation of chronic inflation, such as is illustrated by the intersection of LM' and IS'. Whether one can imagine this position as one of "equilibrium" is more doubtful. Once inflation gets under way, there are powerful forces that tend to make it cumulative. With an astute monetary and fiscal policy, however, it is possible to keep inflation for years within fairly narrow limits, as has happened in fact in several of the ICCs.

Once economists accepted the idea that either chronic unemployment or chronic inflation was a possible state in a capitalist economy, and that there need not *necessarily* be any automatic forces to restore equilibrium with full employment and without inflation, the stage was set for the "knife-edge theory;" that is, the idea that the conditions for steady growth, with full inflation and a stable price level, are so demanding that they are unlikely to be attained; and even if per chance some economy finds itself on the knife edge, it is very likely to fall off it, in one direction or the other, and experience either inflation or unemployment. To this basic concept was added another, perhaps even more disturbing; that movements away from equilibrium, in either direction, tend to become cumulative.

Domar's "Knife Edge"

In the economics literature one encounters frequent references to the "Harrod-Domar thesis," as though the arguments of these two economists, demonstrating the essential instability of a market economy, were virtually identical. In fact they are quite different. Domar's theory is cast in terms of the mechanics of a market economy at the macro level, and states the conditions necessary, in an essentially tautological fashion, for steady growth of such a national economy, with full employment and without inflation. Harrod is concerned with reactions of individual entrepreneurs and investors to the outcome of the interplay of market forces, and the effects of these reactions on subsequent outcomes in the market. His theory rests upon a particular set of behavioral assumptions.

Domar assumes that some national economy is growing steadily with full employment and stable prices, and asks what conditions must be met for it to stay like that. He uses the following symbols: Y_d is the level of effective demand, or national income; accordingly, ΔY_d is the (annual) increase in national income; I is investment, ΔI, the (annual) increase in investment; Y_s is the level of effective supply, or total annual output of goods and services, with full employment and full use of capacity; K is the stock of real capital; σ is the marginal propensity to save (proportion of increases in national income saved) and $\frac{1}{\sigma}$ is therefore the Keynesian multiplier relating increases in national income to increases in investment; α is the incremental output: capital ratio, relating increases in national output to increases in net investment. ($\Delta Y/\Delta I$). We then have the following equations:

$$\text{level of effective demand } Y_d = \frac{I}{\alpha} \tag{1}$$

$$\text{level of productive capacity } Y_s = \sigma K \tag{2}$$

$$\text{equilibrium condition } Y_d = Y_s \text{ or } \frac{I}{\alpha} = \sigma K \tag{3}$$

$$\text{increment of demand } \Delta Y_d = \frac{\Delta I}{\alpha} \tag{4}$$

$$\text{increment of capacity } \Delta Y_s = \Delta K = \sigma I \tag{5}$$

$$\text{equilibrium condition } \Delta Y_d = \Delta Y_s \text{ or } \frac{\Delta I}{\alpha} = \sigma I \tag{6}$$

$$\text{growth rate of investment } r = \frac{\Delta I}{I} = \alpha \sigma \tag{7}$$

Thus for steady growth,

$$\text{the growth rate of demand must be } \frac{\Delta I_d}{I_d} = \frac{\Delta I/\propto}{Y_d} = \frac{\Delta I \propto}{I \propto} = \frac{\Delta I}{I} = \alpha \sigma \tag{8}$$

Thus, steady growth requires investment to grow at the same percentage rate as national income, and that rate must be equal to a specific figure, the marginal propensity to save X the incremental capital: output ratio. Starting with full employment and stable prices, if investment falls below this required figure, unemployment will occur; if investment rises above this figure, the result will be inflation. Since there are no automatic forces in a market economy that could assure that these equilibrium conditions are met, even if, by some miracle, a national economy enjoys a period of steady growth with full employment and stable prices, this happy state of affairs almost certainly will not last, unless the economy is astutely managed through monetary, fiscal, and other policies.[3]

Harrod's Cumulative Causation

Harrod posits a certain type of universal entrepreneurial behavior whereby investment decisions (and presumably other related decisions as well) are based on a certain anticipated rate of growth. Harrod casts growth in terms of national income. While in industrialized countries the increasingly sophisticated business community does pay a good deal of attention to forecasts of national income, and of national rates of unemployment and inflation as well, no doubt expectations as to what will happen to their own sales play an important role in their decision-making. These will of course be influenced by what happens in the economy as a whole, but they will also be affected by factors specific to each enterprise. Harrod of course is well aware of all these factors, but to keep his analysis simple he uses growth of national income as a kind of shorthand or blanket term to cover all of them. Harrod also assumes that if things turn out exactly as expected, the investment decisions of the last period will be repeated in the next. If growth exceeds expectations, investment will be increased; and if growth is disappointing, investment will be diminished.

Harrod's basic equation is GC = s: where G is the growth during a unit of time; $\Delta Y/Y$; C is net capital accumulation in the period (including goods in process and stocks), divided by the increase in output in the period, $I/\Delta Y$; and s is the average propensity to save, S/Y. Thus, the equation is really a restatement of the truism that *ex post* savings equals *ex post* investment. It could be written:

$$\frac{\Delta Y}{Y} \cdot \frac{I}{\Delta Y} = \frac{S}{Y} \text{ or } \frac{I}{Y} = \frac{S}{Y} \text{ or } I = S$$

Harrod's second fundamental equation, $G_w C_r = s$, expresses the equilibrium conditions for a steady advance. G_w, the "warranted rate of growth," is the value of $\Delta Y/Y$ that barely satisfies entrepreneurs; C_r, the "capital requirements," is the value of $I/\Delta Y$ that is needed to sustain the warranted rate of growth. It will be noted that s is the same in both equations. Thus, in dynamic equilibrium (stable value of $\Delta Y/Y$), $G_w C_r =$ GC; the actual, or *ex post* value of I/Y, equals the equilibrium value, which is a subjective phenomenon. Moreover, G must equal G_w and C must equal C_r. For if G exceeds G_w, then C will be below C_r; that is, entrepreneurs will consider the amount of capital accumulation inadequate to sustain the increase in total output and will increase their orders for capital goods (and conversely). But then G will depart still further from G_w in the next period, and a cumulative movement away from equilibrium will set in. Thus, "Around the line of advance which, if adhered to, would alone give satisfaction, centrifugal forces are at work, causing the system to depart further and further from the required line of advance."[4]

There are two possible interpretations of Harrod's argument that if G exceeds G_w, C must be below C_r, and vice versa. If $G_w C_r$ = GC = s by assumption, then the proposition follows by mere arithmetic. Harrod's presentation, however, suggests that he thinks $G_w C_r$ *must* equal GC for economic and definitional reasons, in much the same way that *ex post* savings *must* equal *ex post* investment. It is hard to see that such is the case. It is clear enough that G and C must vary inversely with a given I/Y or C. But why should the equilibrium ratio of (*ex post*) savings and investment to income (i.e., the ratio that satisfies entrepreneurs, or $G_w C_r$ = equilibrium $\frac{(I \cdot S)}{Y}$) be continuously equal to the *actual* ratio of savings investment to income (GC, or actual $\frac{I=S}{Y}$)?

Harrod's main argument does not depend upon the equality of GC and $G_w C_r$ anyhow. It depends rather on the acceleration principle (or better, on the "relation"). For if G exceeds G_w, what this really means is that the rate of increase in total spending is greater than necessary to call forth the current rate of investment, and consequently investment will increase. By definition, if the rate of investment is above the equilibrium level, C_r is below C. Such a situation would be inconsistent with an excess of GC (actual I/Y = S/Y) over $G_w C_r$ (equilibrium I/Y = S/Y), since investment cannot be simultaneously above and below the equilibrium level, but it would be quite consistent with an excess of $G_w C_r$ over GC. That is, C-C_r may exceed G_w - G; entrepreneurs may consider actual investment low, not only relative to the actual rate of increase in consumer spending, but also relative to the level of income. In this case there would be a double incentive to increase investment in the next period. The movement away from equilibrium when G > G_w, and *in addition* GC > $G_w C_r$, will be greater than if G > G_w but GC = $G_w C_r$.

Harrod anticipates the criticism that his formulation gives too much weight to the acceleration principle, and he suggests that the criticism could be met by rewriting the first equation $GC = s - k$, where k is investment not due to the current increase in orders for output. It is not quite clear how much investment is meant to go into k and how much into C. C would presumably not include primary investment induced by innovations—let us say, building of automobile factories in the early stages of the automobile long wave, or "Kondratieff." But would the petroleum refineries, rubber plantations, and roadside restaurants brought into being by the automobile Kondratieff go into C or into k? Harrod says k will include "capital outlay which no one expects to see justified or not justified in a fairly short period."[5] How long is that? It is not a matter of indifference how investment is distributed between C and k.

Another problem arises in connection with C and C_r. The "relation" usually expresses the extent to which investment increases as a consequence of increases in demand for the final products of plant and equipment of a given type. For the "relation" to operate in the economy as a whole (without any change in the period of investment, which is not closely related to rates of consumption, and which Harrod excludes from this part of his analysis), there must be a change in the rate of consumer spending. The relation might be expressed as $I = r \cdot dC_n$. Harrod argues throughout as though an increase in income necessarily entails an increase in consumption, and also as though as increase in investment would always bring with it an increase in consumption. Why else would the increase in investment, $C_r \Delta Y$, resulting from an excess of G over G_w, (excess of C_r over C) carry the system *further* from equilibrium?

Harrod's point is, it will be remembered, that the greater investment brought about by $C_r > C$ will raise G still further above G_w. In the context of his argument, this proposition must mean that the increase in investment in the next period will bring with it an increase in the rate of expansion of consumer spending $\Delta C_n / C_n$. Now, if the increased investment is deficit financed, it is quite likely that the increase in rate of expansion of consumption that accompanies an increase in investment, $\frac{d}{dI}\left(\frac{dC_n}{C_n}\right)$, will be positive; for then the multiplier will operate on the increase in I and so raise consumer spending substantially. But in most of Harrod's argument, savings and investment are always equal; if entrepreneurs consider their investment too low, they also consider their saving too low. An increase in investment financed by an equal and simultaneous increase in saving will not raise income at all, and consumption will actually fall. In this event, investment in period two will be too high, rather than still too low, and will be reduced rather than raised in period three, and so on. The initial excess of G over G_w would in this case set up a series of damped fluctuations, and in the absence of a new disturbance, the system would tend toward a new equilibrium with the actual $\frac{I=S}{Y}$ equal to the equilibrium $\frac{I=S}{Y}$, and so with $G = G_w$ and $GC = G_w C_r$.

The manner in which new investment is financed is crucial to Harrod's analysis. Unless he can demonstrate beyond a shadow of doubt that it is *impossible* for enough of an increase in investment to be financed by new savings to make $\frac{d}{dI}(\frac{dC_n}{C})$ zero or negative, he can argue that an initial divergence of G and G_w *may* start a cumulative movement; but he cannot argue that it *must* start a cumulative movement.

Harrod's third fundamental equation is $G_n C_r$ may or may not be equal to s; here G_n is the "natural rate of growth" or "that steady rate of advance determined by fundamental conditions."[6] What G_n really seems to be is the rate of increase in output at full employment, given the rate of population increase and the rate of technological progress. A better term would have been *potential rate of growth*; there is nothing very natural about full employment. It will be noted that, whereas Harrod seems to feel that $G_w C_r$ *must* equal GC, he stresses the possibility that $G_n C_r$ may not equal GC, by making $G_n C_r$ equal, or not equal, to s.

With the introduction of G_n, Harrod is able to develop a theory of increasing underemployment for advanced economies. If G_w exceeds G_n (as it well may when population growth tapers off, or the rate of improvement in technique or discovery of new resources tapers off), G will also tend to lie below G_w, C will be chronically above C_r, and the economy will be chronically depressed. (After all, G can exceed G_n only in the recovery phase of the cycle.) Conversely, in a rapidly expanding economy (where population growth, or technological progress, or geographic expansion is at a high level) there will be a chronic excess of G_n over G_w, and also of G over G_w, and thus a chronic excess of C_r over C, and a perpetual tendency for inflationary boom to develop. We might call economies of the former type *deflationary gap* economies, and of the latter type *inflationary gap* economies. Harrod's general conclusion about the "virtue of saving" should surprise no one; it is a "good thing" in an inflationary gap economy, and a "bad thing" in a deflationary gap economy.

The causal relation between G_w and s is one of many problems that could have been made clearer by an elaboration of the central concept,

G_w. The term *warranted rate of growth* is not a very happy one for what Harrod seems to have in mind. Nor is "the line of entrepreneurial contentment"[7] a very clear-cut definition of G_w. In his *Economic Journal* article of March, 1939, he defines G_w as "that rate of growth which if it occurs, will leave all parties satisfied that they have produced neither more nor less that the right amount"; it is the rate that "will put them in the frame of mind which will cause them to give such orders as will maintain the same rate of growth." Thus G_w is subjective, but not, apparently, *ex ante*; it is the rate of growth that makes entrepreneurs satisfied with what has happened, rather than a plan for the future.[8]

Although reference to the article makes Harrod's concept of G_w a bit clearer, it still does not tell us what Harrod thinks are the determinants of G_w; and what determines G_w is obviously all important, for C_r depends on G_w; it is, indeed, defined in terms of G_w. G and C cannot be changed except as a result of entrepreneurial decisions, and these decisions depend on G_w. Thus, what happens in Harrod's dynamic economy depends ultimately on G_w. Harrod nowhere presents an analysis of the determinants of G_w, but in the course of his discussion he does indicate the following relationships: G_w varies (1) inversely with C_r (capital requirements); (2) directly with s (the average propensity to save); (3) inversely with the volume of public works; (4) inversely with the volume of investment that is independent of the current rate of growth, k; and (5) directly with the rate of interest r (since k and C_r vary inversely with r, and s probably varies directly with r).

The first of these relationships is arithmetic. Given s, G_w must vary inversely with C_r, just as G varies inversely with C. There are no clues to entrepreneurial behavior here. The second relationship has already been discussed; it, too, seems to be a matter of definition rather than of business behavior. Relationships three and four really amount to the same thing. Public works are one kind of investment that need not depend solely on the current rate of growth of income and that may, therefore, be included in k. Since $G_w C_r = s - k$, by definition, any increase in k must, other things being equal, be accompanied by a reduction in G_w.

The fifth relationship is a product of several others:

1. s varies directly with r, and since G_w varies directly with s, G_w varies directly with r;

2. k varies inversely with r, G_w varies inversely with k, and therefore, G_w varies directly with r;

3. C_r varies inversely with r, G_w varies inversely with C_r, and therefore, G_w varies directly with r.

The relationship between s and r is a true causal relationship; s(r) is a savings function with psychological meaning: savings depend on the interest rate. The same is true of the k(r) function, which is really the marginal efficiency of capital schedule: investment depends on the rate of interest. The $C_r(r)$ function is the period of investment, which also has meaningful content: as the interest rate falls, the capital-output ratio will be increased. But $G_w(r)$ has no meaning of its own whatsoever; given the other relationships, the dG_w/dr is given by definition. Thus not one of these G_w relationships is a truly causal one, with meaning in terms of entrepreneurial behavior.

Finally, Harrod adds two refinements. If d represents the fraction of income needed for capital involved in lengthening the production process ("deepening"), then $G_wC_r = s - d$. If inventions are capital saving, d is negative, and the equilibrium rate of growth is enhanced. Thus, any tendency toward chronic underemployment resulting from $G_w > G_n$ will be aggravated by capital-saving inventions. Harrod thinks falling interest rates might tend to lengthen the period of production and so keep d positive.

In his fourth chapter, "The Foreign Balance," Harrod points out that when we move to an open economy, the appropriate equations are GC = s - b and $G_wC_r = s - b$, where b is the foreign balance. The equation expresses what is already well known: in a country with chronic underemployment, $G_w > G_n$ and a favorable balance of trade on goods and services account helps to reduce the deflationary gap—and conversely for countries with a chronic inflationary gap.

Notes

1. There is a relationship between Hansen's theory and Schumpeter's or Perroux's where innovation is concerned. However, Hansen's policy conclusions were diametrically opposed to Schumpeter's. Hansen was an intellectual leader of the New Deal, while Schumpeter saw the New Deal destroying the spirit of entrepreneurship.
2. Certainly the rate of population growth has tapered off in most ICCs. It would be argued that, in comparison with 1950–1970 period, the rates of resource discovery and technological progress have also tapered off, although "K" and "T" are difficult to measure.
3. See Evsey D. Domar, *Essays in the Theory of Economic Growth* (New York: Oxford University Press, 1957, chap. 4, 83–108).

4. See Roy F. Harrod, *Toward a Dynamic Economics* (London: Macmillan, 1948, 86).
5. Ibid.
6. Ibid.
7. Ibid.
8. Ibid.

4

Interactions of Cycles and Trends

My own work on interactions of cycles and trends belongs to the immediate postwar era. It arose particularly from the Hicks theory of business cycles, with influences from Harrod, Domar, Kalecki, and Kaldor. It was presented originally in the *Economic Journal* for December, 1955. I present it here substantially as it was written, in order to preserve its flavor. It antedates the era of trade-off curves, loops, and Phillips curves; but when combined with these, as we shall see, it constitutes a powerful argument for a regionalized fiscal policy. My starting point is the view that relationship between cycles and trends is a two-way street; one can conceive of growth without fluctuations, and of economic fluctuations without economic growth. The essential causal factors of fluctuations and growth can, and should, be analyzed separately. At the same time, actual fluctuations will be greatly influenced by the growth factors, and the actual trend will be much affected by economic fluctuations. For the purposes of this chapter, I shall begin with the hypothesis of an autonomous trend, based on autonomous investment; and enquire as to the effects of this trend on the amplitude and timing of economic fluctuations.

The following symbols are used:

I_A Autonomous investment (gross)

I_A^R Autonomous investment in real terms (at constant prices)

O_P "Potential" output (gross national product at full employment with constant prices)

O_A Gross national product (at constant prices) produced by autonomous investment alone

O_h Actual "historical" or statistical trend of output (actual gross national product at constant prices)

Y_h Actual (historical) gross national income

L Labor force (population)

K Stock of known resources

Q Stock of capital

T Level of technique. [If f is the production function, $O_p = T.f(L, K, Q)$]

t Time

Ł dL/dt

Ķ dK/dt

Ť dT/dt

S Savings

k Any positive constant

M Super-multiplier

We shall assume that there is an autonomous long-run investment function:

$$I_A = \phi(L, K, T) - \phi(Q). \quad . \quad . \quad . \quad . \quad (1)$$

By "autonomous" is meant that this category of investment is dependent only on long-run rates of population growth, resource discovery, and technological change, and to a lesser degree on the long-run rate of capital accumulation, but is not affected by current short-run changes in the rate of output, level of profits, or the like. "Induced investment," on the other hand, is a function of the level and change in output, whether directly or through profits. Autonomous investment is thus considered causally independent of short-run fluctuations, and not as a mere statistical residue derived by "eliminating" cycles.

Since we are conducting our analysis in terms of gross investment, the long-run growth of the stock of capital, Q, will have a twofold effect: it will in itself increase the need for replacement; and in the long run, as in the short, capital accumulation will in itself act as a drag on the flow of new investment decisions. The first effect will probably be small, especially if, as Professor Hansen maintains, innovations are increasingly capital saving. The second effect may be more substantial, although small relative to the impact of the "growth factors." The net effect will almost certainly be negative, and may be significant. At this stage, however, we shall assume that the two effects offset each other, so that $\phi(Q)$ can be ignored in a first approximation.

For the time being, we shall also assume $S = S(O_h)$. In other words, we shall treat the trend of savings as a series of short-run positions, unaffected by separate long-run causal factors. This treatment is an abstraction, but it is a useful simplification. Trends in the propensity to save, arising from such factors as the increasing ability to think in terms of and provide for a remote future, stressed by Harrod, can be introduced at a later stage of the analysis.

For lack of information about the trend of technological progress, we shall assume that $dT/dt = k > 0$, so that $d^2T/dt^2 = 0$. This formal simplifying assumption may not be an unrealistic one. Lacking adequate measures of technological progress, it is virtually impossible to say whether the rate of technological progress, in the relevant sense of a factor governing autonomous investment, is higher today than it was in the nineteenth century, and whether it was higher in the nineteenth century than in the eighteenth. However, changes in the rate of technological progress can also be easily introduced into the analysis where and when appropriate.

We shall also assume that population growth and discovery of new resources follow a normal growth curve. In more precise terms, L and $K > 0$; d^2L/dt^2 and d^2K/dt^2 are first > 0 and then < 0. Judging from available information, these assumptions are realistic enough.

On these assumptions,

$$dI_A/dt = \frac{\partial \Phi}{\partial L} \cdot \frac{d^2L}{dt^2} + \frac{\partial \Phi}{\partial K} \cdot \frac{d^2K}{dt^2} .$$

Accordingly, I_A will itself follow a normal growth curve, unless $d\phi/dL$ moves in an offsetting manner, so as to produce steady growth, a slim possibility that we shall ignore.

Now let $O_A = M.I_a^R$. In this context M is the super-multiplier; but unless the rate of increase in autonomous investment produces rates of growth that inevitably call the accelerator into action, the super-multiplier will approximate the simple Keynesian multiplier. The super-multiplier comes into play only in periods of relatively rapid growth, when fluctuations would arise anyhow. This point will be discussed further below. For the moment, however, we shall assume that the relevant multiplier is constant. Consequently, the trend of total output O_A will also follow a smooth growth curve, as in figure 4.1.

According to the analysis presented in an earlier article,[1] the curve O_h of actual "historical" output would tend to follow the curve of O_p, of real income at full employment without inflation, until dI_A^R/dt begins to fall significantly, as a result of the falling rate of population growth and resource discovery (L and K), after which a gap will appear, and d/dt $(O_p - O_A) > 0$. In money terms $(Y_A - O_p)$ may be positive and even growing up to the inflection point in O_p; that is, there may be a chronic inflationary gap. Whether the actual trend will be consistently above the trend of full employment at constant prices, in this range, would depend partly on the parameters S and $\emptyset$ in the above equation.

In view of the power of the accelerator, once brought into play, it may be asked whether smooth development along such a growth curve (as distinct from *steady* growth) is conceivable at all. This question is different, it should be noted, from asking whether it is likely; about the latter question there can be little doubt. However, in order to distinguish between the causal effects of growth factors as such and the causal role of economic fluctuation, it is, in my opinion, both possible and useful to conceive of growth along a smooth curve. There are three sets of conditions that might produce smooth growth. First, it would be possible to assume simply that the system *is* moving along O_A, and that changes in dO_A/dt are too small to bring the accelerator into action, unless "shocks" occur greater than those introduced by growth factors alone. Second, one could simply assume that government stockpiling or counter-speculation is undertaken, so as to prevent sharp changes in dO^h/dt, and thus to eliminate the cycle, leaving the growth factors alone to influence economic development. Any situation that could be produced by policy has analytical significance. Third, we might regard the trend $O_p - O_A$ merely as an indication of the magnitude of price-cost adjustments that are necessary for continuous full employment without inflation. With any one of these three assumptions, the trend of output, based on autonomous investment alone, has a clear significance and is a useful analytical tool.

It is therefore possible to distinguish at least six concepts of trend; all of which can differ from each other: O_A, the trend of gross national product, at constant prices, produced by "autonomous" investment alone; Y_A, the trend of national income produced by autonomous investment, [O_A - Y_A] reflecting any trend in prices; O_p, the trend of gross national product at full employment and constant prices; Y_p, gross national income at full employment, but allowing for price trends; O_h, the actual historical, or statistical trend, which will be some sort of average position of actual

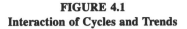

FIGURE 4.1
Interaction of Cycles and Trends

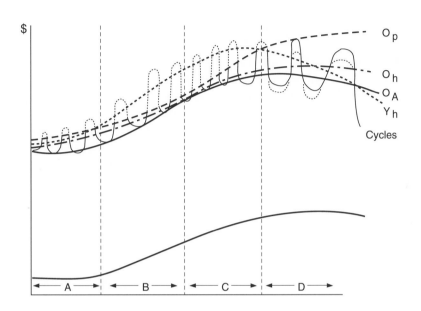

national real income over the course of cycles of various kinds; and Y_h, the analogous statistical trend of national income, including price changes.

For the purpose of determining what policies are best designed to maintain full employment without inflation, it is useful to distinguish between Y_h and the statistical or historical trend as it would have been without government interference of any kind, which we might denote by Y_f, the "free" historical trend. Up to 1940, it is hard to say what the sign of $(Y_h - Y_f)$ would be; in most countries, and for the most part, it appears that government action has accentuated both booms and depressions, while accelerating growth through development works and subsidies to private investment of a developmental nature. In advanced countries this effect has probably been weaker since 1913 than it was during the eighteenth and nineteenth centuries. Since 1940, because of the continuing high level of government spending, there can be little doubt that $(Y_h - Y_f)$ is positive, especially in the United States.

The question may be raised as to whether $O_A = O_p$. Suppose growth were a slow, and slowly changing, affair, based on long-run factors alone, so that the accelerator never came into action. Would there not be price-cost adjustments that would bring full employment? Hicks's whole analysis implies that $O_A < O_p$; it takes induced investment to raise income to full-employment levels. Considering how rare a phenomenon full employment is, if one considers all countries, I am inclined to agree with Hicks. I do not wish to reopen the debate on price flexibility and employment; my own views on the subject have been expressed elsewhere.[2] But even in advanced countries, full employment has occurred only during wars and at the peak of the booms, while in underdeveloped countries mass unemployment is the rule. It seems to take an unusually favorable combination of growth and cyclical forces, including government policy, to produce full employment for any length of time. Until faced with strong evidence to the contrary, therefore, I shall accept Hicks's view that $O_p > O_A$.

We can now distinguish four phases of economic growth (see figure 4.2):

A, where dO_A/dt is low, and $d2O_A/dt^2 > 0$;
B, where dO_A/dt is high, and $d^2O_A/dt^2 > 0$;
C, where dO_A/dt is high, and $d^2O_A/dt^2 > 0$;
D, where dO_A/dt is low, and $d^2O_A/dt^2 > 0$.

Now let us introduce a cycle of the Hicks type, generated by any shock—say a war scare—that lasts only one period. Clearly, the nature of this cycle will vary, according to the phase of economic growth. Six separate causal factors in the cycle will be influenced by the rate of economic growth.

1. The slope of the "ceiling" (O_p). The Hicksian boom comes to an end because of the decline in the rate of growth of output involved in the shift from expansion based on his "super-multiplier" to a rate of growth determined by the slope of his "ceiling," which in my terminology is "the trend of potential output," or national income at full employment and constant prices. Now the potential trend, as well as the autonomous trend, will, of course, taper off when the rate of growth in population (labor

FIGURE 4.2
The Great Depression

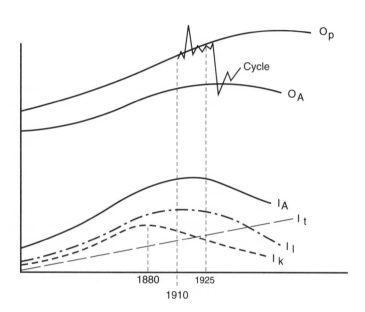

force) and supply of known natural resources tapers off; if the rate of technological progress is constant, there is no reason why it should taper off earlier, and if the marginal propensity to save is also constant, there is nothing to prevent a deceleration of the rise in O_p, if the supply of labor and of natural resources grows less quickly. Thus, at about the same time as the gap between potential and historical trends occurs, booms will weaken. While the "ceiling" is rising rapidly, the shift from expansion based on the super-multiplier to "creeping along the ceiling" does not involve a sharp fall in the rate of expansion, and with lags of significant length the boom can go on for some time. But when the "ceiling" is flattening out, the drop in the rate of expansion when the ceiling is hit becomes greater and greater, and the boom cannot last long after the ceiling is hit. Since there are really a number of "ceilings" in different industries, a slow rate of growth in full employment income might mean that downturns would occur even before full employment is reached in all industries, particularly if there is some immobility of factors of production. Thus the effect of the changing rate of growth on cycles will be such that booms will be of short but increasing duration in phase A, of moderate to long and increasing duration in phase B, of long to moderate but decreasing duration in phase C, and of short and decreasing duration in phase D.

There is an aggravating effect of the trend on the slope of the ceiling, which is more indirect. "Full employment" is in reality not a point but a zone, and the extent to which it will pay to expand the effective labor force, by double or triple shifts, postponing retirement, attracting housewives into employment, and the like, will depend partly on the size of the capital stock. If the "trend" factors are such as to call forth vigorous booms, the stock of capital will tend to grow rapidly in the early stages of the upswing. This accumulation of capital will in itself make the slope of the "ceiling" steeper, postponing the downturn. Thus, if a slackening of growth factors tends to weaken booms (for reasons given below), there will be an *additional* tendency for the ceiling to flatten, because of the slower rate of capital accumulation—which will shorten booms further— and so on. This cumulative effect will be partly, but only partly, offset by the accompanying alleviation of the "drag" imposed on new investment decisions by capital accumulation. Unfortunately, the unfavorable drag on investment decisions depends mainly on the *level* of Q, which grows so long as there is any net investment. The favorable effect through making the ceiling steeper depends mainly on the rate of increase in Q in the early phases of the upswing. If the capital accumulation in the early upswing is reduced through a weakening of growth factors, but is still positive, the net effect of the consequent flattening of the ceiling, on the one hand, and the slower *rate of increase* in the "drag" of capital accumulation on new investment decisions, is bound to be unfavorable. The effect on the slope of the ceiling will also depend partly on the composition of new investment. For example, additions to the stock of housing will increase the slope of the ceiling less than new manufacturing plant.

2. The slope of the "floor." The upturn in the Hicks model comes from the shift in direction of movement in hitting the "floor," which is essentially the equilibrium rate of growth, based on the "autonomous" investment alone. If this equilibrium rate of growth is rapid, the upturn will come very soon after the floor is hit. If the rate of growth in slow, the

depression can last a long time. Thus, so far as this factor is concerned, depressions will be long but shortening in phase A, of moderate to short and diminishing length in phase B, of short to moderate but increasing length in phase C, and long and lengthening in phase D.

3. The change in g, the equilibrium rate of growth. It will be recalled that in Hicks's model the "middle point" for the accelerator coefficient, above which cycles become explosive, is $(1 + g)^2$, where g is the equilibrium rate of growth. Obviously, the lower g, the lower is the middle point. With a given value of the accelerator (above unity), a declining g means that the accelerator is farther and farther above the middle point, and accordingly cycles would become more and more violent. Since in real terms, or employment terms, amplitude can increase in the downward direction only, a declining equilibrium rate of growth would mean more rapid downswings. Of course the "floor" is reached sooner if the downswing is more rapid, but when the effects of the downswings on expectations and Marrama's "rationality factor" (which Hicks ignores) are taken into account, it seems likely that the more violent downswing will mean that the "transformation" of the accelerator in the downswing will last for some time after the floor is reached. That is, it will take a longer period of sustained increase in output to start induced investment and launch an upswing. When the effect of the decline in g on the position and slope of the "floor" is also taken into account, it seems clear that the net effect will be more violent downswings and longer depressions; the combined effect will increase the average unemployment during depression, pulling down the historical, statistical trend.

Even if Hicks is wrong and the accelerator of the real world is below the middle point, a decline in g would cause increasing underemployment in the form of a growing gap between the potential and historical trends. For the closer is the accelerator to the middle point, the slower is the rate of damping of cycles induced by "erratic shocks"; as the middle point drops, unless the accelerator drops too or shocks become weaker (and there is no obvious reason why either of these thing should happen), the average amplitude of cycles induced by erratic shocks will increase—which in real terms means increasing in the downward direction.

Thus, in phase A fluctuations will tend to be extreme to moderate—in *percentage* terms—but diminishing; during phase B their amplitude will be moderate to small, and diminishing; during phase C their amplitude will be small to moderate but increasing; and in phase D their amplitude will be large and increasing, in both percentage and absolute terms. Since in real terms booms are limited by the full-employment ceiling, this means that during phase D, the booms are shortened, while the amplitude of the downswing is increased.

4. The changes in the stock of capital. The stock of capital will start very small, and grow continuously except in deep depression. An industrially mature nation will have a large stock of capital, and consequently a low marginal productivity of capital (apart from technological progress). Now Hicks's "floor" to the downswing is determined partly by minimal autonomous investment, and partly by the maximum amount of net disinvestment. Obviously, the more capital an economy has, the more disinvestment is possible, and the lower the floor to the cycle can be. This relationship provides another reason for supposing that in an economy where total output is growing at an increasing rate, the historical (statistical) trend (in real terms) will be close to the potential trend (in real terms). In such an economy the stock of capital is usually small; while in a economy where output is rising at a decreasing rate, and the stock of capital is large, the historical trend will fall farther and farther below the potential trend.

In other words, the "downward displacement" of the floor grows, at least until downswings become very violent and depressions very long.

5. For completeness, we should introduce the possibility of a long-run rise in the marginal propensity to save. This might weaken upswings by reducing the multiplier. However, by diminishing the degree of change in rate of growth when the full-employment ceiling is hit, an increasing marginal propensity to save may prolong the boom, so long as the accelerator is high. Thus, the effect of this factor is uncertain. Regular cycles require a constant multiplier. If the marginal propensity to save rises with national income in the long run—as seems likely—the upswings will be weakened. The downswings will be less affected, because of the operation of the "Modigliani factor" and of Hicks's "transformation" of the accelerator. According to the Modigliani principle, the marginal propensity to save is reduced in the downswing, the degree to which savings are squeezed out in the downswing depending on the extent of the fall in national income from the previous peak. The lower the peak, the less saving is squeezed out, and the less the downswing is damped. Also, according to Hicks's principle of "transformation," the floor to the downswing is set by the rate at which capital can be consumed, which does not depend on the multiplier at all. Thus the long run tendency for the multi-

plier to fall, as very high levels of national income are reached in advance countries, will weaken booms without shortening depressions or checking downswings.

6. The accelerator itself might rise as the production structure becomes more complex, and businessmen become more cycle conscious. If so, this factor in itself will tend to accelerate and shorten booms as the economy grows. However, this factor operates in the opposite direction from the trend in the multiplier, and consequently the super-multiplier may not change markedly in the course of economic growth. We can justifiably, therefore, concentrate on the first four of the six factors influenced by economic growth.

The results of our analysis thus far are summarized in figure 4.1. We began with a curve of autonomous economic development (O_A), based on autonomous investment (I_A), which follows a growth curve because population growth and discovery of resources follow growth curves, while the other major determinant of autonomous investment, technological progress, proceeds at a steady rate. We then introduced a cycle of the Hicks type. We showed that in phase A fluctuations will have considerable amplitude, measured in *percentage* of national income. The historical trend, O_h, will lie below the potential trend, O_p, but will gradually approach it. Because of the long, deep depressions, the historical trend of national income, Y_h, will also lie below the historical trend of real income, O_h. However, the gap will not be large.

Since in this phase of development both investment and savings are small, any event which brought a substantial increase in investment would tend to produce an explosive boom. With such a small base, any substantial investment means a high percentage increase in investment, while the increase in income (dY/dt) will still be small for some time, so that the increase in savings (dS/dt) will also be small. In this sense, and only in this sense, there will be a "chronic inflationary gap"; *given* any phenomenon calling forth a significant amount of investment, an inflationary boom will tend to set in.

Toward the end of this phase, as booms are strengthened and depressions weakened by the appearance of a significant rate of economic growth, the curve of historical national income (Y_h) may cross the curve of national real income (O_h). Thus the curve of Y_h *will be below* O_p, in the earliest stages of economic growth, and towards the end of the first phase may rise above it.

In phase B, up to the inflection point, booms get longer and stronger, and depressions shorter and weaker. By definition, the statistical or historical trend, O_h, must lie below the trend of national income at full employment without inflation, O_p; but toward the end of the second phase these two curves will be very close together, because of the combination of inflationary booms, and a "chronic inflationary gap" in the *trend* sense as well, arising from the increasing rate of growth, the curve Y_h will lie above the curve O_p. *A fortiori,* therefore, Y_A will lie above O_h.

In phase C the booms will be long and strong, but shortening and weakening. The depressions will be short and shallow at first, but will deepen and lengthen as time goes by. Thus the curve O_h will fall farther and farther below O_p, both from the effect of long-run trend factors on the two curves and also as a result of the changing pattern of economic fluctuations. For the same reason, Y_h will eventually fall below O_p as well.

In this phase the depressions will be more serious than in phase A, although the rate of growth may be the same. The large volume of capital that has been accumulated permits a bigger "downward displacement" of the floor, and imposes a greater "drag" on new investment decisions. Depressions may also be deeper, and booms weaker as a result of a lower multiplier (higher marginal propensity to have). Also, the rate of growth is slow but accelerating in phase A, and is slow and decelerating in phase D.

Thus the impact of the trend on the pattern of economic fluctuations *aggravates* the inflationary and deflationary gaps arising from trend factors alone. In the neighborhood of the inflection point, in the late B and early C phases, a chronic inflationary gap will appear, through the impact of long-run factors, quite apart from the cycle. The expansion of growth factors is high, calling for high levels of investment, while national income is not yet very high, so that savings tend to lag behind. This *chronic* inflationary gap is widened by *cycles* with strong, long booms and short, shallow depressions. The inflationary gap $(Y_h - O_p)$ may be substantial.

In phase D, on the other hand—the "mature economy"—there is a chronic and growing deflationary gap, as a result of trend factors alone. Income and savings are high, but the rate of growth, and autonomous investment, are low. These factors, if not offset, would in themselves create a growing gap between actual and potential national income. However, this gap is accentuated by the effect on the pattern of cycles of the slackening rate of growth; the upswings become more "disappointing," to use Schumpeter's term, while depressions become more devastating. Given a cycle of the Hicks type, "increasing underemployment" will occur in phase D, quite apart from the growing gap between the *trend* of investment and the *trend* of *ex ante* savings. Indeed, so long as *either* the ceiling or the floor follows the normal growth curve, the Hansen thesis will be substantiated, through the effect of the declining rate of growth on cyclical behavior alone. Given the combined effects of flattening ceiling and floor, capital accumulation and rising national income, on the *cycle,* as well as the gap produced by the *trend* factors alone, increasing underemployment in phase D is inevitable, unless appropriate policies are pursued.

Let us now apply this analysis to the great depression of the 1930s in the United States. The critics of the Hansen "stagnation" thesis make two main points: first, they contend that growth can be maintained by technological progress alone; second, they point out that population growth declined, and frontier expansion ended, well before 1929. I shall show that the timing of these factors, far from destroying the Hansen thesis, actually fortifies it.

In figure 4.2, I_L shows investment based on the actual trend of population growth. It will approximate a normal growth curve, with a peak in 1925. (We shall for the moment ignore the post-Second World War increase in population growth.) Curve I_k shows investment based on rate of resource discovery. No statistics of discovery of new natural resources exist, but the Bureau of the Census does publish figures of the centroid of population. The westward movement of this centroid is a fair indication of the rate at which the "frontier" was opened up in the United States, and this in turn approximated closely the rate of resource discovery in the relevant sense. As Professor Hansen rightly insisted, the influence of movement to new territory is not only a matter of discovering and opening up new agricultural land and new mineral resources; it is also a matter of "frontier spirit." This curve also approximates closely a normal "growth" curve, with its peak about 1880.

Adding these two curves together, we get a curve of autonomous investment which, depending on the relative strength of $\partial\Phi/dL$ and $\partial\Phi/dK$, will reach its peak somewhere between 1880 and 1925, and probably about 1910. The curve of O_A, representing the real income produced by autonomous investment and the super-multiplier, will reach a peak at about the same time. If technological progress proceeds at a constant rate, and if the super-multiplier does not change, the peak of O_A will, of course, coincide with the peak of I_A. Because of the offsetting effects of economic growth on multiplier and accelerator, no marked trend in the super-multiplier need be expected. As for the rate of technological progress, we have assumed that it is constant. Considering how rapid technological progress was during the eighteenth and nineteenth centuries, it seems unlikely that the *rate* of technological improvement could have continued to rise steadily since. There is also some evidence that innovation is increasingly capital saving. Thus there is good reason to suppose that the autonomous investment arising from technological progress also tapered off in recent decades. However, we do not need this argument to make our case, and accordingly we shall assume that I_T is a straight line. In the absence of evidence to the contrary, we could also assume that the net effect of any increase in replacement needs, and of the "drag" imposed by capital accumulation, is to reduce the flow of investment decisions; but this assumption, also, is not necessary to prove our hypothesis.

Now let us consider Hansen's argument that the presence of "stagnation" (or "increasing under-employment," as I prefer to term it) since, say, 1910 was part of the reason for the peculiar depth and duration of the "great depression" of the 1930s. The *trend* of savings was undoubtedly upwards throughout the whole period under consideration, following the upward trend of national income. In particular, the trend of savings out of the full-employment income was upwards following the trend in full-employment income. In this connection, it is important to note that the relevant savings trend is the trend of *ex ante* savings at full employment, and figures of *ex post* savings, which are, of course, identical with *ex post* investment, are quite irrelevant. Since autonomous investment began to fall after, say 1910, while *ex ante* savings continued to rise, "stagnation," or increasing underemployment as a *trend* factor must have begun at about that time.

But if "stagnation" began, in say, 1910, why didn't it show up before 1930? I would argue that it *did* show up; the boom of the 1920s succeeded in establishing full employment only in the best months of 1929. The relationship between the trend and the cyclical movement is illustrated in figure 4.2. The downswing of 1913–1914 was quite sharp; my own guess is that the "great depression" might have started then, if the First World War had not come along, which not only brought temporary prosperity, but built up a backlog of replacement demand, and accelerated the automobile, aircraft, and chemical Kondratieffs. The backlog of housing demand was particularly important, although it tapered off with the decline in population growth after 1925. But because of the underlying gap between the *trend* of investment and the *trend* of *ex ante* savings at full employment, these strong, expansionary, cyclical factors failed to create inflationary conditions; prices sagged and full employment was reached only at the peak. Only with the weakening of the *cyclical* factors toward the end of 1929 did "stagnation" reveal itself. Thus the historical course of national income between 1910 and 1940 was perfectly consistent with Hansen's thesis, as reinterpreted here. The lag between the onset of "stagnation," perhaps prior to the First World War, and its becoming effective as a factor governing the cycle, far from being a disproof of the Hansen thesis, is, in the light of the above analysis, one of its most persuasive empirical bulwarks.

A sharp break in trend could in itself cause a downswing, through the decline in the rate of increase in output that it entails. Of course, a *sharp* break in trend is unlikely; but if the effects of the changing trend are delayed the result may be the same. And it appears that this sequence of events actually occurred. The inflection point in both the potential and the autonomous trends probably came between 1910 and 1920; but the effects of the change in trend were delayed by the war and the secondary post-war boom. By 1930 the drop in the potential and autonomous rates of growth was probably substantial; an unusually deep and long depression was to be expected.

As for the "disappointing Juglar," there are several reasons for expecting a weak boom after so long and so deep a depression. One is Hicks's "transformation of the accelerator" (see especially page 106 of his essay). A second is the increased effect of Marrama's "rationality factor."[3] In a depression as deep and as long as that of the 1930s, especially one with its peculiar configuration, with a brief recovery in 1934 and 1937, the "wait-and-see" attitude common to long depressions would become still more deeply entrenched. Finally, the accumulation of debt during the depression resulted in a high marginal propensity to save in the upswing, and consequently a lower multiplier.

There were, of course, other factors involved in the "great depression" besides those analyzed here. The financial crisis of 1931–1933, which was partly the result of purely institutional weaknesses, the psychological impact of the breakdown of the gold standard, "technological stagnation" in the United Kingdom, and the still greater degree of "maturity" on the continent of Europe, where population growth and resource discovery had virtually disappeared in some countries, accentuated the depth of the world depression, which, of course, had some impact on the United States. Nevertheless, it appears that the interaction of cycle and trend, with the factors stressed by Hansen given pride of place in explaining the trend, and with a theory of fluctuations along Hicksian lines, provides a neat explanation of the "great depression."

Summary and Conclusions

The above analysis is far from being an exhaustive exposition of possible interrelations between cycles and trends. It is not difficult, however, to discern from this analysis the directions in which it could be complicated or varied. I have experimented with some of the more obvious variations and complications, and I have not found that they alter fundamentally the conclusions already reached.

First, a model that relies on the Hicks theory of cycles is subject to any imperfections inherent in that theory; and the impact of the trend on the pattern of cycles is less apparent when other cycle theories are used. In Kalecki's theory, for example, the full-employment ceiling is less strategic; expansion can continue "through" the ceiling in an inflationary boom in which profits continue to rise at an increasing rate. There is no modern theory, however, in which investment is not dependent in some way on the rate of overall expansion of the economy, whether expressed in terms of income, sales, profits, or output. There is, accordingly, no theory in which cyclical patterns are wholly independent of the underlying trend. Moreover, my choice of the Hicks model to demonstrate my argument was not dictated solely by its convenience for my purpose. *Employment* must depend on the rate of *physical* expansion; and the rate of *physical* expansion must be affected by the slopes of Hicks's ceiling and floor.

Second, it would be possible to treat autonomous and induced investment together, lumping all factors influencing total investment together in one equation, *e.g.,* $I = I_i(0) + I_A(L,K,T) - \psi(Q)$, where I_i is induced investment. However, the rate of increase in output will itself depend on growth factors, except that the current increase in output will depend on the expansion of population and resources in actual *employment,* and the rate at which improved techniques are actually *applied,* and not on the rate at which these factors become *known* and *available.* Let us lump together the expansion of growth factors *available (L, K, T)* as *G,* and the rate at which they are actually utilized as G^l. Then our equation becomes: $I = I_i(G^l, 0) + I_A(G) - (Q)$. Clearly, G^l reaches a ceiling at full employment, and total investment must fall at that point unless long-run growth accelerates sufficiently, or unless expansion takes place continuously along the full-employment ceiling, as in a "steady-growth" model. Such a formulation has some attractions in terms of neatness, but does not alter the conclusions.

Third, account should be taken of the possibility that the growth factors themselves may show a cyclical pattern, with changes in rates big enough to bring the accelerator into play. Personally, I doubt whether cycles in population growth would take place apart from major "shocks," such as wars; but resource discovery and technological progress may come in waves. However, this possibility introduces no serious new problems. The curves in figure 4.1 would then relate to a long wave, or "Kondratieff" cycle, and the pattern of the Juglar will depend on the phase of the Kondratieff. In this case, however, we need another concept of "trend"—a movement over periods longer than the Kondratieff. Why should this trend be a rising one? The *trend* of potential output, O_p, will be upwards so long as the *trend* of $d/dt\{T.f(L,K,Q)\} > 0$. *If* successive booms are launched so that full employment is reached periodically, the *peaks* will be higher and higher. Whether or not this will happen will depend on the whole complex of very long-run trend, Kondratieff, and Juglar. There is room for much more work here.

However, none of these complications seems to destroy the major conclusions already reached:

1. There is a two-way relationship between cycles and trends, the one amplifying the other. An underlying rapid growth brings vigorous and prolonged booms, short and shallow depressions, so that the *actual* trend of real income stays close to the potential trend of real income at full employment—and vice versa.

2. If population increase and resource discovery follow growth curves, while technological progress is, more or less, constant, the economy will pass through four phases of economic development:

a) Where autonomous growth is small but increasing. In this phase there will be a substantial gap between the autonomous and potential trends of real income, first growing and then diminishing. Booms will be weak but strengthening, depression severe but ameliorating. The cyclical factor will widen the gap between potential and historical trends of income at the beginning of the phase, narrow it towards the end. There may be a downward price trend as well during the early part of this phase.

b) Where autonomous growth is rapid and increasing. The gap between income produced by autonomous investment alone and potential income will narrow. Booms will be long and vigorous, depressions sharp and shallow. Thus the trend of historical real income will approximate the trend of potential real income. The price trend will be upwards; there may be a "chronic inflationary gap."

c) Where autonomous growth is rapid but decreasing. Income produced by autonomous investment will fall farther and farther below potential real income. Booms will weaken, depressions deepen and lengthen. The historical trend of real income will also, therefore, fall farther below the trend of full-employment income.

d) Where autonomous growth is small and diminishing. Real income produced by autonomous investment will fall far below the full-employment level. Booms will be weak and short, depressions long and deep. Because of the greater "downward displacement" of the floor, depressions will be longer and deeper in this phase than with the same autonomous rate of growth in phase A. In the absence of appropriate government action, the trend of historical real income will fall far and increasingly below the full-employment level. Prices will also show a downward trend.

3. This kind of interaction between cycle and trend helps to explain the peculiar depth and duration of the "great depression" of the 1930s in the United States. Resource discovery (frontier development) reached its peak around 1880, population growth in 1925. The delayed effect of the slackening of growth, due to the First World War and its aftermath, only intensified its impact.

In sum, the model seems to suggest a fruitful approach to a generalized theory of economic development, which would take account of both cyclical and trend factors.

Conclusion

With the addition of the theory of underemployment equilibrium, the concept of chronic inflation, the doctrine of secular stagnation (or secular inflation) in mature economies, the theory of the "knife-edge" and cumulative movements away from equilibrium and interactions of cycles and trends, to the earlier theories of business cycles, we move a long way in the direction of the realities of the 1990s. But we are not yet there. Underlying all the theories that are discussed in this chapter and the previous one is still the basic notion that unemployment *or* inflation are alternatives and that policy need be directed only towards curing one or the other at any one time. We do not have as yet a theory to explain simultaneous, and even simultaneously increasing or decreasing, unemployment *and* inflation. Still less do we have a theory to explain what seem to be shifts in trade-off curves and cyclical loops that are just as regular and systematic as the prewar economic fluctuations. Has there been some basic structural change in the economies of the ICCs? If so, what, why, and how, and what do the changes imply with regard to needed changes in policies to deal with unemployment and inflation? To these questions we now turn.

Notes

1. Higgins, Benjamin, "The Theory of Increasing Underemployment," *The Economic Journal* (June 1950).
2. Higgins, Benjamin, "The Optimum Wage Rate," *Review of Economics and Statistics* (May 1949).
3. Marrama, V., "Short Notes on a Model of the Trade Cycle," *The Review of Economic Studies* XIV (4): 34–40.

Part III

Postwar Economic Fluctuations as Shifting Trade-Off Curves and Loops

5

Concepts and Definitions

In our review of the theories of economic fluctuations that were elaborated before shifting trade-off curves (or cyclical loops) took over the world economy, we found several concepts, ideas, and constructs that seem still to be relevant today, and which help to explain the functioning of regional, national, and global economies. Let us reassemble these, in order to isolate the elements that are missing, and which must be added in order to have reliable basis for the formulation of policies to promote economic stabilization and growth in today's world.

Rather than a single "cycle," the economy is characterized by several interacting cycles of varying lengths, from some forty months (the Kitchin cycle) to about fifty years (the Kondratieff cycle). In between are the Juglar (seven to eleven years) and the Kuznets or construction cycle of about sixteen to twenty years. There may be more or less regular cycles in employment and output in other sectors and industries as well, such as iron and steel, transport, and energy; but these are less clearly established. There is debate still about the regularity and periodicity of all the cycles. The main point is, however, that observed economic fluctuations are an extremely complex phenomenon, and we should not expect to find some one simple "law of motion" that would lead to some one simple policy to assure steady growth of the economy.

The observed movements of the economy reflect a combination of "impulses" and "propagation." The impulses, such as investment in capital equipment, may themselves follow a fairly regular cyclical pattern, but it is not clearly established why they should do so. However, the mechanism of the economic machine is such that the propagation process is constrained within limits; and a model consisting of random, exogenous shocks combined with a constrained propagation mechanism, can generate fluctuations as regular as those actually observed in the real world. It is not necessary, therefore, to find "the" impulse that regularly generates each cycle. It is enough to have occasional shocks, favorable or unfavorable, to explain the sort of fluctuations that actually take place.

If, however, we were to attempt to pick out one type of impulse that is intrinsic to the economic system, and which is sufficiently irregular in its occurrence to explain observed fluctuations, it would be innovations. The role of these in generating business cycles has been well explained by Schumpeter.

With regard to the propagation mechanism, the most satisfactory model thus far is one consisting of interactions between the multiplier and the accelerator, constrained by a ceiling and a floor. In this model, interactions among savings, investment, and consumption are of paramount importance. Since these interactions are greatly affected by the operation of the banking system, interest rates, and monetary expansion and contraction, these are important factors in the explanation of economic fluctuations. Purely monetary theories of the trade cycle, however, are inadequate. The behavior of the monetary system is itself determined in large measure by real factors.

All structures of capital (average periods of production or investment, capital-output and capital-labor ratios) are not compatible with all structures of interest rates. Consequently, unforeseen changes in interest rates can make existing structures of capital inappropriate and unsustainable, causing serious trouble. This is the element of truth in the Hayek theory. We are not obliged to choose between over-savings and under-savings theories of crises; both can be right. If savings dry up and interest rates rise unexpectedly in the course of a process of capital expansion, there can be a crisis. But excess savings and its obverse, inadequate consumer spending to absorb the products of new capital, can also bring a crisis. This is the core of the "knife-edge" theory. Many things can make the economy fall off the knife edge.

Since the pattern of long waves and longer run trends can affect the slopes of the floor and ceiling, cycles and trends will interact.[1] Regional or national economies experiencing rapid long-run growth will be relatively stable, with long periods of prosperity and short depressions. Stagnant economies will be unstable as well, with short booms and long depressions. The best way to stabilize a stagnant economy may be to accelerate its long-run growth.

These seven pillars of wisdom, together, provide considerable insight into the functioning of the economy and provide guidance towards ways of improving it. They do not, however, provide a complete explanation of the fluctuations taking place in national or regional economies today. Accordingly, they do not in themselves provide a solid base for designing policies to eliminate—or at least substantially reduce—unemployment and inflation, nor for solving the related balance of payments problems. Since today's fluctuations take a form that can be described as shifting trade-off curves or cyclical loops, it is these phenomena that we must analyze if we are to have a solid basis for policy. In this part of this volume we present such an analysis. However, since the phenomena to be explained, and the tools used for analyzing them, are unfamiliar, we begin by clarifying concepts and endeavoring to provide precise definitions.

The Concept of Trade-Off Curve

Let us recall that the concept of the trade-off curve (TOC) was introduced after Phillips introduced his curve showing the long-run relationship between unemployment and the rate of wage increases. Why should anyone have expected such a relationship to exist? Microeconomic theory told us that employment (N) is a function of the wage rate (w); and since unemployment (U) is equal to the labor force (L) minus "N" (U = L-N), we would expect that U = f(w). But there is no logical necessity for unemployment to fall when wages rise more rapidly; from our micro theory we might expect the reverse. Of course, if wages are rising because of rising labor productivity, increased demand for labor, and overall economic expansion, we might expect unemployment to fall as the rate of wage increase ($\hat{w}$) accelerates. The point is that the relationship shown in the Phillips curve depends on the operation of the whole economic system, including variables that are not shown in the diagram. The curve does *not* depict a simple functional or causal relationship, $U=f(\hat{w})$.

The same observation holds when we move to the trade-off curve. It is important to be clear from the beginning that the curve *does not* depict a simple functional or causal relationship between "U" and "P," rate of price increase, in the way that a demand curve shows a direct relationship between price and quantity demanded, or a consumption function shows a direct relationship between consumer spending and incomes. It depicts a series of combinations of unemployment and inflation emerging as a consequence of the manner in which *the entire economic system functions,* including the impact of government policy. It is, therefore, an extremely complex concept. At any point of time, of course, only one combination of U and $\dot{P}$ can be observed; but the concept of a curve implies that all the other points on it *could have been achieved* at that point of time if something, notably policy affecting the supply of money, had been different.

In other words, the more familiar curves of economic analysis are based on observations of individual behavior, and on plausible assumptions about that behavior derived from those observations. It is reasonable to assume that individuals will buy more of a commodity when its price is lowered, and empirical study shows that they do. Similarly, it is reasonable to expect that individuals will spend more on consumption when their incomes rise, and budget studies show that they do. Macroeconomic relationships like the consumption function for a national economy can be derived by aggregation of individual consumption functions, and then the macroeconomic relationship can be verified and quantified by statistical and econometric analysis. But we have no widely applicable rule of individual behavior that says that people normally tend to drop out of the labor force (stop looking for work) if the rate of price increase or wage increase rises, thus reducing the unemployment rate; and return to the labor force if the rate of wage or price increase falls, thus raising the unemployment rate. Nor do we have a behavioral law stating that individual employers tend to take on more workers when wages rise more rapidly and let them go when wages rise more slowly. They may take on workers when prices rise more rapidly, but only if wages or interest rates do not rise still more rapidly. A Phillips curve or a trade-off curve is a kind of report card on the functioning of the entire economy, and its position, slope, configuration, and shifts depend on a host of things not shown in the diagram itself.

Clearly, in order to speak of shifting TOCs, the TOCs must exist. We say that a series of observations for successive periods of time lie on the same TOC when two conditions are met:

1. The observations *appear* to lie on a single curve: that is, a curve can be drawn that gives a good fit to the data.

2. It is reasonable, on the basis of general knowledge of the situation prevailing in a particular country in a particular period, to conclude that during the period covered by observations thought to lie on a single "stable" TOC, the government could have selected any of the combina-

tions of unemployment and inflation indicated by the curve as a policy objective, and achieved that objective by money-management policies alone. In other words, the TOC is a set of optional goals of monetary and fiscal policy.

Of course this concept of TOC will not satisfy quantitatively minded economists. There is no way of testing now whether in fact the government of Esperanza could have produced, through policies to control the money flow alone, 10 percent price increases and 8 percent unemployment in 1960, instead of the 8 percent price increase and 10 percent unemployment actually observed. The fact that these two options, together with a few others, *look as though* they lie on the same curve is scarcely proof enough. But economics made a good deal of progress in the seventy years after 1870 with theoretical concepts that did not lend themselves easily to empirical testing, and it is better to work with variables which are the real causal factors but are not easily quantified, than to stick to variables which are readily available in statistical form but do not explain what is going on in the world.

Thus, in this analysis the term *trade-off curve* does not refer to an econometrically derived functional relationship between the rate of inflation and the rate of unemployment; nor even such a relationship with one or two variables thrown in, such as the rate of increase in the United States price level, so favored as an added variable by Canadian econometricians in deriving TOCs or Phillips curves from the data.[2] On the contrary, the theory is that in any period of time—a year or a quarter or a month—the operation of the entire economic system, including actions of government and links to the world economy, produces some increase in prices and some average level of unemployment. Each such observation of one level of unemployment and one rate of increase in prices constitutes one point on a trade-off curve.

The question then is: How many points lie on the same TOC? Conceivably, if the TOC is completely unstable there may be only one point on each curve, in which case it is hardly worthwhile calling it a curve. Similarly, if the points lie on a vertical straight line (as they seem to do for some countries in some periods), and still more if they seem to lie on a curve sloping upward to the right, there is little point to calling it a trade-off curve since no trade-off is involved. For a trade-off to exist there must be several points, representing options between more inflation and less unemployment or *vice versa,* which can be considered to lie on the same curve, in the sense that all points are available at each point of time throughout the entire period of time covered by the curve. Since the observed points emerge from the operation of the whole economic system, the question as to which points lie on the same curve cannot be answered by merely deriving a single equation for a curve and then measuring the deviation of particular points from this curve. One would need to know whether or not the operation of the entire economic system had changed in some fundamental way. Conceptually, saying that unemployment/price increase combinations lie on the same TOC means first of all that the observations look as though they might all lie on the same curve. Secondly it means that, in fact, at any point of time during the period covered by the curve, the government in question could have chosen any of the options represented by the curve, and achieved the option selected as optimal (minimum discomfort point) through standard monetary and fiscal policy (management of the money supply) alone.

It is of course extremely difficult to determine empirically what points lie on the same TOC defined in this manner. Given sophisticated models of entire economies in which one has confidence, one could substitute, for actual policies pursued in each year covered by the presumed TOC, different monetary and fiscal policy variables; and see whether the resulting simulated levels of unemployment and inflation conform to those which in fact occurred in other years, and which are presumed to lie on the same TOC.

It is the author's current conviction that TOCs in this sense did exist in some countries between about 1955 and about 1967, and perhaps again in the late 1970s. In between the observations were shifting upward and outward so rapidly that it is a matter of debate whether any curve could have been said to exist. There is some reason to doubt that TOCs have stabilized now in many countries, in the sense that there are real options of better employment and worse inflation or *vice versa,* to be obtained by ordinary monetary and fiscal policy alone.

The Concept of Shifting TOCs

What do we mean by a shift of the TOC? We mean that both unemployment and inflation have moved together, up or down, so that any preexisting "trade-off" is destroyed. We shall turn to the detailed analysis of the data at a later point; here we want only to explain the concept of shifts. It is clear that all the points observed for any country or region cannot be interpreted as lying on the same TOC. As we shall see, in Canada and the United States throughout much of the period covered, inflation and unemployment were increasing together; any TOCs that existed were valid for only a limited period of time, and were in the course of shifting upward to the right. In other words, the overall situation was deteriorating. In the last few years, there has been some improvement; the TOC may be shifting downward to the left, whether as a result of improved policy or of improved operation of the national economies, a question to which we shall return below. In between, there have been short periods of relative stability, in the sense that inflation and unemployment moved in opposite directions. In these periods we might say that a trade-off curve existed, in the sense that the combinations observed *during* the period were continuously attainable *throughout* the period, through management of the money flow alone.

The recognitions that there are cyclical shifts in TOCs, and that these shifts may be systematic, has come only recently to the economics profession. Indeed, Professor Robert Solow of M.I.T. leans toward the view that the shifts are haphazard, while recognizing the possibility of systematic shifts.[3] Professor Jay Forrester, of the systems analysis group of the same institution, however, on the basis of a large model with interacting cycles of various lengths, concludes (as we do) that the shifts are generated by the operation of the entire economic system. The interactions of the "business cycle" (about four years), the Juglar cycle (eight to twelve years), the "Kuznets cycle" (fifteen to twenty-five years), and the "Kondratieff long wave" (fifty years) may explain why recessions since 1945 were less severe than prewar cycles; we may be on the upswing of a long wave. Professor Forrester adds, "our work to date suggests that the balance of inflation and unemployment in the economy depends in a complex way on the many modes of behavior in the economy as well as on the government policies being followed...changes in money supply or changes in the position of the economy relative to the long-wave fluctuations will tend to cause shifts in inflation and unemployment that cannot be described in terms of simple movements along a fixed trade-off curve."[4] Forrester provides a diagram to illustrate how the long-wave and expansionary monetary policy, together, could bring shifts in trade-off curves. Our own view is similar in contending that the shape, position, and shifts of TOCs emerge from the operation of the economic system as a whole—

government policy included. But within that system we put primary emphasis on discontinuous shifts in the "accelerator" (relating investment to increases in output) and in employment multiplier (relating increases in employment to investment).

Our argument is not dependent on the existence of long waves, but proof that long waves do exist would tend to strengthen our position; that is, a long-sustained boom in the capital goods industries would tend to lengthen the "period of investment," raise capital: output ratios, lower the employment multiplier without lowering the income multiplier, and thus aggravate tendencies towards simultaneous inflation and unemployment.

It would facilitate forecasting if we knew precisely how the curves behave; if the shifts are not foreseen, policy must be more flexible than if they are. For purposes of public spending policy, however, the important thing is that the TOCs exist and that they do shift. Unsystematic elements certainly play a role. There can be little doubt that the hike in oil prices in 1973 contributed to the shift upward to the right of TOCs in virtually every country in the world. The world economy is more closely integrated than ever before, and the timing of fluctuations more closely synchronized than ever before. Rising prices anywhere are quickly transmitted into rising costs elsewhere, and the business cycle has become a world cycle as a result. We are confident, however, that further research will show that the present day cycle of shifting TOCs is at least as systematic as was the prewar cycle of alternating inflation and unemployment, and that the importance of systematic factors, as compared to haphazard events, is as great today as it was before World War II.

Since we are laying so much stress on the replacement of the prewar cycle by cycles in the form of shifting TOCs and loops, and since there has been so much confusion in the discussion of TOCs, some words of clarification are in order.

1. We conduct our analysis in terms of trade-off curves, representing sets of options with regard to combinations of inflation and unemployment, rather than in terms of the original "Phillips Curve" showing unemployment in relation to rates of increase in wages. The reason is simple: the policy problem consists in trying to achieve the best possible combination of inflation and unemployment, ideally full employment without inflation, in practice the closest possible approximation to this ideal. Wage increases as such are not a "problem" but rather a laudable objective of economic and social policy; all governments maintain that they would

like to see workers better off, providing more important objectives are not sacrificed as a result.

2. We are not concerned with empirical proof that a stable relationship has existed between inflation and unemployment over long periods in the past. On the contrary, our argument is that the relationship is highly unstable, and that the shifts in the relationship are the essence of postwar economic fluctuations. Thus failure to find a statistical trade-off curve, described by some simple equation, which provides a "good fit" to points of price increase and unemployment observed over long periods in the past, in no way challenges the validity of our position, and in some respects supports it.

3. We do not maintain that unemployment is a function of price increases alone, or vice versa. On the contrary, both the level of unemployment and the rate of price increase are the end result of the operation of the entire economic system.

4. As in the case of any other *ex ante* (forward-looking) curve in economic analysis (a demand curve, a consumption function), only one point on the curve can actually be observed during any time period for which data are collected. If for example quarterly data are used, only one observation regarding price (average for the quarter) and sales (total for the quarter) can be made. That is the only point *observed* on the demand curve. The *concept* of the demand curve, however, implies that if prices were lower, sales would be greater, and so on. Similarly, only one combination of price increase and unemployment can be observed in any quarter. The curve describes a set of possibilities applicable at a point of time, and continuing through some period of time however long or short. But the concept of the curve implies that, other things being equal, if unemployment were lower price increases would be greater, and so on. Again, the curve is valid at a point in time, but may continue unchanged through a period of time.

5. Since the position, slope, and shifts in trade-off curves depend so much on government policy, the curves cannot be described, nor their values estimated, without stating what the policy framework is. Any government can produce (statistical) full employment without inflation, as most socialist countries did for substantial periods, and as other allied nations did between 1941 and 1946. Our analysis suggests that the curve can be shifted downward to the left by policies designed to reduce regional disparities. Thus when we say, "In the first quarter of this year,

unemployment is 9 percent and the annual rate of price increase 4 percent; but the options are open to have 12 percent unemployment and 3 percent price increases, or 6 percent unemployment and 15 percent price increase," we are really saying that these are the options open to government, without substantial changes in the *instruments* of policy used. We shall therefore *define* the trade-off curve as the set of options regarding combinations of inflation and unemployment open to government through the use of traditional monetary and fiscal policy, designed to affect economic activity mainly through changes in the money supply. We can then pose meaningful questions as to how much the trade-off curve can be improved by introducing other types of policy—wage-price controls, rationing, manpower allocation, lowering barriers to trade, effective policies to reduce regional gaps, and the like.

6. With the trade-off curve defined in this way, it is difficult to determine whether particular points observed during some period in the past lie on the same *ex ante,* hypothetical curve, or whether the curve has shifted one or more times during that period. The same problem presents itself with any such hypothetical curve—demand curve, consumption function, saving function, investment function, and the like. To draw any such curve on the basis of *data* implies that the curve has been stable throughout the period of observation, so that several points of observation can be assumed to lie on the same curve. If the curve is constantly shifting we would never have statistical curves at all; we would have only points. The problem of deciding whether or not a set of observations all lie on the same curve is particularly difficult in the case of trade-off curves because the actual outcome with respect to inflation and unemployment depends on virtually everything affecting the behavior of trade unions, employers, and governments, as well as on a number of technical factors such as capital: output ratios, employment multipliers, and the like, all of which can change. Demand curves, for example, tend to shift only if there is a change in consumer incomes or in tastes; otherwise they tend to be stable. But a whole host of things may shift a trade-off curve. Not being in a position to conduct the elaborate econometric studies that might enable us to separate movements along a curve from shifts of the curve, we have adopted a very simple, pragmatic device. Where observations seem to lie along a single curve, giving a reasonably good fit, and nothing specific has happened that might shift the TOC, we assume that the curve has been stable; on the other hand, where the observations do

not fit a single curve well, and at the same time there have been events that could be expected to shift the curve, we assume that the curve has shifted.

Notes

1. Higgins, B. "Trade-off Curves and Regional Gaps." In J. N. Bhagwati and R. S. Ecklaus (eds.), *Economic Development and Planning: Essays in Honour of Paul Rosenstein-Rodan.* London: Allen & Unwin, 1972.
2. Lipsey, R. "The Relationship between Unemployment and the Rate of Change of Money Wage Rates in the United Kingdom, 1862–1957: A Further Analysis." *Economica* (new series) 27 (February 1960): 1–21.
3. Solow, Robert M. "On Theories of Unemployment." *The American Economic Review* (March 1980): 1–11; and "Jobs, Jobs, Jobs: How to Create Them Without Reinflation." *Across the Board* X1V, 1 (January 1977): 29.
4. Forrester, Jay. "Business Structure, Economic Cycles and National Policy." *Futures, the Journal of Forecasting and Planning* 8, 3 (June 1976): 195–214.

6

Unemployment and Inflation in Canada

We turn now to a detailed examination of unemployment and inflation since 1950 in three countries: Canada, Australia, and the United States. In making the comparison among the three countries, we shall be concerned with differences, as well as similarities, in their experience with unemployment and inflation, and with the policy implications of both. We begin with Canada for three reasons: I began my own study of unemployment and inflation in recent decades in Canada; it is the country among the three that provides the clearest evidence of postwar fluctuations in the form of shifting trade-off curves and cyclical loops; and since reducing regional disparities has been a major objective of whatever party has been in power since World War II, Canada has excellent data at the regional level.

Let us start with data at the national level. Let us imagine that we have never heard of Phillips Curves, trade-off curves, or cyclical loops, but that we want to establish the relationship of unemployment and inflation to fluctuations in Gross National Product (GNP). So we plot all three as time series, expecting to find the familiar pattern of prewar fluctuations, with falling unemployment and rising prices accompanying rising GNP, and rising unemployment and falling prices accompanying falling GNP. But when we look at figure 6.1 we get some shocks. There are indeed some periods when the prewar pattern prevailed, unemployment, and inflation moving in opposite directions; but there are other periods when unemployment and inflation fell together; and most shocking of all, still other periods when they *rose* together. What's going on here? We find some evidence that the periods when unemployment and inflation rose together were periods of stagnation or recession in GNP, and periods when they fell together are periods of relatively rapid rise in GNP; but the correlation is far from perfect. The overall situation seems to be some-

FIGURE 6.1
GNP, CPI, and Unemployment, Canada 1950–1994

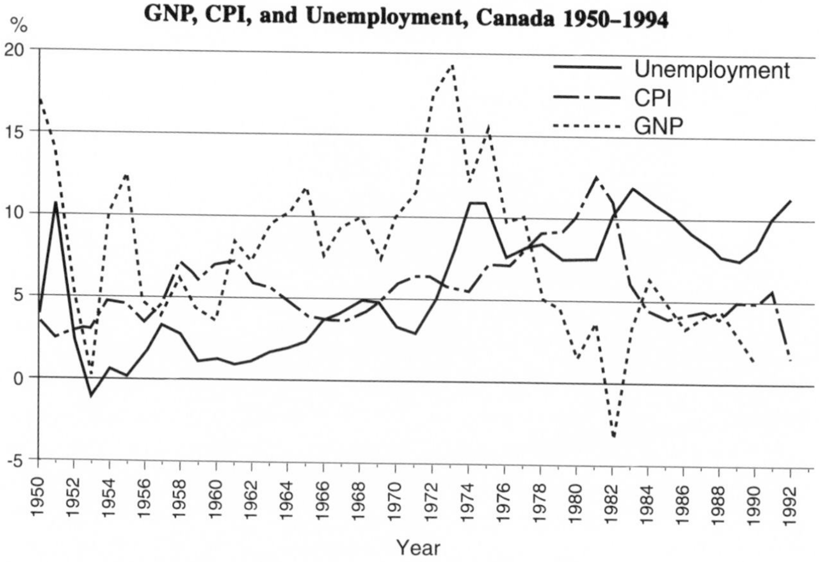

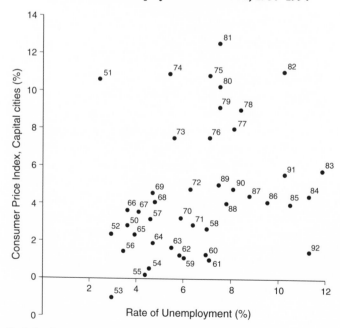

Source: Statistics Canada, *Canadian Economic Observer,* cat. 11-010

FIGURE 6.2
Inflation and Unemployment in Canada, 1950–1994

Source: Statistics Canada, *Canadian Economic Observer,* cat. 11-010.

FIGURE 6.3
Inflation and Unemployment in Canada, 1950–1994

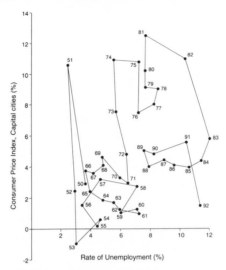

Source: Statistics Canada, *Canadian Economic Observer,* cat. 11-010.

FIGURE 6.4
Trade-off Curves for Canada, 1950–1994

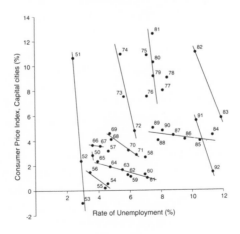

Source: Statistics Canada, *Canadian Economic Observer,* cat. 11-010.

thing of a muddle. The comparatively simple world of the prewar business cycle seems to have disappeared.

Now let us suppose that in order to understand this strange new world better, we plot *combinations* of unemployment and inflation, with unemployment on the horizontal axis and price increases on the vertical axis, to see how they move. The result is a scatter diagram like figure 6.2. What does it tell us? At first glance, it seems like total confusion, although it is clear that things got a lot worse between 1950 and 1994. To see more clearly how the points moved, let us join them, in sequence, by straight lines, as in figure 6.3. Now a kind of pattern appears, although it isn't exactly clear *what* kind. Do some of the points lie on the same curve as others? Let's see. The result this time is figure 6.4, and the concept of shifting trade-off curves emerges.

Now let us confess that we have heard of Phillips Curves and trade-off curves. Figure 6.4 certainly gives no evidence of a Phillips curve that is stable (or reasonably so) over long periods. Between 1950 and 1955 the Canadian trade-off curves were highly unstable. There appear to be at least half a dozen of them, or even more if we regard as TOCs curves with only two points. Starting at the origin, the first curve that might qualify as a TOC is the very steep line joining the points for 1951, 1952, and 1953. The next connects the discomfort points for 1954, 1955, and 1956. Clearly the two points for 1957 and 1958 do *not* lie on the same curve as those for 1954 to 1956. There is not much of a "trade-off" entailed either; the two points indicate a substantial increase in unemployment with virtually no reduction in inflation. The points for 1959 to 1965 form a good TOC, but rather flat. This TOC is substantially lower than the previous one.

The discomfort points for 1966 and 1967 lie close together. They hardly represent a "trade-off," and are better regarded as a temporary quasi-equilibrium. The points for 1968 through 1971 form quite a good TOC; so do the points for 1972 to 1974, though it is a surprisingly steep TOC—if it is a TOC at all. In any case, it brought a steep increase in inflation with almost no reduction of unemployment. The curve for 1975 through 1981 requires a fairly wide envelope to encompass all the points. It represents a further deterioration of the economy. The next two years brought a sharp increase in unemployment with virtually stable inflation, then a sharp reduction in the rate of inflation with virtually stable unemployment. During the 1970s and early 1980s, the Canadian authorities seem to have lost control of the economy altogether; perhaps the oil-price shock was the explanation. Very high rates of inflation brought almost no reduction in unemployment, and the rate of unemployment associated with a given rate of inflation increased steadily. Between 1965 and 1983 the situation was clearly deteriorating. In 1983 a substantial reduction in inflation was achieved with a comparatively slight increase in unemployment, and from 1984 to 1988 there was marked improvement. Then things started to get worse again. Between 1991 and 1993 inflation virtually disappeared, but unemployment was still uncomfortably high.

Thus, the Canadian experience since 1950 can be described as a series of shifting trade-off curves, the shifts being mainly to the northeast but occasionally to the southwest. But suppose we look more closely at figure 6.3 and it suddenly occurs to us that a series of loops, or a spiral, might describe the data as well as a series of trade-off curves. So we try linking the discomfort points in that fashion, and obtain a very interesting result, shown in figure 6.5. Gaston Haddad Luthi prepared such a diagram for the period 1955 through 1978, and I have added the later years. What does the figure mean? Luthi has an interesting idea:

> We observe in this figure three distinct general loops starting in 1955 and spanning over a period of approximately 20 years. The average duration of each of these general loops built into the general loops we note a quite consistent sequence of 4 and 3 years.... Subsequently, could it not be that these loops are in effect representations of Juglar cycles for the general configuration, and Kuznets' cycles when decomposed? In any case, the evidence correlating the cyclical pattern of the economy of the loops of the inflation and unemployment spiral is quite suggestive. (Luthi, 1979, 155)

It is worth stressing the fact, obvious though it may be, that when movements of unemployment and inflation are interpreted as loops, there are periods when the two variables are moving together, in one direction or another. A trade-off exists only in periods when the inflation rate is falling and unemployment increasing or vice versa. Luthi finds for the annual Canadian data that the majority of the observations suggest a trade-off; but with 1979 to 1993 added, it can also be said that a significant proportion of the observations do *not* suggest trade-off, since both unemployment and inflation are either rising or falling together. The figure could indicate shifts in TOCs, rather than movements along them; or that the movements are so powerful that it is useless to speak of a trade-off curve at all.

FIGURE 6.5
Inflation and Unemployment in Canada, 1950–1994

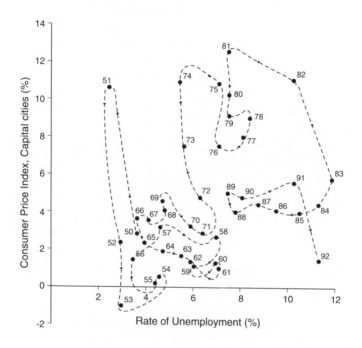

Source: Statistics Canada, *Canadian Economic Observer,* cat. 11-010.

Provincial Patterns of Unemployment and Inflation

We turn now to an examination of provincial patterns of unemployment and inflation, to discover what similarities and differences there are
in comparison with patterns at the national level. Price indices are not
available for regions or provinces. Thus, the TOCs must be constructed
by using unemployment data for provinces or for regions (Atlantic provinces, Prairies) and price data for principal cities. While unemployment
data for such regions are available, there are three cities for the Prairies
and four for the Atlantic provinces. One must choose one of them for
constructing a TOC, and the price movements are not identical for all

FIGURE 6.6
Trade-off Curves for Ontario, 1950–1994

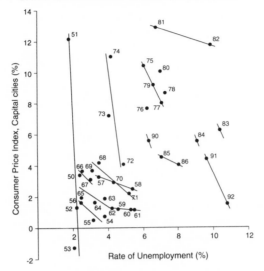

Source: Statistics Canada, *Canadian Economic Observer*, cat. 11-010.

FIGURE 6.7
Trade-off Curves for Quebec, 1950–1994

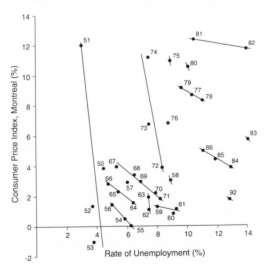

Source: Statistics Canada, *Canadian Economic Observer*, cat. 11-010.

cities. Also, there are differences among the price-unemployment experiences of the three Prairie provinces and of the four Atlantic provinces that have some interest in themselves. It therefore seems preferable to present and analyze the provincial TOCs as such, rather than aggregate the three Prairie provinces and the four Atlantic provinces into two regions.

Figure 6.6 shows TOCs for Ontario. Since Ontario is so large a proportion of the Canadian economy, accounting for about half of GDP and 40 percent of total employment, it is to be expected that the general pattern of fluctuations in Ontario would resemble those of the country as a whole. However, the rate of unemployment has been consistently below the national average. The rate of inflation in Ontario has also been slightly lower than in Canada as a whole.

Quebec is also a substantial part of the national economy, and the general pattern of its economic fluctuations also resembles that of Canada as a whole. However, in contrast to Ontario, Quebec's rate of unemployment has been consistently and significantly *higher* than the national average, and the amplitude of its fluctuations is greater. Moreover, its TOCs tend to be somewhat flatter than Ontario's, suggesting that unemployment can be reduced with less aggravation of inflationary pressure in Quebec than in Ontario (figure 6.7). The rate of inflation has been much the same in Quebec and Ontario.

Apart from Newfoundland, British Columbia had the most unstable of all the regional economies in Canada. For the 1960s, it is hard to distinguish any pattern at all for movements of unemployment and inflation (Figure 6.8). After 1971, the behavior of British Columbia's TOCs resembles more closely those of Canada or the two bigger provinces. Up to 1990, they were closer to Quebec than to Ontario, in that unemployment was persistently above the national average. From 1991 through 1993, British Columbia's unemployment, like Ontario's, has been below the national average.

Alberta's economic fluctuations have been greatly influenced by the oil boom and bust. During the 1960s and early 1970s the pattern was not greatly different from that of Canada. During the period 1972 through 1981 Alberta experienced the same upward shift of its TOC, but the *double* shift that took place in the national and other provincial economies does not appear in Alberta. A further outward shift did take place in 1982. Since 1983 Alberta has experienced reductions in both unemployment and inflation, interrupted by increases in one or the other (figure 6.9).

FIGURE 6.8
Trade-off Curves for British Columbia, 1950–1994

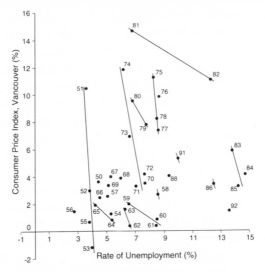

Source: Statistics Canada, *Canadian Economic Observer,* cat. 11-010.

FIGURE 6.9
Trade-off Curves for Alberta, 1966–1994

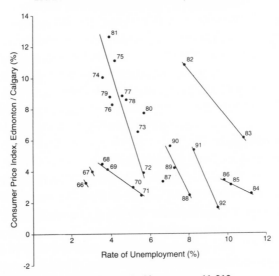

Source: Statistics Canada, *Canadian Economic Observer,* cat. 11-010.

Saskatchewan's story is somewhat different from the others. The double shift between 1971 and 1981 does appear, but there seems to have been an erratic downward shift in 1970 and 1971. The picture for 1984 through 1988 is quite different, with no clear shift to the left. Saskatchewan's unemployment has been consistently below the national average, no doubt partly because of the continuing importance of agriculture in its economy (figure 6.10). Manitoba also presents a somewhat confused picture. For the late 1960s there seems to have been an *upward* sloping curve, which cannot be described as a trade-off; and which implies constantly shifting TOCs, upward and outward, in this period. This experience is followed by three outward shifts to 1983, and then the leftward shifts noted for other provinces, except that in Saskatchewan unemployment was slightly higher in 1988 than in 1987 (figure 6.11). Between 1990 and 1993 Manitoba's unemployment increased by two percentage points.

Like Quebec, New Brunswick has chronically a higher level of unemployment than Canada as a whole. Its pattern of unemployment and inflation is unique. The movement of the discomfort points from 1966 to 1972 and from 1985 to 1989 could be described as two small cyclical loops each, first clockwise and then counterclockwise. Probably, however, the movements in those years are better considered as erratic short-run fluctuations. In 1971 through 1972 came a distinct upward shift, followed by two outward shifts. The years 1981 through 1986 seem to form a trade-off curve. The shift to the southwest does not come until 1986, followed by several years of instability (figure 6.12).

In Nova Scotia, the observations for 1966 through 1970 follow a virtually straight line. There is no "trade-off" between unemployment and inflation; the level of unemployment seems independent of the rate of inflation. The same is true of the observations for 1971 to 1974. The rate of inflation has increased significantly, but it seems to be independent of the rate of unemployment. The years 1974 to 1979, on the other hand, seem to form a well-behaved trade-off curve. Then comes another shift in 1980 and 1981 to a much worse trade-off curve. The observations for 1983 through 1986 appear to lie on yet another vertical straight line; the rate of unemployment is virtually unaffected by the degree of inflation (figure 6.13).

Newfoundland is also unique. Its level of unemployment is nearly double that of Canada as a whole, and two or three times—in some years nearly four times—that of Ontario. On the other hand, price movements

FIGURE 6.10
Trade-off Curves for Saskatchewan, 1950–1994

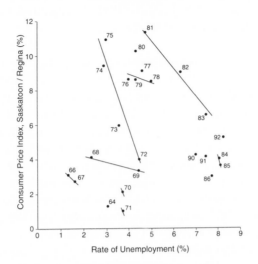

Source: Statistics Canada, *Canadian Economic Observer,* cat. 11-010.

FIGURE 6.11
Trade-off Curves for Manitoba, 1950–1994

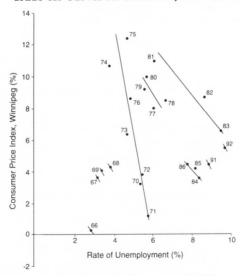

Source: Statistics Canada, *Canadian Economic Observer,* cat. 11-010.

follow those of Canada. The fluctuations of unemployment are quite violent, making for a turbulent economy. As in New Brunswick, the years 1981 to 1985 seem to form a trade-off curve, but a very bad one. From 1986 to 1990 there was some improvement (figure 6.14).

Loops at the Provincial Level

As could be expected, the general pattern of cyclical loops for most provinces is similar to that of Canada as a whole. The provincial loops are somewhat more erratic than the national loops, and show deviations both from the national pattern and from each other. The national loops are a sort of weighted average of the provincial loops, and when some of the provincial loops move in opposite directions, the national loop tends to be ironed out to some degree. All provinces, however, show the same increase in amplitude of loops during the 1970s and 1980s as does the national economy.

As could also be expected, Ontario and Quebec show the closest resemblance between the pattern of their loops and the national pattern. There being no data for the consumer price index in British Columbia for 1987 through 1990 and for 1991, it is more difficult to make a comparison with Canada; but the general configuration seems similar. Alberta was greatly affected by the oil boom and bust; unemployment was lower than the Canadian average during the 1970s, but increased more during the 1980s. Saskatchewan shows much the same configuration as Canada, but at lower levels of both unemployment and inflation; the exception was between 1990 and 1992, when inflation was reduced substantially in Canada but increased in Saskatchewan. Manitoba had a remarkably low rate of inflation from 1966 to 1971 as compared to Canada, and a somewhat lower rate of inflation during the early 1980s. However, unemployment rose in 1991 and 1992, whereas in Canada it fell substantially.

In New Brunswick and Nova Scotia the configuration is much the same as in Canada for those years for which data are available. For Newfoundland, however, the configuration is totally different, and we reproduce the loops here to demonstrate just how much one province can stray from the national path in this regard. From 1956 to 1959 the "loop" consists of an almost horizontal straight line, unemployment increasing from about 6 percent to nearly 20 percent while the rate of inflation remained virtually constant. For 1961 through 1964, it was virtually a

FIGURE 6.12
Trade-off Curves for New Brunswick, 1966–1994

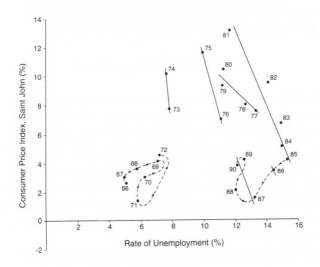

Source: Statistics Canada, *Canadian Economic Observer,* cat. 11-010.

FIGURE 6.13
Trade-off Curves for Nova Scotia, 1966–1984

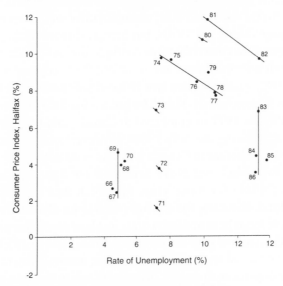

Source: Statistics Canada, *Canadian Economic Observer,* cat. 11-010.

FIGURE 6.14
Trade-off Curves for Newfoundland, 1950–1994

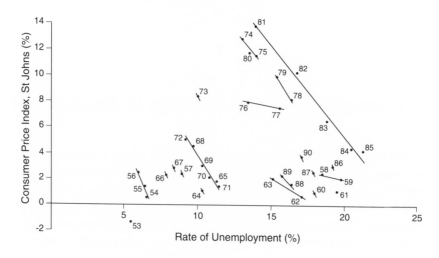

Source: Statistics Canada, *Canadian Economic Observer,* cat. 11-010.

straight line again, the rate of inflation remaining almost constant at a lower level while unemployment was reduced to just over 10 percent. Then there is a shift to the northeast for one year, to yet another horizontal straight line for 1965 through 1966. There follows a counterclockwise loop for 1966 through 1971. From then on the Newfoundland loop follows the Canadian loop more closely, but at much higher levels of unemployment. The Newfoundland economy is a small one, and conditions, especially unemployment, can reflect the situation prevailing in one major industry, such as fishing. Here again, in examining the evidence on differences among provincial loops, we find short-run or long-run variations in experience with unemployment and inflation, that with flexibility, fine tuning, and a differential fiscal policy, provide opportunities for combatting unemployment, inflation, and regional disparities all at the same time.

References

Luthi, Gaston Haddad. "Business Cycle Theory and Stabilization Policy in a World of Shifting Trade-off Curves." Unpublished University of Ottawa Ph.D. thesis. Ottawa, 1979.

7

Unemployment and Inflation in Australia

We turn next to Australia, the second country where I studied unemployment and inflation since 1950. Like Canada, Australia is a large, thinly settled, resource rich, regionalized, and affluent country. Like Canada too, it is an ex-British colony, a Westminster-style parliamentary democracy with many British institutions, and with a federal constitution. One might expect a similar pattern of economic fluctuations, unemployment, and inflation, but in fact there are some striking differences.

Australian economic history since 1950 can be divided into distinct periods, corresponding to changes in government. The first period covers the long rule of the Liberal party, from 1949 to 1972. This was a period of economic turbulence, with violent fluctuations in the rate of growth of Gross Domestic Product and in the rate of inflation, but with essentially full employment throughout. Then came the brief interlude of the Whitlam Labor government from 1972 through 1975, which saw the demise of full employment and a steep rise in the inflation rate as well. The Fraser Liberal government that succeeded it (1975–1983) did not succeed in bringing inflation under control, and brought some sharp increases in unemployment, despite high growth rates. The Hawke-Keating Labor government, which has been in power since (at least to 1996), has concentrated on reducing inflation, at the cost of increased unemployment. The interesting thing is that while the Whitlam government brought a sharp shift to a new TOC much further to the northeast, the Australian economy seems to have been on that TOC ever since, throughout both the Fraser and the Hawke-Keating years, except for the discomfort points for 1983 and 1989.

Figure 7.1 shows time series for unemployment, inflation, and GDP from 1950 to 1994. Imagine, as we did for Canada, that we are examining this figure without having ever heard of trade-off curves. We note

155

that, as in the case of Canada, sometimes unemployment and inflation moved in opposite directions, in accordance with prewar experience; but sometimes they decrease together, and sometimes they increase together. There appears to be some tendency for them to move up together in periods of "stagflation" or recession, and to move down together in periods of recovery or prosperity. There is a suggestion of some kind of cyclical movement, although, to be sure, a very peculiar one in comparison to prewar business cycles.

Now let us suppose that, as in the Canadian case, we plot combinations of unemployment and inflation for the same years, as in figure 7.2. What does the figure tell us? At first glance, it seems like chaos. If we had no concept of a TOC, it is unlikely that we would be led to it by this scatter diagram alone. We can see that, as in Canada, things got worse between 1950 and 1994; especially where unemployment is concerned.

In contrast to the Canadian case, there is not much point in joining the discomfort points by straight lines in order to discern a pattern of some kind in their movement through time. Too many of the points are so close together and there are so many changes in direction of their movement, that no distinct pattern emerges. For the same reason, it is difficult to interpret the movements as cyclical loops. So we are left with trade-off curves; these are shown in figure 7.3. However, the TOCs look quite different from the Canadian TOCs, or from the American TOCs to come. How can we interpret them?

First of all, if we define "full employment" as the situation prevailing when there is no more than three percent (structural and frictional) unemployment, then Australia enjoyed full employment during the whole period from 1950 to 1974. That being so, there would be no reason to expect a TOC to appear; with unemployment already down to the minimum attainable (because structural and frictional barriers prevent instantaneous shifts from one job to another) even a considerable degree of inflation, such as occurred between 1950 and 1952, would not reduce unemployment significantly. Under such circumstances, employment and unemployment become essentially independent of monetary factors, and depend on "real" factors instead. Thus, it was possible for inflation to range from 0.00 percent in 1963 to 12.75 percent in 1952 and 12.85 percent in 1974 without having much effect on unemployment. It is worth noting too that if "without inflation" is defined as price increases of less than 2 percent, there were a good many years during this period when Australia enjoyed "full employment without inflation."

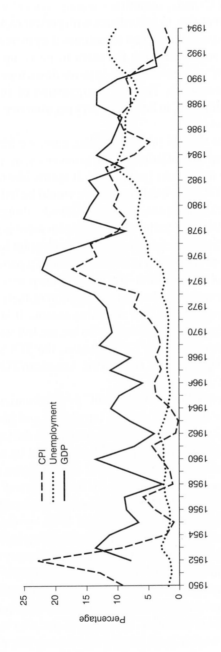

FIGURE 7.1

GDP, CPI, Unemployment Rates in Australia, 1950–1994

Sources: Australian Bureau of Statistics, *Time Series; Commonwealth Yearbooks*

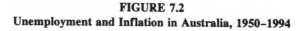

FIGURE 7.2
Unemployment and Inflation in Australia, 1950–1994

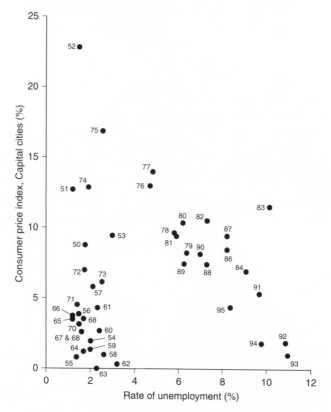

Sources: Australian Bureau of Statistics, Time Series; New South Wales Yearbooks

We have drawn a straight line through the points from 1950 to 1974, which with a reasonable "envelope" or "zone" to encompass points on either side of it, gives a quite good fit. Some economists call such vertical straight lines the "long-run Phillips curve" or the long-run "trade-off curve," which exists when expectations are fulfilled and "equilibrium" prevails. However, for such economists (Milton Friedman and Edmund Phelps, for example) such curves can exist at almost any level of unemployment; their argument is that in the long run unemployment tends to find its "natural" level, and cannot be permanently cured by any degree

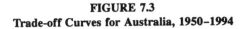

FIGURE 7.3
Trade-off Curves for Australia, 1950–1994

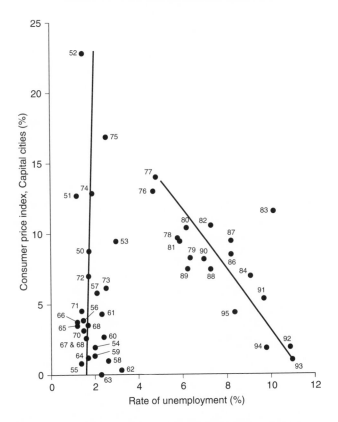

Sources: Australian Bureau of Statistics Time Series; New South Wales Yearbooks

of inflation. We shall deal with this general argument in chapter 9. Here, we will only point out that since no trade-off exists, and the vertical straight line does not represent the locus of points available to the authorities through monetary management alone, it is not a trade-off curve as we define it. For example, no conceivable monetary and fiscal policy could have produced in 1951 the low levels of unemployment and inflation observed in 1955. These years were too disturbed to expect a single TOC to emerge for the whole period. The final phase of postwar readjustment and reaction to the abandonment of controls was scarcely over when the Korea boom-and-bust set in, with the new Menzies government just trying its wings after a long period of Labor party rule. The Commonwealth Arbitration Court reduced the working week by 10 percent in 1948 and granted a stiff increase in the basic wage in 1949; both produced cost-push effects that made it impossible to restrain inflation in 1950 and 1951 by monetary policy alone, without sharper increases in unemployment than actually occurred. It was not long after the Korean War that the build-up began in Vietnam.

While the vertical straight line therefore cannot be regarded as a "trade-off" curve, it is not without meaning. It reflects a long period of full employment, during which the authorities occasionally lost control of the price level. It states that between 1950 and 1974 Australia was in the happy position of "full employment equilibrium" in its labor market, unemployment ranging from 1.1 to 2.9 percent; while it was in the unhappy position of having a very unstable price level, annual increases in the consumer price index ranging from 0.00 to 22.8 percent. The interesting phenomenon brought out by this "curve" is that far from there being a "long-run trade-off" between unemployment and inflation, during this period the rate of unemployment was almost totally unaffected by the rate of increase in prices.

Between 1975 and 1995, something that looks very much like a trade-off curve appears, although it is a very steep one. The era of "full employment equilibrium" was definitely over; but it seemed that prices could be brought down substantially at the cost of a modest increase in unemployment.

The Whitlam Government

Because of the way in which the Whitlam government was dismissed by the Governor-General, after less than three years of office, thousands of pages have been written about its policies, including a recent book by Gough Whitlam himself (Whitlam, 1985). In July, 1975 a Labor party senator from Queensland died, and the Premier of Queensland, ignoring tradition, appointed a replacement who was aligned with the Opposition, instead of appointing a person of the same party as the former senator. That action gave the Opposition a majority in the Senate. At the time, the general public, as well as the Opposition, was concerned with the mounting inflation, as well as with the government's unorthodox methods of financing its deficits abroad. Malcolm Fraser, the new leader of the Opposition, warned that the Senate would not pass the government's Supply Bills, and called for a general election. The government refused, and the business of government came to a grinding halt. In November, the Governor-General dismissed the government, named Fraser acting prime minister, and the next month the Liberal-National-Country party coalition, under Malcolm Fraser, won a smashing victory, with a majority in both houses.

The debate as to whether or not the Governor-General's action was appropriate still goes on to this day. It is a debate that we shall not enter here. But there can be no doubt that the Whitlam regime was responsible for the shift from the vertical straight line to the TOC in 1972 through 1975. There were many reasons for the eventual shift, beginning in the very first year of the Whitlam regime. The Whitlam government embarked almost immediately on a program of increased social expenditures and encouraging wages and salary increases. According to R. B. Scotton, the timing was all wrong; it was the worst time since the Korean War for such policies.

Scotton says that "there can be no doubt that the two central policies of the Government—the expansion of public social expenditures and the encouragement of substantial wage and salary increases—contributed to the intensity of both problems (inflation and unemployment) and the difficulties of subsequent readjustment" (Scotton, 1980, 24). Then the government, frightened by accelerating inflation, introduced a restrictive monetary policy and a sharp cut in tariffs, while wages continued to rise. It is primarily to these factors that Sheehan and Stricker attribute "the collapse of full employment" (Sheehan and Stricker, 1980, 28). The hike in oil prices at the end of 1973 added to cost-push factors. When allowance is made for the substitution of other sources of energy for oil, the rise in total costs of production may not have been disastrous, but it was substantial and the increased price of oil certainly added to uncertainty and to expectations of further inflation. It is quite likely, as Mallou suggests, that the natural rate of unemployment consistent with price stability (with no resort to policies other than money-flow management) rose (Mallou, 1977, 1–20). Rapid shifts in policy also contributed to uncertainty. The rise in labor productivity slowed down and the real wage overhang appeared. Anti-inflation measures were eroded by the continuing export boom and capital inflows. The labor market became increasingly fragmented.

For the Whitlam government, increased public spending was not a necessary evil forced upon it by unfortunate circumstances, but part of its basic philosophy. It *wanted* to enlarge the role of government in the economic and social life of the nation, expand social programs, and raise labor's share of national income. It also wanted to create jobs. The rate of unemployment was still low on international standards, but it was higher than it had been, and a Labor government could not simply ignore it. For the most part, they seemed to have pursued a rather simplistic Keynesian approach: They wanted to increase social expenditures anyway, and the increased spending should reduce unemployment. There were, however, splits regarding monetary and fiscal policy within the Cabinet and among its advisors. After some internal debate, the antitreasury view of Dr. James Cairnes prevailed in the 1973 budget: "Crucial as the fight against inflation is, it cannot be made the sole objective of government policy. The government's overriding objective is to get on with our various initiatives in the fields of education, health, social welfare and urban improvements. The relatively subdued conditions in prospect for the private sector provide the first real opportunity we have had to transfer resources to the public sector" (Cairnes, 1974). Later, when William Hayden replaced Cairnes in the Treasury, at a time when inflation and unemployment were increasing together, Mr. Hayden sounded almost like a Friedman-Monetarist. In his 1975 budget speech, he said: "We are no longer operating in that simple Keynesian world in which some reduction in unemployment could, apparently, always be purchased at the cost of some more inflation. Today, it is inflation itself which is the central policy problem. More inflation simply leads to more unemployment" (Hayden, 1975). At any rate, total public expenditures rose from 31.3 percent of GDP in 1972–1973, to 38.8 percent in 1975–1976, and social expenditures from 14.3 percent to 21.2 percent.

The government's policy regarding federal-state financial relations strengthened the states financially, but somewhat reduced their independence. The fields where Commonwealth expenditures grew most rapidly—urban and regional development, health, and education—were those that had been traditionally regarded as state responsibilities. The expansion was financed by specific purpose grants that grew at a rate of 64.6 percent per annum. Some state governments resented this apparent loss of freedom to determine the shape of their own budgets; but, of course, the increased flow of funds for these purposes released state revenues for other purposes. Moreover, general revenue assistance to the states also grew at 18.9 percent per year, as compared to 8.5 percent over the previous decade under the conservative coalition. In absolute amounts, specific purpose payments increased from $906 million to $4,213 million and general revenue grants from $1,923 million to $3,112 million over the same period. In his 1985 book, Whitlam reiterated his profound and enduring faith in the public sector as the source of human welfare: "The quality of life depends less and less on the things which individuals obtain for themselves and can purchase for themselves and depends more and more on the things which the community provides for all its members from the combined resources of the community" (Whitlam, 1985, 183). Hugh V. Emy quotes Whitlam as saying, "A national government has a responsibility to intervene as a countervailing power on behalf of Australian citizens and consumers to regulate the impact of the private sector on the rights of the individual" (Emy, 1993, 21–22).

With such views, the Whitlam government was bound to run into conflict with senior civil servants inherited from the long period when the conservative opposition was in power, and particularly with the Treasury. It was precisely during the Whitlam regime that the Treasury moved from the Keynesian view, until then generally accepted among Australian economists, to a monetarist view. According to Greg Whitwell, this view entailed skepticism about government's capacity to assure full employment: "From the mid-1970s the Treasury argued consistently against the use of an expansionary policy (in the form of larger budget deficits) as a means of reducing unemployment. In its view such policies simply did not work any more; indeed, they were positively harmful. [They argued that] the large budget deficits and substantial absolute increases in public expenditures which occurred under the Whitlam government `proved ineffective and the upturn in activity in the first half of 1975 which they had sought to foster proved to be unsustainable`" (Whitwell, 1993, 53). This Treasury view finally crystallized into a prescription to "fight inflation first," and in order to do so, to reduce the size of the public sector (Whitwell, 1993, 50).

In the circumstances of the time, the Treasury might well have been right; but they were accustomed to having a monopoly over advice on monetary and fiscal policy and were not about to help the government carry out *its* policies. The result of this situation was that the Whitlam government surrounded itself with a rather mixed crew of economic advisors of its own, which presented it with conflicting advice on the very complicated economic (and political) situation that confronted the government at the time. The result was that economic policy under the Whitlam regime became "confused and confusing," and could not cope adequately with either unemployment or inflation (Whitwell, 1993, 50). For example, in 1973 the Whitlam government reduced tariffs, as an anti-inflationary measure, because of Whitlam's conviction that "the more highly protected the economy, the more resources are devoted to inefficient uses, the more productivity is stifled so that producers are more susceptible to increases in wage and other costs and the more the economy is reactive to inflationary pressures" (Whitlam, 1985, 192). Yet in 1974, when it became clear that the tariff reduction was causing difficulties for some industries and increasing unemployment, the government provided protection for certain industries in the form of import quotas.

When in 1972 the Labor party came to power after twenty-three years in the wilderness, few Labor MPs or Cabinet ministers had any experience with actual government, and their revolutionary zeal was not matched by their political skills and know-how. Moreover, most of the senior civil servants had been appointed by and served conservative governments, and regarded any proposal for radical change with distaste and apprehension. Instead of enthusiastic support from the bureaucracy, that might ease the government through its youthful growing pains, it encountered, instead, stubborn resistance to its program of reforms. The Whitlam regime was imaginative, bold, innovative, and essentially on the right track, but it is generally regarded as a dismal failure. The resistance to the program from top bureaucrats was only one reason for the failure. Opposition from state governments was another. Inexperience was a third. Finally, the Whitlam government was never given the opportunity to learn by doing.

One of the principal economic advisors to the government was Professor Fred Gruen, of the Australian National University. In 1976, Gruen wrote: "Labor's cumbersome machinery of government—its 27-man Cabinet with a possibility of reversal by a 90-member caucus—would have made it very difficult to agree on any order of priority, even if Labor had been convinced at the time that there was need for the establishment of such priorities. Individual members cared too much for *their* individual programs to make decisions in the interests of either the government as a whole or of its total aims" (Gruen, 1976, 27). This indecisiveness on the part of the government may be one reason for the wage-price explosion in 1974 and 1975. The consumer price index rose by 13 percent in 1974, and average weekly earnings (seasonally adjusted) by 28 percent, with still higher increases in 1975. Of course, there were other factors, such as the oil price hike; but in 1975 there was a steep increase in unemployment as well. Australia left the vertical "full employment" line for a trade-off curve in 1975, and has been on it ever since.

From a perspective of thirteen years, Gruen's appraisal of the Whitlam years is a bit more balanced: "Until the May 1974 election, the Whitlam Labor Government's economic measures met with widespread professional support among those who might be regarded as being in a reasonable position to judge its performance. Thus during the election campaign, 172 academic economists signed a letter arguing that the Government had performed well" (Gruen, 1988, 177).

The Fraser Years

Once in power, the Liberal-National-Country party coalition, under the leadership of Malcolm Fraser, set out to destroy Gough Whitlam's innovations as quickly as possible. Even for a leader of Australia's conservative party, Fraser is a remarkably thoroughgoing and consistent conservative. A member of the "rich squatter" (large-scale landowner) class, he has been labelled a "physiocrat" because of his belief that ultimately all wealth springs from the land. He was unapologetic for his demands that real wages and labor's share of national income be cut, to increase profits and stimulate the investment that could reduce unemployment. He is Monetarist to the core, believing that unemployment cannot be reduced below its "natural" rate, and that the only way to reduce unemployment at all is to curb inflation and so reverse inflationary expectations. Naturally enough, he therefore believed—contrary to his predecessor—that government, and particularly central government, should be reduced in scale to an absolute minimum.

These views were expressed in Fraser's opening speech to Parliament in 1976:

At the root of the economic crisis is a steadily increasing tax burden required to finance, at the expense of the private sector, an ever growing public sector. Measures to deal with this crisis will advance Australia toward the long-term goal of a society based on freedom. The government's strategy to achieve its objectives can be summarized as follows: (i) there will be a major redirection of resources away from government towards individuals and private enterprise; (ii) the internal structure of the government is being made more economical and effective; a responsible Cabinet system has been instituted which will permit effective and coordinated decisions to be taken and implemented; (iii) historic reforms will be made to reverse the concentration of power in the federal government. (Fraser, 1976)

With these views, Fraser was vehemently opposed to Whitlam's idea (never clearly expressed) of using regions, and differences among them, as building blocks for fighting inflation and unemployment simultaneously.

The Fraser government inherited the 1975 discomfort point on the TOC, as a point of departure, from the Whitlam regime; but instead of trying to get back to the vertical straight line of the "full employment" era, it concentrated instead on reducing inflationary pressure. In that effort they succeeded, but at the cost of increased unemployment. The discomfort points began to shift east in 1982. Responsibility for the bad performance in 1983 to some extent falls on the shoulders of the outgoing Fraser government; they hesitated to cut expenditures enough to curb inflation in an election year.

It is worth nothing that, unlike the Whitlam government, the Fraser government embraced the Treasury line; Whitwell says, "If it seems that I have dwelt excessively on the Treasury, then I should reiterate that its views, or sometimes a diluted version of them, became the basis for much of the Fraser government's rhetoric. This rhetoric represented a shift away from the conventional wisdom espoused during most of the long postwar boom" (Whitwell, 1993, 57). It cannot be said that the Fraser government did a much better job on unemployment and inflation than its predecessor. In its early years it moved along the TOC that it inherited from the Whitlam regime, reducing inflation substantially at the cost of a modest increase in unemployment. But then in 1982 it suffered a significant rise in unemployment with some increase in inflation as well; and it was largely responsible (because the newly elected Labor government did not bring down a budget until August) for a dramatic increase in unemployment and a further increase in inflation in 1983. Of course, there were unfavorable shocks, of which the election itself was one and the global recession was another; but following Treasury advice seemed not to make the Fraser government markedly better equipped to deal with shocks than the Whitlam government had been.

The Hawke Labor Government

The replacement of the Fraser Conservative government by the Hawke Labor party government brought no such abrupt changes in direction of government policy as did the replacement of Whitlam by Fraser. Instead, the first major action of Hawke as prime minister was to assemble representatives of employers, labor, agriculture, and other social groups to work out an accord on wages, prices, and other important aspects of economic policy. In some respects Hawke was more successful in pursuing conservative policies than his predecessors: wage restraint, deregulation, privatization, limitation of price increases, a cautious anti-inflationary monetary and fiscal policy. The reaction of the Australian public to these policies is reflected in Hawke's reelection in 1986. As Gruen puts it: "Since [1983] the Accord has worked well to restore a more favorable economic climate and to give us very high growth rates by current OECD standards—although these very high growth rates have created their own problems. We are now confronted with a current account deficit that is not sustainable for long" (Gruen, 1988).

Once in power, the Hawke government was quick to distance itself from the previous Labor government of Gough Whitlam. This was particularly true of Whitlam's urban development program and the Department of Urban and Regional Development. Patrick Troy, a professorial fellow in the Urban Research Unit at the Australian National University, who was an advisor to the Whitlam regime, states that "the Hawke government, in its determination to avoid what it saw as the failures of the Whitlam government, eschewed interest in urban affairs.... By the 1988 Platform all references to the cities had disappeared" (Troy, 1993, 160 and 164). The change in outlook of the Labor party between 1972 and 1983 was partly a matter of ideology, and partly a matter of necessity. Hugh V. Emy puts the difference in the circumstances faced by the two governments thus: "In 1973 Labor came to power at the tail-end of a long period of sustained growth when economic prospects still seemed fairly good. In 1983, Labor came to power in the wake of a severe recession facing high levels of both unemployment and inflation and, by the standards of the time, a massive public deficit. Expenditure control very soon became a major priority. Commonwealth budget outlays, which peaked at 30 percent of GDP, in 1984–85, were cut back to 23,5 percent, to the level of 1973, by 1990–

91. Undoubtedly, Labor in 1983 drew certain lessons from what happened to the Whitlam government" (Emy, 1993).

The newly elected Labor government under Bob Hawke did not present a budget until August of that year. The bad performance on the employment side was due to the global recession, no doubt aggravated by the shock delivered to the business and financial community by the election of a Labor government. By 1984 that community had discovered just how far to the right the new Labor government was, and confidence was largely restored. The Accord between the government and the Australian Council of Trade Unions assured them that there would be no wage blowout (the Labor government actually reduced real wages) and it soon became apparent that the new government would not embark on a spending spree either.

Since 1983, all the discomfort points seem to fall on the same trade-off curve as before, given a narrow envelope, except the observation for 1989. That is the only observation that is "clearly not on the trade-off curve." The curve continues very steep; one could say that Labor bought a six- or seven-point drop in the inflation rate at the cost of a three-point increase in unemployment. Whether or not this "trade-off" constitutes an improvement is impossible to say; we do not know the shape and position of the "community indifference curves" between unemployment and inflation. But we do know that the Labor government has been determined to fight inflation at any cost; and since other OECD governments were similarly inclined, it was no doubt easier to fight inflation than to fight unemployment. In any case, it is a remarkably stable trade-off curve that has resulted.

Moreover, during this period the trade-off curves of the six states and one territory were remarkably similar to the TOC of Australia, and to each other, as a glance at figures 7.4 to 7.10 will show. The Northern Territory TOC somewhat differs from the TOCs of the states, being much more thinly populated, less urbanized, more tied to natural resources, and overall less developed. But among the six states, the years of peak unemployment, the years of minimum unemployment, the years of peak inflation, and the years of minimum inflation, were virtually identical; and the actual figures for high and low unemployment were very close together. The results are summarized in table 7.1.

The differences in timing and amounts of inflation and unemployment are so small as to make a policy of combatting both by a differentiated

FIGURE 7.4
Trade-off Curves for New South Wales, 1950–1994

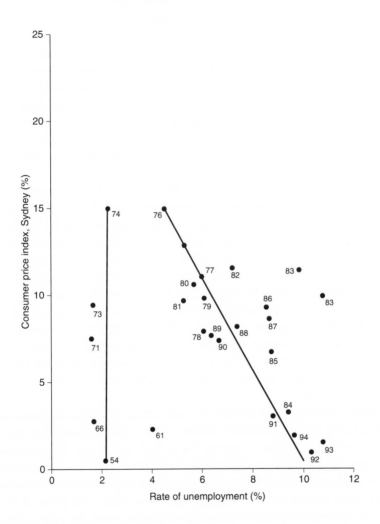

Sources: Australian Bureau of Statistics Time Series; New South Wales Yearbooks

FIGURE 7.5
Trade-off Curves for Victoria, 1959–1994

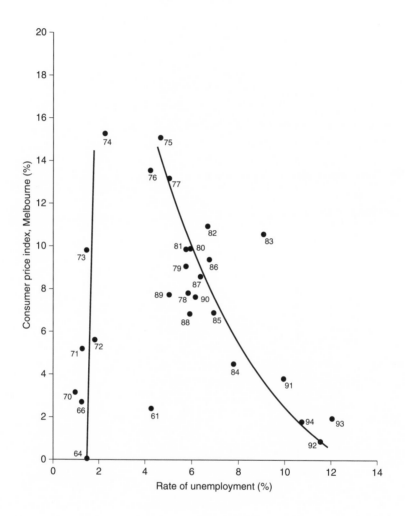

Sources: Australian Bureau of Statistics Time Series; Victoria Yearbooks

FIGURE 7.6
Trade-off Curves for Queensland, 1950–1994

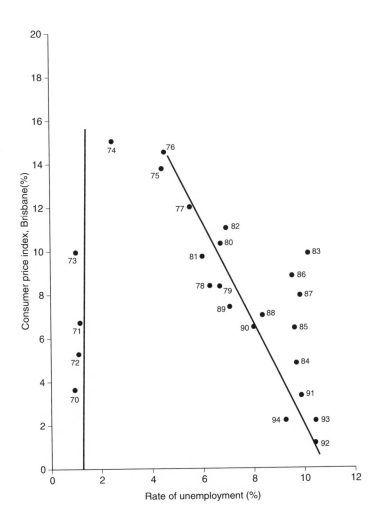

Sources: Australian Bureau of Statistics Time Series; Queensland Yearbooks

FIGURE 7.7
Trade-off Curves for South Australia, 1950–1994

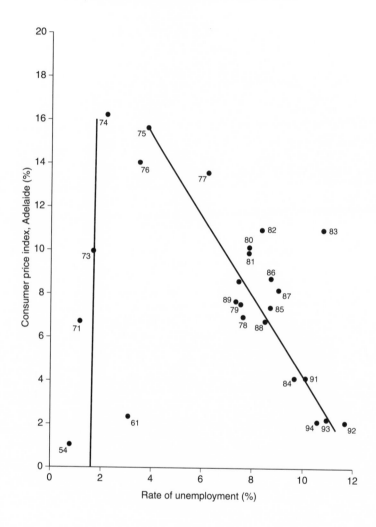

Sources: Australian Bureau of Statistics Time Series; South Australia Yearbooks

FIGURE 7.8
Trade-off Curves for Western Australia, 1950–1994

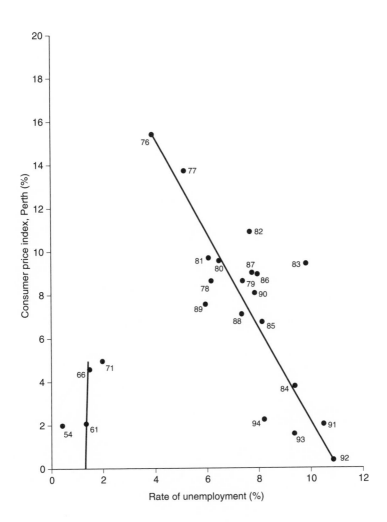

Sources: Australian Bureau of Statistics Time Series; Western Australia Yearbooks

FIGURE 7.9
Trade-off Curves for Tasmania, 1950–1994

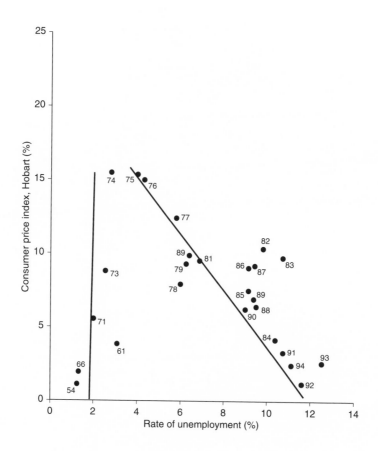

Sources: Australian Bureau of Statistics Time Series; Tasmanian Yearbooks

FIGURE 7.10
Trade-off Curves for Northern Territory, 1982–1994

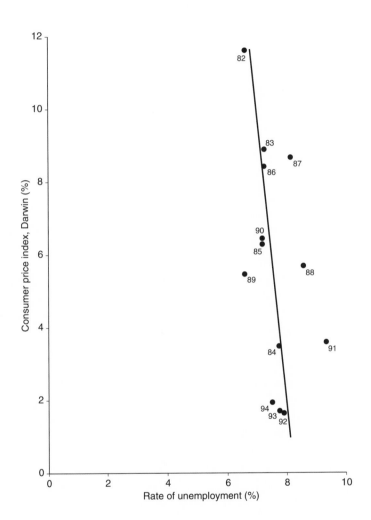

Sources: Australian Bureau of Statistics Time Series

TABLE 7.1
High and Low Points of Unemployment and Inflation After 1983

	Unemployment				Inflation			
	High	Year	Low	Year	High	Year	Low	Year
Australia	10.9	1993	6.2	1989	9.32	1987	1.90	1992
New South Wales	10.8	1993	6.3	1989	9.23	1986	0.85	1992
Victoria	12.1	1993	5.0	1989	9.30	1986	0.86	1992
Queensland	10.5	1993/2	7.0	1989	8.54	1986	1.11	1992
South Australia	11.7	1992	7.3	1989	8.64	1986	2.07	1992
Western Australia	10.9	1992	5.9	1989	8.97	1987	0.28	1992
Tasmania	12.5	1993	8.9	1990	9.13	1987	1.15	1992
Northern Territory	9.3	1991	6.5	1989	8.65	1987	1.64	1992

fiscal policy among *states,* increasing public expenditures in states where unemployment is concentrated, and cutting government expenditures in states where inflationary pressure is generated, would require very fine tuning, and would be extremely difficult. This situation reflects the fact that the states grew up almost together and in the same way, so that the glaring differences in occupational structure and product mix that exist among Canadian provinces, and even to some extent among American states, do not exist among Australian states. The differences in occupational structure and product mix that occur in Australia are to be found among much smaller regions than states, such as the ministry of Industry, Technology and Regional Development's ninety-six regions. It is in terms such as these that a differential fiscal policy, to combat unemployment, inflation, and regional disparities all at the same time, must be designed.

Differences Among Trade-off Curves of Australia and the States: 1984–1993

Let us note certain features of the recent Australian trade-off curve, from which some of the state TOCs differ:

1. The discomfort point for 1993 lies north of the point for 1992;

2. The point for 1989 seems clearly not to lie on the curve.

New South Wales:
1. The discomfort point for 1993 lies south of the point for 1992;
2. The points for 1986 and 1987 (as well as the point for 1983) seem clearly not to lie on the TOC.

Victoria:
1. The point for 1993 lies to the east of the one for 1992.

Queensland:
1. As in New South Wales (but not in Australia) the points for 1985, 1986, and 1987 seem not to lie on the TOC, while the points for 1980, 1981, 1988, and 1989 seem to lie on the curve.

South Australia:
1. The point for 1993 lies to the west of the one for 1992.

Western Australia:
1. The point for 1993 lies well to the west of the one for 1992.

Tasmania:
1. The point for 1993 lies well to the east of the one for 1992;
2. The point for 1989 could lie within the curve's envelope, or trade-off zone. (If we draw the curve so as to incorporate the points for 1991, 1984, and 1993, then 1992 lies "clearly off the TOCS.")

Northern Territory:
1. The point for 1992 lies well to the west of those for 1991 and 1993, and seems to be "clearly off the curve." It is also slightly above the point for 1993;
2. The point for 1989 lies well to the east of the TOC, and seems to be clearly off the curve, but to the east rather than the west.

These are not substantial differences for so large a country.

Points "Clearly Off the Trade-off Curve"

To say that a point is "clearly off the trade-off curve" means, according to our definitions, that it is a point that could not have been attained or avoided by orthodox management of the money supply through macroeconomic monetary and fiscal policy alone. It implies that something unusual happened in that year, a shock or a windfall gain or improvement, over which the authorities determining the money supply had no control, and probably did not foresee. It also implies that the effects of the shock or windfall were temporary, so that the economy returned to the "normal" TOC; otherwise, there would be a shift of the curve in one direction or another.

The discomfort point for 1983, which appears well to the right of the "normal TOC" for the Commonwealth, the six states, and the Northern Territory, was clearly such a point; the sudden increase in unemployment could not have been avoided through macroeconomic monetary or fiscal policy alone. Similarly, the sharp decline in unemployment that took place between 1986 and 1989 was probably due less to policy than to spontaneous recovery, which did not last.

It could be said that in Australia there is a long-run trade-off between inflation and unemployment; inflation can be reduced substantially at the cost of a relatively small increase in unemployment. The question is whether too high a price has been paid in increased, and especially in long-term unemployment to achieve a modicum of price stability. Only the electorate can answer that question.

Why Only One TOC?

Why should the discomfort points generated by an arch-conservative government like that of Malcolm Fraser appear to lie on the same trade-off curve as the discomfort points produced by a Labor government under Hawke and Keating? Doesn't the fact that they do seem to fall on the same TOC prove that the fundamental nature and mechanism of movement of the economic system is what really matters, and that economic policy is relatively impotent? I think the answer is "no"! The policy under Hawke and Keating (the latter as treasurer to Bob Hawke and then as prime minister) was essentially the same as policy under Malcolm Fraser, only Labor was able to pursue the policy more consistently and more effectively. Both governments have concentrated on reducing inflation, hoping that market forces would reduce the level of unemployment. The Fraser government, having inherited an inflation rate of nearly 17 percent from Whitlam in 1975, and a somewhat tangled fiscal situation, had to do something about it. They had brought down inflation to 9.35 percent by 1981, at a cost in increased unemployment of less than one percentage point. But then in 1982 and the early months of 1983 they lost control of both unemployment and inflation, and ended up (almost certainly, unless the Australian Community Indifference Curve is a very curious one) in a worse position than when they began, with more than twice as much unemployment and still with three quarters as much inflation. Labor cut inflation to 4 percent and unemployment to 8.5 percent in less than one year. From then on, they moved up and down the TOC, ending up with a very low inflation rate and a rather high unemployment rate. But as a *Labor* government, with a prime minister for three terms who had been a successful Head of the Australian Council of Trade Unions, and was still popular with members of the Trade Union movement, Labor was able to do what Fraser could not, much as he would have liked to do so: reduce real wages and labor's share of national income, and increase profits and investment, without labor unrest. It may also be, although I can't prove it, that a government has more room to maneuver at the bottom of a TOC than at the top of the same curve. This question deserves further study.

References

Cairnes, James. *Budget Speech.* Canberra: Commonwealth Printer, 17 September 1974.

Emy, Hugh, "A Policy Overview: From Social Democracy to the Social Market Economy." In Hugh V. Emy, Hughes Owen, and Mathews Race (eds.), *Whitlam Revisited: Policy Development, Policies and Outcomes.* Leichhardt, N.S.W.: Pluto Press, 1993, 16–31.

Emy, Hugh V., Owen Hughes, and Race Mathews (eds.). *Whitlam Revisited: Policy Development, Policies and Outcomes.* Leichhardt, N.S.W.: Pluto Press, 1993.

Fraser, Malcolm. "Governor General's Speech Opening Parliament." *House of Representatives Debates, 1976.* Canberra: Commonwealth Printer (1 February 1976), 12–13.

Hayden, William. *Budget Speech.* Canberra: Commonwealth Printer, 1975.

Gruen, Fred H. G. "What Went Wrong? Some Personal Reflections on Economic Policies Under Labor." *The Australian Quarterly* 48 (3), 1976.

———. "Of Economics and Other Things." In Karl Bitman (ed.), *Strauss to Matilda: Viennese in Australia 1938–1988.* Wenkhardt Foundation, 1988.

Mallou, J. S. "Causes of Economic Problems in the 1970s." *Economic Papers* 56 (October 1977), 1–20.

Scotton, R. B., and Helen Ferber (eds). *Public Expenditures and Social Policy in Australia, vol. 1—The Whitlam Years, 1972–75.* Melbourne: Longman Cheshire, 1980, 24.

Sheehan, P. J., and P. P. Stricker. "The Collapse of Full Employment." In R. B. Scotton and H. Ferber (eds.), *The First Fraser Years, vol. II.* Melbourne: Longman Cheshire, 1980, 28.

Troy, Pat. "Love's Labor Lost: Whitlam and Urban and Regional Development." In Hugh Emy, Owen Hughes, and Race Mathews (eds), *Whitlam Revisited: Policy*

Development, Policies and Outcomes. Leichhardt, N.S.W.: Pluto Press, 1993., 142–67.

Whitlam, E. G., *The Whitlam Government.* Ringwood: The Viking Press, 1985.

Whitwell, Fred. "Economic Affairs." In Hugh Emy, Owen Hughes, and Race Mathews (eds), *Whitlam Revisited: Policy Development, Policies and Outcomes.* Leichhardt, N.S.W.: Pluto Press, 1993, 32–62.

8

Unemployment and Inflation
in the United States

We now have enough concepts, theories, and facts based on experience in Australia and Canada to tackle the world's biggest economy—the United States. What has been the story of unemployment and inflation in the United States since World War II? Is it the same, or similar to, the story in Australia and Canada or is it different? If there are differences, what are they, and what is the explanation?

Let us look first at the time series for unemployment, inflation, and percentage changes in GNP. As we can see from figure 8.1, there was a spurt of inflation in the immediate postwar period, but it was short lived. There was a backlog of pent-up demand for consumers' durables and for capital goods of various sorts. As controls were lifted, prices rose in response. There was also a reserve of government bonds and savings certificates that could be liquidated to finance the spending spree. Unemployment rose briefly as conversion from a war economy to a peacetime economy took place. The GNP fell briefly in 1955 and again in 1958, but recovered rapidly in both cases. Nothing like the expected "primary postwar recession," let alone the "secondary postwar depression" of the period between the wars appeared. On the whole, despite minor year-to-year fluctuations, the 1960s were a decade of unprecedentedly high and steady growth. During this decade the rate of inflation rose and the rate of unemployment fell, while the *trend* in growth of GNP remained more or less stable. In this period there was little to shake the faith in the Keynesian system or the Keynesian policies. The appearance of simultaneous unemployment *and* inflation worried few people. At around 5 percent, neither was very serious.

The "new economy" and the breakdown of the Keynesian system appeared in the 1970s. With the oil price shock of 1972, inflation reached

FIGURE 8.1

U.S. Unemployment, Inflation, and GNP Growth Rates in Percent (1950–1993)

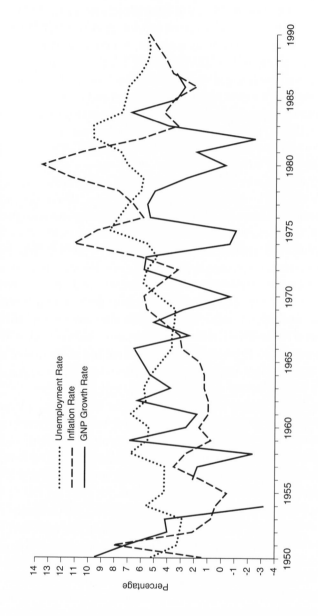

Source: United States Department of Commerce, *Statistical Abstract of the United States,* 1994.

11.0 percent in 1974, recovered briefly, but rose again to 11.3 percent in 1979 and 13.5 percent in 1980. But unemployment, instead of falling as in previous inflationary periods, rose too and growth of GNP, instead of rising, fell during the decade as a whole, reaching negative figures in 1974 to 1975 and again in 1980. The early 1980s were recession years, with falling, and even negative, rates of growth of GNP, and increasing unemployment. Since then both unemployment and inflation have shown a tendency to fall when growth of GNP is rising and to rise when growth of GNP is falling. The Keynesian world had disappeared.

Let us now look at the scatter diagram of "discomfort points" (rates of unemployment and inflation for various years) shown in figure 8.2. As in the case of other scatter diagrams of this sort, if we had never heard of Phillips curves, trade-off curves, or cyclical loops, this diagram might seem like total disorder and leave us mystified. However, it might occur to us to link the successive discomfort points with straight lines, to see how the points have moved through time, as in figure 8.3. When we do so, the semblance of a pattern begins to emerge. We start in 1950 with a fairly high rate of unemployment (for those days) and virtually no inflation. Then in 1951 we see a precipitous rise in the rate of inflation, accompanied by a slight fall in the rate of unemployment, followed immediately by a steep fall in the rate of inflation, with a modest decline in unemployment. In 1954, we have a near doubling of the rate of unemployment, with a slight fall in the already very low rate of inflation. In 1955, there was an actual drop in the consumer price index, and a decline in the rate of unemployment as well. Was this remarkable performance due to astute policy, the inevitable forces of the postwar business cycle, or an accident? We would need something like the *Business Annals* that Merle Thorpe used to do for the National Bureau of Economic Research in the 1920s to find out for sure, but my guess is that it was a combination of all three.

Whatever the explanation of the almost-perfect performance of the American economy in 1955, it didn't last long. In the next two years, prices rose substantially with no reduction in the rate of unemployment. It appears that in these years the authorities were struggling desperately to bring both unemployment and inflation under control and not quite succeeding. During the 1960s, however, the authorities were moderately successful in stabilizing the American economy. Unemployment ranged from 3.5 to 6.7 percent, while inflation ranged from 1.0 to 5.5 percent.

FIGURE 8.2
Scatter of Discomfort Points (1950–1993)

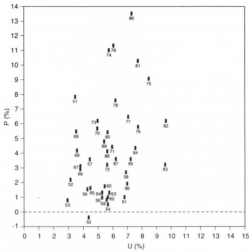

Note: New England; U = Massachusetts, ΔP = Boston

Source: United States Department of Commerce, *Statistical Abstract of the United States,* 1994.

FIGURE 8.3
Sequence of Discomfort Points (1950–1993)

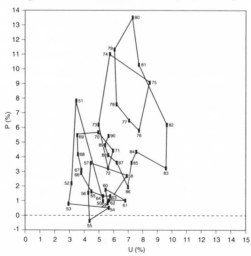

Note: New England; U = Massachusetts, ΔP = Boston

Source: United States Department of Commerce, *Statistical Abstract of the United States,* 1994.

But with the energy crisis of the 1970s the economy got away from them once again. There was an almost-vertical rise in the rate of inflation from 3.2 percent in 1972 to 11.0 percent in 1974. Over the next two years, inflation was brought down at the cost of a substantial increase in unemployment. Then for two years inflation got away again and reached a new peak of 13.5 percent in 1980. In that year unemployment also rose to 7 percent and GNP fell slightly.

From then on (under Reagan as president and Volcker as chairman of the board of governors of the Federal Reserve System) monetary policy was fairly successful in stabilizing the American economy. The rate of inflation was brought down to 3.2 percent in 1983 while the rate of unemployment increased to 8.2 percent. Then the rate of unemployment was brought down to 5.5 percent in 1988, while the rate of inflation increased only to 4.1 percent. In 1990, unemployment stood at 5.5 percent and the rate of inflation at 5.4 percent.

Trade-off Curves

Now—since we *are* acquainted with TOCs—let us ask: "What do the American data tell us about trade-off curves in the United States? Figure 8.4 endeavors to answer that question.

First of all, the year 1950 seems to stand alone. That is, it is unlikely that any standard monetary and fiscal policy, by itself, could have produced in 1951 the same discomfort point that was actually observed in 1950. It is probable that it would have taken considerably more than 5.2 percent unemployment to offset the inflationary pressures present in 1951. The years 1951 to 1953 appear to lie on the same almost-vertical straight line, but to call it a "trade-off" curve seems inappropriate, since no trade-off of reduced unemployment for increased inflation was involved. The observations for 1955 through 1957 seem to lie on a similar almost-vertical straight line, less high and further to the right. The same caveat applies. Then come nine years that seem to provide an excellent fit to a single TOC, and perhaps they did. As already noted, that was a period of remarkably steady growth, which in accordance with my theory, would have meant that both unemployment and inflation were relatively easy to keep within limits.

The years of the early seventies appear to form another TOC higher and further to the right. Then comes a distinct break, presumably due

FIGURE 8.4
TOCs (1950–1993)

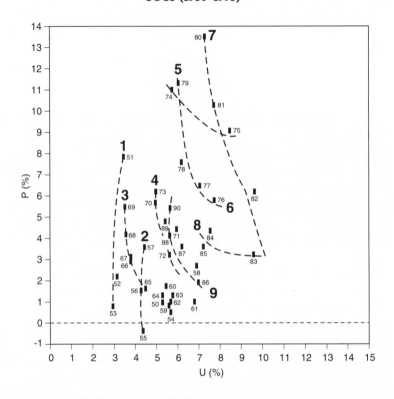

Note: New England; U = Massachusetts, ΔP = Boston

Source: United States Department of Commerce, *Statistical Abstract of the United States,* 1994.

to the loss of control by the authorities in the aftermath of the oil crisis. It is hard to say whether or not the two observations for 1974 and 1975 form a TOC or not. We have treated them as such, but so short-lived a relationship hardly deserves the name "trade-off curve." During 1976 through 1979 control seems to have been reestablished, although on a TOC much higher and further to the right than the previous ones. The years 1980 through 1982 saw a further shift of the TOC upward to the right. It is hard to say whether the year 1983 lies on the 1980–82 curve or on the 1984–85 one. We have chosen the 1984–85 TOC; it is unlikely that the authorities would, even if they could, have chosen in 1983 any of the points for 1980, 1981, or 1982, paying so high a price in increased inflation for so little reduction in unemployment. The years 1986 through 1990 (TOC$_9$) were relatively good ones, but not so good as to inspire confidence regarding the future.

Cyclical Loops

The United States story of unemployment and inflation since World War II is not so easily reduced to regular, clockwise, cyclical loops, steadily increasing in amplitude, as the Canadian one. The lone observation of falling prices in 1955 (figure 8.5) seems to have been an aberration. Ignoring it, we have a clockwise cyclical loop from 1950 to 1956. But then there is a counterclockwise loop until 1959. The observation for 1960 seems to be another aberration. Since between 1959 and 1960 unemployment moved down only 0.1 percent and inflation moved upward only 0.9 percent, it could be regarded as an "equilibrium" in which no cyclical movement took place. Indeed, the whole period 1959 to 1964 could be regarded as a "dynamic equilibrium," with minor changes in GNP, unemployment, and inflation adding up to "steady growth." Alternatively, one could construe a new clockwise loop as beginning in 1961 and completing itself in 1972, as we have done in the diagram. Then comes another clockwise loop, situated further to the northeast and much greater in amplitude, from 1972 to 1976. Finally, there is another clockwise loop from 1976 to 1984, again further to the northeast and greater in amplitude.

The movement from 1984 to 1988 appears to have been counterclockwise, and a new clockwise loop appears to have started in 1988 to 1990. If this new loop turns out to be further northeast and greater in amplitude than the 1976–84 one, the United States may experience both unemployment and inflation well into the double digits.

A question arises concerning the observation for 1981. Was it on a loop, or was it an aberration? The inauguration of President Reagan may have brought a wave of optimism in 1981, which resulted in a temporary drop in unemployment, while the true cyclical movement resumed in 1982 with a sharp drop in inflation, due to a tight monetary policy, while unemployment continued to increase. I have drawn the diagram both ways. The reader may choose.

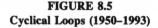

FIGURE 8.5
Cyclical Loops (1950–1993)

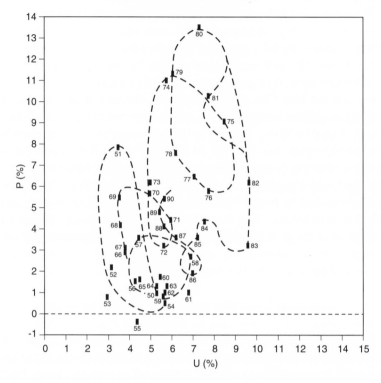

Note: New England; U = Massachusetts, ΔP = Boston

Source: United States Department of Commerce, *Statistical Abstract of the United States,* 1994.

Conclusions on Unemployment and Inflation in the United States

The United States most resembles Australia and Canada in the fundamental disorder that it presents. Since 1950, there have been times when
unemployment and inflation went up together, times when they went down
together, and times when they moved in opposite directions. It is tempt-
ing to say that they go up together in periods of recession and down
together in periods of recovery or prosperity, but even that relationship is
imperfect. A case can be made for treating economic fluctuations in this
period as a matter of shifting TOCs or cyclical loops, or both together,

but the case is not absolutely watertight. Most of the time the movement is clockwise, but sometimes it is counterclockwise.

What we seem to be watching are not the "natural" movements of an economy driven by "market forces" alone, but powerful market forces offset by almost equally powerful monetary policy, a weak and aberrant fiscal policy, and occasional intervention by other policies concerned with foreign trade, foreign investment, foreign exchange, industrial relations, and the like. One of the most potent factors in private decision-making is rational expectations about government policy. With the information revolution, decisions of private enterprise is increasingly influenced by events taking place all over the world. The precise outcome of this extremely complicated game is increasingly indeterminate. We are faced with oligopoly on a global scale, and the "I think that he thinks that I think that he thinks" element in decision-making plays a greater role than ever before. With the growing tendency for expectations about the course of the global economy to be the same everywhere, the global economy becomes inherently unstable. It is a wonder that it has been as stable as it has been for four decades.

American Unemployment and Inflation by Region

In Australia, there are only six states that are treated as "regions." Since there is some interest in differences in unemployment and inflation by *states,* it is possible to construct trade-off curves and loops for "regions." In Canada, since World War II, reduction of regional disparities has been a major objective of national economic policy, and so good figures exist on unemployment and inflation both for the ten provinces and for the five regions. In the United States, reduction of *regional* gaps has never been an objective of *national* policy, although there have been sporadic programs devoted to particular regions, such as the Tennessee Valley Authority and the Appalachian Regional Commission. As a consequence, there exist virtually no statistics for unemployment and inflation by region. The Bureau of the Census does distinguish nine regions, and for the single year 1950 there are figures for unemployment and inflation for those regions. From 1950 until 1968, there are no unemployment figures even for states. From 1968 to date, there are unemployment figures by state grouped into the nine regions. There are consumer price index figures for metropolitan *cities* for the whole period.

Accordingly, we have taken the figures for unemployment and inflation for each of the nine regions for 1950, which gives us a solid base. We then skip to 1968, and choose the most important state in each region, and the most important city in each state, to get figures for unemployment and inflation. Unfortunately, there are no consumer price data for any city in the East South Central region; so we have been forced to use a nearby city (Washington, D.C.), with a reported consumer price index, as a surrogate. This rough-and-ready method is obviously a very imperfect way of measuring *regional* gaps in unemployment and inflation, but it enables us to make approximate comparisons that are nonetheless interesting.

We thus have the following "regions": New England—unemployment in Massachusetts and price increase in Boston; Middle Atlantic—unemployment in New York State and price increase in New York City; East North Central—unemployment in Illinois and price increase in Chicago; East South Central—unemployment in Tennessee and price increase in Washington; West South Central—Texas and Houston; Mountain Colorado and Denver—Pacific California and Los Angeles.

New England

Let us now proceed in the same manner that we have for other countries and regions. Looking first at the scatter diagram (figure 8.6), the diagram for New England does not tell much at first glance, except that things were obviously getting worse up to about 1975 through 1980 and have been getting somewhat better since. If we link the points by straight lines, we can see this sequence more clearly and in more detail (figure 8.7). Up to 1975, it was unemployment that got worse. From 1975 to 1978, there was marked improvement. Then in 1979 there was a vertical quantum leap in the rate of inflation, more than 2½ fold in two years. The inflation was brought quickly under control during the next two years at a modest cost in terms of increased unemployment. Then unemployment was brought under control at a modest cost in terms of aggravated inflation. Between 1984 and 1986 both unemployment and inflation were reduced to very low levels, whether as a result of astute policy or of rising GDP. But then came another, although less drastic, vertical leap in the rate of inflation, followed by stable rate of price increase, but a steady increase in unemployment to 1990, when

FIGURE 8.6
Scatter of Discomfort Points (1950–1993)

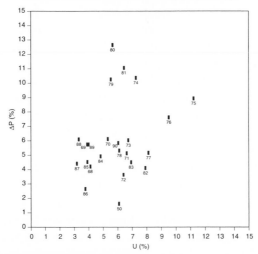

Note: New England; U = Massachusetts, ΔP = Boston
Source: United States Department of Commerce, *Statistical Abstract of the United States,* 1994.

FIGURE 8.7
Sequence of Discomfort Points (1950–1993)

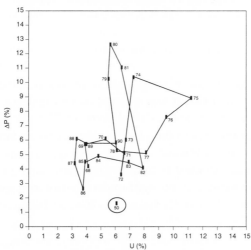

Note: New England; U = Massachusetts, ΔP = Boston
Source: United States Department of Commerce, *Statistical Abstract of the United States,* 1994.

with both inflation and unemployment around 6 percent the economic situation was hardly satisfactory.

How does this experience translate into trade-off curves? Figure 8.7 gives an indication of how this question might be answered. The observations for 1950, 1968, and 1969 look as though they might fall on the same TOC, but considering the instability of the national economy during this period, especially with respect to prices, it seems highly unlikely that the New England TOC did not shift in somewhat the same fashion as the national TOC. In 1970, there was clearly a shift of the New England TOC to the right. By stretching the concept of "curve," we could imagine a triangular "trade-off zone" encompassing the observations for 1971 through 1973. Then comes the almost vertical shift upward; perhaps the observations for 1974 and 1975 lie on the same (very short) TOC. By allowing a fairly wide envelope, one can imagine a TOC very steep for the years 1978 to 1982. A series of shifts to the left, followed by shifts to the right, next occurred.

However, the behavior of so unstable an economy is better described as a series of cyclical loops. Here we see once again big loops and smaller loops, possibly corresponding to the Juglar and Kitchin cycles in a post World War II setting. The year 1990 is an awkward place to stop. From the configuration in figure 8.8, it appears that the "Juglar" has improved in recent years. But where are we heading? We have no idea where the next loop may take us.

New England and the United States

The diagrams for New England and those for the American economy as a whole resemble each other, as one would expect them to do, since New England is a "leading region" within the American economy in more than one sense. Looking first at the diagrams showing the discomfort points connected by straight lines in sequence, one difference becomes immediately apparent. The New England diagram is more constrained on the inflation axis than the American one, and less constrained on the unemployment axis than the American one. The New England lines go much further along the unemployment axis than the American ones; the American lines go further along the inflation axis *in both directions,* even in the period 1968 to 1990. In terms of our analysis of "hysteresis" above, it appears that the forces pushing north and south are stronger in

FIGURE 8.8
TOCs (1950–1993)

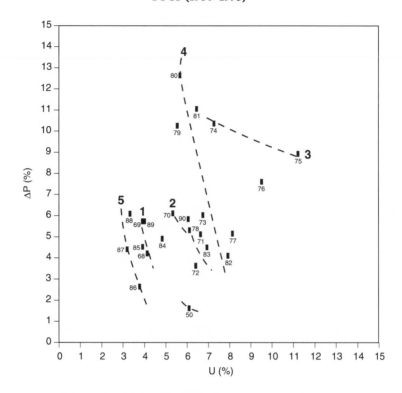

Note: New England; U = Massachusetts, ΔP = Boston
Source: United States Department of Commerce, *Statistical Abstract of the United States,* 1994.

the United States than in New England, and the resistance to increases and decreases in unemployment is also greater in the United States than in New England. Considering that it is the federal government that controls monetary policy, that fiscal policy has been weak, and that monetary policy has been aimed almost exclusively at checking inflation, letting unemployment pursue its own course, this result is somewhat surprising. It may be related to New England's somewhat peculiar occupational structure, with its high proportion of high-tech industries and sophisticated services. Such a labor force may be more subject to fluctuations than the labor force of the country as a whole. It is also clear

FIGURE 8.9
Cyclical Loops (1950–1993)

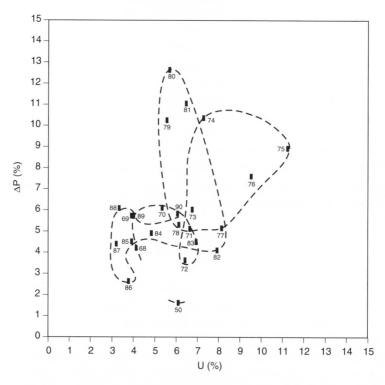

Note: New England; U = Massachusetts, ΔP = Boston

Source: United States Department of Commerce, *Statistical Abstract of the United States,* 1994.

that New England was much more successful than the United States was at a macro-economic level in the late 1970s and 1980s. Perhaps for the same reason, New England's labor force was of a kind that was finding jobs in that period. However, the two economies ended up in 1990 in much the same position (see figure 8.9).

The same differences show up, of course, in the trade-off curves for New England and the United States. The United States seems to have a series of well-defined TOCs, shifting upward to the right and then downward to the left. New England shows the same general pattern, but its TOCs are less clearly defined and the degree of instability has been such that it is possible to discern fewer of them for New England than for the United States.

New England experience shown greater regularity when interpreted as cyclical loops. The same differences from the United States as a whole, however, still appear. Ignoring the dramatic leap in the price increase in 1951, the United States loops for 1950 to 1960 and for 1960 to 1977 are located lower on the price increase axis than the loops for New England and cover about the same range on the unemployment axis. For the United States, the loop for 1972 to 1978 took place *to the left of the 1970 to 1986 loop*. The converse was true for New England. The incomplete United States loop, which began in 1986, shows steeply rising inflation with a slight reduction of unemployment while the New England loop shows a steep rise in inflation up to 1988 followed by a substantial increase in unemployment, with no increase in inflation to 1990.

The Mid-Atlantic

The scatter of discomfort points of the mid-Atlantic region is more constrained or "bunched" than the New England scatter and, therefore, is more different from that of the United States. The rate of inflation never fell below 3.0 percent nor rose above 11.3 percent. The range of unemployment was from 3.5 percent to 10.3 percent, compared to 3.2 percent and 11.3 percent for New England, or 3.4 percent and 8.5 percent for the United States. In New England, the range was from 2.6 percent and 12.7 percent; in the United States from 0.4 percent to 13.5 percent (fig. 8.10). The relatively limited range of the mid-Atlantic scatter becomes even more apparent when the discomfort points are linked with straight lines (figure 8.11). Since in the same country prices can never for long differ more than the transportation costs between the urban centers—and Boston and New York are close together—it seems a bit strange that the differences in rates of inflation exceeded the difference in rates of unemployment.

There is more similarity in the mid-Atlantic and New England TOCs. The exception is that the (two-year) TOC_3 of the mid-Atlantic intersects TOC_4, while in New England TOC_3 is well to the right of TOC_4, and New England's TOC_5 is well toward the inflation axis, but does not appear at all for the mid-Atlantic (figure 8.12).

FIGURE 8.10
Scatter of Discomfort Points (1950–1993)

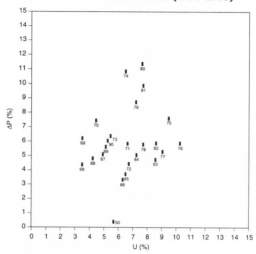

Note: Middle Atlantic; U = New York, ΔP = New York City

Source: United States Department of Commerce, *Statistical Abstract of the United States,* 1994.

FIGURE 8.11
Sequence of Discomfort Points (1950–1993)

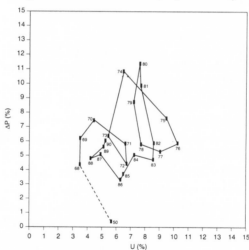

Note: Middle Atlantic; U = New York, ΔP = New York City

Source: United States Department of Commerce, *Statistical Abstract of the United States,* 1994.

FIGURE 8.12
TOCs (1950-1993)

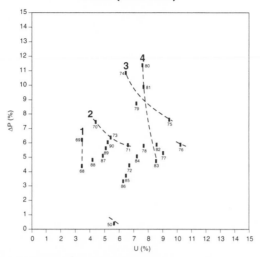

Note: Middle Atlantic; U = New York, ΔP = New York City
Source: United States Department of Commerce, *Statistical Abstract of the United States,* 1994.

FIGURE 8.13
Mid-Atlantic Unemployment and Inflation Rates (1968-1993)

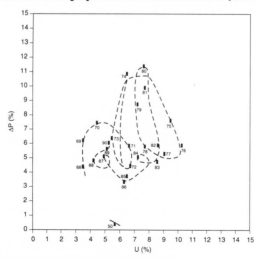

Note: Middle Atlantic; U = New York, ΔP = New York City
Source: United States Department of Commerce, *Statistical Abstract of the United States,* 1994.

On the other hand, the cyclical loops display marked differences. In the mid-Atlantic region the loop beginning in 1968 was at the extreme left of the diagram; in New England that position was occupied by TOC$_5$, during the accelerated inflation of 1986 to 1988. During 1970 to 1976, on the other hand, the patterns were much the same (figure 8.13).

East North Central

The scatter for the East North Central region is more dispersed than that of the mid-Atlantic region or of New England. Unemployment ranged from 3.0 to 11.4 percent, inflation from 2.1 to 14.4 percent (figure 8.14). The peak inflation year for all three regions was 1980 as it was for the United States as a whole. However, the peak unemployment year for the East North Central region was 1983, whereas it was 1976 for the mid-Atlantic, 1975 for New England, and 1982 to 1983 for the United States. The minimum inflation year was 1986 for all three regions, and during the period 1969 to 1990 for the United States, as well. The minimum unemployment year was 1968 for the East North Central region and for the mid-Atlantic region and 1987 for New England. For the United States, unemployment was marginally lower in 1969 than in 1978.

Between 1968 and 1975 the general configuration of the discomfort points, when linked by straight lines (figure 8.15) was much the same for all three regions, but carried unemployment to higher levels in New England than in the mid-Atlantic region, and to much higher levels than in the East North Central region. The patterns diverged considerably in the next few years, but all three regions ended up in much the same position in 1990.

The East North Central region appears to have very orderly TOCs, although with a fairly wide envelope to TOC$_3$ covering the period 1974 to 1979. The curves move progressively northeast until 1983 (TOC$_4$) and then southwest in 1984 to 1985 (TOC$_5$) and again in 1986 to 1990. Neither New England nor the mid-Atlantic regions appear to have quite such orderly TOCs. Only New England established a trade-off curve (TOC$_5$) for 1986 to 1988 further west than the curve for 1968 to 1969 (figure 8.16).

These same differences appear. of course, in the cyclical loops. For the East North Central region the 1976-84-85 loop lies almost entirely *east* of the 1972–76 loop; for New England and the mid-Atlantic regions

FIGURE 8.14
Scatter of Discomfort Points (1950–1993)

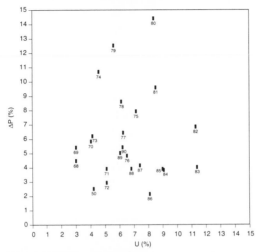

Note: East North Central; U = Illinois, ΔP = Chicago
Source: United States Department of Commerce, *Statistical Abstract of the United States,* 1994.

FIGURE 8.15
Sequence of Discomfort Points (1950–1993)

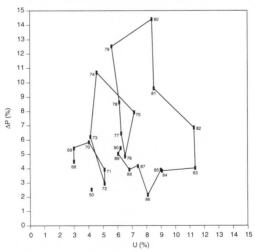

Note: East North Central; U = Illinois, ΔP = Chicago
Source: United States Department of Commerce, *Statistical Abstract of the United States,* 1994.

200   **Employment Without Inflation**

FIGURE 8.16
TOCs (1950–1993)

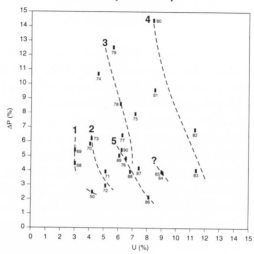

Note: East North Central; U = Illinois, ΔP = Chicago

Source: United States Department of Commerce, *Statistical Abstract of the United States,* 1994.

FIGURE 8.17
Cyclical Loops (1950–1993)

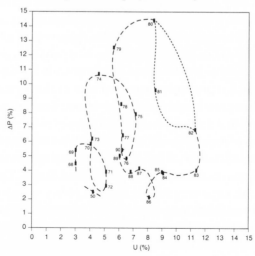

Note: East North Central; U = Illinois, ΔP = Chicago

Source: United States Department of Commerce, *Statistical Abstract of the United States,* 1994.

the 1976-84-85 loop is mainly to the *west* of the 1972–76 loop. Another difference is that for New England the most favorable loop is the (incomplete) 1986–90 one; in both the other regions, it is the 1968–72 one (figure 8.17).

Comparing the East North Central region with the United States, we note once again the wider east-west scatter of the East North Central region. The range of observation for the rate of inflation is also wider; 1.9 percent to 13.5 percent for the United States; 2.2 to 14.4 percent for the region. From 1968 to 1972, and for 1972 to 1976, the pattern is much the same. For 1976 to 1986, however, the patterns are quite different. In the East North Central region, the configuration—and the loop— is almost entirely outside (northeast of) the 1972–76 configuration and loop; for the United States, the reverse is true. For 1986 to 1990 the configurations and loops are similar. Starting in 1968, the United States has seven possible trade-off curves; the East North Central region has five, or six, if we consider the two observations for 1984 and 1985 to be a "curve." They are so close together that they might be regarded as a single point, a temporary equilibrium.

Interim Conclusion

We have already shown that there are significant differences in the movement of rates of unemployment and inflation among regions in the United States. To compare each of the nine regions with all of the other eight would be a tedious task (seventy-two comparisons) and would not add enough to *general knowledge* to be worthwhile for the purposes of this volume, which is primarily concerned with exploring *theoretical* differences between prewar and postwar economic fluctuations. But there is an implication that there are enough differences in the amplitude, pattern, and timing of regional economic fluctuations to permit, by a finely tuned and differentiated fiscal policy, tackling unemployment, inflation, and regional disparities *all at once* in the United States. The possibility is certainly worth exploring further. From a *policy* viewpoint, detailed investigations to establish more precisely the structural differences among regional economies could be very rewarding. For the remainder of this chapter, we shall content ourselves with comparisons of each region with the national economy as a whole, to isolate any major peculiarities in the behavior of each regional economy.

West North Central

The starting points in 1968 were very similar: the United States economy had unemployment of 3.5 percent and an inflation rate of 4.2 percent, and the West North Central region registered unemployment of 3.2 percent and inflation rate of 4.8 percent. (They might well have been on the same community indifference curve.) The movements between 1968 and 1970 were also very much alike. The years 1970 through 1972 were virtually stable in both the nation and the region. The inflation rate declined to 3.2 percent in the United States and to 3.1 percent in the region. In 1972 the West North Central region did slightly better on both counts than the United States as a whole. Between 1972 and 1974 the price level became unstuck in both, the price increase rising to 11.0 percent in the United States and to 11.5 percent in the region. From 1974 to 1976, the pattern was still the same. In the latter year the United States had 7.6 percent unemployment and 5.8 percent inflation while the region had 5.9 percent unemployment and 5.2 percent inflation (figures 8.18 and 8.19).

After 1976, the two patterns start to diverge. The reduction in unemployment to 1979 was considerably greater in the West North Central region than in the United States. In the United States, inflation reached its peak in 1980 while unemployment also increased from 1979 to 1980. In 1982 there was a considerable drop in the inflation rate, accompanied by a slight increase in unemployment. The West North Central region experienced almost the reverse movements: a slight drop in the inflation rate in 1980, with a substantial increase in unemployment. The peak rate of inflation in the United States was 13.5 percent (in 1980) and in the region was 12.3 percent a year later. Both experienced declines in unemployment between 1983 and 1984, accompanied by increased rates of inflation; but whereas the United States managed to reduce both its rate of unemployment and inflation between 1984 and 1985, the region suffered a slight acceleration of its inflation rate. The configurations from 1985 to 1990 are similar, except that the region had a slight fall in its inflation rate in 1989 while the United States had a continuous rise in its inflation rate. In 1990 the region was in a considerably more favorable position than that of the United States, with unemployment of 4.8 percent and inflation of 4.1 percent, compared to 5.5 percent and 5.4 percent for the United States.

FIGURE 8.18
Scatter of Discomfort Points (1950–1993)

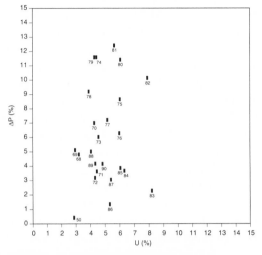

Note: West North Central; U = Minnesota, ΔP = Minneapolis-St. Paul

Source: United States Department of Commerce, *Statistical Abstract of the United States,* 1994.

FIGURE 8.19
Sequence of Discomfort Points (1950–1993)

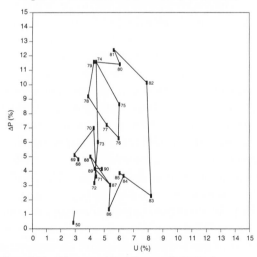

Note: West North Central; U = Minnesota, ΔP = Minneapolis-St. Paul

Source: United States Department of Commerce, *Statistical Abstract of the United States,* 1994.

The trade-off curves for the West North Central region are very similar to those of the United States (figure 8.20). TOC_1 WNC seems to be the equivalent of TOC_3 US, although it is difficult to tell from only two observations, and for the short distance it goes, TOC_1 WNC seems considerably flatter than TOC_3 US. TOC_2 WNC is much the same as TOC_4 US, but the position of individual points is different and TOC_2 WNC is more nearly vertical. TOC_3 WNC and TOC_5 US are similar, if they are trade-off curves. TOC4 WNC is much the same as TOC_6 US although the discomfort point for 1979 is clearly not on the regional TOC and appears to be on the national TOC. We then have a clearcut shift to the northeast to TOC_5 WNC and TOC_7 US. However, the national curve is much further east than the regional curve, the discomfort point for 1983 is clearly not on the regional curve but could be on the national curve. TOC_6 WNC is similar to TOC_8 US. However, TOC_9 US is considerably further to the east than TOC_7 WNC.

The West North Central region displays regular clockwise loops from 1968 to 1985; then they reverse to counterclockwise loops until 1990 (figure 8.21). The US loops are much the same, except that they appear to be clockwise again in 1987 to 1990. Both unemployment and inflation were lower in the West North Central region than in the United States between 1986 and 1990.

South Atlantic

The South Atlantic scatter does not extend quite so far to the west as the United States one. Maximum unemployment of 8.1 percent was reached in 1976 compared to 8.5 percent in 1982 and 1983 for the United States (figure 8.22). The lowest level of unemployment was attained in 1969, 2.9 percent, compared to the United States low of 3.4 percent in that same year. The peak rate of inflation was registered in 1980 for both the nation and the region, 13.9 percent for the South Atlantic and 13.5 percent for the United States. The minimum rate of inflation was recorded in 1986 in the region, 3.0 percent compared to 3.4 percent (for the period 1968 to 1990) for the United States. The configuration of the sequential scatter diagram remains much the same in the region and in the country for the period 1968 through 1983, except that the rate of inflation fell slightly from 1969 to 1970 in the region, whereas it rose slightly in the United States (figure 8.23).

FIGURE 8.20
TOCs (1950–1993)

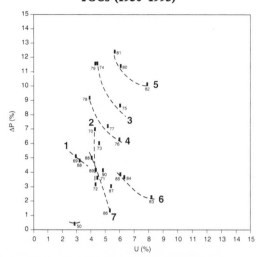

Note: West North Central; U = Minnesota, ΔP = Minneapolis-St. Paul

Source: United States Department of Commerce, *Statistical Abstract of the United States,* 1994.

FIGURE 8.21
Cyclical Loops (1950–1993)

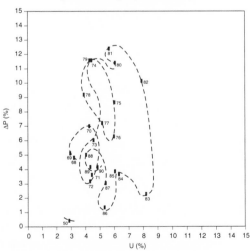

Note: West North Central; U = Minnesota, ΔP = Minneapolis-St. Paul

Source: United States Department of Commerce, *Statistical Abstract of the United States,* 1994.

FIGURE 8.22
Scatter of Discomfort Points (1950–1993)

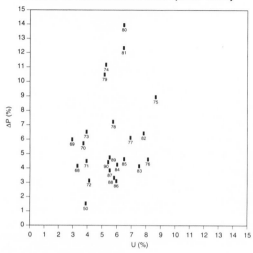

Note: South Atlantic; U = Georgia, ΔP = Atlanta

Source: United States Department of Commerce, *Statistical Abstract of the United States,* 1994.

FIGURE 8.23
Sequence of Discomfort Points (1950–1993)

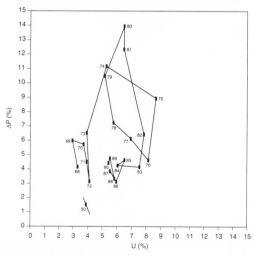

Note: South Atlantic; U = Georgia, ΔP = Atlanta

Source: United States Department of Commerce, *Statistical Abstract of the United States,* 1994.

FIGURE 8.24
TOCs (1950–1993)

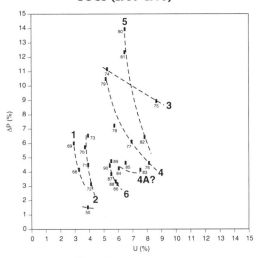

Note: South Atlantic; U = Georgia, ΔP = Atlanta
Source: United States Department of Commerce, *Statistical Abstract of the United States*, 1994.

FIGURE 8.25
Cyclical Loops (1950–1993)

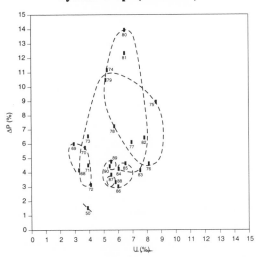

Note: South Atlantic; U = Georgia, ΔP = Atlanta
Source: United States Department of Commerce, *Statistical Abstract of the United States*, 1994.

After 1983 all resemblance disappears. In the United States both the rate of unemployment and the rate of inflation fell steadily from 1984 to 1986; both rose from 1986 to 1987; from 1987 to 1988 the rate of inflation rose while the employment rate fell, and both rose between 1989 and 1990. However, in this whole period the annual movements were so slight as to be insignificant, and might be regarded as being contained in a "zone" of dynamic equilibrium, subject to only minor random shocks rather than cyclical movements.

As for the trade-off curves, TOC_1 in the South Atlantic is equivalent to TOC_3 in the United States and TOC_2 in the South Atlantic is equivalent to TOC_4 in the US, except that TOC_4 US is further to the east (figure 8.24). TOC_3 SA is equivalent to TOC_5 US; TOC_4 SA is equivalent to TOC_6 US, except that the latter is further east and TOC_5 SA is equivalent to TOC_7 US. There is some doubt about the discomfort point for 1983 in both the region and the nation. Does it belong to TOC_5 SA and TOC_7 US or to TOC_{4a} SA and TOC_8 US? The movements are small in any case, and could once again be interpreted as economies in dynamic equilibrium but subject to minor random shocks.

When it comes to loops, the configurations for 1968 to 1983 are the same, except that for the United States the 1979–82 loop is east of the 1972 loop, and for the South Atlantic it is west of the 1972–79 loop (figure 8.25). The loops from 1983 to 1990, for the South Atlantic, show little change in the rate of inflation and modest reductions in unemployment while the United States shows a significant reduction in unemployment and a significant increase in the rate of inflation.

East South Central

The scatter diagrams for the East South Central region and for the United States are very similar. The peaks and troughs of employment and inflation occur in the same years for both the region and the country as a whole (figure 8.26). The region's peak for unemployment is higher than that for the United States (11.8 versus 8.5 percent) and the peak inflation rate is lower than the national figure (11.9 percent versus 13.5 percent). When the discomfort point are connected by straight lines, some differences do appear (figure 8.27). Between 1969 and 1970, the rate of inflation rose slightly in the United States but fell substantially in the region. Between 1970 and 1972 unemployment rose in the United States but fell in the region. In 1975 unemployment was higher than in 1981 in the United States, but substantially lower than in 1981 in the region. Between 1984 and 1989 the patterns were much the same. However, between 1989 and 1990, both unemployment and inflation increased slightly in the United States, while unemployment increased, but inflation dropped significantly in the region.

The East South Central region was too unstable between 1969 and 1973 to permit any trade-off curves to be distinguished, whereas the United States appears to have had quite good TOCs between 1965 and 1969, and between 1970 and 1973. In both the United States and the region, a question arises regarding the treatment of the observations for 1974 and 1975. Should they be regarded as a short-lived TOC? There is no way of determining the answer for sure; we cannot now go back to 1974 through 1975 and see whether some different monetary policy could have produced other points on the curve connecting the two actual observations for those years. It *looks* like a TOC, and we have treated it as such. One thing that *is* for certain is that there was a marked outward and upward shift in those years, followed by a westward and downward shift to a curve with a much steeper slope in both the United States and the region. TOC_2 ESC is equivalent to TOC_6 US and TOC_3 ESC is equivalent to ESC_7 US (figure 8.28). Then comes a market shift to the northeast for both country and region in 1980 through 1983. There could be a TOC_8 US for 1983-85, with no equivalent in the region. Finally, TOC_4 ESC is equivalent to TOC_9 US, except the TOC for the United States includes 1986 and 1987 while the TOC_4 for the region includes only the years 1988, 1989, and 1990.

The loops for 1968 to 1972 appear to be the same, except that there was a much sharper drop in the rate of inflation in 1970 for the region than in the United States (figure 8.29). The configurations for 1973 to 1976 and 1976 to 1983 appear to be the same, except for the question as to whether the point for 1981 lies on the loop for the United States or is an aberration. It clearly lies on the loop for the region. The configurations for 1983 to 1986 are also the same. However, the period 1986 to 1990 is one of steadily rising rates of inflation for the United States, whereas in the region the rate of inflation fell from 1987 to 1990.

West South Central

One difference that is immediately apparent in the scatter of the West South Central region is that the price level actually fell in 1986 (figure

FIGURE 8.26
Scatter of Discomfort Points (1950–1993)

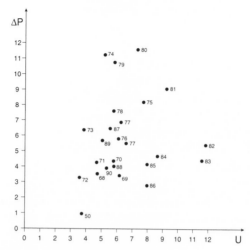

Note: East South Central; U = Tennessee; ΔP = Washington, D.C.

Source: United States Department of Commerce, *Statistical Abstract of the United States,* 1994.

FIGURE 8.27
Sequence of Discomfort Points (1950–1993)

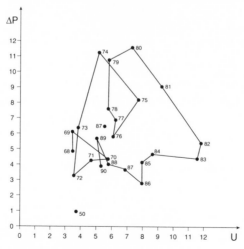

Note: East South Central; U = Tennessee, ΔP = Washington, D.C.

Source: United States Department of Commerce, *Statistical Abstract of the United States,* 1994.

FIGURE 8.28
TOCs (1950–1993)

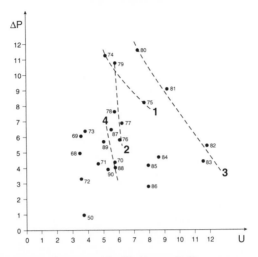

Note: East South Central; U =Tennessee, ΔP = Washington, D.C.

Source: United States Department of Commerce, *Statistical Abstract of the United States,* 1994.

FIGURE 8.29
Cyclical Loops (1950–1993)

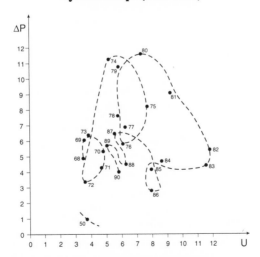

Note: East South Central; U = Tennessee, ΔP = Washington, D.C.

Source: United States Department of Commerce, *Statistical Abstract of the United States,* 1994.

8.30). The drop was only 1.0 percent, but the West South Central was the only region to record a price fall between 1968 and 1990. In the United States the best performance on inflation during this period was a rise in the consumer price index of 1.9 percent in 1986. The West South Central region also outperformed the United States with respect to the minimum unemployment in this period: 2.7 percent in 1968 compared to 3.4 percent in 1969 for the United States. The maximum unemployment was also lower for the region than for the country: 8.9 percent in 1986 compared to 9.5 percent in 1982 and 1983. Finally, the peak inflation in the region was 13.2 percent in 1974, slightly below the United States' peak or 13.5 percent in 1980. Thus, the region performed better than the country on all counts.

When we join the discomfort points by straight lines, we see sharp differences in the configuration of the scatter for the West South Central region and the United States (figure 8.31). The rate of inflation increased in 1970 in the United States and declined in the region. It fell between 1971 and 1972 in the United States and rose slightly in the West South Central region. Inflation accelerated sharply between 1972 and 1974 while unemployment increased slightly in both the country and the region, but the rate of inflation in the region was almost the same in 1975 as in 1974, while in the United States it dropped substantially. In the region, the rate of inflation in 1977 was slightly less than in 1976; in the United States it was higher in 1977 than in 1976. Inflation in the United States peaked in 1980; in the region it peaked in 1979. From 1980 to 1983 the configurations are much the same, but in the United States the rate of inflation increased in 1984, while in the region it fell slightly. From 1984 to 1990 the pattern for inflation is much the same, but from 1984 to 1986 unemployment fell in the United States while it increased substantially in the region. In 1990, the United States ended up in a slightly more favorable position on both unemployment and inflation than the region.

The differences are even more striking when it comes to trade-off curves. TOC_1 WSC is not equivalent to TOC_3 US (figure 8.32). The discomfort point for 1968 does not seem to lie on TOC_1 WSC, nor does the point for 1973. On the other hand, all the points from 1969 to 1972 do. The year 1973 seems to have been an aberration in the region while in the United States it clearly seems to fall on TOC_4. The years 1974 and 1975 *may* constitute a short-lived TOC in the United States. There is no question of a TOC for those years in the region, since no trade-off is

FIGURE 8.30
Scatter of Discomfort Points (1950-1993)

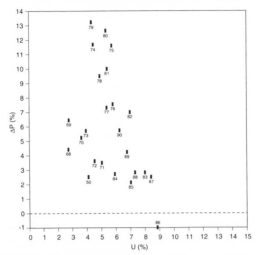

Note: West South Central; U = Texas, ΔP = Houston

Source: United States Department of Commerce, *Statistical Abstract of the United States,* 1994.

FIGURE 8.31
Sequence of Discomfort Points (1950-1993)

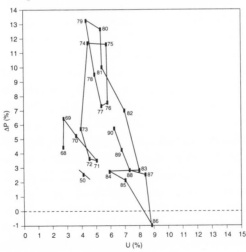

Note: West South Central; U = Texas, ΔP = Houston

Source: United States Department of Commerce, *Statistical Abstract of the United States,* 1994.

involved. TOC_2 WSC covers the years 1976 to 1979 and is more or less the equivalent of TOC_6 US. TOC_3 WSC, covering 1980 to 1983, is more or less equivalent to TOC_7 US. The observations for 1984 and 1985 in the region *may* constitute a TOC, but it is scarcely the equivalent of TOC_8 US; the year 1983 clearly does not lie on it and the positions of the discomfort points for 1984 and 1985 are quite different from those of these years in the United States. The United States has no equivalent of TOC_5 WSC. In the United States, the years 1987 and 1988 fall on TOC_9. Of course, with a not very wide envelope, we could put *all* the observations of trade-off curves 2, 3, 5, and 6 and the years 1974 and 1975 as well, for the West South Central region, on the same curve. In the same fashion, we could run TOC_1 and TOC_4 together into one curve. We would then have a shift from 1968 to a TOC, and a second shift to the northeast to another curve, then a shift back to the first curve, and finally a shift back to the second curve. That would mean that after 1968, the authorities responsible for unemployment and inflation in the West South Central region would have had just two sets of options to choose from, depending on the forces in the economy, one more favorable and one less favorable. The two curves would both have been very steep; substantial reductions in the rate of inflation could have been attained at very little cost in increased unemployment. The question is then, with so much more attractive options available to them, why did the authorities ever let inflation rates go so high?

Interestingly enough, with so much difference in the TOC patterns, the loops look much the same, except for the peak inflation in the region in 1979, and the drop in the price level in 1986 (figure 8.33). In general, there seems to be more similarity in the configuration of loops than of trade-off curves: the points must *look* as though they lie on the same curve, and from general knowledge of the economic conditions prevailing in the period, there is reason to believe that through alterations of monetary policy plus, perhaps, simple changes in macroeconomic fiscal policy, the government could have chosen any of the points on the curve instead of the one they did choose. There is no way of testing now whether or not all the policy options represented by a particular TOC were in fact available. The fact that the curve gives a good econometric fit to all the points is not conclusive proof that they were all available. Given a very big model of the economy, one could, of course, simulate various policy options, and see whether or not they work, according to the model. But

FIGURE 8.32
TOCs (1950–1993)

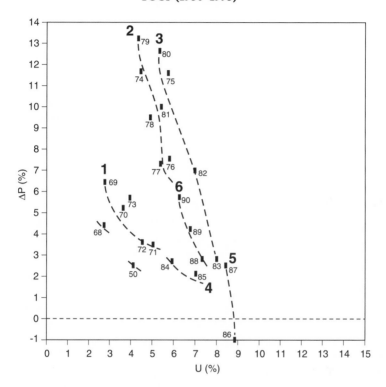

Note: West South Central; U = Texas, ΔP = Houston
Source: United States Department of Commerce, *Statistical Abstract of the United States,* 1994.

even that would not be absolute proof. The points on the loops, however, are all observations of what actually occurred, as distinct from specula-tions about what *would have occurred* in any period of time had policy been different. As a description of reality, therefore, we can have more faith in the loops than in our fabricated TOCs.

The Mountain Region

For the Mountain region the price index (Denver) is available only from 1972 to 1990 (fig. 8.34). Unemployment ranged only from 3.4 per-

FIGURE 8.33
Cyclical Loops (1950–1993)

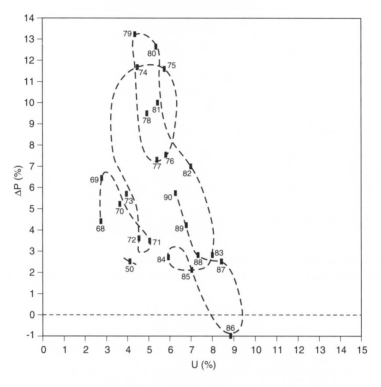

Note: West South Central; U = Texas, ΔP = Houston
Source: United States Department of Commerce, *Statistical Abstract of the United States,* 1994.

cent in 1973 to 7.7 percent in 1987. The rate of inflation varied from 0.7 percent in 1985 to 15.5 percent in 1979, the highest peak attained by any region except the Pacific. The configuration of discomfort points, when joined by straight lines, departs considerably from the United States model (figure 8.35). Up to 1976 the patterns were much the same, but then the differences appeared. Contrary to the course of events in the United States, in the Mountain region unemployment increased in 1977. Inflation was reduced in 1978, peak inflation was registered in 1979, unemployment fell in 1981 and 1983; inflation fell in 1984; unemployment increased in 1986 and again, slightly in 1987; the rate of inflation diminished in both

FIGURE 8.34
Scatter of Discomfort Points (1972–1993)

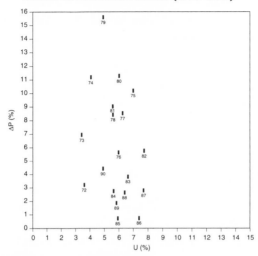

Note: The Mountain Region; U = Colorado, ΔP = Denver
Source: United States Department of Commerce, *Statistical Abstract of the United States,* 1994.

FIGURE 8.35
Sequence of Discomfort Points (1972–1993)

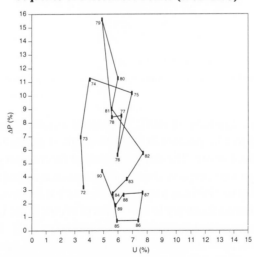

Note: The Mountain Region; U = Colorado, ΔP = Denver
Source: United States Department of Commerce, *Statistical Abstract of the United States,* 1994.

1988 and 1989 and then rose steeply in 1990, with a small decrease in unemployment. In the United States, inflation increased steadily from 1986 to 1990, with a slight increase in unemployment in 1990.

As for trade-off curves, it can hardly be said that they exist at all in the Mountain region. Two pairs of discomfort points appear to be on the same *lines,* 1972 and 1973, and 1974 and 1975 (figure 8.36). But the first of these lines is too nearly vertical to suggest a "trade-off," and the second is too nearly horizontal to inspire any confidence in its being a genuine trade-off curve. However, apart from these two lines, if we allow a wide enough envelope, we can put *all* of the points on the same nearly vertical line (plus its envelope). What this interpretation would mean is that the level of unemployment is scarcely affected by the rate of inflation; so the authorities might as well bring the rate of inflation down as close to zero as was in fact achieved in 1985 and 1986. Since the rate of inflation was the same in both years, what excuse did the authorities have for not choosing the 1985 position as an optimum? And if, indeed, this configuration represents a real trade-off curve—a set of options available by standard monetary and fiscal policy alone—what earthly excuse would the authorities have had for allowing inflation to reach the second highest rate of all regions in the country, except ignorance? The powers of a single state to control inflation and unemployment are, of course, limited but the State of Colorado has a budget and the Federal Reserve System has a branch in Denver. I suspect that the configuration is *not* a true TOC in the sense in which we have defined it, and that all the points in it were *not* continuously available during the whole period from 1976 to 1990.

Curiously enough, this disorderly behavior when interpreted as TOCs becomes very orderly when interpreted as cyclical loops. True, the loops were not quite identical to those of the United States. The 1976–84 and the 1984–89 loops are quite different from those of the United States. The Mountain region loop is counterclockwise for the whole period 1982 to 1989, then turns clockwise for the single year 1990, with unemployment in that year below that of any year in the 1980s (figure 8.37). The United States figure for unemployment is above that for 1989, the same as in 1988, and below other years in the 1980s. In 1990, the Mountain region was clearly on a higher community indifference curve than the United States, with unemployment at 4.9 percent and inflation at 4.4 percent, compared to 5.5 percent and 5.4 percent for the United States.

FIGURE 8.36
TOCs (1972–1993)

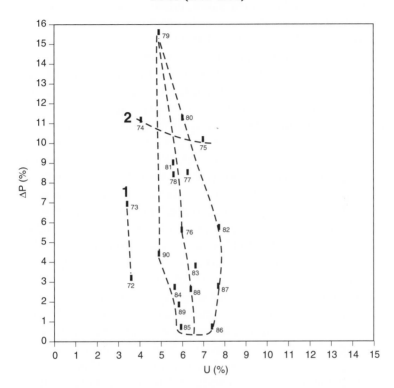

Note: The Mountain Region; U = Colorado, ΔP = Denver
Source: United States Department of Commerce, *Statistical Abstract of the United States,* 1994.

The Pacific Region

At first glance, the scatter diagram for the Pacific region seems more concentrated in the center of the lower half of the diagram than the United States one (figure 8.38). Closer examination reveals that the reason for this impression is that between 1968 and 1990 the United States had seven years with inflation above 7.5 percent, and the Pacific region only four (figure 8.39). Inflation showed considerably less acceleration between 1968 and 1969 than the United States, and between 1968 and 1974 the Pacific had consistently lower rates of inflation

FIGURE 8.37
Cyclical Loops (1972–1993)

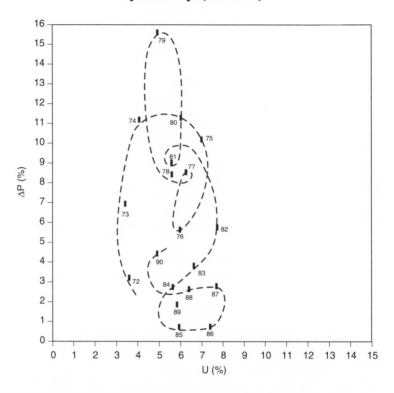

Note: The Mountain Region; U = Colorado, ΔP = Denver

Source: United States Department of Commerce, *Statistical Abstract of the United States,* 1994.

than the United States. The range of variation in unemployment is much the same. Unemployment in the Pacific ranges from 4.4 percent in 1969 to 9.9 percent in 1987, compared to 3.5 percent (1969) to 9.5 percent (1982 and 1983) in the United States. The inflation rate in the Pacific ranged from 1.8 percent in 1983 to 15.7 percent in 1980, the highest figure recorded by all regions, worse than the Mountain region by 0.2 percent. Otherwise, the main difference is that whereas the 1972 to 1976 cycle lies almost entirely *inside* the 1976 to 1983 cycle in the United States, in the Pacific the first cycle lies mainly *outside* the second. The movements from 1983 to 1986 brought more reduction in

FIGURE 8.38

Scatter of Discomfort Points (1950–1993)

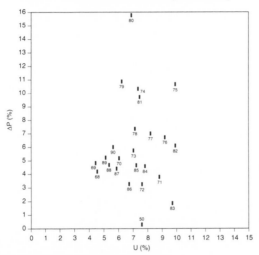

Note: The Pacific Region; U = California, ΔP = Los Angeles

Source: United States Department of Commerce, *Statistical Abstract of the United States,* 1994.

FIGURE 8.39

Sequence of Discomfort Points (1950–1993)

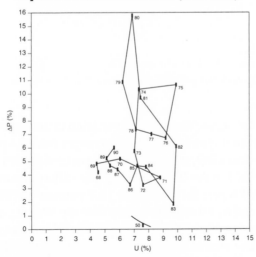

Note: The Pacific Region; U = California, ΔP = Los Angeles

Source: United States Department of Commerce, *Statistical Abstract of the United States,* 1994.

unemployment in the United States than in the Pacific. The movements from 1986 to 1990 are similar.

The differences are sharper when expressed as trade-off curves (figure 8.40). The two observations for 1968 and 1969 are much the same in the United States and in the Pacific, except as already observed, there was much more acceleration of inflation in the United States. They form part of TOC_3 covering 1965 to 1969. But TOC_4 US for the early 1970s does not appear at all in the Pacific. Instead, there is a clustering of points within a narrow range, combined with constant movement. Once again, we might regard 1970–73 as a period of dynamic equilibrium, disturbed by minor random shocks. Whereas the points for 1974–75 might possibly be regarded as a short-lived trade-off curve in the United States, they clearly could not be so regarded in the Pacific; unemployment increased substantially in 1975 and the rate of inflation rose slightly; no trade-off was involved, and there was obviously a shift, although whether of TOCs or merely points, is hard to say. TOC_2 PAC is equivalent to TOC_6 US, but is flatter in its lower portion, inflation falling less and unemployment increasing more. TOC_3 PAC is more or less equivalent to TOC_7 US. The observation for 1983 seems less likely to fall on the same TOC as the observations for 1980 to 1982 in the Pacific than in the United States. TOC_4 US is roughly equivalent to TOC_8 US, but is longer and steeper, covering about the same reduction in unemployment but more decline in inflation. TOC_5 PAC is equivalent to TOC_9 US, although TOC_9 US is much steeper than TOC_5 PAC, encompassing less reduction of unemployment but considerably more increase in inflation. Also, it is reasonable to include the observation for 1990 in TOC_9 US, but not in TOC_5 PAC.

The loops for the Pacific region are very similar to those for the United States—once again providing a reason for having more credence in loops than in trade-off curves (figure 8.41). In both the region and the country, a question arises concerning the interpretation of the discomfort point for 1981: Was it a temporary aberration, the result of some temporary shock, quite apart from the stronger and more durable forces causing the cycles, which we have analyzed above under the heading of hysteresis or the topocross? It seems likely that it was, but those forces are so many and so varied and so imperfectly understood that we can't be sure. It is worth noting that in both the region and the country the loops move clockwise except for the period 1984–86 when the movement was for a short time counterclockwise—another mystery to be solved.

FIGURE 8.40
TOCs (1950–1993)

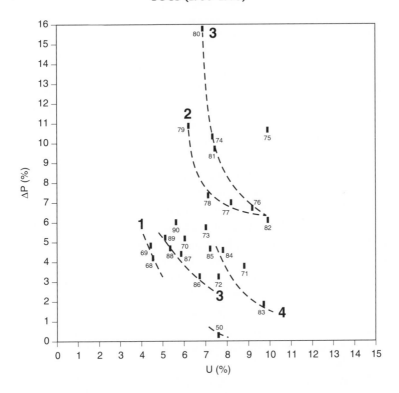

Note: The Pacific Region; U = California, ΔP = Los Angeles

Source: United States Department of Commerce, *Statistical Abstract of the United States,* 1994.

Conclusion

Our interim conclusion still stands and it is an important one: even in the United States, which is presumably more integrated than is Australia or Canada, there are enough differences in cyclical behavior among regions, to make it worth exploring the possibilities of reducing *both* unemployment and inflation by a differential fiscal policy among regions. By "differential" we mean a policy of determining both the *timing* and the *placing* of government spending and incentives to private spending according to the forces causing unemployment and inflation in each region. In this chapter, we have been working with nine regions because

FIGURE 8.41
Cyclical Loops (1950–1993)

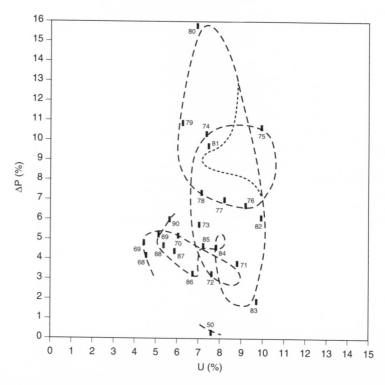

Note: The Pacific Region; U = California, ΔP = Los Angeles
Source: United States Department of Commerce, *Statistical Abstract of the United States,* 1994.

that is what the United States Bureau of the Census does, and then only imperfectly. We could not work with states because there are no data on inflation for many states, nor for cities within them. For the kind of policy we have in mind, even states would be too big.

In Australia the Office of Regional Development of the Commonwealth Department of Industry Technology and Regional Development has designated ninety-six regions, and documented differences among them, which turn out to be substantial, despite the apparent similarities among Australian *states*. With the establishment in 1993 of the Department of Industry, Technology and Regional Development, the appointment of a high-level Task Force on Regional Development, the Commission Inquiry on Regional Industry Adjustment, the Ministerial Council of Industry, Technology and Regional Development, the government requirement that all proposals coming before Cabinet should include an assessment of their regional impact, the selection by the government of a private consulting firm to prepare a major study of factors influencing decisions of private enterprise concerning location of industry, especially in "the regions" (outside major metropolitan centers), the studies by the Office of Regional Development of the problems and potential of its ninety-six regions, and the various initiatives for regional development at the state and local level, Australia should soon be in the best position of any country in the world to launch a differential fiscal policy to fight unemployment and inflation simultaneously.

9

Canada, Australia, and the United States: Similarities and Differences

We now have before us detailed accounts of unemployment and inflation in three countries, on the whole rather similar: large, regionalized, resource rich, mainly English speaking, economically advanced, with many institutions in common inherited from the days of British colonialism, parliamentary democracies with federal constitutions. One would expect the behavior of their economies to be much the same. We have found that it is—in broad outline; but when it comes to the details, there are vast differences.

Similarities

In all three countries the postwar period has been one of intense economic instability, without bringing a repetition, as many people feared it would, of the great depression of the 1930s. Indeed, it was the longest period of uninterrupted economic growth since the Napoleonic Wars. What made the period strange and disturbing, however, was that, while there were short periods where unemployment and inflation moved in opposite directions, inflation going up and unemployment coming down, or vice versa, there were other periods when unemployment went up together or down together. Particularly disturbing, of course, were the periods when both unemployment and inflation got worse, plus the fact that no one seemed to understand completely *why* they should do so; nor for that matter, why they should go down together either. There seemed to be some suggestion that in periods of stagnation or recession both inflation and unemployment went up, whereas in periods of rapid economic growth they fell; but that was only a suggestion, not a well-proven and widely accepted fact. Finally, there was a general deterioration of economic conditions from the 1950s to the 1990s, especially with regard to unemployment, balance of payments, and foreign indebtedness. The phenomenon of chronic and growing long-term unemployment was shared with most of the OECD countries, and some developing countries in the world.

The three countries were also broadly similar in the economic policies pursued. Monetary policy has been the main instrument of stabilization, reducing and containing inflation the major objective. In that objective they have all been quite successful, but at the cost of high and growing levels of unemployment. Keynesian fiscal policy, cutting taxes and increasing government expenditures when unemployment was high, and reversing policy when the opposite situation appeared, has been eschewed by all of them; and probably rightly so, since unemployment and inflation were both omnipresent, and sometimes even increased together. But sometimes the governments deliberately followed an *anti*-Keynesian policy. Thus early in 1995, with unemployment at 9 percent and inflation running around 1.5 percent, the Australian government decided that the Australian economy was "overheating"; inflation threatened to rise again, and the balance of payments was dangerously negative on current account. So they decided to raise interest rates, reduce government spending, and raise taxes, counting on a spontaneous boom in private investment to reduce unemployment. None of the governments has learned how to control unemployment, inflation, and the current account balance all at once, and all of them are prepared to accept a very high "Non Accelerating Inflation Rate of Unemployment" rather than risk increasing inflation and balance of payments difficulties.

Differences

While the general profile of inflation and unemployment is similar in all three countries, there are differences in timing and amplitude of economic fluctuations, especially at the regional level. Thus the United States enjoyed its minimum level of unemployment in 1953; Canada in 1956, and Australia in 1950 to 1951. The United States and Canada achieved minimum unemployment rates of 3 percent and 3.5 percent. The Australian rate was 1.1 percent. The United States suffered a maximum unemployment rates of 9.5 percent in 1982 to 1983. Canada's maximum unemployment rate was 11.8 percent in 1983, and was almost equally high in 1992 to 1993. Australia, having a very different pattern of inflation and unemployment, reached its highest rate of unemployment in 1993, 10.9 percent.

The United States recorded a slightly negative rate of price change in 1955, -0.3 percent. Canada also had its lowest rate of inflation in 1955, 0.36 percent, but the figures for 1959 and 1961 were much the same. Australia's minimum inflation was achieved in 1963, when the price level was stable (price increase of 0.0 percent). The United States had its worst year for inflation in 1980, when the price level rose 13.5 percent. Canada's worst year came in 1981, when prices rose by 13 percent. Australia's worst year for inflation was 1952, when prices rose by 22.8 percent.

The United States had its lowest rate of growth in 1955, -0.3 percent, and its highest in 1980, 13.5 percent. Canada had its lowest rate of growth in 1982, -3.5 percent, and its highest in 1973, 19.4 percent. Australia's nadir was reached in 1958, 2.5 percent, and its peak in 1975, during the minerals boom, an astounding 21.7 percent. These figures seem to reflect historical shocks unique to each country, rather than the impact of a global cycle or economic policy.

During the period covered, the United States had five brief intervals when unemployment and inflation increased together; 1956 to 1957, 1969 to 1970, 1972 to 1974, 1979 to 1980, and 1989 to 1990. Except for the last, these were all intervals of recession. Unemployment and inflation fell together during 1951 to 1953, 1954 to 1955, 1958 to 1959, 1975 to 1976, and 1985 to 1986. The first and last of these were periods of falling growth rates, the other three were intervals of rising growth rates.

Canada experienced simultaneously increasing unemployment and inflation in 1956 to 1957, 1959 to 1960, 1976 to 1978, 1979 to 1980, 1988 to 1989, 1990 to 1991. Only the first of these periods coincides precisely with the periods of simultaneous rise in unemployment and inflation in the United States. The only periods when unemployment and inflation fell together were 1963 to 1964 (barely) and 1983 to 1988 (substantially). Again, there is no close relationship to the United States.

Australia's picture is different again. The periods of simultaneously increasing unemployment and inflation were 1955 to 1957, 1969 to 1977, and 1981 to 1983. None of these periods corresponds precisely with either those of the United States or of Canada. Moreover, these were all periods of high to very high growth of GDP. The intervals of simultaneously falling unemployment and inflation were 1953 to 1955, and, briefly and very mildly, 1980 to 1981, 1983 to 1985, and 1987 to 1988. Again, there is no relationship to either American or Canadian experience. The growth rate of GDP was not markedly different in these periods from periods of increasing unemployment and inflation. During the entire period from 1976 to 1994, as we have noted, nearly all the observations lie on or close to a single trade-off curve (TOC), sometimes with steeply rising inflation and only modest reductions in unemployment, as between 1984 and 1987, but with sharp reductions in inflation and modest increases in unemployment during the period as a whole.

When unemployment and inflation are not rising together or falling together, which is a necessary phenomenon if we are to describe the fluctuations in the form of loops, they should fall on a trade-off curve. In chapters 11 and 12 we offer some explanations of observed behaviour; here we are merely reporting the behavior itself. But it is worth reporting here that shifting trade-off curves and cyclical loops do *not* cover all observations; some behavior is too erratic for that. If the observed economic fluctuations were completely systematic, combinations of unemployment and inflation repeating themselves in a regular fashion period after period, we would expect all observations to fall on a trade-off curve, concave or convex to the origin, or on a loop. When the TOCs are shifting so rapidly, up or down, that no trade-off occurs, the discomfort points would be on a loop, but not on a TOC. We have not found that degree of regularity in the real world. The Canadian case comes closest to it, but the 1972 observation is neither on a TOC or a loop, the loop for 1976 to 1979 goes counter-clockwise instead of clockwise, and the loops themselves are shifting, not just the TOCs. In the Australian case, the data do not provide sufficient evidence of regular loops; except for 1983 and 1989, from 1976 to 1994 the discomfort points all seem to lie on one TOC. In the United States, all the observations except the one for 1950 can be allotted to some TOC, although some of them are so nearly vertical that the term "trade-off" curve seems inappropriate, since no trade-off is involved. Nearly all the points can be allotted to some loop or other; but for the years 1951 to 1954, 1984 to 1989, and 1991 to 1993 the movement seems to be counter-clockwise, not clockwise. "Maverick" discomfort points on neither a trade-off curve or a cyclical loop are probably *sui generis,* due to some particular shock, favorable or unfavorable; the oil crisis of the early seventies, the 1983 Australian election, the Gulf War, the Kobe earthquake. Some of these shocks would have an impact on several national economies; others would be unique to a particular country. In this respect they are no different from the shocks that occurred between the wars. Observed events are the result of a combination of such shocks and reactions to them, and of more or less regular cyclical forces.

In the United States, it would be possible to interpret the observations for 1951 to 1953 as falling on (or close to) a vertical straight line, because the U.S. experienced full employment in those years. The discomfort points for 1955 to 1957 might also be interpreted as falling on a vertical straight line, with unemployment almost constant at about 4 percent; but it is not a TOC and certainly not a long-run "Phillips Curve." The observations for 1959 to 1969 seem to fall on a stable trade-off curve, which prevailed for eleven years before a shift to the northeast occurred. Altogether we distinguished eight trade-off curves between 1950 and 1993, enduring for two to four years each; it will be recalled that we raised the question as to whether a line joining only two points can be properly called a "curve."

Canada has a plethora of two-point-curves between 1955 and 1993: 1955 to 1956, 1956 to 1957, 1966 to 1967, 1972 to 1973, 1975 to 1976, 1982 to 1983, and 1989 to 1990. The longest-lasting TOCs were 1961 to 1965, and 1977 to 1981, five years each. There was one TOC of four years duration, 1958 to 1971, and one of three years duration, 1991 to 1993. Excluding the two-year curves, there were six TOCs between 1955 and 1993; including them, there were twelve. Altogether, Canada has a more unstable economy than the United States, and suffered from more erratic policy.

Cast in these terms, Australia had a more stable economy, and a more consistent policy than either the United States or Canada, although its peak rates of unemployment and inflation were much the same. Excluding the vertical straight line during the period of full employment, Australia has had only one discernible TOC during the whole period from 1950 to 1993, with a sharp shift to the northeast from 1975 to 1976. The curve is rather steep, but displays a distinct trade-off, with substantial reductions in inflation bringing relatively small increases in unemployment, rather than a fixed, "equilibrium" rate of long-term unemployment which no amount of inflation can dislodge.

Canada probably provides the strongest case for interpreting postwar fluctuations as shifting TOCs and cyclical loops, whether at the national or regional level. No doubt the structural differences among Canadian regions is part of the explanation. Being a neighbor and the chief trading partner of the United States, and since the two countries are at approximately the same level of development, if postwar economic fluctuations in both countries take the form of shifting TOCs and/or cyclical loops, one would expect the patterns to be the same. But a glance at the diagrams of trade-off curves and loops for the two countries reveals that in fact they are very different. How is that possible?

I think the answer lies in the analysis of "the machine, the structure and the game" presented in chapter 12. These days, the machine—the basic mechanisms of the mixed market economy, interactions of multiplier and accelerator, and all the factors entering into pre-World-War II theories of the business cycle—are less important in determining what happens in any country than either the structure or the game. Neighboring countries need not pursue identical government policies, the behavior of trade union leaders and employers' representatives may differ, expectations regarding any of these factors can vary a great deal. If two championship chess matches are played simultaneously in the United States and Canada, by equally famous and equally brilliant players, while the same fundamental rules and strategies may guide them, the results will still be unpredictable.

Postwar Economic Fluctuations, Phillips Curves, Trade-off Curves, Loops: What Have We Learned?

What can we say *in general* about economic fluctuations since 1950, and about the role in them of Phillips curves, trade-off curves, their shifts, and loops, on the basis of our three case studies? A good many "mainstream economists" are prepared to make generalizations about these matters that are not borne out by our observations in these three countries, and it is interesting to make the comparison. A very good short summary of the "mainstream" viewpoint is the article in the London *Economist* for 19 February 1994, and we shall use it as a point of departure. It is entitled "A Cruise around the Phillips Curve," and it is on pages 70 and 71.

The first thing worth noting is that the argument is based entirely on United States data. It is assumed implicitly that the United States is a "representative country" like Marshall's "representative firm," and that what holds for it will hold for all countries, or at least for all economically advanced market economies, in the same fashion that the original Phillips curve assumed implicitly that the United Kingdom was a "representative country." The second thing worth noting is that the author of the article makes no distinction between Phillips curves and trade-off curves, and uses a single index called "inflation" to cover increases in both. In other words, price and wage inflation are assumed to move precisely together. This device may be alright as a simplifying assumption in a first approximation, but leads and lags between wages and prices are ultimately very important in the overall picture, as the author's later argument makes abundantly clear.

The author begins his analysis with figure 9.1, showing (American) unemployment and price increases for the 1960s. In that period the Phillips or trade-off curve still held; "the points fall on a fairly neat, downward sloping line." But then the author presents figure 9.2, for 1970 to 1993, in which the Phillips curve has obviously broken down. (It is worth remarking, however, that for the years 1971 through 1993 the observations form a series of cyclical loops, apparently increasing in amplitude.) Macroeconomic policy could no longer be a relatively simple matter of striking the best balance between inflation and unemployment, trading off more of the one for less of the other.

Toward the end of the 1960s the concept of Phillips curves or trade-off curves came in for attack, first on theoretical grounds, and later on empirical grounds. The theoretical argument centered around "the money illusion" and the distinction between money and real wages. Friedman and Phelps argued, for example, and the author of the *Economist* article agrees, that in the long run it is real wages, not money wages, that determines the level of employment and unemployment. Whatever happens to money wages, if real wages remain the same, there is no reason to expect the level of employment and unemployment to change. In the short run, to be sure, an *unexpected* increase in the rate of inflation, which reduces real wages, may bring a reduction of unemployment. But when workers discover that their real wages have fallen, they will demand—and get— an increase in money wages. When real wages have been restored, unemployment will also return to its former level.

The process is illustrated in figure 9.3. The economy begins at A, with unemployment at U_1, and an inflation rate of P_1. The government pushes the inflation rate up to P_2, unemployment falls to U_2, and the economy

FIGURE 9.1
The Vanishing Phillips Curve
American Unemployment Against Inflation, Annual Averages

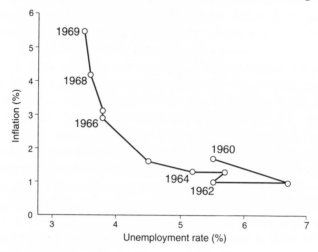

Source: U.S. Bureau of Labor Statistics.

FIGURE 9.2
The Vanishing Phillips Curve
American Unemployment Against Inflation, Annual Averages

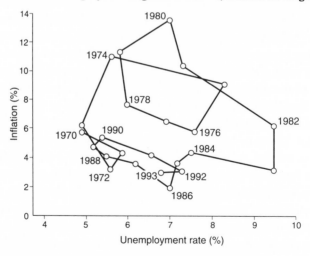

Source: U.S. Bureau of Labor Statistics.

moves to U_2 on the short-run "Phillips" curve. But expectations gradually adjust, the economy moves *toward* equilibrium, and the economy
moves to point C on the long-run "Phillips" curve. Inflation remains at
P_2 but unemployment has risen. "When expectations have adjusted fully
and the economy is back in equilibrium, the long-run Phillips curve is
actually vertical, as shown in Chart 4. With inflation still at P_2, the
economy has moved to point D. Unemployment has returned to U_1" (71).
The economy is worse off than it was at the beginning; unemployment is
as bad as before, but inflation is higher (83). The only way to hold unemployment at U_2 is to make sure that inflation constantly exceeds expectations, so that the economy is always out of equilibrium. In the best case,
lower unemployment can be bought only at the price of perpetually increasing inflation. "In the worst case, the short-run curve would snap to
the vertical, as workers cottoned on to the government's inflationary approach to job-creation. The economy would endure ever accelerating inflation without even a temporary gain in jobs."

Phillips thought that in the long run, or over very long periods, there
was a trade-off between more unemployment or more inflation. In the
United Kingdom between 1861 and 1957, and for shorter periods in other
countries, empirical and econometric studies show that this belief was
indeed justified. Phillips found that for the United Kingdom during the
period studied unemployment of about 2.5 percent was associated with a
wage increase of about 2 percent. Taking account of growth in productivity, this situation was consistent with more or less stable prices. Higher
unemployment was associated with falling prices, lower unemployment
with rising prices. Unemployment varied inversely with inflation.

Since such a trade-off, and a highly stable one at that, is the very
essence of the original Phillips curve, it seems inappropriate to call the
vertical line in *The Economist*'s chart 4 (figure 9.4) a "long-run Phillips
curve," since no trade-off exists. If such a curve exists, it would be better
to call it a "curve of long-run equilibrium in the labour market." In our
three case studies, whether at the national level or at the regional level,
we have found no evidence of the existence of such a curve, nor of a
tendency to move toward it, except in Australia *during the period of
"full employment" from 1950 to 1974.* If general conditions are such in
any country that full employment is maintained throughout a certain period, it is obvious that the curve relating unemployment to inflation will
approximate a vertical straight line for the duration of that period. Changes

FIGURE 9.3
The Vanishing Phillips Curve
American Unemployment Against Inflation, Annual Averages

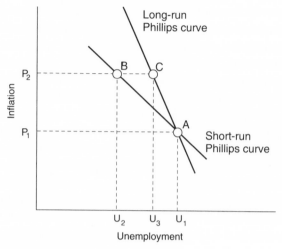

Source: U.S. Bureau of Labor Statistics.

FIGURE 9.4
The Vanishing Phillips Curve
American Unemployment Against Inflation, Annual Averages

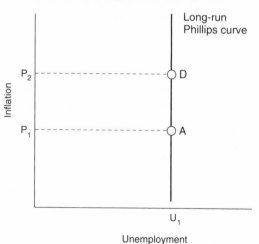

Source: U.S. Bureau of Labor Statistics.

in the rate of inflation, by definition, cannot have any significant effect on the rate of unemployment. We have not found any evidence of such a curve at high rates of unemployment, or of a tendency to move toward such a curve. On the contrary, we have found a high degree of instability in the relationship of unemployment to the rate inflation, the two sometimes rising together, sometimes falling together, sometimes moving in opposite directions. We have, to be sure, found some trade-off curves that were quite steep, but they survived for only short periods, and gave little sign of being either "long-run" or "equilibrium." Perhaps if there were no government intervention *of any kind,* and a set of expectations appropriate to genuine *laissez-faire,* some "long-run equilibrium" would emerge toward which economies would tend. But how can we ever tell?

Expectations of the existence of a stable, long-run trade-off curve, and related expectations that an increase in the rate of inflation *as such* will reduce unemployment, belong to the era of the original Phillips curve. Surely no economist today thinks that unemployment can be cured by simple expansionist Keynesian policy, such as deficit-financing current government expenditures or burying bank notes in garbage tips and letting contracts to dig them up, as Keynes suggested.

This brings us back to the Non Accelerating Inflation Rate of Inflation, or NAIRU. As *The Economist* rightly says, "the Nairu itself is an economic variable not a constant" (71). Even Friedman and Phelps have high hopes for such devices to reduce unemployment as increased flexibility of labor markets, a higher degree of mobility, training and retraining and generally upgrading the labor force. Removing such barriers to employment as payroll taxes, and substituting jobs and wages for unemployment insurance, would also help. *The Economist* stresses the importance of increasing the credibility of government policy, so that the conditions of "equilibrium"—that expectations are confirmed—will be met. But to increase the credibility of government policy, the policy must be credible. The surest way of gaining credibility is to create jobs, in the public or the private sector, in a noninflationary manner, as explained in chapter 15.

Our three cases do not suggest any common pattern of unemployment and inflation and of movements of both toward a common "equilibrium," of the sort depicted in the *Economist*'s chart 4. There is some suggestion of a tendency for the short-run TOCs to become steeper as time goes by, but there is no tendency for the TOCs to become more stable. Australia's vertical straight line between 1950 and 1974 was "stable," in the sense that it reflected a long period of full employment. More recently the Australian picture has shown the swap of a lot of inflation for a limited increase in unemployment, but it scarcely reveals a "long-run equilibrium." There are too many movements along the curve, in both directions, for that.

The common pattern in the three countries consists of the following features: they all reveal periods when the observed discomfort points seem to lie of trade-off curves (although the number of TOCs distinguishable, the number of years covered by each TOC, and the years covered varied a good deal); they all have periods when unemployment and inflation rose together and others when they fell together; over the entire period the situation has become worse in all of them; they all have observations that do not seem to fall on either a TOC or a loop, and which must be explained by particular events in each country; and the actual observations in each country are the result of a combination of events occurring, policy responses, expectations regarding both, and interactions among all three.

Why should Australia have only one TOC (apparently) and Canada and the United States several, during the same period? This is another mystery that I can't resolve completely without a good deal of further research; but I have a hunch that it has to do with the lack of disparities among large regions, like the Australian states. When the timing of settlement, the product mix, and occupational structure of all such regions are roughly the same; when two thirds of the population live in the six state capitals on the coast, and there is no city of even 100,000 people not situated on the coast, except Canberra, the national capital and an artificially created city; when the system of wage determination is such that incomes earned from a given profession, occupation, or trade are substantially the same everywhere in the country; then not only will per capita incomes be much the same in all large regions, but it is almost impossible to have inflationary pressure generated in some regions and unemployment to be concentrated in others. Then shifts in *national* TOCs cannot take place because of events, trends, and forces occurring in certain *regions*. To find significant regional differences in Australia one has to get down to regions as small as the Department of Industry, Technology and Regional Development's ninety-six. And since low-income, high-income, low-unemployment, and high-unemployment regions are scattered throughout the country, the disparities among them cannot have a great deal of effect on *national* unemployment and inflation.

The patterns for the Atlantic provinces, Alberta, and British Columbia differ from those of the other provinces in that up to 1984 or 1985, unemployment was still increasing, and reached very high levels in those years. There is some suggestion that the TOCs have become steeper in both the Atlantic provinces and British Columbia; that is, reducing unemployment by standard Keynesian expansionary policies risks greater aggravation of inflation than it would have done in the 1970s. Over the entire period covered, the Ontario and British Columbia economies show the most marked deterioration. The Newfoundland economy is in the worse condition, but the situation in that province has been unsatisfactory since the early 1950s. Quebec showed a marked improvement during the 1980s, but still had a very high level of unemployment, from which not even Montreal was spared.

Given the overall economic situation, there were during the 1960s and 1970s opportunities for a stabilization policy in the form of restraining inflation where it was generated (the Prairie provinces, British Columbia, and Ontario) and attacking unemployment where it was concentrated (the Atlantic provinces and Quebec), without increasing either total government spending or budget deficits, and at the same time reducing regional disparities. By the early 1980s the TOC for Canada as a whole had become so unstable that the question arises whether the situation might not be described better in terms of cyclical loops than in terms of shifting TOCs. The years 1984 to 1988 saw a mild recovery in the Canadian economy, and the TOC shifted toward the origin. During the early 1980s the situation was marked by the appearance of very high unemployment, even in Ontario, and by sharp reductions in the rate of inflation throughout the country. In Ontario the TOC continued to shift to the east until 1983, when there was a sharp decline in the rate of inflation and a slight increase in unemployment. In 1984 there was clearly a shift toward the origin. In Alberta there appears to have been a shift to the north in 1972, and a second shift to the east in 1982, but no clear evidence of a shift toward the origin in 1984. Saskatchewan displays a pattern somewhat similar to Alberta's. Except for the 1970s and early 1980s, when the TOC clearly shifted three times to the right, Manitoba scarcely shows any pattern at all; although in 1984 the Manitoba TOC clearly shifted toward the origin, as the Canadian TOC did.

Altogether, there is enough evidence of differences in the behavior of unemployment and inflation among provinces to warrant an attempt at a differential fiscal policy. To be successful, such a policy would need to be fine-tuned and flexible. It would require detailed knowledge of the provincial economies, as well as the national economy, on the part of the designers of such a policy. It would also require collaboration and coordination of fiscal policy among all the provincial and the federal governments. The potential gains, however, in terms of simultaneous reductions in unemployment, inflation, and regional disparities, would make such an attempt well worthwhile.

Australia, Canada, and the United States

In my 1982 paper on "The Postwar Trade Cycle as Shifting Trade-Off Curves: The Case of Australia," I expressed doubts as to whether either trade-off curves or loops could be clearly distinguished for Australia. I presented a scatter diagram of discomfort points for Australia from 1950 to 1980, which I labelled figure 4 and a time series diagram for unemployment and inflation, which I labelled figure 3. With regard to figure 3, I wrote:

> The first thing that emerges strikingly from the juxtaposition of the two series is the obvious deterioration of the overall situation (increased discomfort) over the period as a whole. Both unemployment and inflation show a strong tendency to become worse, while fluctuations in both have become more violent.... Except for the interval from March 1961 to December 1974 might reasonably be described as one of full employment.... Thus it can be said that the "without inflation" objective was abandoned a full decade before the "full employment" objective. The second point that emerges from figure 3, although less clearly than the first one, is that there seem to have been three fairly distinct periods with regard to interactions of unemployment and inflation. Until September 1969 the two series tended, on the whole, to move in opposite directions, suggesting the presence of a trade-off between inflation and unemployment. Starting with December 1968 and ending with June 1977 they tended on balance to move together. The trade-off seems to have broken down; either the economic system was out of control, or the TOC was shifting up and out, or both. From September 1977 through to December 1979 the observations have once again tended to move in opposite directions, indicating that a new TOC may have been established, although at a much higher level of discomfort.

Turning to the scatter diagram, I remark that at first glance (as with most scatter diagrams of discomfort points), it looks like total chaos. But with a liberal use of envelopes it is possible to distinguish three possible TOCs, one for 1950 to 1954, a second for March 1956 through September 1970, and the third from December 1970 to June 1974. With regard to the first, I say: "Opinions are likely to differ as to whether or not all these points lie on the same TOC in the sense we are defining it." With regard to the second TOC, two questions arise: (1) is there reason to believe that, during this second interval the government could, in fact, have attained any of the points on the curve (or at least within the envelope) in any quarter, by money management alone? and (2) is there reason to think that in fact the TOC has shifted outward, in the sense that the points on the first curve, or within the first zone, were no longer available by money management alone? The third period is short, but provides a very good fit to a single curve. After 1974, the diagram becomes very disorderly and no trade-off curves can be distinguished. The three curves that were isolated are all extremely steep. Would it really have been possible in those years to get rid of inflation at so small a cost in increased unemployment?

As for loops, while it is possible to discern loops for some periods, essentially clockwise, moving northeast, and increasing in amplitude, there is enough irregularity in the movements to warrant doubts about such an interpretation of the data.

Canada probably provides the strongest case for interpreting postwar fluctuations as shifting TOCs and/or cyclical loops whether at the national or the regional level. No doubt the structural differences among Canadian regions is part of the explanation. Being a neighbor and the chief trading partner of the United States, and since the two countries are at approximately the same level of development, if postwar economic fluctuations in both countries take the form of shifting TOCs and/or cyclical loops, one would expect the patterns to be the same. But a glance at the diagrams of trade-off curves and loops for the two countries reveals that in fact they are very different. How is that possible?

I think the answer lies in the analysis above of "the machine, the structure and the game." These days, the machine—the basic mechanisms of the mixed market economy, interactions of multiplier and accelerator, and all the factors entering into pre-World War II theories of the business cycle—are less important in determining what happens in any country than either the structure or the game. Neighboring countries need not pursue identical government policies, the behavior of trade union leaders and employers' representatives may differ, expectations regarding any of these factors can vary a great deal. If two championship chess matches are played simultaneously in the United States and Canada, by equally famous and equally brilliant players, while the same fundamental rules and strategies may guide them, the results will still be unpredictable.

Reference

"Schools in Brief: A Cruise around the Phillips Curve." *The Economist* 19 (19 February 1994): 70–71.

10

The New Long-Term Unemployment

There is today widespread recognition, not only among economists but among politicians, bureaucrats, journalists, trade union leaders and employers, and even among members of the general public, that there is something unusual going on in the labor markets of the world. Just *how* unusual is one of the matters for debate. There has been an awareness of technological displacement and long-term unemployment ever since the "Luddite" machine smashers of the early industrial revolution in the nineteenth century. But the persistence of large-scale unemployment even in countries where the growth of GNP is respectably high, and particularly the growing numbers of long-term unemployed, concentrated among the young and the old, the unskilled and poorly educated, is a cause for concern the world over.

The reaction within the economics profession is varied. Those with the strongest faith in the market, and in the "natural" tendency toward "equilibrium" with something approaching full employment and stable prices—or at least a low and stable rate of inflation—are inclined to define the problem out of existence. They define the "natural rate of unemployment" as the level of unemployment consistent with stable prices; or at least the rate consistent with a "non-accelerating rate of inflation" (NAIRU). And since this natural rate of unemployment is the best achievable in this best of all possible worlds, there is nothing to be done about it. But why is the NAIRU so high, and increasing, in so many countries—not to speak of the zero-inflation natural rate of unemployment? Faced with this question, many members of this school maintain that most of the long-term unemployment is really voluntary anyhow. They then adduce *individual* reasons as to why the unemployment is "voluntary," because of various changes in the social structures of economically advanced countries. The growing number of two-employee families

243

makes it easier for one of them to spend more time in job search, to have a reserve price for their services that they regard as "normal," to be reluctant to move elsewhere in search of work so long as they share a home with a partner who is still working. Many countries have unemployment insurance schemes generous enough to permit such behavior.

Others blame the trade unions for the inflexibility of wages, and argue that when trade union members accept unemployment rather than accepting a wage cut, they are also going into "voluntary unemployment." Employers, by not lowering their "administered prices" enough to maintain their sales, also contribute to long-term unemployment. The combination of "sticky wages" and "sticky prices" guarantees the persistence of unemployment.

Those who feel that the rate of unemployment is inexcusably high, and that something must be done about it, point to the demoralization involved in youth unemployment, and the related high incidence of youth suicide; the loss of skill entailed in prolonged unemployment, so that the long-term unemployed become virtually unemployable; the impoverishment, broken homes, and shattered dreams that long-term unemployment entails. The "something" recommended is seldom Keynesian policy pure and simple; most economists recognize that increased government spending alone would not work, although various combinations of Keynesian deficit spending and other programs, including various form of retraining, might.

Technological Displacement and Long-Term Unemployment

As the 1990s flow on it becomes increasingly clear that the world is confronted by a problem that is in some respects as old as the industrial revolution of the late eighteenth and early nineteenth centuries; but in other respects is as new as the "New Industrial Revolution" of the late twentieth and twenty-first centuries. Technological displacement and consequent long-term unemployment may go back two centuries; but today's phenomenon has elements that are brand new, and hence is imperfectly understood. Let us begin by trying simply to itemize these differences between today's long-term unemployment and that of yesterday.

In the first place, yesterday's technological displacement was a matter of greatly increasing the output per man-hour through the introduction of machines, or more productive machines. Thus it was tools, or less productive machines, that were actually displaced, not labor. Provided output was increased at a sufficiently rapid rate, full employment could still be maintained. Today, however, the increasing use of robots for repetitive assembly operations displaces labor completely. Increased output increases the demand for high level managers, scientists, and technicians, but not for labor; even comparatively skilled tool users, or machine-tool users, are not needed for operations entrusted to robots.

In the second place, the core of the New Industrial Revolution is the information revolution; and the speed of that revolution is such that the education industry cannot keep up with it. The information industry, which has become the biggest employer in North America, requires specific knowledge and skills. Acquiring them means making the right decisions about choice of educational streams quite early in the education process; at least as early as undergraduate training. Too few students make the right decisions, and thus do not acquire the knowledge and skills that would qualify them for employment in the major growth industry of the industrialized (or post-industrial) world. The result is that unemployment in such countries (let us call them the OECD countries as a convenient shorthand, although the phenomenon is not confined to the OECD) is heavily concentrated among youth.

In the third place, the new long-term unemployment is subject to cumulative causation: long-term unemployment results in more and longer-term unemployment because of the loss of skills entailed in long-term unemployment. In the nineteenth and early twentieth centuries, the skills involved in handling the new machines were relatively simple, and could be retained for fairly long periods—like the ability to ride a bicycle. But today's long-term unemployed not only lose the skills they had when they lost their jobs, but they fail to acquire the new and higher skills they might have learned on-the-job. (At least that is how the employers look at it, which is enough to keep the long-term unemployed jobless.)

Fourth, there is today a much higher participation rate for women, including a good many wives. Women are more willing to accept part-time work at relatively low wage rates. This fact not only makes it more difficult for men to get full-time jobs at what they consider an appropriate wage; the fact that men have working wives and can collect unemployment insurance changes their job-search behavior. It becomes unnecessary for them to take any job offered at whatever wage or salary is attached to it.

Fifth, labor markets today are segmented. Trade union rules and other regulations reduce the mobility of labor, between industries or sectors, and between one place and another.

In these circumstances, some economists regard the increase in long-term unemployment and withdrawals from the labor force as inevitable. These tend to treat the nonaccelerating inflation rate of unemployment as the equilibrium or "natural" rate, the best that can be achieved. Others view the tendency for the NAIRU to increase in OECD countries with alarm, and seek ways of combatting it. In an article entitled "The Cursed Dole," the London *Economist* writes:

> Today's tolerance of unemployment would have astonished people in the 1960s. Despite having one worker in ten on the dole, many a government in Europe can now expect not only to survive, but to win re-election boasting of its economic prowess. Everywhere voters and politicians have grown used to unemployment that is indefensibly high. Yet there is no great mystery about why unemployment happens, or how to reduce it. The only mystery is why an avoidable misery has proved so politically tolerable. (*The Economist,* 28 September 1991, 16)

The NAIRU in many countries has become much too high, *The Economist* continues; it may be far above "full employment." The challenge to governments, therefore, is to bring the NAIRU down. This is mainly a matter of supply-side policies, not of Keynesian demand management. For one thing, unemployment benefits should stop after six months, as in Japan and the United States. "Open-ended entitlement to unemployment benefits is bad policy." At the same time, governments should help the unemployed to find work, as in Sweden, which has the best record on unemployment in Europe. Government should also provide high-quality training, and pay a wage subsidy to employers, again as in Sweden (and Australia); "and if all this fails, a guarantee of public employment." The net cost to the taxpayer, instead of paying unemployment benefits, "is small at worst"; and the system improves morale and preserves skills. The system also includes scrapping all minimum wage laws, and curbing trade union power.

What is the "New Industrial Revolution"?

J. Blazejczak seeks to evaluate the "long-term effects of technological trends on the structure of employment" (Blazejczak, 1991, 594). He first asks, "What is the new technology?" He answers this question as follows:

There is broad consensus on the following points:

* The most important basic technology at present is commonly believed to be microelectronics;

* Bio-technology will have an increasing impact, although it is expected to reach its full potential only after the year 2000, with advances in genetic engineering;

* A key role for innovative solutions is attributed to new materials, the features of which can be designed with respect to specific applications;

* Further technologies that are judged to be of basic importance are membrane and surface technology, lasers, new computers, software techniques and artificial intelligence.

He then adds an observation:

* "The economic importance of information will be further strengthened as new technologies allow better quality and more rapidly available information."

He then develops a three-dimensional technique for evaluation of new technology (sectors of the economy, fields of application of new technologies, and economic mechanisms) and applies it to changes in the sectoral structure of employment of Germany in the 1990s.

Richard Florida also tries to pin down the nature of the new technologies, but sums up the characteristics of all of them combined as "the new industrial revolution" (Florida, 1991, 559). He notes that there is still disagreement as to whether the next stage of capitalism will be characterized by "the rise of networks of small, flexible specialized firms" or "the return and continued dominance of big firms" (560). However, he agrees that "what is new about the new industrial revolution is to be found in the rise of the new technologies of the microelectronics revolution (e.g. semiconductors, computers, software) and the new organizational forms that have emerged to harness them" (560). In his view:

Moreover, at the core of the new industrial revolution lies a sweeping organizational transformation at the point of production. This reorganization I refer to as "the new shop floor," by which I mean the blurring of the distinctions between the factory floor and the R & D lab, as innovation becomes more continuous and the factory itself becomes a laboratory-like setting.... In doing so, the organizational forms of the new shop floor mobilize and harness the collective intelligence of the workers as a source of continuous improvement of products and processus, increased productivity and value creation (560–61).... In the new industrial revolution, knowledge itself is increasingly important to production and to the further advance of technology and the productive forces. (561)

He makes a distinction between old-fashioned Fordism, with its top-down management, and "Toyotism," with its emphasis on teamwork. He quotes Akio Morita, former chairman of Sony:

> A company will get nowhere if all the thinking is left to management. Everybody in the company must contribute, and for the lower level employees their contribution must be more than just manual labor. We insist that all of our employees contribute their minds. (567)

Florida maintains that the need to involve the knowledge and brains of the entire staff is well documented by what is currently happening in the field of manufacturing. "Although the microelectronic industry is still relatively young, it is the leading manufacturing employer in the U.S.A., with more than 2.6 million employees—three times as many workers as the automobile industry and nine times more than in steel fabrication" (565).

In conclusion, Florida is full of praise for the new emphasis on teamwork:

> The team is the mechanism through which workers are used to solve production problems and innovate. It becomes the source for adapting to production bottlenecks as workers use their own intelligence and knowledge to devise cooperative strategies to overcome such bottlenecks. The team is a simultaneous source of motivation, discipline and social control for team members, driving them to work harder and more collectively. (570)

Does "New Industrial Revolution" Mean Technological Unemployment?

This description of the new technology, or the new industrial revolution, sounds like a beautiful new world, where workers, owners, and managers work together as members of a single happy team, sharing in innovation and all contributing ideas, based on their intelligence and knowledge. It sounds like a prosperous, high-productivity world as well. There is just one drawback. To contribute their intelligence and knowledge, the workers must be intelligent and have some kind of advanced education or training. What happens to workers who have no such skills? The answer is simple: they join the swelling ranks of long-term unemployed, or drop out of the labor force altogether. It is true that some of the new technologies are so advanced that the machines do all the work on the basis of artificial intelligence, so that the "machine-minders" need not possess any advanced skills themselves. All the evidence suggests, however, that on balance, the new industrial revolution is leading to growing long-term unemployment or nonparticipation of unskilled or semi-skilled workers. Let us turn to a brief review of this evidence.

The Facts

Let us look at some known facts, then review some of the explanations of the facts, and finally explore some policy proposals. We shall begin with the article on "The Rise in Unemployment: A Multi-Country Study" by C. R. Bean, P. R. G. Layard, and S. J. Nickell (*Special Supplement on Unemployment* of *Economica,* 1986). The article is somewhat out of date, but has the advantage of covering all OECD countries, and being in a highly prestigious journal. It shows that nearly all the OECD countries have been suffering from increasing unemployment for some decades (table 10.1). The article begins with the following statement:

> One of the most remarkable features of recent economic history has been the remorseless rise in unemployment throughout the industrialized countries. However, while the trend to higher unemployment is universal, the experience of individual countries also differs widely. The increase is especially marked within the European Community, where unemployment rates rival those reached in the interwar years. By contrast, in the Scandinavian countries and Japan unemployment is lower and has risen very much less. Experience in the United States lies somewhere between these extremes, and in the last few years unemployment there has fallen sharply.

Contrary to a frequently expressed opinion, they say, the rise in unemployment is not due to a growth of the labor force, with the supply of jobs lagging behind the demand for them. Despite the increased female participation in the labor force in recent years, the labor force as a whole has not been increasing markedly faster than in the 1960s.

The United States

In a long paper prepared for the Brookings Institution, Chinhui Juhn, Kevin M. Murphy, and Robert H. Topel ask "Why has the natural rate of unemployment increased over time?" (Juhn, Murphy, and Topel, 1991). It is a study of "the evolution of male unemployment and nonparticipation in the U.S. labor force since 1967" (75). They found that "both

TABLE 10.1
OECD Standardized Unemployment Rates, 1956–1984
(period average)

	1956–66 (%)	1967–74 (%)	1975–79 (%)	1980–83 (%)	1984 (%)
Australia	2.2	2.1	5.5	7.2	8.9
Austria	2.4	1.5	1.9	3.0	3.8
Belgium	2.6	2.6	7.0	11.5	14.0
Canada	4.9	5.2	7.5	9.4	11.2
Denmark	2.3	1.3	6.5	9.9	n.a.
Finland	1.6	2.5	5.1	5.4	6.1
France	1.5	2.5	4.9	7.5	9.7
Germany	1.4	1.1	3.5	5.4	8.6
Ireland	5.4	5.6	7.0	9.7	n.a.
Italy	6.5	5.6	6.8	8.6	10.2
Japan	1.7	1.3	2.0	2.3	2.7
Netherlands	1.2	2.2	5.3	9.9	14.0
New Zealand	0.1	0.3	1.0	3.6	n.a.
Norway	2.3	1.7	1.9	2.4	3.0
Spain	2.1	2.7	5.8	14.6	20.1
Sweden	1.7	2.2	1.9	2.8	3.1
Switzerland	0.1	0.0	0.4	0.5	1.2
United Kingdom	2.5	3.4	5.8	10.9	13.2
United States	5.0	4.6	6.9	8.4	7.4

Source: All except Denmark, Ireland, and New Zealand OECD *Economic Outlook*; Denmark, Ireland, and New Zealand, Grubb, 1984.

nonparticipation and unemployment contribute to a strong *secular increase* of nonworking time" (77). Most of the secular increase in nonwork is accounted for by "an increased incidence of long jobless spells. Overall, nearly 80 percent of the long-term increase in nonwork is accounted for by spells lasting more than six months" (77). "Based on observable indicators of skill like experience and education, it is well-known that unemployment is greater among less skilled individuals" (79). Curiously, they found that rising unemployment has been associated with a long-term *decline* in sectoral mobility. One would think that rising unemployment would result in increased demand for retraining, and consequent increased sectoral mobility, a point to which we shall return below. Jobless men, especially those with long spells of nonwork, are much more likely to be single, and to rely on extended family for support. The number of jobless men has increased, and the wages they can command has fallen; but the real household income of jobless men has been more or less constant; since household incomes of working men has risen, the *relative* welfare of the jobless has declined.

The incidence of short spells of unemployment (less than fifteen weeks) has remained nearly constant through time, but the higher incidence of long spells (more than six months) accounts for about two-thirds of the total increase in unemployment. The rising incidence of very long spells of unemployment also accounts for the rising rate of nonparticipation.

Nearly all of the long-term increase in the two jobless rates falls on less skilled individuals. For the least skilled workers, the jobless rate rose by nearly 16 percentage points between 1967 to 1969, and 1987 to 1989. The demand for labor has shifted toward more skilled workers. When unemployment rises, it rises more for unskilled workers. Inflexible wages are of little importance in the long run. Workers in the lowest decile of the wage distribution experienced a long-run rise in unemployment more than three times the average for the sample as a whole. Not only are nonworkers less skilled, but they are in categories in which wages have fallen over time. Employment and wages in different regions of the U.S. tend to rise or fall together.

In conclusion, the authors of this paper make the following points:

> We have shown that virtually all of the trend toward rising male joblessness in the United States is accounted for by the rising unemployment and nonparticipation of less skilled persons. For this group, increases in unemployed weeks are mainly attributable to an increase in the incidence of very long spells of nonwork.... In many interpretations, the natural rate of unemployment is a fixed number toward which the labor market tends to gravitate. Our results challenge that view.... A long-run decline in the demand for various types of labor may increase the natural rate because the rewards to employment decline for marginal workers. Our results also imply that current unemployment rates have a far different meaning than comparable rates in the not-too-distant past.

> The composition of unemployment has shifted toward less skilled workers, who suffer comparatively long spells of joblessness and whose rewards from work have fallen sharply. In both respects, they resemble the growing class of men who have simply withdrawn from the labor market.... Our evidence shows that many workers with very low skills have either left the labor force completely or spent long periods without jobs. If joblessness itself generates declining market skills,

either through depreciation of human capital or reduced on-the-job training, then the effects of reduced demand on work incentives will be reinforced. As a result, even an increase in demand for less skilled workers could not quickly reproduce the low jobless rates of the past. Past patterns of demand have altered the stock of human capital, rising future natural rates of unemployment and nonparticipation. (124–26)

The United Kingdom

Peter E. Hart, basing himself primarily on United Kingdom experience, maintains that there are several types of "structural" unemployment (Hart, 1990). He begins his article with this warning:

> World markets are changing rapidly. If a small open economy such as the United Kingdom does not adapt quickly enough to these changes, its firms will become uncompetitive and, if institutional rigidities prevent firms from adjusting, unemployment will persist. Such unemployment is said to be structural. It reflects a chronic disequilibrium in labor markets. (213)

Structural unemployment is aggravated by segmentation, which makes sector-to-sector movement difficult, so that a general expansion of demand leads to increases in wages, prices, and imports rather than increased employment. Rigid policies to prevent inflation in some sectors only reduce output and employment in others. There are substantial differences in regional Philips (or trade-off) curves. Unemployment in some regions will reduce the rate of increase in earnings there without diminishing the inflationary tendencies in other regions. Thus "wage adjustment and labor mobility cannot be relied upon to correct regional imbalances in employment opportunities" (215).

As early as 1930, John Maynard Keynes recognized the existence of technological unemployment, but thought it would be temporary. The microelectronics revolution, however, by reducing the demand for unskilled and semiskilled labor, has made technological unemployment chronic. There is a mismatch of skills and available jobs, which could be removed by adequate training and retraining programs, but "our training programs are *not* adequate and indeed have not been for a long time, and the result is that the necessary adjustments do not take place and the disequilibrium in the labor market persists" (217). There is also a geographic mismatch. The variation in unemployment by regions increased from 0.8 to 2.9 percent in 1960 and 5.2 to 11.2 percent in 1988.

Three demographic shifts contribute to structural unemployment; increased female labor force participation; a growing proportion of young people; and an increasing number of elderly people. Women search less intensively for jobs; youths have higher turnover and take longer to find new jobs; elderly people have difficulty in acquiring new skills.

Employers may respond to a need for extra labor by hiring part-time workers who do not qualify for employers' pension contributions or holiday payments. Many of the long-term unemployed are "unemployable" as a result of chronic illness or disability, for which compensation is more generous than it was some decades ago. Such structural factors in current unemployment are important, "because they obstruct both neo-classical and Keynesian attempts to decrease aggregate unemployment" (226–27).

Demand for Retraining

An obvious solution for unemployment among the unskilled and semi-skilled is retraining. An econometric study of the demand for retraining in the United Kingdom, however, contains little good news (Allen, McCormick, O'Brian, 1991). Their findings were as follows:

> We have found that the demand for retraining amongst unemployed workers in a depressed region of the United Kingdom follows a pattern which is consistent with our framework. The probability of application: declines with age after 27 years; is greater where expected unemployment is greatest, namely, those leaving industries in long-term decline (engineering and shipbuilding) and least in industries in which unemployment is an equilibrium feature of the cyclical pattern of jobs in the industry (construction) in which turnover is high (services); is greater amongst those who are most distressed in unemployment in comparison with their last job; is less amongst union members; is greatest for workers with formal qualifications (O/A levels) and least amongst those with vocational training (City and Guilds/CSE/Apprenticeship). Thus it would appear that mid-career flexibility may be enhanced by formal qualifications and inhibited by earlier vocational training. (201)

In other words, it appears that retraining is unlikely to be sought by two categories of workers for whom the incidence of unemployment is particularly high; young school drop-outs with neither formal qualifications nor experience, and older workers without much by way of formal education or higher-level skills.

The Australian Unemployment Picture

In December 1993, the Commonwealth Government of Australia published a report of the Committee on Employment Opportunities, entitled *Restoring Full Employment: A Discussion Paper*. It contains an opening chapter providing a general survey of labor market trends. The picture given by this chapter is similar to the unemployment picture in Canada, the United Kingdom, and the United States—and indeed, the picture in all OECD countries. During the 1980s Australia enjoyed the most rapid job growth of all OECD countries; but in the 1990s even strong output and employment growth failed to bring unemployment back to the levels achieved prior to the 1982–83 recession. Since 1983 Australian unemployment has been above the OECD average in every year but 1989, when it was about equal to the average. As in other countries, particularly disturbing was the growth of long-term unemployment:

> Since 1990, the number of long-term unemployed people (those unemployed for one year or more) have risen to unprecedented levels. By August 1993 over 35 percent (nearly 340,000) of those unemployed had been unemployed for two or more years. (18)

The highest unemployment rate was in the fifteen to nineteen age group, and the numbers of unemployed were greatest in the twenty to twenty-four group. This latter group also had the highest rate of long-term unemployment. As in other countries, the rate of unemployment varied significantly with educational attainment. Only 6.2 percent of those with university degrees were unemployed, while 14.8 percent of those who failed to reach the highest level of secondary school were unemployed. Long-term unemployment also tended to diminish with the level of education attained. Over the past twenty years the dominant factor in growth of the labor force has been increased participation of women, particularly married women. This trend has been accompanied by a large increase in the number of casual and part-time jobs. This experience is shared by all OECD countries. In this connection, the report observes:

> This shift, however, does not appear to be directly associated with high unemployment for men. Countries with the highest participation rates for women have been those with the lowest rates of unemployment for men. (39)

The Australian government recognizes that recovery from recession and accelerated economic growth may encourage enterprises to install new technologies, displacing lower-skilled workers. It may also encourage some drop-outs to return to the labor force. Thus the decline in unemployment may not match the increase in employment. One solution is to make sure that all members of the labor force have knowledge and skills that make them employable with the new technologies:

> The Commonwealth, State and Territory governments have sought to reform Australia's training system with an important objective being to improve our international competitiveness. Government initiatives include: more emphasis on making training relevant to the needs of industry; a greater focus on the outcomes of training—what an individual can do, rather than how long he or she has spent in the system...(and) improved access to training for disadvantaged groups. (76)

Canada

In September 1993, Statistics Canada published in the *Canadian Economic Observer* an article by Miles Corak on long-term unemployment in Canada (Corak, 1993, 1–20). It begins with the startling statement: "Most (65 percent) of an increase in the unemployment rate reflects a longer duration of unemployment, not an increased number of newly unemployed" (1). Corak proceeds to present a detailed comparison of the effects on unemployment of the recession of 1990 to 1993 with that of the recession of 1981 to 1982. Although the unemployment rate in the 1981–82 recession was higher, he says, the average duration of terminated unemployment was the same, about 19.6 weeks. In the more recent recession the short-term unemployed (less than three months) terminated their unemployment sooner than they did a decade earlier; but the long-term unemployed stayed that way longer than they did in the earlier recession. Older people in particular remained unemployed for longer spells than in 1981 to 1982 (26.2 weeks compared with 22.8 weeks during 1983); while younger persons were unemployed for shorter periods (14.8 weeks versus 17.7 weeks).

The coexistence of economic growth and high unemployment is not unusual in Canada, Corak points out. The unemployment rate rises sharply during the onset of recession, but declines slowly during recovery. In the 1981–82 recession the unemployment rate rose sharply from 7.5 to 11 percent within one year, and took seven years of strong growth to return to its pre-recession level. "Increases in the incidence of unemployment are responsible for the sharp rise of the unemployment rate during the onset of recessions, while increases in duration are largely responsible for the very slow decline during recovery and expansion even as the inflow of newly unemployed starts to tail off" (2). Comparing the two recessions, Corak maintains, shows that "the unemployed faced very different conditions in the two recessions depending on how long they had been unemployed. One of the major findings is that the recession of the early 1990s had a much deeper impact on specific groups in the economy, who are experiencing longer spells of unemployment than in 1981–82" (2). To bring out these differences Corak uses as a measure of duration of unemployment "the average *completed* duration of unemployment, for a cohort of individuals who begin their spell of unemployment at the same time," as distinct from the Labor Force Survey measure of the average length of time that the current unemployed happen to have been without work. The two measures give quite a different picture of the behavior of unemployment during recession and recovery. It is of interest to note that Corak says of his measure of the length of time between the beginning and termination of unemployment, "There is a loop in the data, but it is a very muted clockwise movement" (5).

Corak also presents a table showing the "exit rates of leaving unemployment" for selected years, according to the duration of unemployment, for the two cycles. The table shows that a person becoming unemployed in 1992 had a 33 percent probability of regaining employment in less than a month; a person who had been unemployed for at least a month had a 27 percent probability of regaining a job in less than two months, and so forth. During 1992, as in most years, the chances of getting a job back fell with each month of unemployment. Comparing 1992 with 1983, we see that the chances of being reemployed were better for the short-term unemployed in 1992, but lower for the long-term unemployed. The figures also indicate a tendency for the ratio of long-term to total unemployment to increase.

Corak then makes a gesture toward taking account of regional differences in cyclical behavior by comparing Ontario with the "rest of Canada." He reports:

The unemployed in Ontario fared worse in 1992 than in 1983 as did those aged 45 and older. Job leavers, those permanently laid off in regions outside Ontario, and the young actually experienced unemployment spells that were 2 to 3 weeks shorter during 1992 than during 1983. The Ontario economy fell into recession earlier and more steeply than the rest of the country. The extent of the change in the Ontario labor market stands out.

The overall average of unemployment increased by nine weeks, and by more than 13 weeks for those permanently laid-off...the average duration for those permanently laid off in Ontario increased by 62 percent between 1981 and 1982 but soared 107 percent in the latest downturn. In the rest of Canada, the average duration for those permanently laid off increased by 36 percent between 1981 and 1982, but by only 25 percent during the latest recession before declining in 1992.... In other words, if 100 individuals had been laid off in Ontario in 1989, about 41 would have left unemployment within one month, but in 1992 only 17 would have done so. (6–9)

Explanations

The main facts seem reasonably clear: all over the industrialized world there is a medium- to long-run tendency for unemployment to increase; and the people suffering from unemployment are either young, or beyond middle age and relatively uneducated and lacking in skills, especially the skills demanded by the "new industrial revolution." What are the explanations offered by economists for these facts?

Let us return first to Bean, Layard, and Nickell. They conducted a whole array of empirical tests, but they really haven't much to say by way of conclusion. They say that trade union power is difficult to measure, because the unionization rate "may mean different things in different countries," but nevertheless, "the results are not very supportive of the notion that unions *per se* inhibit the efficient functioning of the labor market." As to whether the unemployment results from demand or supply factors, "it is six of one and half a dozen of the other." The analysis of international differences in labor market performance "is perforce very crude." In order to explain international differences in unemployment, "one also needs to look at both the external shocks impinging on the economy and the stance of government policy" (Bean, Layard, and Nickell, 1986, S19–S20).

John, Murphy, and Topel really have no general theoretical explanation of increasing unemployment in the United States. Their paper is a detailed description of the nature of the unemployment problem in that country. They provide some clues as to what the causes are not: the growing unemployment is not due to inflexible wages (102). They make the interesting observation that sectoral mobility of labor has actually declined during the period of increasing unemployment (105). They make a guess that "since female labor market participation and earnings rose dramatically during the period we study, it is plausible that male labor

supply could fall because of optimizing behavior within households"—
in other words, because his female partner is working, the male partner
who loses his job does not search very hard for other work (107). Single
men who lose their jobs have not become markedly poorer, which suggests that they have other sources of income, such as families who will
take care of them (109). They also point to marked contrasts among
regions in the United States in experience regarding wage movements
and employment and unemployment (115). There is a suggestion that a
major reason for rising unemployment is the failure of increasing numbers in the labor force to match their education and training to the increasing demand for new types and higher levels of skills. "As a result,
even an increase in the demand for less skilled workers could not quickly
reproduce the low jobless rates of the past" (135–36). In short, at least
some of the unemployment is in *some* sense "voluntary."

Unemployment Causes Unemployment

There is general agreement that long-term unemployment causes more
long-term unemployment. Christopher Pissarides, for example, maintains
that "if unemployed workers lose some of their skills during unemployment, aggregate employment can exhibit persistence that outlasts both
the duration of the shock that moves it from the steady state and, more
importantly, the maximum duration of unemployment" (Pissarides, 1992,
1371). In his terminology, the market becomes "thin," because job seekers as a whole have "less human capital" than before. The thin market
leads to more job shortages, which perpetuates the thinness. The effects
of the shock persist, and the economy can get stuck at a low-level equilibrium. Employers may discriminate against the long-term unemployed,
preferring a short-term unemployed worker with more recent work experience. The intensity of search for a new job may also fall with the duration of unemployment. Reduced intensity of search reduces the matching
rate of vacancies and job seekers.

Richard Jackman and Richard Layard reach the same general conclusion based on British experience between 1969 and 1988. They compare
the rates of exit from unemployment with rates of new entry into unemployment for the period. They find that during the period as a whole the
overall exit rate fell to 17 percent of its original level, while the exit rate
of new entrants fell to 42 percent of its former level; the ratio of the two

exit rates combined fell by 60 percent. These results, they maintain, are inconsistent with the hypothesis that the short-term and long-term unemployed consisted of two different groups, so that the long-term and short-term had quite different probabilities of being rehired at the moment of losing their jobs; and the results confirm the hypothesis that long duration unemployment reduces the individual's probability of being rehired. They "explain the overall fall in the UK exit rates from unemployment by the combined effect of (1) a fall in the ratio of vacancies to unemployed and (2) a higher proportion of the unemployed being long-term unemployed, and hence being demoralized and stigmatized in the eyes of employers" (103).

Dr. Helen Hughes, Director of the Full Employment Project at the University of Melbourne's Institute of Public Affairs, goes so far as to maintain that long-term unemployment is becoming "hereditary."

> Unemployment has become hereditary. The proportion of young people not working in households where one or more parents are unemployed is double that of households with employed parents. Some 700,000 children under 15 (in Australia) are affected by parents' unemployment. (Hughes, 1994, 9)

She also makes the point that nearly 60 percent of the single women heads of households are unemployed.

Hysterisis?

One of the most thorough and most interesting efforts to expound the "unemployment causes unemployment" thesis is a long article (sixty-three pages) by Oliver J. Blanchard and Lawrence H. Summers, entitled "Hysterisis and the European Unemployment Problem," published by the National Bureau of Economic Research in their *Macroeconomics Annual* for 1986. The increase in unemployment in Europe since 1970, they maintain at the outset, cannot be explained by either conventional classical or by Keynesian macroeconomic theories. It also challenges the premise that there exists some "natural" or nonaccelerating rate of inflation rate of unemployment toward which economies tend to gravitate, and where they would be in "equilibrium." "The European experience compels consideration of alternative theories of 'hysterisis' which contemplate the possibility that increases in unemployment have a direct impact on the 'natural' rate of unemployment.... We are particularly interested in the current European situation; we seek explanations for the pattern of high and rising unemployment that has prevailed in Europe for the past decade.... The central hypothesis we put forward is that hysteresis resulting from membership considerations plays an important role in explaining the current European depression in particular and persistent high unemployment in general. The essential point is that there is a fundamental asymmetry in the wage-setting process between insiders who are employed and outsiders who want jobs.... Shocks that lead to reduced employment change the number of insiders and thereby change the equilibrium wage rate, giving rise to hysteresis. Membership considerations can therefore explain the general tendency of the equilibrium unemployment rate to follow the actual unemployment rate" (15–16).

In the course of their analysis they find many similarities between the current European depression and the Great Depression of the 1930s in the United States. Many people now hold the view that unemployment in Europe will never again fall to pre-depression levels. "These pessimistic views are premised on the conviction that structural problems are central to high unemployment in Europe, and that causes of persistent high unemployment go beyond a sequence of adverse shocks." Similarly, in the United States around 1937 many people had given up hope that unemployment would ever return to pre-crash levels. "Yet the American depression of the 1930s was ended by the expansion of aggregate demand associated with rearmament. Unemployment recovered to pre-depression levels" (65). "The finding of so many parallels between the current European depression and the American depression suggests to us that hysteresis in Europe may be more the result of a long sequence of adverse shocks than the result of structural problems. Perhaps most telling is the observation that the apparent natural rate of unemployment drifted upwards following the actual unemployment rate during the American depression just as it has in Europe" (71).

From the historical record, the authors conclude, the "membership effects" become important in bad times, "and are not crucially dependent on presence of unions." By way of a general conclusion, the authors state, "Our argument is that Europe has experienced a sequence of adverse shocks...each of which had a fairly permanent effect on the level of employment.... Unlike simple Keynesian explanations for the European depression which stress only aggregate demand, our theory explains increases in the apparent natural rate of unemployment" (72). This conclusion, they say, "has a number of fairly direct policy conclusions." One is that efforts should be made to "enfranchise" as many workers as possible, through work sharing and other devices. If more workers share in wage-setting decisions, "they may lead to reduced wage demands and increased employment" (72).

The big question is, however, whether to adopt policies to increase aggregate demand and reduce unemployment, running the risk of aggravating inflation. The authors ask in their final paragraph, "Do the many parallels between the American and European depressions imply that a major expansion in aggregate demand would create the same miracles in Europe as it did in the United States?" They answer their own question with a cautious "yes." Even if unemployment resulted initially from adverse shocks, expansionary policies that succeeded in raising employment will yield permanent benefits. The apparent increase in the natural rate of unemployment does not mean that demand expansion cannot possibly succeed. Much depends on achieving a surprise that suddenly reverses expectations. Here they enter a *caveat*: "The likelihood of achieving a surprise may well have been much greater in the United States after a decade of major deflation than it is in Europe today after a decade of stagflation." However, they end their paper on a note of optimism:

> On the other hand, the very political infeasibility of expansion in Europe suggests its possible efficacy. Certainly the protracted high unemployment caused by the deflationary policies of the recent past stands as a testament to the potent effects of macroeconomic policies (73).

Technological Displacement?

There are any number of economists who are willing to explain the rise of long-term unemployment by the speed and nature of "The New Industrial Revolution," which introduces shocks too severe for our lumbering mixed economies to handle smoothly. Peter Senker's article "raises some concerns about the implications of 'Capitalism Triumphant' for the worldwide distribution of products, services, and work" (Senker, 1991, 351).

In an article in the September 1990 issue of *Futures,* Egon Matzner, Ronald Schettkat, and Michael Wagner report on a major study of technological displacement in Germany, known as "The Meta Study." This study, they say, "applied various methods to investigating the direct and indirect employment effects of new technologies at different levels of the economy. The methods employed by the participating research institutes...ranged from detailed enterprise-level case-studies to use of highly aggregated economic macro models" (Matzner, Schettket, and Wagner, 1990, 687). For example, the team used "dynamic input-output analysis" to determine the impact of industrial robots on employment. They found that in the first two years the use of robots in the production process resulted in a slight net gain in employment because the production of robots precedes their use in the production process. However, in the longer run, employment is reduced "semi-permanently"; the production of new robots fails to keep pace with labor displaced by their use in the production process. The spread of the new technology changes skill requirements. Use of a dynamic econometric model showed that the overall effect of recent technical progress in Germany is labor saving. Older workers are particularly affected by changing skill requirements; the skills they learned when making their choice of trade or profession are now outdated. Younger workers exhibit a skill profile that more closely resembles modern requirements. The persistent high level of "structural unemployment" in Germany results from the time between changes in skill requirements and the adjustment made by workers. The risk of becoming unemployed is not higher in the highly innovative branches of industry than in less innovative branches. Their general conclusion is that "it is only under favorable conditions that an increase in innovative activity leads to higher employment than the status quo trend. However, even with pessimistic assumptions, an increase in innovative activity would appear to be more advantageous in terms of employment than a decrease. In addition, a higher level of innovative activity enables a higher level of income generation" (706).

Structural Slumps

We cannot close this chapter on the literature concerning long-term unemployment without some reference to Edmund Phelps's latest book, *Structural Slumps: The Modern Equilibrium Theory of Unemployment, Interest, and Assets* (Phelps, 1994). True, the book analyses the big swings in unemployment, and so aims at explaining prolonged booms as well as prolonged slumps; but while it analyses the boom from 1950 to the early 1970s, it also analyses the slump from the early 1970s to the early nineties, and so offers some explanation of the long-term unemployment that emerged during the latter period.

Phelps begins his introduction to the volume with the following statement:

> The aim of this book is to uncover the nonmonetary mechanisms through which various nonmonetary forces are capable of propagating slumps and booms in the contemporary world economy. The approach is to synthesize out of some modern as well as neo-classical elements a theory which could be called *structural unemployment* and its path through time.... The theoretical sections are built around the *equilibrium* case in the expectational sense of the term: the case of correct expectations about the course of the economy. The product is therefore a theory of the equilibrium path of unemployment. (Phelps, 1994, 1)

In contrast to earlier theories, which treated the natural rate of unemployment as a constant, or as a parameter that moves exogenously with time, Phelps defines the natural rate as the current equilibrium steady-state rate of unemployment; the natural rate becomes endogenous, a variable of the system, "the moving target that the equilibrium constantly pursues" (1). The theory is elaborated in a series of mathematical models of such things as the "labor-market equilibrium locus," the "product-market equilibrium locus," "capital market equilibrium, neoclassical and modern," " a turnover-training model," " a customer-market model," "a two-sector fixed-investment model," "wages, wealth, and interest in shirking decisions," and so on. The analysis is closely reasoned, difficult, and virtually impossible to summarize. What we can do is to summarize its main findings and conclusions, and present its policy recommendations concerning long-term unemployment.

Chapter 6, "Key Factors in the Structuralist Theory of Unemployment Fluctuations," presents a useful summary of the argument up to that point in the volume. Phelps there states that among the causal factors—the shocks—"there are two at least two factors—real interest rates (external or induced internally by public or time-preference shocks) and transfer payments—that have a central role in the structuralist theory and yet play little or no part in any of the principal theories" (59). Productivity shocks and supply shocks "constitute an important category of factors in virtually every macroeconomic school of thought" (59). In the structuralist models permanent productivity shocks are capable of having effects on the equilibrium path of employment, positive or negative depending on whether the shock reduces or raises costs. But "a shock seldom disturbs just one equation of the model; the above cost shocks also operate to shift the equilibrium labor—market locus—the wage curve—by impacting on the nonwage income of workers which works in the opposite direction. Furthermore, in general a shock will disturb the path of the interest rate, the shadow price of the assets, and thus the derived labor demand" (60).

External interest rate shocks, caused by "a surge of investment opportunities external to the country" (61) will contract the demand for labor. The welfare state, expressed in the form of transfer payments, will (probably) "have the side-effect of decreasing employment." Whether or not protective tariffs expand or contract domestic employment is a complicated question for structuralist theory; the answer is "it depends." The same is true of an increase in time preference. An increase in public debt "seems to be contractionary for the employment rate" (65). As for public expenditures, if these consist of purchases of output that would otherwise have gone to consumers, there will be "an abrupt increase of interest rates and a drop of asset prices," with unfavorable effects on employment. But if the government purchases capital goods it will drive up their prices and stimulate the derived demand for labor.

From this brief summary, we can see that Phelps's "structuralist theory" takes account of many factors not usually considered in Keynesian or neo-classical theory. For example, the high cost to employers of workers "quitting" or "shirking," and the effects of "incentive wages" to offset these costs on the equilibrium employment path, do not normally enter into either the standard Keynesian or neo-classical models.

In chapter 17, Phelps tests his theory econometrically, using seventeen OECD countries as his sample. He is quite pleased with his results. At the end of the chapter he says, "Clearly it would be impossible to look back on the foregoing results without some degree of satisfaction. What is most remarkable about these findings is that there were no fundamental failures of the theory, only a handful of mild surprises that could readily be understood in terms of the theory and hence did not require a revamping of the theory." Among the most clear-cut and significant results are the following:

1. World wealth (capital plus public debt) drives up the world real interest rate while the world capital stock drives it down. In the national-unemployment-rate equations the world real rate of interest is a key variable.
2. The real price of oil is also statistically significant.

3. An increase in national consumers' wealth is expansionary, "though only mildly so." (318)

4. The national tax rate "was found to be importantly contractionary." (318)

5. The increase in world public debt has a large effect on world employment (negative, instead of positive, as one might expect from simple Keynesian theory).

From the standpoint of explaining the new world long-term unemployment, the most interesting chapter in the book is number 18, "A Concise Nonmonetary History of Postwar Economic Activity," in which Phelps endeavors to explain the wide swings in world unemployment since 1950 in terms of his theory. He considers the period of 1945 to 1950 to be one of reconstruction, and so begins his story with 1950 to the late 1950s. He asks first of all, since the world public debt was at an all-time high and the world capital stock at an all-time low, why was the world unemployment not extraordinarily high at the beginning of this period? He argues that there were counterbalancing factors. The levels of public expenditures were low, and the rates of interest and taxation were also low. He suggests that fighting the Korean War with so little wage-price inflation, "the expenditures of the U.S. government in prosecuting the Korean War served to contract the equilibrium unemployment rate itself" (338).

The period from the end of the 1950s to the early 1970s Phelps calls "A Golden Age," and states that "our equilibrium theory 'predicts' almost no change in the world employment rate during this period" (338). The continuing decline of the world public debt "continued to operate toward lowering the world unemployment rate. The continuing but weaker growth of the world capital stock relative to the augmented labor force operated in the same direction, but weakly. In this period the declining real price of oil is another force tending to reduce unemployment. But the steeper rises of government purchases and tax rates now operate in the opposing direction, in contrast to the first period" (339–40).

The next period includes the oil shock, from the mid-1970s to the early 1980s, and also marks the rise of long-term unemployment. According to Phelps, "the oil-price increase of 1973 was the most important shock for the equilibrium path of the world unemployment rate over this period" (342). But the marked reversal of the path of world public debt was "half as important as the first oil shock" (342). Another neglected factor, according to Phelps, was the slowdown in the pace of world capital accumulation in relation to the augmented world labor force.

During the 1980s the growth of world public debt accelerated. World public expenditures also increased, and world interest rates soared. These shocks "gave impetus to a major increase of the equilibrium unemployment rate" (342). Rising income-tax rates also made a contribution to rising unemployment rates.

The early 1990s brought plenty of shocks, but additional data are needed for a quantitative analysis of their impact on unemployment. The Berlin Wall was torn down, Germany was reunited, the Soviet Union broke up, the cold war came to an end. China and East and Southeast Asia continued their rapid growth. Phelps ventures only "a few surmises." The decline in the supply of savings and major rise in the major rise in investment demand in the united Germany, combined with the appearance of other new bidders for the world supply of savings, explains why real interest rates have remained high. Public debt has continued to climb, and capital stock outside the "new areas" has continued to slow down relative to the augmented labor force. In the OECD countries fiscal policy has also been contractionary. Phelps states that "it is not surprising that the world unemployment rate, which had been tending downward in the late 1980s, has resumed its climb" (347).

Phelps's final chapter, "Economic Policies to Which the Structuralist Theory Might Lead," is a bit disappointing. One senses that the author was reluctant to write it. He says that readers of his volume would be "consternated if this volume remained silent on the policy question. The issue has to be joined. Yet numerous pitfalls await any attempt at formulating appropriate policy toward structural fluctuations in the global economy. What follows is an informal reconnaissance of the terrain, not the construction of a formal model, which can come only at a later stage.... The purpose of this final chapter then is to begin the necessary discussion" (359).

To "begin the discussion," Phelps first makes the point that if the cause of high unemployment is "structural," that doesn't mean that the government can do nothing about it. The government is *part of the structure*. Large shocks require correspondingly large policy responses. Structuralism does not provide grounds for passivity. A cut in direct tax rates while government spending is held constant is expansionary, as Keynes said. But global balanced budget cutbacks seem also to be expansionary, contrary to the Keynesian view. Employment subsidies, "a non-Keynesian sort of measure, also warrants a closer look." In the Keynesian view, every dollar of additional spending is expansionary; but in the structuralist perspective, some expenditures would have far less impact on derived demand for labor than others. In approving deficit spending, the Keynesian school unleashed a perplexing time-inconsistency problem. A temporary fiscal stimulus may do more harm than good if it does not vanish or decline enough as a slump comes to an end. From a structuralist perspective the main trouble with Keynesian policies is that unilateral actions by a large country, or a collection of smaller ones, may have adverse repercussions on the rest of the world. Yet one can only be puzzled by the fact that in the 1990s several countries have responded to contractionary forces by measures to *cut* their deficits. "It would be prudent to postpone these measures in the hope that the external climate improves" (365).

A more reliable policy is the application of employment subsidies. "The suggestion here is that, with a system of employment subsidies in place, it would be natural to add a cyclical supplement that varies with disturbances to macroequilibrium in an employment-stabilizing direction" (366).

At the end of the chapter Phelps discusses several multilateral schemes for "coordination of the *equilibrium* (or *natural*) levels of employment and other *real* indicators in the global economy." He insists, however, that "in bringing up these schemes I do not mean to be making a proposal.... The sketches are ideas for discussion and, if not rejected, for modification, or, if rejected, for use as stepping stones to better ideas" (370).

It is easy to see why Edmond Phelps felt reluctant to discuss policy issues. His theory is so broad in scope, and embraces behavioral assumptions that include many different actors, which may vary from country to country, and from time to time in a single country, that it is hard to be *sure* of the effects of a particular policy in a particular country at a particular time. The final chapter reminds one inevitably of the story of the government that advertised for a one-armed economic advisor, because they were sick and tired of advisors who said "on the one hand this but on the other hand that." In the section entitled "Commentary" which ends the book, however, Phelps does allow himself two definite statements:

> What is paramount in any case is that across-the-board *increases* in government spending, and especially balanced budget increases, are *not* to be used since they have the beggar-thy-neighbour effect of lowering employment while raising it at home—the latter, generally speaking, by a lesser amount than the former—so that

if all countries engage in that policy response to low employment, the consequence is a further general reduction of employment rates....

[W]e may at last be in sight of the day when public policy will shift from social insurance programs that have been the historical mission of the welfare state to programs for economic justice. Unemployment insurance and all the other social-insurance programs that tax away wage income and that undermine work as a way of providing self-esteem will be dismantled and the savings put into raising the wage rated paid for the contributions to society of the less advantaged members of the labor force. (373–74)

Despite the paucity of concrete recommendations of policy measures for reducing unemployment, the book, and especially chapter 18, goes a long way toward explaining the growth of long-term unemployment since the early 1970s, and toward explaining the risks attached to simplistic Keynesian policies to reduce it.

Conclusion

It can hardly be said that there is unanimous agreement among economists regarding long-term unemployment; what it is; how new and different it is; what causes it; and what—if anything—should be done about it. In part, the disagreement among members of the economics profession regarding long-term unemployment can be traced back to fundamental ideological differences, in degree of faith in the market economy on the one hand and in the managed economy on the other; or to the degree of fear of "market failure" and of "government failure." But even if this ideological difference were to disappear altogether, and all economists were to agree on some "optimal blend" of reliance on the market and insistence on some kind and amount of management of the economy, the disagreements on long-term unemployment would remain.

The simple truth is that we still don't understand long-term unemployment very well. We can point to a host of plausible factors that contribute to it; but we do not know *for sure* what their relative importance is as an explanation of the phenomenon, or whether the real world phenomenon is the result of an unfortunate conjuncture of all of them. Some of the contributing factors are more sociological, political, or institutional, rather than "purely economic." Thus various writers stress the role of "the cursed dole," minimum wages, the battle between "insiders" and "outsiders," the pigheadedness of union leaders on one side or employers on the other, collective bargaining rather than enterprise bargaining, the increased participation of women in the labor force and the growing prevalence of the two-earner family, the New Industrial Revolution and the lagging educational system, rather than relying on a simple Keynesian explanation in terms of inadequacy of aggregate effective demand. With so many plausible explanations available, many of them "non-economic" in the sense that they have little to do with cycles and trends in the main macroeconomic variables, it is little wonder that many economists are puzzled by a phenomenon that is not supposed to exist anyhow.

The concept of hysteresis strikes a responsive chord with the present writer. It ties in with the concepts of "cumulative causation" and the "knife edge" that played so great a role in the early postwar period, and which did so much to clarify our thinking about cycles and trends. It also ties in with our discussion of Gaston Luthi's Topocross and chronic unemployment, and of loops of increasing amplitude, in chapter 11. But it does not suffice to give the process a high-sounding, scientific name. We must understand the process itself, in all of its aspects. There is much work to be done.

References

Allen, H. L., B. McCormick, and R. J. O'Brian. "Unemployment and the Demand for Retraining." *The Economic Journal* 102 (March 1991): 190–201.

Bean, C. R., P. R. G. Layard, and S. J. Nickell. "The Rise in Unemployment: A Multi-Country Study." *Economica* 53 (1986): S1–S22.

Blanchard, Oliver J., and Lawrence H. Summers. "Hysteresis and the European Unemployment Problem." *Macroeconomic Annual.* National Bureau of Economic Research, Cambridge, Mass.: 1986.

Blazejczak, J. "Evaluation of Long-term Effects of Technological Trends in the Structure of Employment." *Futures* 23 (July-August 1991): 596–604.

Commonwealth of Australia. "Restoring Full Employment: A Discussion Paper." Committee on Employment Opportunities, Canberra, ACT: December 1993.

Corak, Miles. "The Duration of Unemployment During Boom and Bust." *Canadian Economic Observer.* Ottawa, Statistics Canada: September 1993.

"The Cursed Dole." *The Economist* no. 320 (28 September 1991): 16–17.

Florida, Richard. "The New Industrial Revolution." *Futures* 23 (July-August, 1991).

Hart, Peter E. "Types of Structural Unemployment in the United Kingdom." *International Labor Review* 129, 2 (1990): 213–28.

Hughes, Helen. "Hard Decisions Needed to Give Unemployed Hope." *The Australian* (1 December 1994): 9.

Jackman, Richard, and Richard Layard. "Does Long-term Unemployment Reduce a Person's Chance of a Job? A Time-series Test." *Economica* 58 (February 1991): 93–106.

Juhn, Chinhui, Kevin M. Murphy, and Robert H. Topel. "Why Has the Natural Rate

Unemployment Increased Over Time?" *The Brookings Papers on Economic Activity*, no. 2. Washington, D.C.: 1991, 4.

Matzner, Egon, Ronald Schettkat, and Richard Wagner. "Labor Market Effects of New Technology." *Futures* (September 1990): 22.

Phelps, Edmund. *Structural Slumps: The Modern Equilibrium Theory of Unemployment, Interests, and Assets*. Cambridge, Mass.: Harvard University Press, 1994.

Pissarides, Christopher A. "Loss of Skill During Unemployment and the Persistence of Employment Shocks." *Quarterly Journal of Economics* (November 1992): 1371–91.

Senker, Peter. "Technological Change and the Future of Work: An Approach to an Analysis." *Futures* (24 May 1992): 351–63.

Part IV

Unemployment and Inflation since 1950: Hypotheses, Theories, Explanations

11

Unemployment and Inflation since 1950: Hypotheses and Theories

We now have before us three case studies of experience with unemployment and inflation in three countries since 1950, plus a discussion of the near-universal experience in recent decades with long-term unemployment. Now, we must begin our attempt to explain these phenomena. In broad outline, the experience we have described is similar. In minute detail, we have noted some striking differences. Neither the similarities nor the differences are thoroughly understood. There is no received doctrine and no widely accepted general theory to explain them. In this chapter, we present some hypotheses and theories that *may* explain at least some of them. In the next chapter, we present our own theory of unemployment and inflation in today's world.

In this chapter, we endeavor to relate the concepts of trade-off curves and their shifts and cyclical loops to the earlier business cycle theories. In this way we may see more clearly what has changed and what has not. We shall start with Schumpeter's concept of the *kreislauf,* circular or stationary flow, and the two-phase cycle.

Cycles, Trade-off Curves, Loops

Figure 11.1 represents a trade-off curve. U_n is the natural rate of unemployment, in the sense of the rate at which inflation will not be accelerated. P_n is the "natural" rate of inflation, the rate that must be sustained if unemployment is not to increase. Point E, on the trade-off curve, is the equilibrium point for the whole system; both inflation and unemployment, and by implication per capita output and real incomes, are stable. Let us imagine that this is a well-behaved late nineteenth- or early twentieth-century European or North American economy, and that the "natu-

FIGURE 11.1
Nineteenth-Century Cycle

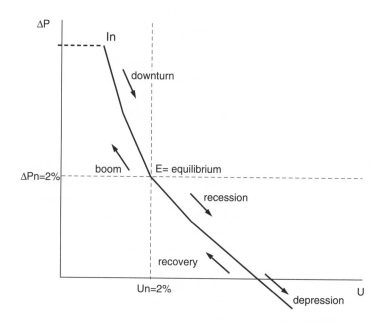

ral" rates of unemployment and inflation are both equal to 2 percent and few people worry about either. Professor Schumpeter sometimes spoke as though his "equilibrium" were one of full employment without inflation; but unemployment can never be literally zero, and few governments today are really striving for a totally stable price level. We do not wish to start with a model too abstract from today's reality.

Schumpeter's stationary flow would mean that the economy remained constantly at E. Now let us introduce his two-phase cycle. Innovations take place, new investment is financed by bank credit, monetary expansion ensues, prices rise more rapidly, and a wave of prosperity ensues. The economy moves up the TOC from E to I_n. Then, the new plant and equipment begins to produce, output increases, bank loans are repaid, the rate of monetary expansion falls, and the rate of inflation drops. However, all this has been foreseen, there is no overreaction, let alone panic, and the system returns to equilibrium, with both unemployment and inflation at 2 percent; but output is higher than before, and if population grows less than output, per capita incomes will rise. The two-phase cycle permits some growth.

Now let us move to the four-phase cycle. During the upswing borrowing and investment are undertaken by the "cluster of followers," some of it not based on sound foresight and wholly rational expectations, savings increase as incomes rise, but nonetheless money becomes tight and interest rates go up, too. Some of the investment undertaken proves to be too roundabout (capital intensive) at the higher interest rates, and some enterprises fail. Some prices may fall, and monetary expansion may actually cease. Panic ensues, and the system moves through E and along the lower portion of the TOC until the price level actually falls. The system enters a depression phase, and remains there until the inappropriate investments of the upswing are liquidated, bank reserves increase again, new innovations appear, expectations improve, and a new wave of investment gets under way. The system moves back up the TOC, but because of the cumulative nature of the expansion, goes through into a new prosperity phase, and the whole cycle is repeated.

The cycle thus described is fairly typical of the fluctuations that actually took place in the more advanced industrial nations from the end of the Napoleonic Wars to the beginning of World War I. But while good use can be made of the notion of a long-run trade-off curve in describing such a cycle, we have not yet made use of the idea of *shifts* in TOCs, nor of cyclical loops. Let us therefore introduce a concept of a *stable loop,* as a step toward a system more closely resembling the real world of the post-World-War II era, allowing for periods in which the rate of unemployment and the rate of inflation move together. Such a system is depicted in figure 11.2. It goes around and around the same loop, and in that sense is "stable" in the long run. However, it is a far cry from the "stationary flow" or the two-phase cycle, or even the four-phase cycle. We have deliberately drawn figure 11.2 so that the portion of the loop that is convex to the origin, and which might be regarded as a TOC, goes through the point E; and so that there are on that portion of the loop, points where the rate of inflation is falling while unemployment is rising. To that extent the diagram looks like a pre-World War II cycle; but only to that extent. Over a large portion of the loop inflation and unemployment are either rising together or falling together.

FIGURE 11.2
Hypothetical Stable Loop

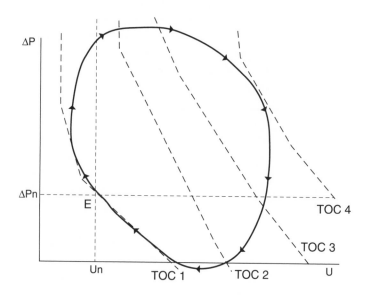

While the various observations comprising the loop obviously cannot all be on the same TOC, it is perfectly possible that every point on the loop also lies on *some* TOC, in the sense that at each point of time, a different monetary policy could have produced more unemployment and less inflation or *vice versa*. In the same manner, in a period of constantly shifting demand curves, first increasing and then decreasing, the actual combinations of prices and sales might well describe a loop, and yet each observation might also lie on a demand curve; if prices had been higher purchases would have been lower, and *vice versa*. I have therefore drawn several TOCs and numbered them successively, to show the shifting of the TOCs through time. The portion of the loop-curve that is concave to the origin might also be regarded as a TOC, since inflation and unemployment are moving in opposite directions. The inflection point on the

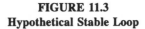

FIGURE 11.3
Hypothetical Stable Loop

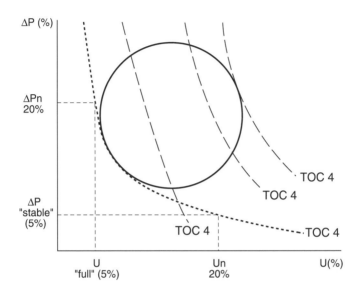

right hand side of the loop, where inflation and unemployment stop moving in opposite directions and start moving together again, must of course be tangential to a TOC, if it is to be on both the loop and some TOC.

Whatever the causal factors behind it, it is clear that the move from a system such as is shown in figure 11.1 to the system depicted in figure 11.2 must reflect a fundamental structural change, and not one that is clearly for the better. Yet even figure 11.2 shows a system that behaves better than the one we actually have. In today's world, unemployment seldom falls below the natural rate, and price levels seldom fall at all. Present-day reality is better described by figure 11.3. Yet even that system is better than the one we actually have, because in reality the loops are not stable, but are shifting upward and outward and increasing in amplitude.

Thus the loops and the shifting TOCs are quite consistent with each other, but they are not fully explained by prewar business cycle theory; still less are *shifting loops* explained by those theories. These are the gaps which we must try to fill in.

How Regular and Periodic Are the Shifts and the Loops?

We have been conducting our theoretical discussion in terms of "the economy" or "the economic system," as though it had been firmly established that the TOCs, their shifts, and the loops exist, that their behavior has enough regularity and uniformity to permit systematic theoretical analysis, and that they are sufficiently universal, at least among ICCs, to treat them as an intrinsic part of the machinery of an industrialized "capitalist" or "mixed" private enterprise system. We are still conducting our analysis largely in terms of variables characteristic of the earlier business cycle theory: individual behavior regarding innovation, entrepreneurship, investment, savings, consumption, and the like. But are we justified in assuming such regularity, periodicity, uniformity, and universality?

The truth is we do not really know. The same questions were still being asked about business cycles when World War II began, and even for a decade or two after it was over. Are they really cycles, or are they just fluctuations, or even sporadic movements? Even if a certain regularity of movement is established in each one of the industrialized capitalist countries, can we be sure that they are so similar in all of them as to establish a strong probability that they have a common cause? These questions regarding business cycles still remain. Yet to date, the nature and causes of the movements of unemployment and inflation since World War II have not been studied nearly as intensively and extensively as the prewar movements were. Considering that the human resources, statistics, computers, and money available for such studies are so much richer than they were in 1940, it is difficult to say why this situation should prevail. Partly, I believe, it is because the phenomenon of inflation and unemployment moving together is so inconvenient and puzzling that economists shy away from it. But we must try to understand it, even if we must accept the probability that our early attempts will be no more successful than the early attempts to understand business cycles.

My own answer to my own question would be as follows. From what we know of TOCs, their shifts, and loops, there is no reason for us to believe that they are intrinsically less systematic, periodic, regular, uniform, and universal than the old cycles of alternating inflation and unemployment. Therefore, there is just as good a chance of finally understanding them, evolving theories to explain them, and formulating policies to deal with today's economic problems based on those theories, as there was a generation or two ago of doing the same with business cycles. But we have to get started; and the first step is to recognize just how much the functioning of our economic system has changed, and thus how much our analytical framework must change in order to deal with it. We will not solve today's economic problems by small alterations of or additions to the analytical frameworks inherited from the past.

Ex Ante or *Ex Post* TOCs?

Having arrived at this point, where we seem closer to astronomy than to engineering, it may be useful to distinguish between *ex ante* and *ex post* TOCs. Phillips, when he invented what came to be known as the Phillips curve, was not thinking primarily of short-run policy options. With his background of natural science and engineering, he was more concerned with discovering and establishing an empirical law. We have been interpreting the concept of TOC in exactly the opposite fashion, as a set of policy options. It is conceptually possible that the movements of inflation and unemployment cannot be controlled by monetary management alone; there may be no *ex ante* TOC. Yet the observations *ex post* might give a good statistical fit to a curve which looks like a TOC, at least over some period of time. We would then be in the position of a gardener whose roses will die if there is a sudden frost early in the spring and whose zinnias will die if there is a sudden frost early in the fall. That is a trade-off of sorts, but not one that allows the gardener to choose a point of minimum discomfort; he cannot select an optimum combination of early and late frost. Of course, if he can forecast accurately, he can adjust his plans so as to reduce his discomfort somewhat, but that is all.

Measuring Business Cycles

If and when it is determined to the complete satisfaction of the economics profession that the postwar trade cycle takes the form of shifting trade-off curves or loops, there is little reason to hope that the task of dating turning points will require less than the heroic efforts of the National Bureau of Economic Research in measuring prewar cycles.

Do the TOCs Shift in a Systematic Fashion?

The discovery that there are cyclical shifts of TOCs, and that these shifts *may* be systematic, is a relatively recent experience for the economics profession. Professor Robert Solow of the Massachusetts Institute of Technology leans toward the view that the shifts are haphazard, while recognizing the *possibility* that they may be systematic (Solow, 1980, 1977). Professor Jay Forrester, of the systems analysis group at the same institution, however, on the basis of a large model with several interacting cycles of various lengths, concludes (as we do) that the shifts are generated by the operation of the entire economic system. The interactions of the "business cycle" (the Kitchin cycle, about four years), the Juglar cycle (eight to twelve years), the Kuznets cycle (fifteen to twenty-five years), and the Kondratieff long wave (about fifty years) may explain why the recessions since 1945 have been less severe than the prewar depressions; we may have been on the upswing of a long wave. Professor Forrester adds: "[O]ur work to date suggests that the balance of inflation and unemployment in the economy depends in a complex way on many modes of behavior in the economy as well as the government policies being followed.... [C]hanges in money supply or changes in the position of the economy relative to the long-wave fluctuations tend to cause shifts in inflation and unemployment that cannot be described in terms of simple movements along a fixed trade-off curve" (Forrester, 1976). Forrester provides a diagram to illustrate how the long-wave and monetary expansion together could bring shifts in trade-off curves. Our own position is similar in the contention that the shape, position, and shifts of TOCs are the result of the operation of the economic system as a whole, including government policy.

Our argument is not dependent on the existence of long waves, but proof that long waves do exist would strengthen our position; that is, a long-sustained boom in the capital goods industry would tend to lengthen the period of investment, raise capital:output ratios, lower the employment multiplier without lowering the income multiplier, and thus aggravate tendencies toward simultaneous inflation and unemployment, as shown in the next chapter.

Our task would be easier if discomfort points moved in systematic fashion, whether as TOCs with regular cyclical shifts, as cyclical loops, or even as a systematic sawtooth or cobweb movement; for if the movement is systematic we can hope to understand and explain it, and we might then be in a position to offset or control the movements. The appeal of the prewar business cycle theory, obviously, was that it promised a means of explaining, offsetting or controlling economic fluctuations. The concepts of shifting TOCs and loops are easily reconciled: when unemployment and inflation move in opposite directions we can imagine a stable TOC; and when they move in the same direction, the TOC is shifting to a position of more or less discomfort. Indeed, if the cyclical loop repeated itself consistently and continuously, the shifts in TOCs would also be regular, after the manner of some of the earlier business cycle theories. If such were the case, and if we were assured that periods of increasing discomfort were always followed by periods of diminishing discomfort, we should have less reason to worry and more hope of controlling or offsetting the movements. Unfortunately, as we well know, we are confronted not by regular cycles of this kind, but by an apparently long-run trend toward increasing discomfort, no matter how the movements are stylized.

The concept of sawtooth movements is disturbing because it is unfamiliar, and suggestive of the chaos that all scientists abhor. Moreover, even if the movements were systematic and understandable, if they were always in one direction they would lead ultimately to intolerable inflation or intolerable unemployment. On the other hand, if the movements were cyclical, sometimes following the teeth southeast along the longer-run TOC and sometimes following it northwest, there would be nothing more alarming about such movements than a regular, longer-run cyclical loop. Much depends, of course, on just how long this longer run is. If deterioration continues throughout the whole of a Kondratieff downswing, it could be serious enough to worry most people and most governments. The electorate is not likely to respond with enthusiasm if told: "Do not worry, this is just a Kondratieff downswing; your children will be better off than you are—although your grandchildren will suffer much the same discomfort as you do."

A Cobweb Pattern?

A final possibility that occurs to me is a "cobweb," illustrated in figure 11.4. The solid line represents a long-run TOC around that fluctuations take place, within the limits of a stable loop. Point A represents an optimal position, with minimum discomfort. However, it leads to infla-

FIGURE 11.4
The Cobweb
Community Indifference Curve (CIC)

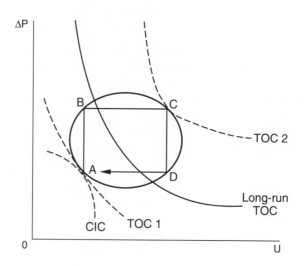

tionary expectations combined with easy money, and the TOC shifts up
to point B. Now expectations are reversed, interest rates rise, and money
is tight. The TOC shifts to TOC₂ and the economy moves to point C.
With unemployment so high the price level cannot be maintained, and if
falls to point D. With prices so low consumer spending picks up, unemployment falls, and the economy returns to A. This cobweb is drawn
so as to be self-repeating; but as with the original cobweb theorem based
on demand and supply curves, it could be converging; or it could be
diverging, corresponding to loops with increasing amplitude.

Figure 11.5 illustrates another type of cobweb relationship that is consistent with the Australian or Canadian data, at least for some periods,
but which is hypothetical rather than empirically derived. The curve TOC₁
is the initial trade-off curve between price increases and unemployment.

The curve labelled "Isocom" is the community indifference curve, or "equal discomfort curve," which is tangent to TOC_1. The Isocoms can also be interpreted as "equal political support" curves. The broken curve marked "Government Response Curve" (GRC) is based upon particular assumptions regarding the way in which the government in question plays "the Game" during the period covered by the diagram. It is assumed that the government uses no policies other than money management (monetary and fiscal policy aimed at regulating the rate of expansion of the money supply) to check inflation or to reduce unemployment. It is further assumed that the government lacks the knowledge and sophistication regarding actual shapes of TOCs and Isocoms, and regarding reactions of unions, employers, and foreigners to their policies to achieve perfect fine-tuning. Policy is designed to move toward "min" (the minimum discomfort point on the current TOC) without any assurance of actually achieving it. Policies are expressed in terms of target rates of expansion of the money supply for the next year (or quarter, perhaps) as measured on the axis O' - ΔM on the right hand side of the diagram. This target rate of ΔM can be read off from the GRC curve by running a horizontal straight line from any point on GRC to the O' - ΔM axis.

The starting point is "S" with unemployment at 3 percent and the rate of inflation at 5 percent. In this quadrant (with "U" below 4 percent and "ΔP" above 4 percent) policy is directed toward checking inflation rather than toward reducing unemployment. At point "S" the target rate of monetary expansion over the next year is 3 percent (or, if policy is more flexible and fine-tuned, the target might be to achieve the equivalent of an annual rate of 3 percent for the next quarter, subject to change in the following quarter). The actual discomfort point reached by this policy is found by dropping a vertical straight line from point "a" on the GRC to the TOC_1. In reality there is no necessity for the point to be vertically below "a," but it could be, and it is a convenient abstraction to assume that it is. The discomfort point achieved is therefore "b," with unemployment at 5 percent and inflation at 2.8 percent. In this quadrant, with unemployment above 4 percent and inflation below 4 percent, policy switches to reducing unemployment. The corresponding point on the GRC is "c" with ΔM at 5.2 percent. But then the discomfort point moves to point "d" with unemployment at only 2.8 percent while inflation is at 5.4 percent, and so on. This cobweb is a diverging one and could become explosive.

FIGURE 11.5
Hypothetical Cobweb

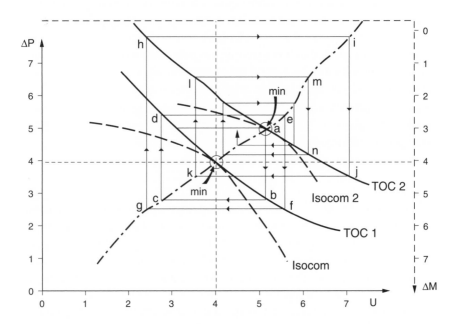

We next assume that by the time the cobweb reaches "g" the public is thoroughly frightened, especially of worsening inflation, so that the "expectations augmented trade-off curve" shifts to TOC$_2$. Now the cobweb process begins again from "h." We have drawn the second cobweb so as to be converging rather than diverging; perhaps the government has learned by experience to calculate the desirable rate of monetary expansion more competently, or unions and employers have become better behaved, or both. With this second cobweb, movements of the discomfort points will become less violent and less erratic in time, and the economy will settle at an equilibrium at min'—until something happens to disturb this equilibrium. Note that this equilibrium, while a minimum discomfort point for the new TOC, is—to use Lionel Robbins's often quoted expression of many years ago—*"only* equilibrium." The society is much worse off than it was at any point on TOC$_1$.

There is of course no necessity for the performance of any particular government to follow precisely this pattern. Our contention is not that the governments behave in identical fashion always and everywhere, but rather than behavior differs from country to country, and that even in one particular country the style of policy may vary from time to time. We do believe, however, that the kind of trial-and-error approach to stabilization policy illustrated in this example has been followed, with variations on a common theme, by a good many governments, including those of Australia and Canada. In any case, it behooves us as economists, to whom governments have a right to look for help in formulating policy, to try to understand how policy is now formulated and to suggest rules (if such exist) that might improve the outcome.

Dynamic Topology

Gaston Luthi and I have worked together, sporadically, on cycles, shifting TOCs and loops, for more than ten years; first at the University of Ottawa, where Luthi wrote his Ph. D. dissertation, "Business Cycle Theory and Stabilization Policy in a World of Shifting Trade-off Curves," under my direction; then at Public Works Canada, and later still at L'Institut Canadien de Recherche sur le Développement Régional at the Université de Moncton (Gaston Haddad Luthi, 1979). It is becoming a bit difficult to distinguish who had which idea first. However, the "topocross" is quite clearly his invention. It is derived through the application of *dynamic topology,* a technique well-known in fields like geography and spatial engineering. François Perroux was working along similar lines at the time of his death in 1987, but otherwise I am aware of no other application in the field of economics.

Since working with three-dimensional space would involve the complex mathematics of volumetrics, Luthi limits his analysis to two-dimensional topological space. The axes of any diagram showing combinations of unemployment and inflation show these two dimensions, and the actual quantities at any point of time show as a point in this particular two-dimensional space. However, the point existing at any moment in time is subject to "propensities," or forces, which tend to move it in any of the four directions: up, down, right, or left; or north, south, east, or west. In order for a point to remain fixed in space as time goes by, the strength of the forces pushing toward each direction must be equal, and remain unchanged. If the forces vary in a regular sequence, eventually returning to their starting point, as in Schumpeter's four-phase cycle, the result could be a stable loop. However, the stable loop need not be a perfect circle, as in figure 11.3; if fluctuations in prices are greater in amplitude than fluctuations in unemployment, the loop will be tall and thin; and short and wide in the reverse case.

Luthi's basic topocross model is shown in figure 11.6. It shows, amongst other things, the relationship between the standard self-repeating cycle and the topocross generated by the four propensities. Luthi is assuming here that the loops are stable. The four phases of the conventional cycle, shown as movements of something (national income, prices, production, employment) from "equilibrium" to peak, then recession through depression to trough, and then through recovery back to "equilibrium," are here translated into observations of unemployment and inflation shown as points in space, determined by the relative strength of the four propensities: north, south, east, and west. In the topocross in the lower part of the diagram, the movement from E to peak is not really a boom; it is a period of "stagflation," GNP is falling slightly, and unemployment is increasing; but prices are rising steeply. Let us suppose that at the beginning the system is in "equilibrium," in the sense that at the moment the four propensities have equal strength and the economy is at point "E," (we are *not* saying that there is any natural tendency of the economy to move towards this point, nor that it is in any way stable). The introduction or strengthening of a purely inflationary force would move the point vertically upward; introduction or strengthening of a force causing only unemployment would move it horizontally to the East; and so on. But in reality, there are always in any economic system, conflicting and complementary forces. If these change in relative strength in a regular, systematic, cyclical fashion through time, the movement of the inflation-unemployment points can form a loop.

It is clear that the configuration of the loops can differ from country to country, and even from region to region within one country. It is also clear that the configuration of loops, as well as their general position in space, can change through time, whether for a country or a region. In Australia during the 1950s, unemployment ranged from about 0.5 percent to 1.5 percent while inflation varied from less than 0.5 percent to nearly 11 percent. The loop is very narrow and very steep, with very little East-West movement but a lot of North-South movement. At time of writing, unemployment was a more serious problem in Australia than

FIGURE 11.6
Topocross

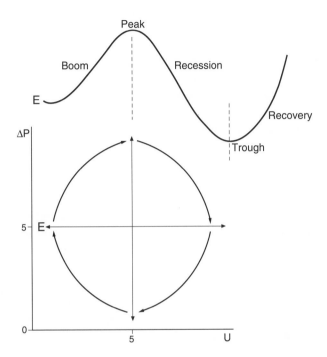

inflation and the loop is more extended East-West than North-South. During the oil-boom of the 1970s and early 1980s, Alberta's loop was much like that of Australia in the 1950s, inflation ranging from 4 percent to over 12 percent (1981), while unemployment was well below the Canadian average, and for a while even substantially below the Ontario average. Now unemployment is about equal to the Canadian average and well above the Ontario figure, while inflation is somewhat below the Canadian average.

Where hyperinflation is chronic, Luthi's topocross looks like figure 11.7. Where there is chronic and serious unemployment, it looks like figure 11.8. However, even if a particular national or regional economy has looked like figure 11.7 or figure 11.8 for some time, that fact in itself does not mean that it will stay that way. Exogenous factors (like the price of oil for Alberta or Texas), changes in government policy, the mechanism of the economy itself, or innovations and resource discoveries, can bring changes in both the position and the shape of the loops.

The *position* in space *of the entire loop,* which is tantamount to the field of operation of the entire economy in terms of these two variables, would depend on the relative strength of the north, south, east, and west forces at the beginning of time; and if each of them always changed in strength in the same cyclical sequence, always returning to their starting point, the same loop would go on repeating itself forever. Put in this fashion, it is intuitively obvious that in a dynamic economy, it is highly unlikely that the loops would be stable for long periods. As an economy evolves in a certain pattern, there will be not only marginal changes in relative strength of the four propensities, in a regular cyclical sequence, but also sharp *shifts* in their strength that will push the whole system into a new and different space, in the manner illustrated in figure 11.8.

We cannot know *a priori* what the movements of the system in space will be. We need empirical evidence and a theory to explain our observations. But let us accept as an hypothesis that Luthi's hunch is correct, and the loops of different amplitude represent the Kitchin, Juglar, and Kondratieff cycles. We could then represent the functioning of the economy by a diagram such as figure 11.9. The loops marked 1, 2, and 3 are Kitchin cycles. We assume that each of them is stable in itself, and that the system returns to its starting point after each complete Kitchin cycle. However, there are the powerful propensities pertaining to the Juglar cycle. These tend to push the entire system, as represented by the Kitchin loops, first to the northeast from loop 1 to loop 2, and then to the southwest to loop 3, and finally northwest and back to loop 1. The Juglar, as drawn, is the envelope for the three positions of the Kitchin loop. Similarly, the still more powerful propensities of the Kondratieff cycle push the system containing the Juglar and the three Kitchins, first to the northeast from Juglar system A to Juglar system B, then to C, and back to A. So with the interactions of the three self-repeating cycles we end up back at the starting point on Kitchin 1.

But, of course, the story does not end there. There may be trends, in one direction or another, longer than the Kondratieff cycle; the K loop can shift as well. It seems clear enough from past experience that it does. Moreover, since countries at different stages of development have different structures, there is no reason to expect that their patterns of economic

FIGURE 11.7
Hyperinflation

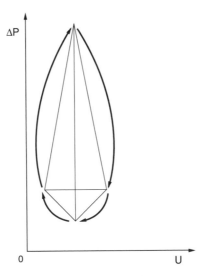

FIGURE 11.8
Chronic Unemployment

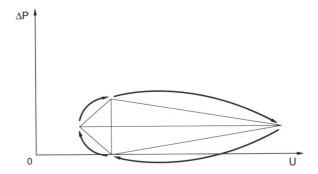

fluctuations will be identical. It may well be that with the increasing internationalization of the global economy and the remarkably fine performance of some of the less developed countries, combined with the halting performances of some of the more advanced industrialized countries and the collapse of socialist ones, the long-run tendency will be toward convergence. Meanwhile, we can never be certain that stabilization policies that work in one country will work in another. Also, since the strongest forces affecting the behavior of national economies in today's world are government policies, and since these differ widely from country to country, there is good reason to expect wider variation in their patterns of shifting TOCs loops than in their cycles before World War II.

Trade-off Zones

In the course of the project undertaken for Public Works Canada on *Growth and Stability in Construction*, Professor Luthi and I developed the concept of trade-off zones, as distance from trade-off curves. The preoccupation with Phillips curves in the years after the concept was first introduced led to efforts to fit single curves to unemployment and price-increase data, which in retrospect prove to have been somewhat misguided. Once we move from the concept of a functional relationship between unemployment and wage increases or price increases, to the concept of sets of relationships between unemployment and inflation that depict the functioning of the entire economy, there is no longer any reason to expect—or even to be pleased by—relationships that all lie on a precise curve, or very close to it. What is interesting and important is that, during certain periods, the unemployment-inflation points *are confined to a limited space,* and that, in other periods, they are confined to a different space. Finally, it is extremely important that some TOZs are clearly preferable to others; the shifts of the TOZs in space are a strong indication that the economy is performing worse or better. Figure 11.10 shows trade-off zones for Alberta, the Atlantic provinces, and Ontario. It is obvious that the Ontario zone is preferable to either of the other two. To decide whether the Atlantic Canada or Alberta zone is preferable, we would, of course, need to know the shape of the community indifference curves between unemployment and inflation (as drawn, the Atlantic Canada zone is worse). Similarly, if the Alberta curve shifted to the position of the Ontario one, we would be certain (other things being equal)

FIGURE 11.9
Shifting Loops

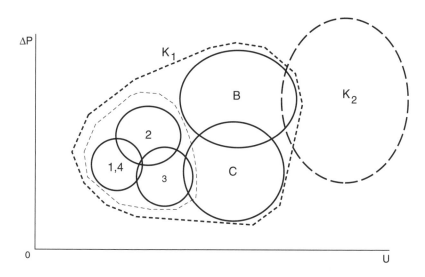

that welfare in Alberta had improved. If the zone shifted to the position of the Atlantic Canada one, we would need the Alberta community indifference curve to decide for sure whether Alberta welfare had improved or not. In any case, such clearly delimited zones may be a better tool for analyzing the behavior of the economic system as a whole than curves to which the actual points do not fit very well.

Economic Fluctuations as Net Results of Countervailing Forces

For those of us brought up on prewar business cycle theory, it is hard to escape the concept of a *sequence* of phases or periods of the cycle; a prosperity phase culminating in a boom and dominated by inflationary forces; a downturn leading to recession and depression, a period dominated by

FIGURE 11.10
Trade-off Zones
Ontario, Alberta, Atlantic Canada

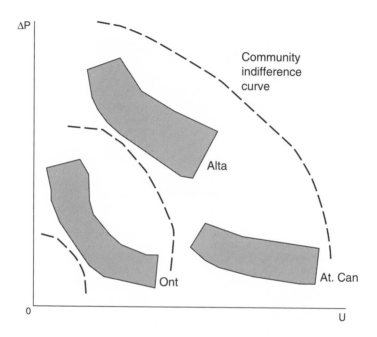

forces bringing increased unemployment, falling prices and output; a reversal of forces bringing a recovery phase; and so on. The concept of an economic system in which there are nearly always some forces pushing or pulling it to the east, others pushing or pulling it to the west, north, or south, is difficult to grasp. Yet, that is what we seem to have. There may be relatively short periods in some economies when the forces are overwhelmingly in one direction, as in periods of hyperinflation, but in today's world these are relatively rare. Most of the present-day economies are both more managed and better managed than most economies were before World War II. Inflation, unemployment, and fluctuations in gross national product are kept within limits. Moreover, the greatly increased sophistication of the business community and the general public leads to "rational expectations" that government policy will succeed in keeping fluctuations within limits. In some ways, the high level of economic literacy complicates the policymaker's problem; people tend to expect the same thing and to act in unison, thus amplifying fluctuations. But it means that the public is much less subject to outright panic.

On the other hand, it seems probable that the forces that caused the prewar cycles are still there beneath the surface; the basic machine of a market economy has not changed its fundamental design. The mechanism of the multiplier and accelerator is still the same. Consequently, it is possible—even probable—that the shifts in relative strength of *other* forces may follow a cyclical pattern. Certainly the available evidence suggests that they do.

What are the forces that push the system in each direction? It seems to me that the answer can be sought within the framework of the Keynesian system, but modified to take account of interactions and feedbacks, and particularly of expectations. The Keynesian system is not wrong; it is so close to being tautological that it could scarcely *be* wrong. It is, however, incomplete as an explanation of today's economies. For example, taking each force in isolation from all others, the system will be pushed to the east by an increase in the labor force; a decline in investment, consumption, government spending, or exports; or a rise in interest rates or taxes. But when interactions and expectations are taken into account, the end result may be quite different. An increase in taxes and the consequent reduction of the budget deficit may lead to expectations of reductions in interest rates, and so to an increase in investment. Falling exports may lead to expectations of new barriers to imports, and so to increased investment in some fields of activity. An increase in wages may be expected to expand consumer spending, and to bring a relaxation of monetary policy, expansion of the money supply, and higher prices, to offset the wage increase; and so lead to a reduction of unemployment. There can be no *general* theory that will provide the policymaker with all the information he or she needs to select the right policies. Response will vary from country to country—even from region to region—and from time to time in the same country. It is simply necessary to *know* how people are likely to respond to a particular change in economic circumstances, or a change in policy, in a particular society at a particular time.

The need for such knowledge should not be a cause for dismay. The knowledge can be acquired. Indeed, most central bankers, to take but one

294 Employment Without Inflation

example, probably already have it, for types of behavior related to monetary and fiscal policy. However, such knowledge cannot be deduced from simple assumptions regarding supposed universal behavior of individuals. It can be obtained only by continuous and close observation of the relevant actors, and groups of actors, in the society concerned.

References

Forrester, Jay. "Business Structure, Economic Cycles and National Policy." *Futures, the Journal of Forecasting and Planning* 8, 3 (June 1976): 195–214.

Luthi, Gaston Haddad. "Business Cycle Theory and Stabilization Policy in a World of Shifting Trade-Off Curves." Unpublished Ph.D. thesis. Ottawa: University of Ottawa, 1979.

Solow, Robert M. "On Theories of Unemployment." *The American Economic Review* (March 1980): 1–11.

———. "Jobs, Jobs, Jobs: How to Recreate Then Without Reinflation." *Across the Board* XIV, 1 (January 1977): 29.

12

The Machine, the Structure, and the Game

Thus far in this book, we have done three things. We have reviewed prewar business cycle theories, and found that while many of them were overambitious in seeking to discover (and sell) *the* theory of economic fluctuations, nearly all of them had an element of truth that is helpful in explaining the observed behavior of prewar economies; and some of them, like the Schumpeter, Hansen, Samuelson, Domar, Harrod, and Hicks models, are very helpful indeed. However, no one theory explains the whole of *post*war fluctuations in the world's economies. Second, we have provided *descriptions* of economic behavior, at both the national and the regional levels, of a number of economies, during the last four decades. Third, we have suggested a number of hypothetical, but plausible, models that, if verified theoretically and empirically, would provide explanations of observed behavior. I have reached the point where the onus is on my shoulders to try to present a cohesive theory to explain these observations.

In doing so, however, I will avoid falling into the trap that captured so many of the prewar business cycle theorists; I will not maintain that there is some single theory that explains the behavior of all the economies in the world, national or regional. There are, to be sure, some uniformities. The world's major economies have tended to go through periods of inflation, unemployment, stagflation, or high growth at about the same time. Moreover, most of them have experienced, at one time or another, periods of quite distinct types of performance: rising income with declining rates of inflation and falling unemployment; periods of recession with rising rates of inflation and of unemployment; periods with rising inflation and falling unemployment; and periods of rising unemployment and falling inflation. It is this regularity in postwar experience that we must try to explain. As suggested above, if we can show reasons for regarding these four types of performance as phases of a cycle; and if we can discover reasons why these phases should follow each other in fairly regular sequence, we would be coming close to a theory of shifting trade-off curves and loops.

For reasons already touched upon above, however, we cannot expect that the patterns of economic fluctuations, or their causes, will be identical in all countries. To begin with, while there is a family resemblance among the policies adopted in countries wedded to monetarism (Australia, Canada, New Zealand, the United Kingdom, the United States), there have been significant differences in details of policy even amongst these countries, and wider differences between each of them and other countries. There are differences in industrial relations, reflecting differences in relative strength of bargaining power of trade unions and employers. There are differences in resource endowment, occupational structure, and product mix. There are differences in political systems, financial institutions, business organization, legal systems, role of government, patterns of foreign trade, and capital flows. Consequently, there are differences in strength of exogenous shocks of various kinds, and differences in the speed, force, and manner in which they are propagated. Any given event—sudden changes in oil prices, the Gulf War, changes in government—will affect different economies differently.

My model has three components. The first is the Machine. By that expression, I mean the underlying mechanism of the economic system itself, particularly the interaction of accelerator and multiplier, Hicks's floor and ceiling, and the interaction of cycles and trends, or of Kitchin, Juglar, and Kondratieff cycles, as presented in Part II. There is no reason to think that these mechanisms have disappeared. Given the essentially tautological nature of the Keynesian system, they *cannot* disappear. Moreover, since the basic relationships among the variables are inherent in any market economy, they must be basically the same in any such economy. The numerical value of the variables can differ, but that's all.

The second component is the Game, played by employers, trade unions, governments, and foreigners. The Game is played continuously, but is played with particular intensity at certain times, as when strategic wage contracts are hammered out or a budget handed down or a new Central Bank interest rate announced. The manner in which the Game is played varies, not only from country to country at any time, but in the same country from one time to another.

The third component is the Structure, which, in turn, breaks down into three components of its own. One of these relates to the degree of structural integration or disintegration of the national economy. For the most part, governments of ICCs have tackled the problems of inflation and unemployment as though the national economies with which they were dealing were in reality the tightly knit, integrated, and homogeneous units of the neo-Keynesian textbooks. In fact, even the most advanced economies are collections of individual regional and sectoral economies, each with a life of its own, and with widely differing degrees of interaction and mobility among them from one country to another. Second, there is the structure of capital, as related to the Austrian School's "average period of investment," which can be approximated for purposes of measurement by the capital: output ratio and the capital:labor ratio. Third, there is the structure of production and foreign trade. The world inherited from the colonial era an international division of labor that had little to do with the actual comparative advantage of various countries, and still less to do with long-run comparative advantage.

The Machine, the Structure, and the Game interact, each having its impact on the operation of the other two determinants of the performance of the economy. But it is the Game that is most important. It is there that the fundamental decisions are made that determine how the economy will behave. It is also the component of the analysis of present day economic fluctuations that is furthest removed from prewar business cycle theory and so most unfamiliar. As I have already indicated, the behavior of the Machine was already explained quite well by prewar theory. The analysis of the Structure also has in it some familiar elements. Let us, therefore, begin with the Game.

The Game

We have stated that there are four sets of players in the Game: big business, big labor, big government, and foreigners. Play among the first three is more or less continuous; Foreigners intervene, and the other players react, more intermittently. The Game is very complex, the rules and strategies pursued are far from clear, and perhaps no one fully understands it. There are many possible variations of the Game, and we will not try to present all of them here. We wish only to provide some insight into the nature of the game and of the way in which it might be analyzed.

For convenience, we shall make the not unrealistic assumption that major wage contracts are negotiated by big business and big labor at regular and not too frequent intervals—say, once a year. Government may take a direct hand in the Game even at this stage; it may make its preferences known, it may offer guidelines, it may require use of arbitration machinery like the Australian Industrial Commission, it may even introduce wage and price controls. Certainly, the Game is not played in an identical fashion in all countries. Trade unions, employers, and governments do not behave in identical ways in all countries, or even at all times in the same country. The fact that the strategies of all players are subject to variations from time to time and from place to place is one of the factors that makes its analysis so extremely difficult. Many economists still conduct their analysis as though unions and employers behaved like collections of individual workers and entrepreneurs, and the government had no impact; this concept may be a source of solace, since standard neo-classical models of behavior can then be used. But it can lead the analysis far from reality.

We shall also assume for convenience—again not unrealistically—that the strategic contracts in major industries set the stage for wage determination throughout the entire economy. Then, according to our model, the employers set their (administered) prices for the year; and the government responds by determining its monetary and fiscal policy for the year. These restrictive assumptions with regard to timing are not essential to the analysis, but they are convenient and do little violence to reality.

Figure 12.1 provides one possible model of the Game. We are leaving Foreigners out for the moment; the players are big business, big labor, and big government. It is possible to construct models in which the role of government is ignored. There may be some analytical advantages in using a first approximation of this sort. But few trade union leaders or employer representatives go to the bargaining table today without some concept of what government policy is likely to be in reaction to various possible contracts. To save time and space, therefore, we introduce government from the start in this presentation.

The diagram is not meant to be a representation of universal behavior of the players, always and everywhere. On the contrary, I am arguing that economic theorists as a group *do not know* how the Game will be played in a particular country at a particular time. Perhaps the specialists in industrial relations or industrial organization will have a better idea than the general theorist; but even they will not always be sure, and in any case their special knowledge plays too small a role in economic theory. It is no use continuing to treat wage price determination as though

FIGURE 12.1
The Game

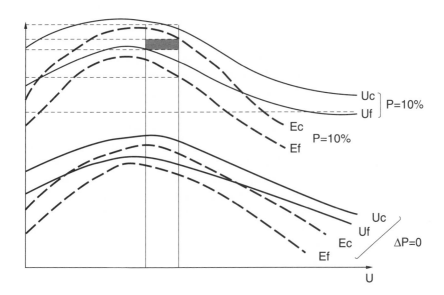

it were a matter of individual decisions, of single employers and employees, if in fact they are the result of decisions made by those who control large organizations—unions, monopolistic enterprises, and governments. Of course, it is embarrassing for economists to admit this truth; most theory rests on very simple assumptions about *individual* behavior, and welfare economics rests on the basic premise that what emerges in the market is a response to what *individuals* want. When we move to today's reality, we must admit that we have no generally accepted behavioral assumptions.

The figure implies that the negotiators for the unions go to the bargaining table with a wage rate they hope to get for their membership, which we call the ceiling, U_c; and a rock bottom level of wages they are willing to accept, which we call the floor, U_f. Both floor and ceiling are affected by the expected level of unemployment, u. As drawn, the curves imply that the union leaders take little account of the level of unemployment in their bargaining until high levels of unemployment are reached, except for the expected reaction of government policy to various levels of unemployment. That is, they are disinclined to make concessions in their wage demands because unemployment is increasing among young people, housewives, older people, unskilled workers, and others who are not members of the union. Only when unemployment reaches levels where it begins to cut into their membership will they relax somewhat in their demands. There is plenty of evidence for this kind of behavior by union leaders. Indeed, in the Canadian construction industry, there is evidence that the leadership has ignored unemployment altogether in the intermediate ranges; some of the steepest increases have been demanded and won during periods of steeply rising unemployment in that industry. One reason, no doubt, is that when unemployment reaches high levels, they expect the government to shift from a predominantly anti-inflation policy to a predominantly anti-unemployment policy, a shift from which the construction industry is likely to benefit more than others. The downward slope of the curves at very low levels of unemployment reflects the converse expectation regarding government reactions. The union leadership is sophisticated enough to know that when unemployment falls to very low levels, the government will shift to a stronger anti-inflation policy, which will put the employers in a position where they can no longer count on being able to offset wage increases with price increases. Clearly, if the union leadership were less sophisticated, or if the employers either were, or were expected to be, less sophisticated, the union leaders might regard lower unemployment as a signal for even tougher bargaining. Instead of turning down, the curves U_c and U_f would become steeper as they approach the vertical axis. Both types of behavior are plausible, and pure economic theory cannot tell us which pattern of behavior is likely to prevail in a particular country at a particular time. We would need to know the unions and their leaders very well.

Much depends on what policies government is expected to pursue. The Mulroney government in Canada, the Hawke and Keating governments in Australia, the Lange government in New Zealand, the Thatcher government in the United Kingdom, and the Reagan and Bush administrations in the United States concentrated on fighting inflation and almost totally ignored unemployment. When governments have behaved in this way for some time, both unions and employers may expect them to go on in the same manner, making the employers tougher in their bargaining stance and the union leaders more maneuverable. On the other hand, in some circumstances they may expect the parliamentary opposition, the unions, and the general public to be strong enough to force reversal of policy, in which case bargaining behavior will be different.

The curves E_c and E_f represent the ceiling and floor for the employers. Their representatives go to the bargaining table hoping to limit wage increases to E_f, and willing to go as high as E_c and no higher. Here, too, expectations regarding government reactions are crucial. In a particular country at a particular time, the expectations of employers and of unions regarding government reaction to a wage contract, and to existing levels of unemployment, are likely to be more or less the same. Governments today usually make their intentions on these matters clear. It is natural for both the employers' curves to lie somewhat below the union's curves; if that were not the case, collective bargaining and arbitration would proceed more smoothly than they do. Employers, too, expect policy to shift to anti-inflation measures when unemployment falls and, consequently, become tougher in resisting wage claims; their curves slope downward below some levels of unemployment. It would be natural for them to become less malleable when high levels of unemployment are reached; they expect the unions' bargaining power to fall, and perhaps hope to find ways around the unions in recruiting a labor force. In between, they are less resistant to wage increases because they expect with confidence that the government will bail them out with anti-unemployment measures and monetary expansion, so that wage increases are easily passed on to price rises.

But the Game is more complicated still. Expectations regarding government policy translate themselves into expectations regarding price increases during the next year. These expectations, in turn, have a feedback into the whole bargaining process. Since there is a limit to the number of variables that can be handled on a two-dimensional diagram, we have treated price expectations in the form of a family of bargaining curves, one pair for each expected prices increase. The lower pairs may be regarded as those pertinent to expectations of price stability, the upper pairs as prevailing with price expectations of, say, 10 percent increase in the next year.

The union leaders and employers' representatives enter the bargaining process with some expectations of next year's unemployment. These expectations are represented by vertical straight lines, Ex_u (unions) and Ex_e (employers). For convenience, we shall assume that both employers and unions expect (at the beginning of the bargaining process) that prices will rise by 10 percent in the next year. Note that the union curves flatten out at high levels of unemployment with these price expectations; that is, we are assuming that the unions will never accept a cut in real wages, no matter how high unemployment goes.

Of course, when a government is as adroit at "union-bashing" as the Hawke Labor government was in Australia, unions may accept cuts in real wages, as they have in fact done in Australia. The reason is that they want to keep labor in power, feel that the opposition would be even worse, and accept the view that the real wage cuts are needed to promote investment, encourage growth, and reduce unemployment. Nonetheless, it is my impression that such cases are rare, but they are possible, and one needs to know the situation to conduct analysis.

As the curves are drawn, there is a small area of overlap, shown by the shaded area, within which bargaining can take place without one or another of the two parties withdrawing in favor of strike or lockout. It is obvious that bargaining can easily break down. Indeed, negotiations may fail if the basic curves are too far apart, if expectations regarding unemployment are too far apart, of if expectations regarding price increases are too far apart. And the curves themselves embody expectations regarding government reactions.

It is also obvious that the curves may shift in the course of bargaining. As discussion proceeds, expectations regarding price increases, unemployment, and government responses may change. The government itself may make statements influencing expectations. In short, the outcome of the Game is wildly indeterminate; even if we were in possession of all the relevant curves at the beginning of the bargaining process, we could not predict the outcome with precision. Not only do we lack the needed knowledge to analyze the Game, but the Game itself is a good deal more unpredictable than an individual game of chess between two champions. One may know that Mr. Kerenski is likely to lead with the Yugoslav variant of the King's Indian Defense, and be quite sure how Mr. Sakharov will respond; but that will not be enough to predict the final outcome with any accuracy.

In any case, out of the Game comes a result; usually a contract. The result of the major contracts each year spread throughout the wage structure and the price structure. The government responds with measures to manage the money supply in a manner it considers appropriate to the outcome of the bargaining process. These policies, together with the decisions of unions, employers, investors, and (finally) individual consumers, are fed into the Machine. The Machine, in turn, cranks out a given level of developmental and induced investment, and so a certain rate of unemployment and inflation. We have one point on a trade-off curve or Phillips curve.

As a consequence of all this, the bargaining curves and expectations lines of employers and unions shift. They go to the bargaining table next year with all these reactions behind them, and start again. The process is repeated, and out of the Machine comes another point for inflation and unemployment, which may be regarded as lying on the same TOC or Phillips curve, or which might be regarded as representing a shift in these curves.

Before turning to the problem of distinguishing movements along TOCs from shifts of TOCs, we must say a word about the other players in the game, Foreigners.

Foreigners

Four kinds of foreigners influence the outcome of the Game: exporters, importers, investors, and migrants. The impact of the migrants is perhaps most direct. They swell the labor force and thus, other things being equal, add to unemployment. Of course, they bring mouths as well as hands, but the lag between their arrival and the creation of new employment opportunities, simply because they are there, can be quite long. I have little doubt that in countries like Canada and Australia, immigration since World War II has in fact raised the level of unemployment; and to the degree that immigrants consume goods and services without producing them, they add to inflationary pressures as well. Exporters are of two kinds: those that export products of cheap labor to ICCs and thus aggravate unemployment; and those that raise prices of strategic imports (oil) and so add to the cost push, which must be offset by monetary expansion to limit unemployment. Importers aggravate inflation and unemployment by buying products of the sectors and regions where inflationary pressure is generated and refusing to buy those of the sectors and regions where unemployment is concentrated. Investors have their main impact by strengthening the tendency toward an increasing average period of investment; they like to invest in natural resource exploration and production, and other long-period projects. All these interventions are mutually reinforcing. Rising costs through higher prices of imported energy and raw materials raises export prices, thus raising costs in importing countries, and so on. The wage-price spiral also raises prices of exports, thus adding to the cost push of countries who must buy them. The Game is extremely inflationary, without necessarily expanding employment opportunities. Given a growing labor force and technological progress of a labor-displacing nature, we have here sufficient explanation of simultaneously increasing inflation and unemployment.

The Structure

Let us now turn to the three elements in the Structure.

Sectoral and Regional Disparities

When Gunnar Myrdal was Executive Secretary of the United Nations Economic Commission for Europe, he organized a study of regional development and underdevelopment in Europe. The results, which were published in the *Economic Survey of Europe in 1954,* were very interesting: (1) regional gaps were large in the poorer countries, small in the richer ones; (2) regional gaps are increasing in the poorer countries, diminishing in the richer ones. In those days Italy, Turkey, and Spain, along with Greece, Yugoslavia, and Portugal, were still regarded as underdeveloped countries. In such countries, with regional inequality defined as the proportion of the population living in regions where the average income was less than two thirds of the national average, the gap was about 33 percent, compared to some 10 percent in such countries as Norway and France, and only "a few percent" in Great Britain and Switzerland (33). Moreover, in countries where regional gaps were large they were also increasing; where gaps were small they were diminishing.

Other economists found that Myrdal's finding for Europe applied to other parts of the world as well. His principle began to take on the aspect of an universal law. Not long afterward came the explosion of interest in Phillips and trade-off curves, and the series of efforts to derive empirical TOCs for various countries from the available data. It was inevitable that the idea would occur to someone to look at the relationship between regional disparities and the position, configuration, and movements of TOCs. This relationship was the subject of my contribution to the 1972 *Essays in Honour of Paul Rosenstein-Rodan,* entitled "Trade-off Curves and Regional Gaps" (Higgins, 1972). Assembling data on both regional disparities and TOCs for the same countries, however, is a monumental task; and despite continued efforts to do so, I have been unable to update my essay in that volume. I am obliged, therefore, to present the same data again, for what they are worth.

Figure 12.2 is the same diagram that I presented in my essay in the Rosenstein-Rodan volume. It presents TOCs for eight countries, together with indices of dispersion in per capita income among regions in the same countries. It shows clearly that as regional gaps become larger, the national trade-off curve shifts upwards and to the right. Figure 12.3 presents similar data for the major regions of Canada, with much the same result, except that in Canada the regional TOCs display marked differences in slope, as well as in position, according to the degree of dispersion among sub-regions with in each of the five major regions.

As pointed out in the earlier paper, the data underlying this analysis are imperfect in many ways. In many ways—economically, politically, and socially—the gap between richest and poorest region in any country is more important than the overall dispersion index for all regions. In a country where there are a large number of regions defined for statistical purposes—Australia's ninety-four, for example—the gap between richest and poorest regions could be enormous, yet if most of the other regions have incomes close to the national average, the dispersion index could be low. Obviously, in measuring gaps one has to use the available statistics, and accept the definitions of "regions" of the authorities collecting the statistics—or else go out and gather them yourself, an impossible task. But when it comes to international comparisons, the regions for which statistics are available may be conceptually quite different for one country to another.

Nonetheless, the figures shown here are highly significant. They mean that the position, and the range through which they move, of TOCs and loops, in any country, are greatly affected by the degree of regional disparity—the extent of regional disintegration. The reason is simple: the size of regional gaps reflects the amount of frictional and structural unemployment, and so goes a long way towards determining the "natural

FIGURE 12.2
Trade-off Curves for Selected Countries, 1960–1965

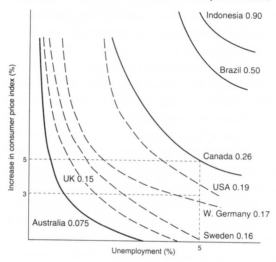

Sources: Bodkin et al. (1966), Williamson (1965), and Chernick (1966).

FIGURE 12.3
Trade-off Curves for Canadian Regions, 1963–1967

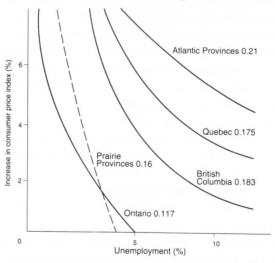

Sources: Chernick (1966), and Bodkin et al. (1966).

rate of unemployment." For similar reasons it has a good deal of influence on "the natural rate of inflation" as well.

A large part of this paper was devoted to providing a theoretical explanation of the close association between bad trade-off curves and wide regional disparities. The only real "theory" of trade-off curves so far is the concept of excess demand for (or supply of) labor, introduced into the literature by Lipsey, and carried further by Corry and Laidler, Marion, and others. The rate of change in wages and prices is related to the excess demand for labor, d-s; and the excess demand for labor is related to the level of unemployment. When d=s, so that excess demand is zero, unemployment will be limited to frictional and structural (sometimes called "natural") unemployment. Thus, the actual position of a trade-off curve will depend on the amount of frictional and structural unemployment in an economy. These in turn will depend on the degree of integration of various markets, as measured particularly by the degree of mobility of factors of production, especially labor, and the speed of movement. Under conditions when regional gaps cannot exist—perfect mobility of all factors or production, perfect knowledge, complete flexibility of wages and prices, well-behaved isoquants, etc.—trade-off curves will not exist either, since simultaneous inflation and unemployment would be impossible. The more unequal is the distribution of unemployment among various markets, the higher will be the trade-off curve. When markets are geographically (and culturally) separated, unemployment will tend to be more unequally distributed. Thus, the conditions that give rise to large and persistent regional gaps also produce unfavorable trade-off curves.

It is part of my argument that in countries where inflationary pressure is generated in one or two regions while unemployment is concentrated in one or two others, much can be done to push the national TOC back toward the origin by deliberate differentiation in fiscal policy among regions. We shall return to this point below. The problem is more complex where the disintegration is sectoral rather than regional. In LDCs, of course, there is usually a major overlap between regional gaps and sectoral gaps; the rich region is the one where the modern sector is concentrated, and the poor region is the one where the traditional sector is concentrated. In ICCs, the relationship between sectoral and regional disparities is often more subtle. In Australia, for example, the leading sector where inflationary pressure is generated consists of modern mining, a bit of scientifically oriented manufacturing, and infrastructure and services related to these. The lagging sector where unemployment is concentrated consists of traditional manufacturing: textiles, clothing, boots and shoes, furniture, metal working. (The relationship of this structural problem to the structural problem of resources engaged in activities where comparative advantage is nonexistent, discussed below, will already be apparent.) These two sectors do not fall neatly into geographic regions, although there is some concentration of the dynamic, inflation-generating sector in the frontier areas to the north, and some concentration of the traditional, high-unemployment sector in the older cities along the southern coasts, from Brisbane to Perth. We shall return to the policy implications of such structural problems below.

The Structure of Capital

Just as the basic system of interactions implicit in Schumpeter-Hansen-Samuelson-Harrod-Hicks models of economic fluctuations is still there beneath the surface of postwar economic behavior of ICCs, so the basic principle of a relationship between the structure of interest rates and expected profits on the one hand and the structure of capital on the other, the hard core of the Austrian theory of capital, is still valid. We cannot expect that all structures of capital are compatible with all structures of interest rates and expected profits. "Capital" is not an amorphous mass floating around ready to alight at will on one or another investment project, provided only that the relationship of interest rates to profits is attractive. Capital is a specific aggregation of particular kinds of plant, equipment, and inventories; and the capital: output ratio and the capital:labor ratio are the outcome of a particular mix of these kinds of capital that is in existence at a particular point of time.

During this period, there was a new wave of investment in capital-intensive, long gestation period, and long-life projects: oil search and mining, other mineral production and exploration (bauxite, uranium, copper, etc.), heavy industry, rubber and oil palm plantations, power, transport, housing, research and development in new fields like electronics and computer technology. These fields were attractive because of innovations, scarcities of energy and raw materials, population growth, and rapidly growing demand. During the 1950s, wartime shortages and destruction still played a role. Certainly, interest rates were no deterrent to investment of this kind; real interest rates may never have been lower.

In many countries, basic interest rates were only slightly above, or even slightly below, expected rates of inflation. This lengthening of the average period of investment meant that a given amount of investment, which could be expected to generate as much monetary expansion as before, would generate less expansion of output to offset the increased inflationary pressure, and less employment.

Moreover, in the recession following 1972 and the recessions of the 1980s and 1990s, according to the hypothesis, as private investment tapered off, the *average* period of investment increased again. Contrary to the Hayek theory of crises, and in contrast to actual experience in the 1929–1933 downswing, during those recessions, it was *not* the long investment period projects that were abandoned. The housing projects, the roads and railroads, the pipelines, the offshore oil search and drilling, the power plants, continued. The decline in private investment was more a matter of letting inventories run down and cutting back on orders for new equipment than abandonment of long-run development projects. In the developmental investment sphere, the recession was more a matter of stagnation than of absolute decline.

These tendencies in the private sector were aggravated by actions taken in the public sector. In order to offset the growing unemployment and its repercussions, governments of ICCs paid unemployment insurance benefits and enlarged public works spending. Treating unemployment insurance as "investment in human resources," it can be regarded as a type of investment for which the incremental capital:output ratio is infinite; it swells the spending stream but generates no offsetting flow of goods and services that could counteract the inflationary impact of such spending. The same is true of most kinds of public works spending. Not only does the output frequently appear only after a substantial time lag, but very often there is no product that is sold in the market to offset the inflationary impact. Even when a marketed product does appear, as in the case of publicly assisted housing or government enterprises in the fields of energy and transport, the lag between initial investment and sale of final product is long, and the resulting capital good is durable and amortised over a long period. When this sort of investment replaces production of shoes or textiles, it is obvious that the average period of investment is lengthened and the incremental capital output ratio raised.

We may summarize the argument in a simple model.

We shall use the following symbols:

P = the general price level

Y = national income

O = total output of goods and services (real flows)

K = the stock of capital; $I = \Delta K$, investment

m = the Keynesian multiplier (treated as a constant)

a = the output:capital ratio (treated as a parameter; a constant but subject to discontinuous shifts as a consequence of exogenous changes)

n = the employment capital ratio (treated as a constant subject to shifts)

N = the level of employment

L = size of the labor force (given)

U = level of unemployment

The model has five basic equations in five unknowns:

$$P = Y/0 \tag{1}$$

$$\Delta P = \frac{\Delta Y.0 - \Delta 0.Y}{0^2} \tag{1a}$$

$$0 = a.K$$

$$\Delta 0 = a.\Delta K + \Delta a.K$$

$$= a.I \tag{2a}$$

$$Y = m.I \tag{3}$$

$$\Delta Y = m.\Delta I \tag{3a}$$

$$N = n.I \tag{4}$$

$$\Delta N = n.\Delta K + \Delta n K$$

$$= n.I \tag{4a}$$

$$U = L - N \tag{5}$$

$$\Delta U = \Delta L - \Delta N \tag{5a}$$

Substituting from Equations 2a and 3a in equation 1a, we have:

$$\Delta P = \frac{\Delta I - a.I.mI}{(aK)^2} \tag{6}$$

Since "ΔI" is small compared to "I," and "K," the total stock of capital is a very large number, it is apparent that a small decline in "ΔI" accompanied by a decline in "a" will be highly inflationary.

Since "n" and "a" are both constants related to "K," "n" can be expressed in terms of "a:"

$N = n.k$ $\qquad\qquad$ $n = N/K$

$0 = a.k$ $\qquad\qquad$ $a = 0/K$

Therefore, $\dfrac{n}{a} = \dfrac{N/K}{0/K} = \dfrac{N}{0}$

Substituting in Equation 5a, 4a,

$U = \Delta L - \Delta N$

$\quad = \Delta L - nI$

$\quad = \Delta L - \dfrac{a.n}{0} . I$

When "I" falls slightly and "a" falls, unemployment increases.

Thus, when "I" falls slightly and "a" also falls, both inflation and unemployment are aggravated.

Structure of Production and Trade

We come now to a more delicate topic: the existence in ICCs of former "infant industries" that grew up behind high protective tariff walls, and which have now become doddering geriatrics in need of more protection than ever. Australia, Canada, New Zealand—even the United States— together with the former European imperialist powers, are now paying a high price for colonial policies of encouraging the growth of manufacturing at home and discouraging it in the colonies. It is obvious that in most of the countries of the third world, at existing wage rates, comparative advantage lies in manufacturing and comparative disadvantage is more marked in agriculture. Yet in many LDCs, the great bulk of the population is still engaged in peasant agriculture. It is equally obvious that in Australia, Canada, New Zealand, the United States, Argentina, Uruguay, and the Netherlands, comparative advantage is more marked in agriculture, particularly production of foodstuffs. Yet in these countries, only a small fraction of the labor force is engaged in agriculture. The imbalance in resource allocation has now reached such proportions that no imaginable series of marginal responses to market signals could bring rapid adjustment of the international division of labor to true, long-run comparative advantage. There is no way that the great majority of

Indian workers can be quickly absorbed into manufacturing and sophisticated services, leaving a small minority in agriculture. And there is no way that the majority of Australian or Canadian workers can be absorbed into agriculture. It would do no good to try; the level of technology in agriculture is such in these countries that doubling the proportion of the labor force in agriculture from 5 percent to 10 percent would hardly raise agricultural output at all; even in agriculture technological coefficients tend to become fixed when a very large scale of production is reached and land-and-capital-intensive technology is used. Of course, a lot of people could be forced on the land and made to use Asian-style, labor-intensive techniques by an authoritarian government; but it is doubtful that agricultural output would be increased thereby and it might even fall. Certainly, living standards of farmers would fall drastically, and just as certainly, no democratic government would dream of such a solution to problems of inflation and unemployment.

What the governments of countries like Australia, Canada, the United States, and other agricultural surplus countries do in fact is to continue protecting traditional industries such as textiles, clothing, boots and shoes, furniture, and metal working, which could not possibly withstand competition from developing countries in a completely free market, despite the formal commitments to give preferential treatment to the manufactured exports of LDCs. Inefficiency in some of these industries in ICCs is so profound (relative to wage rates), protection and subsidies are on such a scale, that they amount virtually to "make-work" projects in the private sector. The consequence is further raising of the capital:output and capital:labor ratios (for society as a whole) and further aggravation of the cost-push. At the same time, enough imports are coming in from LDCs into these ICCs to add to the level of unemployment in them. The amount may not seem large: it is estimated at 0.5 percent to 1.5 percent of the labor force in countries where calculations have been made. But there is also an indirect effect that is estimated to be much greater. In a desperate attempt to remain competitive with low-wage countries, technological improvement has been accelerated. The result is technological unemployment. Thus, this structural problem helps to explain the outward drift of the trade-off curve.

There does not seem to be any simple solution to this problem. The classical argument is that technological displacement is only temporary, and that technological improvement can only be beneficial. In the long run, this argument no doubt remains true; but, meanwhile, there can be little question that technological unemployment is increasing, perhaps in part because unemployment insurance schemes have changed job-search behavior, in part because the rhythm of technological change is so rapid. Similarly, the stock advice of economists to countries like the United States, Canada, and Australia, where traditional enterprises can no longer compete, is "move on to higher technology and abandon the traditional industries." The present writer has given this advice to his own country (Canada) more than once. But which advanced technology industries, and how? Some of the LDCs are in the process of leapfrogging over the backs of such ICCs where technology is concerned. India, Singapore, Hong Kong, Brazil, Malaysia, Taiwan, South Korea, Thailand—these countries are exporting not only textiles but electronics, scientific instruments, turbines, automobiles, computer components, and consulting services. Low wage rates have an effect even here. Of course, no country can produce all of everything the world wants and needs, and as the LDCs progress, they will provide splendid markets for somebody to sell something. But it is not easy to see just where Australia, Canada, or New Zealand, for example, could hope to undersell manufactured goods or sophisticated services produced in Asia. Certainly, it is too much to expect a small-scale manufacturer of clothing or foot valves to undertake the scientific, technical, and market research himself, to discover where he may find a new niche. Government must lend a hand in this process if such small-scale manufacturers are to survive in a world of increasingly liberalized trade. Meanwhile, both inflationary pressures and unemployment emanating from this aspect of the Structure are likely to increase.

We have here another sufficient explanation of simultaneously increasing inflation and unemployment, when all the factors entailed in the operation of the Machine and the aggravations emanating from the Structure are added together.

Interactions

We see, therefore, that we have not one, but several explanations of simultaneous, and even of simultaneously increasing, inflation and unemployment. The Machine produces fluctuations of varying lengths. Left to itself it would no doubt generate fluctuations of the prewar type, with alternating inflation and unemployment. There is good reason to believe that in the long run, an unattended Machine would produce cycles of increasing amplitude, so that over the cycle as a whole, the average level of inflation and unemployment might rise. This tendency is aggravated by efforts to limit unemployment; governments simply do not manage their money supplies so as to produce significant reductions in the general price level, accepting whatever level of unemployment may emerge. Every aspect of the Structure aggravates the tendency toward increasing inflation and unemployment: growing sectoral and regional distortions; the lengthening period of investment; and the increasingly marked disequilibrium in the global structure of production and trade. The Game generates price increases through actions taken by all the players, but with costs and prices rising together, profit margins are little affected, and private investment fails to keep up with the combined effects on unemployment of a growing labor force and technological displacement. There are, moreover, interactions among the three major components of the whole process. The increasing amplitude of the underlying cycles requires accelerated monetary expansion to avoid increasing unemployment; the consequent acceleration of inflation raises expectations regarding price increases of both unions and employers, thus raising both labor demands and employer concessions. Rising unemployment in itself raises expectations regarding monetary expansion, which could induce unions to demand, and employers to grant, higher wage increases. Structural imbalances are themselves self-reinforcing; investment will tend to flow towards those sectors and regions where expansion is taking place and inflation is generated, and away from stagnant sectors and regions where unemployment is concentrated.

References

Bodkin, Ronald G., Elizabeth I. Bond, Grant L. Reuber, and T. Russel Robinson. *Price Stability and High Employment: The Options for Canadian Economic Policy.* Ottawa: Economic Council of Canada, Special Study 5, Queen's Printer, 1966.

Chernick, Sydney, E., *Interregional Distribution of Income.* Ottawa: Economic Council of Canada, 1966.

Higgins, Benjamin. "Trade-Off Curves and Regional Gaps." In Jagdish Baghwati, and Richard Eckaus, *Development and Planning: Essays in Honour of Paul Rosenstein Rodan.* London: George Allen & Unwin, 1972.

Lipsey, R. "The Relationship Between Unemployment and the Rate of Change of Money Wage Rates in the United Kingdom, 1862-1957: A Further Analysis." *Economica (new series)* 27 (February 1960): 1–21.

Williamson, Jeffery G. "Regional Inequality and the Process of National Development." *Economic Development and Cultural Change* (July 1965).

Part V
Policy

13

The Approach to Policy

When it comes to moving from theory to policy, there are some fundamental differences between the business cycle theories outlined in part I and the analysis presented in part III. These differences impose a new approach to policies directed toward the elimination—or, less ambitiously, the reduction to acceptable levels—of unemployment and inflation. Differences that must be taken into account in designing policy include the following:

1. Most of the earlier theories strove to discover and explain *the* cause of economic fluctuations, or cycles. The fluctuations were conceived as taking place around an equilibrium trend, usually thought of as a trend with full employment and a stable price level. In other words, economic fluctuations, or business cycles, with *alternating* inflation and unemployment, were regarded as lapses from the normal condition of steady growth. The economy was normally in equilibrium, and tended to move back to equilibrium if any disturbance took place. This vision of the functioning of a market economy made the task of the policymaker relatively simple: having discovered *the* cause of lapses from steady growth, eliminate it, thus preventing departures from equilibrium. If that aim proves too difficult to attain continuously, at least accelerate the natural return to equilibrium if unforeseen disturbances occur.

Thus, for example, von Hayek identified *the* cause as overinvestment, generated by failure of the banking system to synchronize increases in interest rates with improvements in profit expectations. Policy solution? Easy: *do it*! The task of keeping market interest rates always equal to the "natural rate" that guarantees continuous equilibrium growth is primarily the responsibility of the central bank. It takes a certain degree of skill; but given the skill and the will, steady growth should be assured. Keynes, on the other hand, identified *the* cause of depression and unemployment as oversavings or underconsumption. Policy solution? Also easy: offset the oversaving by deficit-financed government spending, increasing expenditures or lowering taxes, or both. If *instead* the problem is inflation, reverse the procedure, cut spending, raise taxes, and produce a budget surplus. Virtually all the earlier theories implied that unemployment or inflation can be cured by an appropriate combination of monetary and fiscal policy. Only in very rare circumstances, such as major wars, were direct controls, regulations, or other forms of direct intervention in the economy given any consideration, and only then because a degree and speed of structural transformation was required that an unaided free market could not be guaranteed to achieve on its own.

Today there is a pervasive skepticism among economists about the very existence of "equilibrium," and even more skepticism about any "natural" tendency toward it, let alone a natural tendency toward full employment and stable price levels. The analysis in part III makes no use of the concept of equilibrium, except as a purely hypothetical situation whereby, more or less by accident, the north, south, east, and west forces in the "topocross" happen to be equally strong for a while. In my analysis there is no "natural" tendency toward such a situation; on the contrary, it would be highly unnatural and extremely rare. It is not even a situation that would necessarily be good if it did occur. An economy might be stable for a short period, in the sense that the rates of unemployment and inflation did not change, but both might be intolerably high. Instead of aiming to eliminate fluctuations, policy within the analytical framework of part III is seen as a constant struggle against *both* unemployment and inflation. In any case, there would be no sense in eliminating a "cycle" or "fluctuation" which, at the present time, happens to take the form of simultaneous reductions in both unemployment and inflation, even if the economic system is not heading for "equilibrium," and the present phase may be followed by another in which both unemployment and inflation will be increasing. The time to resist market forces is when that starts to happen; until then policy might better be directed toward strengthening market forces and making them continue in the same direction.

Our analysis in part III suggests that there are so many factors that can make an economy fall off the steady-growth "knife edge" that it is highly unlikely that any economy, left to its own devices, will stay on it for very long. The combination of unemployment and inflation existing at any point of time, and *possibly* prevailing through some period of time, is the result of the manner in which the entire economic system functions, including government policy, which is part of the system. Moreover, the causal factors that yield unacceptable levels of unemployment, or inflation, or both, in any particular economy, may be different at different times. Thus to be effective, the policymakers must be continuously aware of *everything* that is happening in the national economy, and in the regional economies of which it is composed. That requirement includes being aware of any and all developments in the global economy that have an impact on the national economy with which they are concerned, which in most cases will include virtually everything happening in the global economy. Policy must therefore be extremely flexible, and there must be many varieties of tools in the toolkit, each highly specialized and adapted to deal with a particular set of circumstances.

2. The earlier theories rested on the assumption that the manner in which the Machine operates is known, or at least knowable; and that this knowledge will lead directly to selection and application of appropriate policy. The theory expounded in part III, however, maintains that while a good deal is indeed known about the operation of the Machine, taken by itself, much less is known about the impact of the Structure and changes in it; and that the outcome of the Game is essentially unknowable, like a poker game or a chess match. This argument does not mean that government is helpless in its efforts to improve the performance of the economy; for government is itself a player in the Game, and, in the end, probably the most powerful player. As the game goes on and government acquires more knowledge of the psychology of the other players, it may even be able to anticipate their moves, and so design its strategy in advance. Unlike opponents in a chess game, or even the players in a poker game, government is always the dealer, and so has an advantage (even if it doesn't cheat). It can learn not only to bluff, but also to warn—saying to big business and big labor, "You had better not make that move, or I will make this one, and you'll be sorry." At worst, government can always respond to moves of the other players in such a way as to minimize their harmful effects.

However, as in a real poker game or chess match, the moves of the government must be continuous; it cannot just make a move, go away, and come back in six months or a year. Moreover, it is not just monetary policy that must be continuously adjusted; the possibility of bringing into play another tool from the toolkit, or of changing the mode of using tools already in use, must be kept under constant consideration. As we shall see in more detail below, playing *this* sort of Game in *this* sort of way requires changes in the organization of government.

More disconcerting than the uncertainties involved in the Game are the continuing uncertainties surrounding the mechanism of the Machine itself. We know that the operation of the Machine has changed since World War II, but we don't know exactly how. Therefore, we cannot be absolutely sure of how it will react to various policy options. We must be prepared, not only to use a wide variety of tools in different situations, but to drop them like a hot potato if they don't work in the way expected—or, if the possibility exists, to use them in a different and more effective manner. For example, we have learned that we cannot hope to eliminate unemployment and inflation, always and everywhere, through macroeconomic monetary and fiscal policy alone. Nonetheless, it is extremely important to know what combination of these policies, on their own, would produce the minimum discomfort point (the best possible combination of unemployment and inflation).

Having achieved that much, we can then consider other policies designed to push and pull the economy to a still better point. Now to achieve an optimal combination of monetary and fiscal policies, it is essential to know, at each point of time and during each period of time, whether the economy is on a trade-off curve, offering a choice of different combinations of unemployment and inflation, all achievable through monetary and fiscal policy alone; or whether it is on a cyclical loop, generated by forces so strong that they cannot be offset, but only modified, by macroeconomic policy. Of course, if unemployment and inflation are moving *down* together, the authorities might be excused if they decide just to relax and enjoy it. But when they are moving *up* together, it is of crucial importance to know whether relaxing anti-inflationary policies will reduce unemployment, or whether lower interest rates and taxes, and higher expenditures, will fail to check the eastward movement; or even, by frightening the business and financial community, accelerate it, increasing rather than decreasing unemployment.

We have no general theory that can provide answers to questions like this. The authorities in a particular country may come to know the leaders in the business and financial communities, and in the trade unions, well enough to make informed guesses as to what will happen. But there is no way of making absolutely sure of what will happen except trial and error. Once again, the importance of extreme flexibility in monetary and fiscal policy is apparent. But of course, other tools are available. There is no sense in limiting policy to the macro level, unless the great majority of the people in the society have a strong and clear-cut aversion to all forms of micro and meso (sectoral and regional) intervention, and would much rather have higher levels of unemployment and inflation than any increase in the role of government in the economy.

What belongs to the Machine and what to the Game? This whole approach is so new that it is not easy to say. Standard, mainstream economics depends on behavioral assumptions. The Game is about behavior too. Why not simply incorporate the Game into the Machine? My reason is that in my view there is a fundamental difference between the two. I regard the outcome of the Game as essentially unknowable; study it as you will, and however familiar you may become with the players, you will never be able to predict the outcome with complete certainty, every time; to revert once again to my analogy, no more than one could predict the outcome of every championship chess match with complete certainty. I think of the Machine as a set of functional relationships that can be described and quantified, as in an econometric model. Such relationships as the multiplier and the accelerator do not change every day; they have a certain stability, and when they change one soon knows it and can quantify the new relationship. The Machine has changed in recent decades, and we do not understand the new relationships well enough to say whether we are currently enmeshed in a system of shifting TOCs, or on a cyclical loop, possibly with only one attainable point at each point of time, or possibly with a few options available to the policymakers. But I do not believe that such relationships are inherently unknowable, and I think that ultimately they will be known.

3. While some interest was shown in regional business cycles before World War II, on the whole, business cycle theory at that time, and the policy recommendations that came out of it, applied to national economies. In countries with federal constitutions there was an effort to integrate federal, state or provincial, and sometimes local, fiscal policy; but there was no thought of using regional differences as building blocks to construct a policy to reduce unemployment and inflation simultaneously. The theory presented in part III leads to a totally different approach to policy. Instead of striving for a uniform policy throughout the land, with

central, state or provincial, and local governments marching together in harmonious goosestep, the theory leads to deliberate discrimination amongst regions in fiscal policy, with increased expenditures (and possibly reductions in taxes) in regions with high unemployment, and reductions in spending (and possibly increases in taxation) in regions generating inflationary pressure. (Differentiation of tax rates amongst regions would no doubt encounter political opposition; but Canada has twice effectively used accelerated or postponed appreciation to encourage some industries or sectors and discourage others; the same device could be used to discriminate among regions.)

It is not just a matter of different levels of total *per capita* spending or tax collection according to the economic situation in different regions; it is a matter of encouraging or discouraging *particular projects* (public or private) in *particular places* at *particular times*. Decisions to encourage or discourage would be based on thorough analysis of the types of human, natural, and capital resources that are unemployed in each region; and of the requirements of various projects for these resources, as well as the value in use of the goods and services that each project would make available. It is a matter also of postponing expenditures on projects (public or private) in overheated regions that are not essential in the near future, and which use excessive amounts of particularly scarce resources.

It follows from this approach that policy cannot be the same in all countries at all times, nor in all regions of one country. For example, in Canada, such a policy could be quite conveniently implemented by discriminating among provinces. Discriminating among states in Australia would achieve little; the differences in economic position among states are too small, to achieve the desired results, Discriminations would have to take place among considerably smaller regions.

We shall examine a number of real-world case studies below. Here, by way of demonstration, let us consider a few examples of policy decisions, which in the present context are hypothetical, but which are based on real situations. The country of Utonia (well-known in economic development circles as the favorite case study of the Institute of Economic and Social Studies in the Hague) has a national unemployment rate of 10 percent and an inflation rate of 5 percent. It has been following a tight monetary policy, of which the business and financial community approves in a general sort of way. Any threat of an expansionary policy that could lead to accelerating inflation would bring pessimistic expectations, which could well increase unemployment by scaring off investment. However, there is growing insistence that government must do something about unemployment, an insistence shared even by the business and financial communities in the more depressed regions where unemployment is highest. Unemployment ranges from 5 percent in the booming region of Siliconia, with its rapidly growing hi-tech industries, to 25 percent in the decadent farming, fishing, and forestry region of Esperanza. However, high unemployment is not limited to regions dependent on primary industry. Unemployment is also high in the former industrial heartland of Smokestackia. There are job vacancies in Siliconia, but only for highly trained and skilled workers who can handle efficiently certain specialized jobs. Unemployment there is as high as it is only because people who have lost their jobs in Esperanza and other lagging regions go to Siliconia in hopes of finding work, but they are incapable of doing the jobs that are vacant. (Readers will quickly recognize the strong resemblance of Utonia's economic situation to that of Australia, Canada, New Zealand, the United Kingdom, and the United States.)

Clearly something must be done, and done quickly, if the government is to be returned to power in next year's election. Equally clearly, Utonia's economic problems cannot be solved by monetary policy alone. It is not at all clear that reducing interest rates would bring down unemployment to acceptable levels. Lower interest rates, if they increase investment at all, are more likely to increase it in Siliconia than in either Esperanza or Smokestackia, thus increasing inflationary pressure, raising wage rates in high-tech industries, and prices everywhere. If inflation shows signs of becoming cumulative, the result may even be that the nervous and hypersensitive business and financial community will reduce investment, thus increasing unemployment throughout the country.

A straightforward policy of encouraging migration—offering free tickets to Siliconia on government owned airlines and railways, and undertaking public investment there in schools, hospitals, low-cost housing, and industrial parks—also would not work. There would be no jobs for the migrants from the high-unemployment regions, and the increased spending in Siliconia would aggravate inflationary pressure there, which would soon spread to other regions.

A policy of encouraging migration combined with a policy of retraining workers to acquire the skills needed in Siliconia, setting up technical schools and colleges and subsidizing on-the-job training by private enterprise, *might* work, but it would be very expensive. It would involve abandoned housing, school places, and hospital beds in the retarded regions, as well as broken families and distorted age structures there; and it would involve heavy investment in infrastructure in Siliconia. Before embarking on such a policy, surely it would make sense to take another hard look at the possibility of job creation in Esperanza and Smokestackia, and of postponement of expensive, capital intensive, high-skill-requirement projects in Siliconia?

The objective is not to kill geese that are laying golden eggs. The purpose is to accelerate growth of the national economy, not retard it. But as a rule infrastructure in prosperous regions is of a higher quality than infrastructure of retarded regions; consequently, there are nearly always public investment projects on the horizon, perhaps even some that are fully planned and ready to go, that can be postponed without imposing real hardship on the residents of the region. In Siliconia the construction of a new high school, planned to begin next year and to be completed in three years, can be postponed for two or three years; all that will happen is that classrooms and athletic facilities in the existing high school will be slightly more crowded. The refurbishing of town halls can also be delayed. Adding new runways instead of building entire new airports can handle the growth of traffic for another few years.

On the other hand, infrastructure in retarded regions is nearly always inadequate in some respects, and "telescoping" (bringing forward in time) of badly needed construction projects (housing, schools, hospitals, parks, parkways, streets) can bring significant benefits to the residents, as well as creating new employment. More important, as experience with regional development planning in virtually all developing countries, and in some industrialized countries, shows, a properly designed regional development planning team, with the right level and the right range of expertise, can *nearly always* find profitable opportunities for *private* investment within the region.

Regions like Smokestackia, and still more regions like Esperanza, after decades of stagnation or decline, cannot be expected to have within their own populations all the entrepreneurial, managerial, scientific, and technical skills necessary to bring about a transformation and resurgence of its economy. But teams that assemble the requisite expertise from *outside* the region can, and often do, bring about that resurgence, in collaboration with such local talent as exists (Higgins and Savoie, 1988).

Examples are legion; but to cite only a few, the regional development planning exercise mounted in 1976 for the Canadian city of Moncton, New Brunswick, by the Department of Regional Economic Expansion, transformed a moribund railway town into the most dynamic city in New Brunswick, and one of the most dynamic in the whole of Atlantic Canada. The United Nations team in Libya, especially the Food and Agriculture Organization experts, converted the Sahara desert, in the vast area between the escarpment and the sea, into a lush garden, with citrus orchards, olive groves, tobacco plantations, and vegetable gardens. The team mounted by the Canadian International Development Agency to prepare a plan for the Malaysian region of Pahang Tenggara provided the foundation for transforming the region from a virtually empty, largely under-developed jungle into a prosperous plantation economy. It is worth noting too that such regional development schemes do not bring a substitution of public for private enterprise. On the contrary, the teams themselves were composed of private consultants, not bureaucrats. They were recruited by private consulting firms or directly from universities. The execution of the plans opened up opportunities for private enterprise, on a scale and with a scope that had not even been dreamed of until the studies were made and the plans prepared (Higgins and Savoie, 1988).

It cannot be denied that in some cases, a tailor-made team of appropriate experts would decide, after careful study, that the only solution for unemployment (and perhaps for poverty) is emigration from the region. There may be some regions in the world that are strictly no hopers, regions where the original base for growth of output, income, employment, and population has completely disappeared (totally exhausted mining and forestry areas, for example) and where there is absolutely no alternative base for future growth in sight. In such cases encouraged emigration and retraining may be the right policy. However, in the range of experience of the present writer, such cases are extremely rare, exceptions that prove the rule.

We have been talking of unemployment and inflation and how to cure them. But note that in talking about regions like Esperanza and Smokestackia we are by implication talking about foreign trade policy and "adjustment" as well. When once-prosperous regions become decadent regions, the reason often is that once-strong exports are no longer competitive in national or world markets. "Adjustment" then becomes essential, unless the national society is willing to accept the inefficiency, costs, and sacrifice of potential income associated with continued, and probably increasing, protection. But "adjustment" is just another way of saying "development," or "solution," for regions with problems like those of Esperanza and Smokestackia. There is no way of separating monetary and fiscal policy from foreign trade policy, and there is no way of separating any of these from regional development policy.

With the approach to policy that arises out of the analysis in part III of this volume, we find that regional development policy, instead of being something apart from the main issues of monetary, fiscal, and foreign trade policy, is in fact an integral and major part of all three of them. There is no hope of finding satisfactory solutions to unemployment, inflation, balance of payments problems, stagnation, and inefficiencies associated with failure to adjust, unless regions are used as building blocks, and unless formulation of policy designed to resolve all these problems begins with analysis at the regional level, and ends with policies that discriminate among regions.

A corollary of this conclusion is that one cannot design effective policy to deal with unemployment, inflation, and balance of payments problems, and obviously not with regional disparities, with knowledge of such macroeconomic variables as level and rate of growth of national income, level of interest rates, employment and unemployment, government expenditures, tax rates, and budget deficits or surpluses, exports and imports, international capital flows, for the national economy alone. One must also have detailed knowledge of regional structures, regional differences and imbalances, and the functioning of the regional economies of which the national economies is composed. Unfortunately, in most industrialized countries, this is a sort of knowledge that central banks, ministries of finance, treasuries, and ministries of trade and commerce do not have, and really do not want to have. If there is within the government structure a department specializing in regional development, it is rarely consulted by the authorities making monetary, fiscal, and foreign trade policy. Formulation of effective policy will require a new mind-set in the old-line agencies of most governments, and a new form of government organization to go with it.

Reference

Higgins, Benjamin, and Donald J. Savoie. *Canadians and Regional Development at Home and in the Third World.* Moncton, New Brunswick: Canadian Institute for Research on Regional Development, 1988.

14

Designing Policy for the Late 1990s and Beyond

From what has been said now several times, particularly in the previous chapter, and perhaps *ad nauseam,* this final chapter on general policy should not be expected to present a concrete and uniform set of policies to cure unemployment, inflation, regional disparities, and other economic ills, valid always and everywhere. Nor should it be expected to provide detailed programs to eradicate these ills in individual countries. The whole thrust of the argument has been that, given the nature and the performance of the global economy in the 1990s, economic policy, if it is to be effective, must differ from country to country, and from region to region within one country, in any given period of time. It must also vary from time to time, as conditions change, in any particular country or region. Sometimes, with drastic and unexpected changes of the situation in the global or national economy, policy may need to be radically revised almost literally overnight. Effective economic policy requires constant vigilance and extreme flexibility. Sharp eyes must be kept, not only on the Machine, but on the Structure and on the Game as well.

It is the Game that gives the most trouble, and which has come to dominate the global economy, and most national economies. For the most part, if no other forces are involved, the Machine operates more or less in the manner predicted by standard micro- and macroeconomic theory. A *marginal* reduction in interest rates or taxes, or a marginal increase in government expenditures, may be expected to bring a marginal increase in investment, employment, and income. Structural changes for the most part take place slowly, are visible, knowable, and quantifiable. Policy can be readily enough adapted to take account of structural change. There are, however, two sets of forces that may prevent the outcome of policy changes from being identical to what standard theory would predict. One of these might be labelled *the Mystery Machine,* which generates those portions of observed cyclical loops where unemployment and inflation are increasing together. The forces that generate these movements seem to last too long, running into several years, to be explained by the vagaries of the Game alone. It is possible, of course, that "the rules of The Game" become established or rigidified for a period of years, in such a way that the pattern of simultaneously increasing inflation and unemployment *must* occur for a certain length of time, in much the way that cumulative movements dictated the pattern of the old prewar cycle. Expectations may solidify, and remain set for years at a time. We don't yet know, and this lack of knowledge limits our capacity to predict the results of policy changes.

It is still worse, however, with the Game, since *its* results are inherently unknowable. The big labor players, and still more the big business players, are as fidgety and jumpy as a thoroughbred stallion; and any drastic and unexpected change in the strategy of big government, or of foreigners, may result in a violent response. As Joseph Schumpeter argued two generations ago, in his critique of President Roosevelt's New Deal policies, any significant change in the rules of the game frightens entrepreneurs and investors, causing them to scramble for safety and liquidity rather than undertaking risky new investment, if they don't actually panic. The result is a drop in investment, employment, and income. For two generations, investors and entrepreneurs have been told by their governments, especially in the industrialized capitalist countries, that inflation is the worst thing that can befall a national economy, and that fighting inflation is the major economic objective of any decent national government. Thus, any sign of abandonment of the battle against inflation is frightening; and reductions in interest rates or taxes, or increases in government expenditures, big enough to reduce unemployment, according to the textbook, may instead frighten entrepreneurs and investors into scrambling for safety and liquidity, reducing investment and increasing unemployment.

As this paragraph was being written, in Australia Prime Minister Paul Keating was struggling with this precise problem. With unemployment still high, the federal government was under severe pressure from both big labor and big business to do something about it; but both big labor and big business are extremely nervous about any policy that might increase the rate of inflation. There is no important conflict of interest between labor and management; both want reductions in both inflation and unemployment. But both are fearful of what may happen if the government loses control of the economy. The general mood is one of extreme uncertainty as to the probable *impact* of changes in policy. The economic and political situation is much the same in Canada, New Zealand, the United Kingdom, and the United States.

Thus, in making economic policy governments cannot simply look at the main indicators of the current position of the economy and the forecasts for next year. They must also understand the *moods* of big business and big labor, and of the relevant foreigners. Indeed, since no government is completely united, the policymakers must understand the moods of big government as well.

Thus economic policymakers today need to be extremely knowledgeable and well informed, brilliantly analytical, sensitive to the moods of all major social groups, intrepid—and, of course, properly advised. It is a tall order. To come closer to an understanding of how effective economic policy might be formulated, let us review a check list of the major branches of economic policy.

Monetary Policy

We begin with monetary policy because it is the most universally used, and the most widely discussed in the media; as a result, it is probably the most widely understood.

We have argued above that monetary policy is ineffective as a device for fighting unemployment and inflation simultaneously, and that its results are uncertain. That doesn't mean that monetary policy is unimportant. On the contrary, a sound monetary policy is the foundation upon which other economic policies rest. Monetary policy must be carried as far as possible toward the achievement of national goals, and then we can see what remains to be done through use of other policy instruments.

If we were sure that the national economy was on a trade-off curve, and that the curve would be stable for some length of time, then the principal objective of monetary policy could be expressed in the manner illustrated in figure 14.1. TOC_1 and TOC_2 are trade-off curves and CIC_1 and CIC_2 are community indifference curves, showing combinations of unemployment and inflation that the population considers equally undesirable, or "uncomfortable" as Okun expresses it. The optimal position is obviously at "O," where the TOC just touches the lowest conceivable indifference curve; "O" is Okun's "minimum discomfort point." We assume that the economy is actually on TOC_2. I have added a second vertical axis on the right of the diagram, showing interest rates (as a shorthand for monetary policies) that are consistent with the horizontally opposite points on the TOC. The interest rate yielding the minimum attainable discomfort point is 8 percent.

The community indifference curve is not revealed in any market, or fully revealed anywhere else. Still, there are various channels for expression of public opinion on this score, and the authorities can form some idea of the shape of the CIC. Indeed, bringing the national economy to point "O" is what central banks have essentially been trying to do for the past three decades; and in my view, with a considerable degree of success. Of course there are other considerations that must be taken into account, notably the balance of payments and the levels of interest rates that will attract or drive away foreign capital, and these may not be totally consistent with arriving at "O." Nonetheless, I feel that the major aim of central banks has been to attain and maintain the best possible combination of unemployment and inflation.

There are, however, more serious technical problems in maintaining an economy at "O". There is no assurance whatsoever that the position at "O" is identical with position "E," or equilibrium, as defined in chapter 5: that is, the position on some trade-off curve where the "natural rate of unemployment" is combined with "the natural rate of inflation." Only at that hypothetical "equilibrium" point is unemployment at the lowest possible level attainable without accelerating inflation, and the rate of inflation at the lowest level attainable without increasing unemployment. It may not exist at all, let alone being the same point as "O." In other words, the TOC may be inherently unstable, and efforts to achieve "O" may only shift it toward higher unemployment, or higher inflation, or even both. This danger is especially severe, of course, if the economy is in phase one of a loop, as shown in figure 14.2. In short, whatever the current situation of the economy with respect to unemployment and inflation, there is no guarantee that good monetary policy alone will make it better; but bad monetary policy could certainly make it worse. National economies and monetary policy are in something the position of a faithful Calvinist: if you are not one of the chosen to begin with, there is no chance of getting to heaven; but even if you are among the chosen,

FIGURE 14.1
The Trade-Off Between Inflation and Unemployment

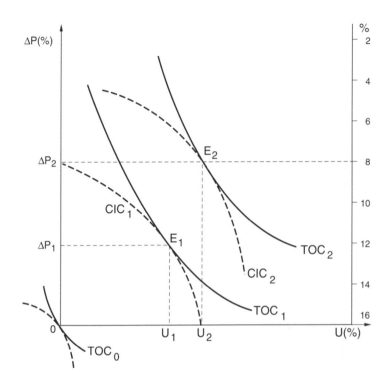

you can spoil your chances of getting to heaven by bad behavior. Just in case, you had better behave. So the monetary authorities cannot know if they are capable of leading the national economy to heaven; but just in case, they must try constantly to do so.

Suppose the economy is on a stable loop, as in figure 14.2. In phase one of the cycle, there is really not much the monetary authorities can do, except to try to prevent the northeast movement from becoming cumulative, so that the economy leaves the cyclical path and shoots off on a path like b-b'. If they know how to do it, they might try to accelerate the cycle, to arrive sooner at phase two, where there is at least a kind of trade-off, so that they can seek a minimum discomfort point on it. Such a policy would probably entail lower interest rates to combat unemployment, and to slow down the drop in inflation rates. In phase three they could, and

FIGURE 14.2
Hypothetical Stable Loop

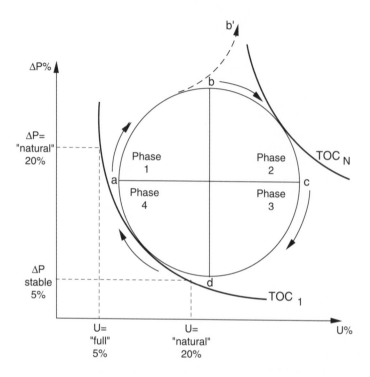

probably would, argue that their policies had been right all along, as evidenced by the current dramatic improvement in economic conditions. They should, if they could, try to prevent the upturn in inflation rates at point d, and to bring further reductions in unemployment without any acceleration of price increases; but that may prove to be beyond their capacity. On the other hand, between "d" and "a" the economy *may* be on a trade-off curve, (it looks like one), affording the authorities an opportunity to guide the economy toward the optimal point on the TOC. Once there, the authorities should try to keep the economy there; but the gathering northeast forces may be too powerful for them, and a new phase one of the cyclical loop may set in. Moreover, as we saw in chapter 5, the whole (Juglar) loop may meanwhile have shifted northeast. Any economy that entrusts its stabilization and growth to monetary policy alone is likely to have a rough time, no matter how astute the monetary authorities.

Fiscal Policy

It is important to distinguish between two broad categories of fiscal policy: macroeconomic or aggregative, designed in terms of total amounts of government spending and tax collection in the national economy as a whole; and selective or discriminatory, with deliberately designed differences in treatment of various sectors, industries, social groups, or regions.

Even the first category affords the government greater control over the economic impact than monetary policy has, and is therefore more effective than monetary policy. The monetary authorities must rely on hoped-for reactions of the private sector, even in the first link of the chain. They are therefore involved in the Game, with all its uncertainties, from the very beginning. The fiscal authorities, however, have firm control over the first round of reactions, and can predict with considerable accuracy the impact on spending streams in that first round. That is, the government itself controls its own spending; once a budget is struck, the government can see to it that the amounts stipulated in it are actually spent; and even control to a significant degree the times when they are spent and the manner in which they are spent. There is perhaps more uncertainty as to total tax collections, since the government cannot know with complete accuracy what incomes, consumption, and investment will be over the next year. It can, however, try to make sure that the stipulated taxes are actually collected; and fiscal authorities have become rather skilled at forecasting the amounts that will be paid in taxes. In the second round, of course, involving the initial reactions of the private sector to the amounts spent (and announced to be spent) and collected (and announced to be collected) the fiscal authorities are in the Game too.

Let us go through the cyclical loop of figure 14.2 once more, in terms of macroeconomic, aggregative fiscal policy. In phase one the fiscal authorities are almost as helpless as the monetary authorities, but not quite. They can at least control directly their own contributions to, and deductions from, the spending stream. If the northeasterly forces are strong, nothing can be done to prevent both inflation and unemployment from being aggravated, while phase one lasts, by means of macroeconomic fiscal policy alone. No government can simultaneously increase and reduce budget deficits. More spending will in itself increase inflationary pressure; it ought to create new jobs. The outcome is uncertain, however; if the increased spending swells the budget deficit, one of two things might happen to frustrate the favorable impact on employment. If the central bank has a good deal of autonomy, it may raise interest rates to offset the increased inflationary impact of the budget, and investment may fall and unemployment rise. If on the other hand the Bank cooperates with the fiscal authorities in their efforts to fight unemployment, and does *not* raise interest rates, the business and financial community, fearing runaway inflation, may panic, and unemployment may increase anyhow.

If a government wants to increase (decrease) its budget deficit, which side of the budget should it change, spending or taxation? This question is a very complex one, and cannot be answered in terms of economic theory alone. There are to begin with administrative complications, which vary from country to country and even from region to region within a country. Is it easier to pinpoint the impact of a change in the budget, in terms of timing and in terms of placing, through the tax side or through the spending side? Public works spending, for example, is sometimes downgraded as an instrument for employment creation because of the lag between legislation authorizing the expenditure and the time when actual hiring begins. In defense of public works planning, it is argued that such lags can be avoided, if shelves of ready-to-go projects are accumulated, complete to the point of preparing working drawings and acquiring sites in advance. Tax laws may seem easy to revise, but there can be a long lag between legislating a new income tax system and its actual impact on incomes and spending of households and firms. One cannot generalize; each government must study its own situation to arrive at the right answer as to whether taxation or expenditures can be most conveniently changed.

There are also differences in taste between one society and another with regard to preferences for public and private goods. There is today a widespread feeling that governments have become "too big." If budget deficits are to be increased to raise total spending and create employment, many people would prefer tax cuts, so that they can decide for themselves how to spend their increase in disposable income. But there are nonetheless societies where many people would like increased government spending on public health, education, transport facilities, and communications, even if it means foregoing a tax cut. Again, it is impossible to generalize about such decisions.

In the other phases of the cyclical loop the considerations for fiscal policy are similar to those of monetary policy, except that the impact of changes in fiscal policy can be more direct. In phase two, the emphasis should be on employment creation, which can be done directly. The drop in inflation rates may be slowed down, but that is a small price to pay; and the government should seek the optimal point on the TOC (if there is one) and perhaps speed up the process of reaching the point where both unemployment and inflation start to fall (if they can). Once again, in phase three the government will no doubt sing its own praises for producing such marvelous prosperity and superb performance, and try to keep inflation from accelerating again, without launching a new trend toward higher unemployment. If they fail in this effort, and find themselves quite definitely on a TOC instead (phase four) they should try to find the minimum discomfort point on it.

Adding macroeconomic, aggregative fiscal policy to monetary policy gives the government a somewhat better chance of improving the economic situation as the cycle continues. It does not, however, guarantee reductions in both unemployment and inflation in all phases of the cycle. For that objective, selective and discriminatory fiscal policy is necessary.

Selective Fiscal Policy

The basic principles of a selective fiscal policy are very simple, and the nature and significance of such a policy are best demonstrated by citing real world examples, as is done below. Virtually no economy in the world—not even in the small island nations of the South Pacific—is so perfectly integrated that all regions, sectors, and social groups experience equal degrees of unemployment and inflationary pressure at every point of time. In most countries there are wide differences among regions and sectors in the extent to which inflationary pressure is generated, or unemployment concentrated, within them. Frequently unemployment is concentrated within distinct social groups as well, such as young school and university drop-outs, women, older workers, and less highly trained workers. These differences afford opportunities for selective fiscal policy, relieving inflationary pressures where it is most severe, and creating jobs in regions, sectors, and social categories where unemployment rates are highest, rather than simply managing the total money supply and leaving it to "the market" to do the rest.

But while the basic principles are simple, their application is not, as we shall see in greater detail below. Implementing a selective fiscal policy efficiently and successfully requires a great deal of intimate knowledge of the economy, not just at the level of the national economy, but at the level of the region and community, the sector and industry. Even in the affluent industrialized countries, all the required knowledge is not there; and just as in the less developed countries, acquiring it requires teams of highly trained professionals in a whole range of disciplines, who can make detailed, on-the-spot studies with enough depth and breadth to provide answers to questions like "What can best be done with Cape Breton? With Northeast New Brunswick? With Appalachia? With Detroit, Cleveland, Buffalo, Pittsburgh? With Glasgow, Birmingham, Manchester, Sheffield?"

Wage Policy, Training, Manpower Planning

Obviously levels of employment and unemployment do not depend entirely on how much money is spent on what, when and where. They also depend on structures of wage rates and of productivity and skills. Productivity and skills depend in turn on the amounts, types, and quality of training that members of the labor force are able to acquire. Finally, they depend on the degree to which future labor requirements are foreseen, and the extent to which training programs are designed to fit those requirements—that is, on the effectiveness of manpower planning, whether undertaken by the private or the public sector.

In most of the industrialized capitalist countries, a good many less developed countries, and virtually all of the former socialist countries, there is today a reaction against regulation of the labor market, minimum wages, compulsory arbitration, and complex wage-fixing systems like the Australian Industrial Relations Commission and its State associates. The trend is toward deregulation and individual rather than nation-wide or union-wide bargaining. This trend is a response to earlier periods of excessive, inefficient, or ineffective wage control systems. In the long run, if skillfully managed, this trend could improve the efficiency of allocation of labor and other resources, increase mobility, raise per capita GNP and reduce unemployment. In doing all that it might reduce rates of inflation as well. However, in the field of wage policy as in all others, the road to a genuinely "free market" is strewn with land mines and full of dangerous pitfalls.

In the first place, it must be remembered that a "free" market is not the same thing as a perfectly competitive, or even a purely competitive market. Unless we are to go back to the dark days before 1825 and make trade unions illegal, and unless we can really do the unthinkable and enforce antimonopoly legislation that eliminates monopoly power completely, a "free" labor market would be one in which the structure of wages would be the outcome of a more or less haphazard distribution of monopoly power among various employers and various trade unions. There is little evidence that such a wage structure would reflect marginal value product of various groups of workers more accurately than the present one, and it would well be worse. True, "the market" is likely in time to eliminate unions or employers who use their monopoly power to excess, and push too hard for wage increases or reductions; but von Hayek's "bigger and better bankruptcies" is not really an ideal solution for either unemployment or inflation. Besides, in today's ICCs most trade union leaders and most employers' representatives know better that to push too hard; they are more likely to play the Game so as to arrive at a satisfactory wage and a comfortable profit, ganging up together against the consumers. Most specialists think that compulsory arbitration systems like the Australian one have aided the employers rather than the workers, delaying through a cumbersome and time-consuming arbitration process wage increases that a free market would have brought sooner. (In Australia, for example, the Australian Council of Trade Unions hesitates to bring a case for a higher basic wage before the Commission until it can show that market conditions warrant it; and the case may take two years or more before a decision is handed down.) Thus, deregulation could bring a wage blowout, leading to an acceleration of inflation, and quite possibly higher unemployment as well.

If deregulation leads to greater mobility of labor, it is likely to increase inflation, unemployment, and regional disparities as well. Migration to the more dynamic and prosperous regions will accelerate growth, and reduce amplitude of fluctuations there; but many of the migrants from lagging and stagnant regions will lack the training and skills required to get jobs in the prosperous region. The increased pressure on infrastructure in the prosperous region will impose inflationary pressures there. In the lagging region emigration will have cumulative effects, raising unemployment there still further. To the extent that migrants do find employment in the dynamic region, they will raise its level of income directly and indirectly, increasing the disparity between it and the lagging region—as we saw in chapter 2 under the heading of "cumulative causation."

People to Jobs or Jobs to People?

Neo-classical economists who criticize regional development programs on the grounds that they hamper the functioning of the market, and that accordingly a free market with flexible prices would have done a better job of reducing regional disparities, base their arguments on the following assumptions: (1) In a free market, with no artificial supports to wages and other prices, in regions where incomes and productivity are relatively low and unemployment relatively high, wages will fall; (2) In consequence, labor will migrate to more dynamic regions to obtain jobs at higher wage rates; and (3) In addition, capital will be attracted to the disadvantaged regions by the lower wage rates, and the increased investment there will reduce employment, raise marginal value product, and ultimately raise incomes in the retarded regions.

Two quite separate kinds of question arise with regard to this sort of argument: Does it ever happen?, and Is it a good thing if it does? Let us deal with these questions in reverse order.

In the first place, let us be clear that there can be no concept of "efficiency" of performance of national and regional economies apart from its impact on human welfare. In any society, or any large group of people within it, there are many who attach great importance to staying where they are and doing what they are doing. Consequently, policies designed to permit them to do so cannot be dismissed out of hand as "impairing efficiency." There may indeed be a trade-off between what the Government of Manitoba has called "the stay option" and other elements of social welfare. If so, this trade-off has to be appraised, before policy can be "efficiently" formulated. In many developing countries, in the province of Quebec, and in the Atlantic provinces, in Appalachia, in the Great Lakes region, there are a good many people who have a heartfelt desire not to move. It is nonsense to make people suffer needlessly, merely to satisfy some economists' special definition of "efficiency."

There is a difference between "mobility," in the sense of *willingness* to move, and actual movement. One of the studies of Canada's Royal Commission on Bilingualism and Biculturalism showed that the population of

Quebec, especially the women, were extremely reluctant to move, even within Quebec. But the census data on migration showed that the proportion of the Quebec population moving to another place of residence was just as high as in the rest of the country. The juxtaposition of the two sets of data suggests that the pressure on people in Quebec to move was severe, and that there was a high social cost involved in actual movement.

There are other social costs involved in migration. The most obvious is that emigrants leave behind them housing, transport facilities, schools, hospitals, shopping centers, banks, factories, and the like that have to be provided for them at the other end of the line. In addition, we know that in all societies there are certain thresholds of population size at which certain types of economic activity appear or disappear. Studies made in various countries show that a movement of population out of lagging areas, if it is sufficient to exceed natural population growth and lead to an absolute decline in population, can become cumulative, leading not only to depopulation in terms of numbers, but to a decline in the average quality of the population in terms of education, training, and skills, and occupational structure. Anyone who has seen such areas—in east Texas, western Virginia, northern Minnesota, Quebec's Cantons de l'Est, the north and northeast of Brazil, and in west-central Australia—knows how grim they can be. We should not recommend solving the problems of depressed areas by emptying them, as an alternative to regional development, without knowing the costs; and *saving* these costs is one of the benefits of regional development.

The study undertaken for Public Works Canada cited above showed that stability of regional economies is *positively* correlated with the rate of growth. The explanation for this relationship is provided in terms of interactions of cycles and trends, using a Hicks-style model of the trade cycle, as shown in chapter 4. This finding is crucial in deciding between a "move jobs to people" policy and a "move people to jobs" policy. Another consideration, of course, is that if unemployment is currently high everywhere in the country, moving from one region to another is no guarantee of finding a job. All of these factors must be taken into account, and measured as well as possible, in evaluating regional development programs which may have as one of their results holding people in the regions where they now are.

Let us now ask the other question: Does a free market with flexible prices guarantee elimination of regional gaps by factor movements?

Obviously not. Labor does indeed move to jobs and higher incomes when the incentive is powerful enough. But rare indeed are the cases where the movement is sufficient to offset natural population growth and bring absolute declines in the population of large regions. In the United States, with its extraordinarily mobile population, there have been some decades in which the population of the two or three poorest states among the fifty fell; but in those decades those states remained poor, and the more recent increase of prosperity in them has been accompanied by immigration and population growth once more.

As for capital flowing to low-wage regions, there is little clear evidence that low wages by themselves are sufficient to attract enough capital to transform poor countries or regions into rich ones. The universal experience is that for repetitive jobs with a given technology, productivity of labor in developing countries, like Indonesia, Thailand, and Malaysia is as high as in the United States, while wages are a small fraction of the American level. In recent years there has been some flow of capital to take advantage of this situation, but it is an insignificant proportion of total American investment in manufacturing. Many factors weigh more heavily than labor costs in investment decisions. As for technology being adapted to differences in cost and availability of labor, here a veritable hornet's nest of problems arises. There is a vast literature on choice of technology and "appropriate technology," but no clear conclusions emerge from it, except that most sophisticated enterprises adapt technology to scale of production but not to relative costs of capital and labor.[1]

What all this means is that in evaluating regional development programs in the past, and in making recommendations for the future, we cannot simply *assume* that in the absence of such programs, free market forces would have brought about "adjustment," in the sense of eliminating unemployment, inflation, poverty, inequalities, and the like. Here again we are confronted by questions of fact, and no evaluation can be complete unless the facts are ascertained.

Note

1. C.f. Benjamin Higgins. "Appropriate Technology: Does it Exist?" *Regional Development Dialogue* 3, 1 (Spring 1982).

15

Why Not Full Employment?

In formulating policy with regard to unemployment and inflation, what possible reason has any government for choosing an employment target below full employment? By "full" employment we mean unemployment of around 2 or 3 percent of the labor force, the usual estimate of frictional plus structural unemployment. By "choosing" we mean more than expression of pious hopes; we mean that the government has determination to achieve full employment and believes that this goal is attainable. During the immediate postwar years this target was officially accepted by Industrialized Capitalist Countries (ICCs) and by Less Developed Countries alike. During the 1960s and 1970s full employment was gradually abandoned by the ICCs, but remained an official target for LDCs, not just because unemployment is undesirable in itself, but because eliminating unemployment was regarded as one of the most promising roads to economic and social development. This kind of thought reached its height in the 1970s, with the International Labor Organization's World Employment Programme and its World Employment Conference of 1976. During the 1980s and 1990s few indeed are the governments that have declared their intention to achieve full employment.

The main reason, of course, is that the experience of the 1950s and 1960s, and the increasingly widespread acceptance of the trade-off curve, convinced many people, including economists, politicians, and government bureaucrats, that there *is* some kind of trade-off between unemployment and inflation, and that attempts to achieve truly full employment might generate runaway inflation. But the postwar trade-off curve, and the cyclical loops that are associated with them, are to a large extent the product of the kind of policy that has been adopted since World War II. It does not follow that they could not be made to disappear by a *different* kind of policy.

During World War II, in all of the Allied Nations, there was a period of five or six years when overfull employment was accompanied by virtually stable price levels (see figure 15.1).

Moreover, during the period 1940 to 1946, not only was full employment maintained with virtually no inflation, but other objectives of current national economic policy were attained as well: regional gaps were reduced; the inequality of income distribution was also lessened; technological progress and economic growth were accelerated; consumption increased; balance of payments difficulties were avoided; waste of resources and environmental damage (except for actual battlefields) were curtailed. Could we not, if we would, do the same thing in peacetime?

Let us take a look at this excellent economic performance during the war, and see how it was achieved; and then let us see what happened as wartime instruments of economic management were abandoned; using Canada as an example. Perhaps then we will be in a better position to answer this very important question.

From August 1939, when the war began, until late 1941, when the war economy was fully established, the cost of living index was deliberately allowed to rise by about 15 percent. It was felt that the use of wage-price incentives would facilitate the transformation of the economy during this phase. Even that was a slow rate of inflation compared with postwar experience. But once excess capacity and unemployment had disappeared and the war effort was going full blast, controls were introduced; for the next four years the cost of living rose by only four percent (see figure 15.1). Unemployment was replaced by labor shortage. National income had fallen in 1937 and 1938, after a partial recovery from the depths of the great depression in 1933; but between 1939 and 1945 national income doubled, and nearly doubled even at constant prices. Per capita income rose by more than 50 percent, even in constant dollars.

But did not this achievement entail great sacrifices on the part of civilian consumers? It depends what is meant by "sacrifice." Some commodities were in short supply relative to demand and were rationed: gasoline, alcoholic beverages, sugar, butter. New cars and radios were not available. Personal expenditures on goods and services fell, as a *proportion* of gross national product, from about 68 to about 57 percent. But so great was the growth of total national income that per capita expenditures on consumption (at constant prices) *rose* from $337 to $448 between 1939 and 1945.

FIGURE 15.1
Cost of Living
Canada, United States, United Kingdom, Australia
August 1939 = 100

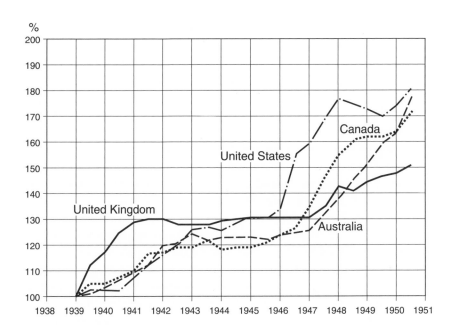

Source: International Financial Statistics, International Monetary Fund, Washington, D.C., Annual Series.

Moreover, this higher standard of Canadian living was much more equally distributed than before the war. Workers benefited most from the elimination of unemployment, which in itself brought a substantial improvement of income distribution. In addition, there was a dramatic shift in tax structure away from commodity taxes (which bear most heavily on the lower income groups) to personal and corporate income taxes (which bear most heavily on the higher income groups). At the beginning of the war income taxes accounted for only one quarter of total revenues of the federal government; at the end of the war the proportion was up to two-thirds. Moreover, the income tax structure was extremely progressive, reaching 50 percent at about $15,000, 70 percent at about $60,000, and 90 percent at about $250,000. The war savings campaigns cut further into spending of middle- and upper-income groups, and the rationing system assured the lower income families that basic necessities would not be bid away from them by people with more money to spend. Given the elimination of unemployment, the rise in incomes, and improved distribution, the standard of living of workers, and of low income groups generally, *rose* substantially in Canada during World War II.

All this progress was accompanied by a marked and permanent improvement in both the sectoral and regional structure of the Canadian economy. On the eve of World War II the prairie economy was still suffering from the collapse of the world wheat market. Unemployment was high, underemployment higher. Incomes were well below the national average. The burgeoning economy of the war period, however, provided employment opportunities to Canadians on the prairies in other fields than agriculture, and in other parts of the country. There was substantial net emigration from the prairie provinces during the war; in Saskatchewan it was so great that the total population actually fell. The share of total employment in agriculture in the country as a whole fell from nearly one-third to less than one-fifth. Structural change of this kind is one of the key elements in economic development. Per capita incomes in the prairies rose by 111 percent, compared to 91 percent for the country as a whole. The Atlantic provinces also had the chance to catch up a bit on the rest of the country; incomes rose by 115 percent. British Columbia was the richest region before the war, but its growth lagged behind the rest of the country during the war, and British Columbia ended the war second to Ontario, which grew at almost the same rate as the national economy. Quebec lagged in growth of income, but industrialization during the war set the stage for accelerated growth in the late 1940s and 1950s and *la révolution tranquille*. On balance, regional disparities were substantially reduced during the war.

As for waste, the control over use of strategic resources was so tight that waste (given the national objectives) was virtually impossible—except, perhaps, by the armed forces, in the early years of the war, before the military leaders learned about scarcities.

It has sometimes been said that the impressive efficiency of the Canadian economy during the war was achieved by astute application of Keynesian principles of monetary and fiscal policy. That is not quite true. Certainly Ottawa was blessed at the time by a group a brilliant young economists, trained in the two Cambridges (England and Massachusetts), employed mainly in the Bank of Canada and the Department of Finance, who understood Keynesian policy very well. The expansion of government expenditures and the increase in government deficits between 1939 and 1941 might indeed be described as "Keynesian," since these are the prescribed Keynesian measures for eliminating unemployment. But once full employment was reached and inflation threatened, pure Keynesian policy would have prescribed high interest rates and budget surpluses. These did not occur. On the contrary, the war was fought on a "cheap money" basis, with interest rates on government securities at an average of about 2.6 percent, and deficits continued to rise throughout the war. High taxes and war loan campaigns helped to keep the expansion of civilian consumption in check; but given the monetary and fiscal policy, there is no way that inflation could have been avoided without the accompanying system of management of the economy by direct controls.

The regulation of production was delegated to the Department of Munitions and Supply, which (like the War Production Board in the United States) determined priority ratings for allocation of scarce materials, and limited their use. In cooperation with industrialists, the department accomplished notable economies in the use of critical materials and sharp *reductions* in the cost of war materials and supplies. The allocation of manpower was improved through the National Selective Service, while the Inter-Departmental Committee on Labor Co-ordination alleviated the skilled labor shortage through a War Emergency Training Program. Control over prices and supplies of civilian goods and services was concentrated in the Wartime Prices and Trade Board. WPTB also regulated consumer credit. It was not an independent agency, but was responsible to the Minister of Finance. This relationship provided a useful link between fiscal policy and direct controls. Restrictions on consumer credit were introduced in the fall of 1941. For most consumer durable goods, a down payment of one-third of the purchase price was required. "Charge accounts" had to be paid by the twenty-fifth of the month after the purchase was made.

A general price ceiling was announced in November, 1941. Maximum prices were set at the highest figure reached between 15 September and 11 October of that year, with the ceiling to become effective on 1 December 1941. This order covered *all* commodities, unless specifically exempted, and a long list of services. Non-farm rents, which had been pegged in some centers under an order of September 1940, were also made subject to a general ceiling in November 1941. A wage ceiling was introduced at the same time, under which employers could not lower wages below the 15 November 1941 level, and could raise them above that level only with permission of the National War Labor Board. A cost-of-living bonus was paid (or retracted) whenever the Bureau of Statistics cost-of-living index rose (or fell) by one point.

Rationing was a fundamental part of the system. By the end of 1943, ration cards had been issued for gasoline, sugar, tea, coffee, meat, butter, and conserves. Liquor was rationed by provincial authorities, and purchases of automobiles, tires, radios, refrigerators, and similar scarce consumer durables, were subject to permit. Meats were divided into four categories, with weekly rations ranging from one to two and one-half pounds per person according to the type purchased; tea and coffee were interchangeable, as were the various kinds of jams, syrups, and so forth, listed under "conserves."

Subsidies, together with remission of import duties and with bulk purchasing, also played a major role in Canadian price control. Subsidies were paid to permit price maintenance in the face of rising costs, generally at whatever stage of the production-and-distribution process had the fewest firms.

While legally a distinct body subject to direction by the Minister of Finance, the Foreign Exchange Control Board was in close working relationship with the Bank of Canada. The main feature of Canadian exchange control was rigorous limitation of capital exports and travel expenditures.

But did not these controls stifle innovation and technological progress? Not at all. On the contrary, there are few periods in Canadian economic history when productivity rose so fast as during the second world war. In any case, profits rose substantially, even after tax, although not so much as total wages.

Decontrol: 1946–1948

With the scrapping of the wartime system of management of the economy between 1946 and 1948, the performance of the Canadian economy rapidly deteriorated. This deterioration set in despite the fact that controls were *not* lifted all at once, but were removed gradually over a period of more than two years. Between October 1946 and October 1947 a large number of wage-price ceilings were lifted, and subsidy payments were also stopped. Meat rationing was maintained until March 1947, and butter rationing until June of that year. Controls on rents and sugar rationing, however, were maintained until near the end of 1948.

What was the result? Despite the gradualness of decontrol, the cost of living, after being virtually stable for five years, leaped upward in 1947 and 1948. During 1947 the overall cost-of-living index jumped twenty-two points, from 124 to 146 (1935–39=100). In the first month of 1948 it jumped thirteen points more, to 159. The picture for food was very much worse: a thirty-four-point rise in 1947 and another thirty-six points in 1948. Only the continued control of rents kept the overall index from rising more than it did. In a belated attempt to stem this tide of inflation, in 1948 the government reintroduced controls on a number of food items and on iron and steel. As may be seen from figure 15.1, Canadian inflation between 1945 and 1949 was worse than in Australia and the United Kingdom, and almost as bad as in the United States, which experienced more rapid price increases after decontrol than during the "greenback inflation" of the Civil War.

True, a part of the inflationary pressure in these years came from the Bank of Canada's efforts to keep interest rates down and consequent excessive monetary expansion, plus the fact that Canadians who had been buying government bonds instead of durable consumer's goods during the war were eager to cash in their bonds and buy cars, clothes, and houses. On the other hand, in 1947 and 1948 the Canadian government was not plagued by unemployment as well as inflation, as it is today. Trade union unemployment was below 2 percent; something close to wartime full employment still prevailed. Curbing inflation alone should have been easy.

After 1948 Canadian economic performance continued to deteriorate. Unemployment reappeared with no relief from inflation, growth rates slowed down, balance of payments problems emerged, distribution of incomes among regions and social groups ceased to show any significant improvement.

One of the main things wrong with policy during the immediate postwar period was cheap money, continued partly because economists and politicians were afraid of another Great Depression, and partly from dislike of enriching bondholders. (Lord Keynes, the number one god in the economics Valhalla of the time, spoke of "the euthanasia of the rentier.") But during the 1950s there was a shift to tighter money, and the sixties brought very high interest rates indeed. The economic situation continued to worsen. But won't monetary and fiscal policy alone do, if it is well conceived and administered? The answer is quite clearly "No!" Up to the 1950s, and even today, many economists and politicians, imbued with confidence in the efficacy of purely Keynesian or monetarist policies, would have answered that question "yes"; but that answer is based only on prewar experience and prewar thought. Then governments were faced only with the problem of checking inflation *or* reducing employment. Unfortunately, as our previous discussion has shown, the problem today is not so simple. The pure Keynesian theory postulated a set of conditions that might produce either inflation or unemployment, but not both at once. The Keynesian policy prescription, reduced to its simplest terms, was, "Expand the money supply through easy credit and budget deficits when unemployment appears, curtail the money supply through tight credit and budget surpluses when inflation threatens." Clearly this prescription will not do when unemployment and inflation exist simultaneously. No country can have cheap money and tight money, or budget surpluses and deficits, at the same time.

As we have also seen above, in virtually every country in the world, industrialized capitalist countries (ICCs) and less developed countries (LDCs) alike, the prewar business cycle, with its alternations of unemployment and rising prices, has been replaced by unemployment and inflation existing side by side, sometimes even increasing together, confronting governments with extremely awkward options with regard to possible combinations of inflation and unemployment. The Keynesian analysis and prescription belong to the prewar world of "business cycles," when depressions with falling prices and increasing unemployment followed booms with rising prices and falling unemployment. But since World War II the combination of nationwide bargaining for wage increases (or close to it), administered prices set by large, monopolistic corporations, and government policies aimed at maintaining high rates of growth but limiting both increases in unemployment and inflation, has replaced the prewar business cycle with shifting trade-off curves, and loops. Trade unions bargain periodically for wage increases, even through periods of rising unemployment; employers grant wage increases in the expectation that they can be offset by raising prices, and governments respond by increasing the money supply so as to make sure that the higher wage-price structure can be sustained without reducing sales, output, or employment. But when costs and prices are rising together profits need not be much affected, and thus the process of inflation need not lead to any increase in real investment or any reduction of unemployment. With a growing labor force plus innovation of a labor-saving type, the co-existence of unemployment and inflation is virtually assured under these conditions.

In recent years, then, it has been clear that there is a powerful world business cycle, in which advanced and developing countries alike are caught up, but with "recessions" that take the form of shifts of the trade-off curves upward to the right, or movement along phase one of a loop, with inflation and unemployment increasing together, rather than an absolute decline in output, income, prices and employment, after the manner of the prewar business cycle. Nearly all countries suffered shifts of their trade-off curves to the right after 1970; that is, unemployment increased with no retardation of inflation, or price increases have accelerated with no reduction in unemployment. The cyclical reductions in private investment that brought depressions in the old, prewar framework, are now translated into a declining rate of increase in employment, and thus, with a growing labor force, increased unemployment, and quite possibly accelerated inflation as well, by government policies that continue to expand the money supply at more or less the old rate despite retardation of the growth of output. The expansion is prevented from being turned into reduced unemployment by trade union-employer policies that continue to raise wages and prices despite an underlying downturn in private investment. The existence of such trade-off curves, while an obvious improvement over economic fluctuations bringing deep depressions like that of the 1930s, is the bugbear of governments today. What to do?

If we wanted to rely on the market as guide and mechanism for resource allocation, and limit the government to monetary and fiscal policy to achieve an optimal result, it would be necessary to smash both large monopolistic enterprises and large monopolistic trade unions, something few governments are prepared to do, and something no political party has dared to propose. The creation of a true "pure competition" market (a situation in which all buyers and all sellers are too small and powerless to influence the price of anything they sell or anything they buy) is certainly one possible route to the improvement of the performance of an economy, but it is perhaps the most "radical" solution of all. And even pure competition would not in itself assure full employment, a stable price level, a satisfactory income distribution, elimination of regional disparities, a high rate of growth, or protection of the environment and the avoidance of waste. It would certainly entail the loss of any extra efficiency that large-scale production brings. It is highly doubtful that atomization of economic activity so as to create the "purely competitive market" which, according to the textbooks assures efficient allocation of resources, can be regarded today as a serious alternative to an "optimal blend" of market and management. And the textbooks also tell us that *without* pure competition, a free market *misallocates* resources. However, it is my view that in the ICCs monopoly power is seldom utilized to the full, and that the separation of management from ownership makes managers more interested in growth of the firm than in maximizing profits by limiting production. Except in cases of blatant exploitation, it is not worth the risks and complexities of tampering with the market. It is better to accept "second best."

Managing a Peacetime Economy

How much of the wartime system of management would be needed to achieve purely peacetime objectives? These objectives include: checking inflation; reducing unemployment; reducing regional gaps; improving income distribution (which implies raising wages *more* than prices, across the board); protecting the physical environment; favoring growth of small and middle-sized cities rather than metropolitan centers; and improving the quality of life. The broad outlines of an effective system of management of the economy to achieve full employment without inflation, can be suggested.

1. The *possibility* of managing wages and prices when necessary, should be accepted. Individual wages and prices should change in response to changes in techniques, costs, and tastes. Where the market is doing a reasonably good job, it should be left alone; but the *principle* of management of the wage-price-profit system should be accepted.

2. A few consumers' goods might have to be rationed. Rationing is called for where demand far exceeds supply at present prices, and where it is important to assure adequate supplies to lower income groups—

generally speaking, food, clothing, shelter, and the consumers' durable goods that constitute a minimum acceptable standard of living in today's society. Not many of these things are scarce at today's prices, and not many would need to be rationed. Each commodity regarded as a "necessity" would require a careful study.

3. Some scarce, strategic, raw materials and equipment might be allocated by use or by industrial sector. Such allocation would simplify the task of rationing, strengthen efforts to avoid pollution and waste, help the federal government in its efforts to redistribute economic activity and change the pattern of urban growth, etc. Petroleum products and electric power might be candidates.

4. Manpower allocation would probably not be necessary. During World War II manpower allocation was needed to build up the armed forces and to staff war industries without excessive wage increases. We have no clear-cut need today to bring drastic and rapid changes in use of manpower. Ordinary wage incentives can be used to assure an adequate supply of labor to sectors considered to be of high priority; larger wage increases could be permitted there than elsewhere. Increased productivity would also justify wage increases. However, with allocation of manpower left to collective bargaining alone, the results will depend on the distribution of bargaining power among various monopolistic groups, rather than on national priorities.

5. Foreign exchange control would not be necessary. With improved management of the economy there should be no flight of capital. There are no strong priorities with regard to the pattern of imports that could not be handled in other ways. However, it might be well to have a system of exchange control in readiness, in case flight of capital or other factors leading to an awkward balance of payments situation should develop.

6. Restrictions on consumer credit should not be necessary, provided restrictions on total credit extension (and so on growth of the supply of money) were adequate. During the war there was a desire to restrict consumption in order to permit more investment, particularly in the war economy; at present the allocation of total credit between financing consumption and financing investment can be left largely to the market. A watchful eye should be cast by the monetary authorities to make sure no serious imbalance appears in this respect, but that is a normal part of the responsibilities of a central bank.

7. During the war little attention was paid to regional gaps as such; the reduction of regional disparities that occurred was essentially a wel-

come byproduct of wartime policy. However, the range of options regarding unemployment and inflation that is open to a government depends a good deal on the extent of regional integration or disintegration of the national economy. A frontal attack on regional gaps would do much to simplify the task of the other elements of economic management, permitting simultaneous reductions in inflation and unemployment.

Fundamentally, the objective of wartime management was higher productivity of the entire economy. The present system of cost-push followed by demand-pull, on the other hand, divorces the structure of wage-price increases from increases in productivity almost altogether. Higher productivity can come through both private and government action. Unions and employers have the major responsibility, in our private enterprise system, of raising productivity. Government can provide tax and other incentives for research and development, and can conduct research itself.

Some people might say—justifiably—that it is worthwhile putting up with a modicum of inflation and unemployment to avoid the degree of government management required to obtain full employment without inflation. If the people of any country are prepared to accept, say, 4 percent unemployment and 3 percent inflation rather than have direct controls, that is their privilege. So long as they provide an unemployment insurance benefit that is adequate, and so long as the demoralizing effects of prolonged youth unemployment are avoided, an unemployment rate of 4 percent—even 5 percent—is tolerable. How much unemployment is consistent with absence of direct management of the economy will vary from country to country. So will the strength of the desire to avoid direct intervention. Each country must make its own choice.

There is, however, an entirely different approach to full employment. Instead of having direct controls, the government can shadow-price labor, and pay a subsidy equal to the difference between the market wage and the shadow price, making it pay employers to achieve full employment. At least that makes more sense than charging a payroll tax, which penalizes employment.

Shadow Pricing Labor

The technology or product mix that provides the highest level of output per capita is not always the most labor-intensive one in particular sectors or industries. But this fact does not imply a "conflict" between output and employment, unless it is impossible to put labor to work without combining it with scarce resources, whose productivity is so high in alternative uses that combining it with unemployed labor instead reduces total output. It is almost always possible to put labor to work doing something useful without using any scarce resources. An example is workers clearing away rubble with their bare hands from the Aswan dam, and carrying it away in simple baskets, made by the workers themselves from raw materials growing wild. The question then is: are the social opportunity costs of employing labor on such projects higher than the output per worker?

Where the only alternative allocation of labor to employment on such projects is total unemployment, the social opportunity costs of putting men and women to work consists only of any additional nutritional requirements of people who are working rather than being totally idle. No society accepts in principle the idea that people without work should be allowed to starve. While there is need for additional research on nutritional requirements of workers versus those of the unemployed, the evidence so far available suggests that costs in these terms are low. Some studies for India, for example, suggested that for a sedentary adult male the daily caloric requirements is about 1800; the additional requirements for four hours of hard physical work per day are 604, for five hours 755, and for six hours 906. Thus, if the society is providing the unemployed with a subsistence diet costing (say) fifty cents a day, the cost of putting a man to work for six hours a day would be about twenty-five cents. It is this additional cost—which we might call OW for "opportunity cost wage"—which measures the true social cost of putting the unemployed to work. Thus, any activity that uses no scarce resources and produces an output worth twenty-five cents per day is profitable from a social point of view. If scarce resources are combined with the unemployed labor, the loss in output through transferring scarce resources from alternative uses to employment-creating activities must be added to the social costs, for comparison with the value of the output obtained from the employment-creating projects. In most cases it would pay to provide workers with simple tools, some of which can be made by other unemployed workers. Capital can be created by labor, even in a "Crusoe economy," through primitive accumulation. In industrialized countries, there may be an additional cost of transport from home to work place; but if there is excess capacity on trams and busses, that cost is zero.

Shadow Wages for the Employed

Thus, for unemployed persons the social opportunity cost of employing them is zero; or more accurately, the cost of the additional nutritional requirements. (If there is excess capacity in agriculture, of course, meeting the additional nutritional requirements may also be costless.) What is too seldom pointed out is that for employed persons with skills identical to those of the unemployed, the true social cost of their employment is also OW. If the only alternative to present employment of those now engaged is unemployment, the cost of keeping them on the job is also the difference in nutritional requirements. If in a group of workers with identical skills the "nth" worker is employed and the "n + 1st" worker is left unemployed, there can be no difference in the OW for the two members of the labor force. Consequently, the appropriate shadow or accounting wage for skills which are represented among the unemployed is OW. If subsidies were paid to all employers, in public or private sector, equal to (minimum wage minus OW), to make money costs to employers equal to the social opportunity costs of employing additional workers, employers would tend to react voluntarily in three ways: (1) Expand total output with existing product-mix and technology, and so increase employment; (2) Shift to a more labor-intensive product mix to take advantage of the lower wage costs, wherever possible; and (3) Shift to a more labor-intensive technology wherever possible.

Shadow Prices for Exports

In some cases the increased output resulting from setting effective wage rates equal to true social opportunity costs might run into marketing difficulties at home. But with the reduced labor costs producers could quote lower prices in the world markets, and consequently exports should increase. If, as is often the case, there is no effective alternative to use of *other* resources except to produce the present product (land under rubber, tin mines, oil wells) it may be that market prices of other factors of production, besides labor of the type represented among the unemployed, are above social opportunity costs. In that case it would pay, from a national welfare point of view, to add export subsidies to the wage subsidies.

Planning for Full Employment while Maximizing Income

In putting together a program to achieve full employment, the proper way to proceed would be to choose projects that will make the most contribution to achievement of stated objectives *other* than employment (which can always be reduced to some measure of national income, if anyone wants to do it that way, with "appropriate" accounting prices for incomes of poor versus income of the rich, etc.). If, as projects are added to the program according to this criterion, the scarcest resource is exhausted while unemployment still exists, then an effort should be made to add further projects, utilizing unemployed labor (and other factors of production) costed at true social opportunity cost, which require only the *second*-scarcest resource; and so on. If in this fashion all other resources are finally exhausted and there is still unemployed labor of certain types, then these types of labor should be combined to produce something, so long as an output above OW can be obtained. Unemployment could be eliminated in this fashion in most if not all countries.

Construction is one field where labor-intensive technology need not be inefficient. It is a striking fact that for projects of the same scale and type, costs on WPA projects, during the great depression in the U.S., were only 13 percent higher on the average than costs of PWA projects, although the former were done on "force account" (direct government hire), with legal restrictions on the amount of equipment and materials that could be used per worker, while the latter were done on contract by private construction firms, using standard *American* technology. If appropriate accounting wages were used, there can be no doubt that the WPA projects were much cheaper—therefore much more efficient. Also, because of the unique degree of durability of housing, public buildings, and the like, there is much more flexibility with respect to timing than with most projects; construction can be delayed or accelerated without anything like the hardship entailed in delaying and then accelerating the production of foodstuffs or textiles, for example. With proper planning public works can be quickly started and quite rapidly tapered off without waste of resources. WPA had 600,000 men at work three weeks after the legislation was passed and something like three million by the end of the year. It should be noted, however, that for a government committed to use of appropriate accounting prices throughout the entire economic system, "public works" lose much of their special appeal. The fact that public works need not be profitable in order to be socially advantageous would then cease to be a special characteristic of public works, and would apply to any and every activity. Undertaking public works instead of subsidizing private investment would have to be justified terms of their value to the community.

Expanding the Educational System

If a country runs out of socially profitable projects with some people still unemployed, there are still things that can be done. One of these is to expand the educational system. In many countries there is a combination of school-age children not in school, unemployed primary and secondary school graduates, and some unemployed university graduates as well. If truly there is no way of employing these human resources without reducing output below OW, why not combine them in various patterns to form educational units? In countries where close to half the population is of school age and educated unemployed are present, there is no obvious reason why half the population should not be in the education system, either teaching or being taught. *A priori* there is no reason why putting people into the educational system as teachers or students should be regarded as "disguised unemployment." If no scarce resources are used, such a programme is worth while if there is any gain in output whatsoever. The gain could take any of three forms: (1) Increased productivity of those trained, at some time in the future; (2) Increased satisfaction, as a consequence of broadened horizons through education, and the like; (3) Increased satisfaction, through teaching or being taught, rather than being idle. There can be little doubt that there would be a "pay off" in one or another of these forms, and probably in all three.

Would scarce resources be necessary? My guess is that they would be negligible. Most communities have some structure that could be used for a school at odd times. Books and materials might provide something of a problem, but some of these (second hand) might be provided through charitable organizations, or by longer runs of textbooks through the government printing office, and the like. The real costs are unlikely to be high.

Shared "Frugal Comfort"

Finally, if all attempts to absorb unemployment without reducing GNP are exhausted and unemployment still exists, there is still no reason for unemployment. With GNP maximized while aiming at full employment, in the fashion described above, income can be shared by sharing employment and leisure, so that no one is poor because he is unemployed. The system of sharing income by sharing work is well-known in traditional village societies. In some of these the result is "shared poverty," to use anthropologist Clifford Geertz's expression. But if every effort is made to use *scarce* resources in such a way as to maximize *their* productivity, most countries might hope for something better than that—let us say "shared frugal comfort," after the expression, coined by Chief Justice Higgins, to describe the standard of basic wages appropriate for Australia in 1904. Of course, a system of "shared frugal comfort" does require redistribution of income from the presently employed to the presently unemployed—which is why there is so much resistance to such programs.

A Generalized Tax and Subsidy Scheme

But is it worth the effort to engage in such a system of shadow pricing? It would be an enormous task to do so across the board; and, as the socialist countries have found to their dismay, getting prices right may not be the be all and end all of economic development, but getting prices wrong may well be the end all. In most ICCs the abuse of monopoly power is probably not all that serious as to warrant the use of shadow prices throughout the entire economy, considering the risks attached. The same questions arise here as with the use of direct controls; if the use of monetary policy, plus macro- and meso-fiscal policy, can produce unemployment of 4 percent (say), would we not be better off to stick to that, with a "cushion" of unemployment insurance and a provision for school drop-outs after six months of unemployment (such as a subsidized "back to school" program)? If any society consciously and deliberately chooses to have minor imperfections in its economy as the price of getting government off its back, why should it not do so? Of course, average unemployment of 4 percent may mean that some regions have twenty percent or more unemployment; but a sensible "meso-fiscal policy" should take care of such regions.

However, conceptually, unemployment can be cured by a generalized tax and subsidy scheme, so broadly applied as to come under the heading of macroeconomics. Providing entrepreneurs are maximizing profits, if governments choose for each firm a "full employment output," and pay a subsidy equal to (marginal costs minus marginal revenue) at that level of output, entrepreneurs will produce that output. A tax may then be imposed on all super-normal profits, which cannot be shifted. Prices would also be lowered by this device.

It can be very simply demonstrated that a subsidy per unit of output equal to marginal cost minus marginal revenue for *any* chosen output $\bar{x}$, will lead to the production of $\bar{x}$, if the entrepreneur maximizes profits and if the demand and cost curves are not altered by the subsidy. Let us denote output by x, total revenue by $R(x)$ and total cost by $C(x)$ and the subsidy per unit as S, which is not a function of x. Then in equilibrium before payment of the subsidy.

$$R'(x) = C'(x).$$

Let us now pay a subsidy $S = C'(\bar{x}) - R'(\bar{x})$. Marginal revenue with the subsidy is then simply,

$$R'(x)_g = R'(x) + C'(\bar{x}) - R'(\bar{x}).$$

Thus if $x = \bar{x}$, $R'(x)_g = C'(x)$. That is, when the subsidy is paid, equilibrium is established with output equal to $\bar{x}$. By the same reasoning, a subsidy per man-hour equal to marginal wages bill minus marginal productivity of labor for any desired level of employment will induce a monopsonistic employer to utilize man-hours, and so forth, and a tax on profits cannot be shifted.

A diagrammatic illustration of the device is given in figure 15.2. For this purpose, demand is $D_2 D_2$ and average cost is *(AC - R)*, marginal revenue is MR_2, and marginal cost is *(MC - R)*. If we define x as the perfectly competitive output (x_2 in figure 15.2) the subsidy per unit will be equal to BC_2 or S. Adding this amount to D_2 we get the curve $D_2 + S$. The curve which is marginal to this one, $MR_2 + S$, will cut *(MC - R)* in C_2, so that equilibrium is established with an output equal to x_2. The geometric proof that $MR_2 + S$ will cut $MC - R$ in C_2 is simple enough, but too cumbersome to be presented here.

An instrument for allocation so powerful on the analytical level deserves examination, despite administrative difficulties which seem more complex than is usual even in the realm of new fiscal policies. The purely

FIGURE 15.2

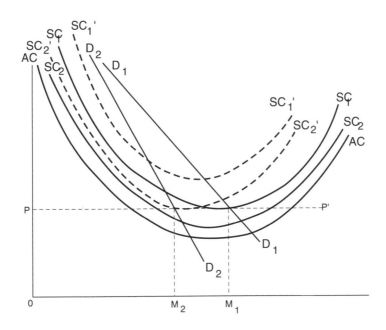

statistical problem of estimating the shapes of cost and demand curves is not an insuperable one. It is a problem met implicitly by any business firm, and by any government agency concerned with allocation, no matter what technique is used. Nothing is gained by using other devices that simply fail to make the problem explicit. Given a reasonably stable economy, the general character of the curves could eventually be determined. By a series of trial-and-error approximations, something approaching the right size of subsidy and tax could be estimated. To begin with, both tax and bounty could be set considerably lower than is estimated to be correct. Any move in the right direction would be a net gain, and it would be better to fall short of perfection than to drive a firm out of business altogether.

Where monopoly is based solely upon differentiation through incurrence of selling costs, one is tempted to suggest a high tax on selling costs. However, the effect of such a tax in itself is to reduce sales as well as selling costs, so that excess capacity is increased rather than diminished. Only if the reduction of selling costs removes the differentiation in the minds of the consumers among rival products, and so flattens the demand curves facing each firm in the "industry", will there be any net gain. To assure this result, it might be well to use the revenues from the tax for the support of a government consumers' research organization which would distribute factual material as to the true nature of various commodities on the market.

If differentiation has a technical basis, so that complete knowledge of the nature of rival products would still leave some consumers with a preference for one product over the others, the definition of one product as "standard," and imposition of taxes on products deviating from the "standard," will not necessarily raise the level of satisfaction. If the tax is made prohibitive for the production of deviations from the "standard," the demand curves for the firms producing a given type of product (say, cigarettes) will indeed flatten and the equilibrium position will come closer to meeting the criteria of a purely competitive equilibrium. On the other hand, the loss of the "preferred" variant of the product will result in a reduction of consumer satisfaction. It is impossible to say which factor will weigh heaviest in any particular case, but the argument for such a tax policy would be strongest where the technical differentiation seems slight and the degree of excess capacity seems large.

With some loss of precision, the administrative problem can be greatly reduced by a "tax on profits in excess of a fair return on utilized capacity." The application of this tax is illustrated in figure 15.3. In this diagram TR_1 is total revenue, TC total costs, and TP_1 total profits. The monopoly equilibrium output is OM_1, the perfectly competitive output OC_1. Suppose profits are taxed 100 percent in excess of, say 10 percent on capital value, and that 10 percent of capital value comes to OA. The curve of total profits, or gains, will follow TP_1 to G, go along GG' to G', and then along TP_1 again. Equilibrium is indeterminate between G and G'. Suppose now that tax-free profits are calculated as 5 percent of *utilized* capacity, with "capacity" defined in such a way as to make it vary directly with output. The curve of net gains now becomes OG'', and the equilibrium position is where this curve cuts TP_1.

In order to establish equilibrium as near to the competitive one as possible, the rate of profit, and the rate at which "utilization" increases with output, should be kept as low as they can be and still have entrepreneurs react to them. The tax must be at or near 100 percent to guarantee

FIGURE 15.3

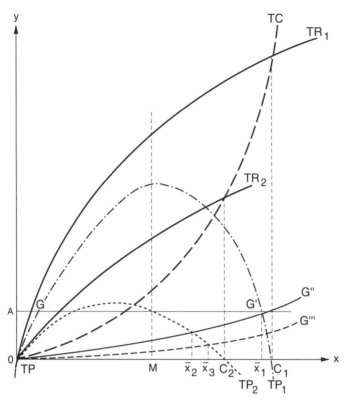

an increase of output with its imposition; otherwise gross profits may fall more rapidly than tax liability as output increases, and no change in output would result from the application of the device.

The attraction of this scheme is its simplicity and its virtually foolproof character. It is unnecessary to know the exact shapes and positions of the cost and revenue curves, or even to have an accurate definition of capacity. It works equally well for monopsony and for monopoly, and for mixed cases. It is only necessary that profits after payment of taxes should rise continuously with output.

Provided the rate at which net profits rise with output is enough to make the entrepreneur aware of it, a movement in the right direction is inevitable. If, therefore, the tax does not result in any increase in output, it is only necessary to raise slightly the rate of profit that is made tax free. It is unlikely that output will be contracted below the previous monopoly level, but if output does shrink it can be stopped in the same manner, by raising the profit rate. The worst that can happen is that the rate is left unnecessarily high, and output accordingly falls short of the competitive level to an unnecessary extent.

This device does not give as perfect results as would precise application of the tax and bounty scheme outlined above; but it will usually result in an output very close to the competitive one, and it is no more complicated from an administrative point of view than excess profit taxes. An advantage of the proposed system over the usual excess profit tax is that since "utilization" is defined in terms of output, there is an incentive not only to utilize existing plant and equipment more fully but to operate the part that is utilized as efficiently as possible. To avoid discouraging new enterprise in risky fields, *bona fide* new firms might be exempt from excess profits taxes for a year or so after production starts, and some allowance for risk might be made for all firms by using a ten-year moving average of profits for tax purposes.

16

Conclusions and Summary

We are now approaching the end of this book. As promised in chapter 1, it has been a long and somewhat tortuous journey, during which we have already arrived at a number of conclusions on particular issues. In this final chapter we want to gather together and restate the most important of the general conclusions reached. We also wish to present a summary, in reverse order, from chapter 15 to chapter 1. In this fashion we hope that we can see where we have arrived and how we got there. The reason of inclusion of each chapter, where it is, may thus appear more clearly. Let us begin with the general conclusions.

General Conclusions

It can be said that unemployment always results from too many people chasing too few jobs, and inflation always is caused by too much money chasing too few goods and services. Beyond such banal generalizations, we have found no single cause for either unemployment or inflation, and thus we can prescribe no single or simple cure for either, let alone for both at once. Of course, unemployment as such can always be cured by a sufficient volume of public spending to create jobs; and inflation can always be cured if the supply of money is cut back enough, at least until stocks of goods disappear. But the first scenario may entail a degree of inflation that no responsible government would wish to face; and if private investment is relied upon at all to provide employment, government spending may not work anyhow, because the resulting inflation may scare off so much private investment that employment falls instead of rising. The second scenario may cause so much unemployment, and so many bankruptcies, as to ruin the economy beyond repair.

The objective of any responsible government must be to reduce unemployment and inflation together, and to keep both within tolerable limits, say four percent for each. To achieve that aim there is no standard remedy, let alone one that can be applied in a once-over fashion, like a course of antibiotics, with the expectation that the malady will then go away. Nor is it to be expected that the appropriate cure, or combination of cures, will prove to be precisely the same in all countries at all times. A national economy is at least as complex and as frail as the human body, and a host of different maladies bring on the same symptoms—fever, palpitations, nausea, high blood pressure, lethargy, and loss of energy. To expect the same remedy for unemployment and inflation to work always and everywhere is like prescribing bloodletting for all ills.

An optimal blend of monetary and fiscal policy that will produce the "minimum discomfort" is a good start. Under exceptional circumstances it may even bring both unemployment and inflation within tolerable limits. But there is no set of forces that will bring any economy automatically to "equilibrium," with stable prices and full employment. There is no assurance that the "minimum discomfort" attainable by an optimal blend of monetary and fiscal policy alone will be tolerable. If a government wants to do better than that, and push the TOC or the loop southwest towards the origin, there are in general three kinds of policy it can pursue:

1. It can stimulate a high rate of long-run growth. We have seen that a high underlying growth rate serves to dampen shorter-run fluctuations, prolonging booms and shortening recessions or depressions. The contribution of the Machine to both unemployment and inflation is thereby reduced. The means of encouraging more rapid growth are well-known: reward innovations; provide incentives for research and development, and for exploration and search for new resources; maintain the highest possible level of scientific, technical, professional, and managerial activity by lavish funding of universities and research institutions; provide excellent technical and vocational training at secondary level; in short, the means used by the United States to catch up with the USSR in space, after the shock of the first Sputnik.

2. It can isolate sectors and regions that are generators of inflation, and others that are pools of unemployment, and pursue differential fiscal policies for each, slowing down the first and speeding up the second. The less integrated the economy by sector or region, the more uncomfortable the trade-off curve is likely to be, but the greater will be the opportunity for pursuing such differential policies.

3. It can establish a system of direct controls similar to those that were so successful during World War II. While the controls would not need to be so extensive as those of World War II, there is nonetheless in many countries a reluctance to reinstall them in peacetime. In some countries, too, despite the prevalence of policies to aid disadvantaged regions or industries, there is a strong feeling that *in principle,* governments should not intervene to discriminate among regions or social groups. If both direct controls and discriminatory fiscal policies are politically impossible, a fourth alternative is to put up with high unemployment and inflation, and offset them by unemployment insurance and indexing. An affluent society can afford to maintain certain groups in idleness, both financially and economically. The social costs, however, can be onerous in the extreme. Prolonged unemployment of experienced people brings loss of skills, motivation, and ambition, which may never be regained. Among younger people, especially those who have never been integrated into the work force, the skills and the motivation to use them may never be acquired. Some of the ablest and best-trained young people can become alienated from society, a sub-culture, permanent drop-outs, not just from the labor force, but from the society. Such a system also causes resentment among those who must work to support those who don't; unemployment insurance results in maldistribution of both income and leisure.

Similarly, if indexing is not to lead to hyperinflation so astronomic that it destroys the currency and results in economic chaos, as in Germany after World War I, every increase in incomes of one social group that exceeds the increase in the value of marginal product of that group must be offset by limiting the increase in incomes of other groups to amounts that are less than the increase in value of marginal product of those groups. In some cases that would mean an absolute decline in real incomes of some groups. Such a system could bring intolerable tensions. It is at best a difficult and dangerous game to play. It is very hard for the authorities in any country to judge at what point inflation will become cumulative and run completely out of control.

In the previous chapter we reached the conclusion that any country that really wants full employment without inflation can have it. "Full employment" in this context means frictional and structural unemployment of 2 to 4 percent. "Without inflation" means less than 4 percent increase in prices per year. What does "really want" mean? That is a more difficult and more subtle concept. But in general, it means that a democratic society exists in the country, and one in which the electorate understands in a general sort of way that measures must be taken to achieve full employment without inflation; and is prepared to vote for a government that will enforce these measures. In this sense, it could be said that the societies of the allied nations "really wanted" to win World War II. They understood that winning the war would require effective allocation of all available resources, including labor; that it would also require a great deal of money; and they "really wanted" to finance the war effort without inflation.

Here we are confronted with a different kind of "trade-off curve." The electorates of the OECD countries, say, "want" full employment without inflation; but they also "want" less government intervention in the economy, smaller bureaucracies, less government spending, and lower taxes. Whether the majority of the electorate in any of these countries "really wants" full employment without inflation, in the sense of being willing to accept all the measures that might be necessary to achieve this objective, is doubtful. Probably a majority of the electorates would gladly accept a rate of inflation or unemployment above four percent if that meant getting the government "off their backs."

The nature of this trade-off is illustrated by figure 16.1. We measure rates of inflation and unemployment, in percent, on the vertical axis, and some index of "amount of government intervention" on the horizontal axis. We assume that in the country concerned inflation can be reduced to 4 percent, or 2 percent, with less government intervention than would be needed to bring unemployment down to the same level. We also assume that the electorate prefers any percentage of unemployment to the same percentage of inflation, and draw the community indifference curves accordingly. The optimal points are 10 percent unemployment achieved with g_u of intervention, and 4 percent inflation achieved with g_i of intervention. This is the kind of juggling act in which governments have been engaged during the past few decades, balancing the amounts and kinds of intervention they *believe* are necessary to achieve various combinations of unemployment and inflation, and the preferences of the electorate regarding various levels of government intervention, unemployment, and inflation. Unfortunately, many governments have misjudged the extent of intervention required to give the electorate what it wants, or the preferences of the electorate, or both; and have been thrown out of office as a result.

FIGURE 16.1
Trade-off of Unemployment, Inflation, and Government Intervention

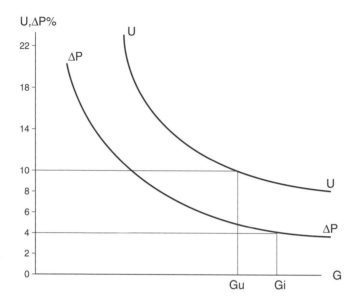

At this point, the economic scientist exits stage right and the moral philosopher enters stage left. The people of a democratic society have every right to maintain that they prefer, say, 10 percent unemployment and 4 percent inflation to the amount and kinds of government intervention that would be required to bring both figures down to 2 percent; but they have no *moral* right to say that, *unless* they are willing to see to it that the unemployed are provided with a subsistence income, and that the low-income groups are protected against inflation. Something like the Australian or Canadian system of unemployment insurance would be necessary to make certain that unemployment did not bring undue hardship; and something like the Brazilian system of indexing to make sure that the low-income groups did not suffer unduly from inflation. For example, wages could be increased every six months, not only to offset the rise in cost of living during the past six months, but the *expected* rise during the *next* six months; rents are adjusted monthly for the rise in prices or are quoted in American dollars; and so on. (When the author was economic advisor to the Brazilian government, at a time when inflation was running at 120 percent per year, the biggest obstacle to the government's efforts to bring the rate of inflation down was the indifference of most of the population to it.)

How did we arrive at the conclusion that full employment without inflation (as defined above) is a feasible objective? Chapter 14 provides a review of various types of policy, in terms of their effectiveness in combatting unemployment and inflation. Monetary policy, we maintained, is ineffective as a device for fighting the two evils simultaneously, and its results are uncertain; but a sound monetary policy is the foundation on which all other policies rest. It should be used to push the TOC—or loop—as far toward the origin as possible. Fiscal policy, when added to monetary policy, greatly increases the control of the authorities over the economy. It does not, however, guarantee reductions in both unemployment and inflation in all phases of the cycle. For that objective, fiscal policy that differentiates among regions, and perhaps among sectors, is necessary. Implementing a selective fiscal policy effectively and successfully requires a great deal of intimate knowledge of how the economy functions, not just nationally, but at the regional and sectoral levels as well—even at the community and industrial level. There is today a widespread reaction against wage controls and regulation of the market; but there is no guarantee that *de*regulation will bring significant reductions in unemployment, nor that it will curtail inflation. It depends on the distribution of power among various employers and employers' associations, trade unions, and other groups. Whenever possible, it is better to move jobs to people than people to jobs; it is less costly in terms of social infrastructure and in terms of social disruption.

It is nearly always possible to put people to work, in the public or the private sector, in a manner that will bring a net gain to society. That is, the value of marginal product of unemployed people provided with jobs will nearly always exceed the wage or salary paid plus the unemployment benefits the persons would otherwise receive. As a last resort, unemployed persons with professional, technical, or artistic training can be combined with selected unemployed young people (recent school or university drop-outs) in especially designed training courses.

Chapter 13 paves the way for the discussion of policies by pointing out that the theories presented in part IV of the book lead to a totally different approach to policy from that suggested by the theories discussed in part II. The latter theories, based on one or another concept of *the* cause of economic fluctuations, sought uniform policy, to be applied throughout the land by all levels of government. The new theories take advantage of regional differences in economic behavior, and recommend deliberate differentiation of fiscal policy, according to the situation regarding unemployment and inflation, trade-off curves and loops, in each region. In other words, not only the *timing* of government spending must be planned according to the phase of the business cycle, but the *placing* must be planned too.

Throughout the whole period from the beginning of the 1960s to the beginning of the 1990s, the governments of the OECD countries behaved as though the major choice was *between* unemployment and inflation. Given the prevalent monetarism of the time, most governments chose to have a high level of unemployment rather than sacrifice the target of combatting inflation. Some of them honestly believed that in fighting inflation they were fighting unemployment too. The whole analysis of part IV shows that the behavior of the ICC economies are not nearly so simple as that. Under some circumstances, as when the economy is in phase one of a cyclical loop, it may indeed be true that by curbing inflation we will at the same time be reducing unemployment. At other times, as in phase two and four of the cyclical loop, fighting inflation will probably increase unemployment.

Part IV offered some explanations, theories, and hypotheses to fit the observed facts concerning unemployment and inflation since 1950. They are admittedly imperfect and incomplete. The brief period of "Keynesian certainty" (roughly from about 1940 to about 1960) had already passed by. But the theory presented in chapter 12 is plausible, and suggestive. It does at least take account of what really happened in the world in recent decades. As explained in that chapter, the main source of uncertainty about economic events is the Game, played by big business, big labor, big government, and foreigners, with interactions in every direction, and with expectations of each actor regarding the intentions and responses of the others playing a major role in the outcome. Chapter 11 is more speculative. It attempts to relate the observations of events in recent decades to the earlier business cycle theories discussed in part II, and to present theories and hypotheses that *could* explain observed events—if they are right.

We begin chapter 11 with a model that includes a trade-off curve along which movements of unemployment and inflation take place, and postulate a Schumpeterian two-phase cycle; we then modify the assumptions to allow a four-phase cycle. We have thus incorporated the TOC into prewar business cycle theory. The model describes cycles of the nineteenth- and early twentieth-century variety; but it does not incorporate or explain either *shifting* TOCs or cyclical loops, and is therefore quite inadequate for analyzing postwar experience. So in our desperate effort to find a model that fits postwar reality, we introduce the concept of a stable loop, which results from repeated shifts in TOCs, with some periods when unemployment and inflation move up together, some when they move down together, and some when they move in opposite directions. Even this model, however, implies more stability and regularity than postwar movements of unemployment and inflation actually display.

So we are forced to the conclusion that in so far as the pattern of postwar economic fluctuations takes the form of loops, formed by shifting TOCs, the *loops* must shift through time as well. Having gone that far in the direction of an equivalent in economics of Heisenberg's uncertainty principle in physics, we devote the balance of the chapter to pure speculation about possible patterns: cobwebs, hysteresis, sawtooth movements, trade-off zones, and various kinds of shifting loops. The movements in different countries will be only as uniform as behavior of major groups (trade unions, employers, consumers, investors), expectations of all these, innovations, resource discoveries, and above all government policies, and interactions among all these variables, are uniform.

Part III presented a series of facts concerning unemployment and inflation since 1950. Chapter 10 dealt with the disturbing new phenomenon of long-term unemployment, a phenomenon that affects most countries, but is particularly serious in the more advanced economies, such as members of the OECD. Chapters 6 through 9 dealt with the cases of Canada, Australia, and the United States, pointing out similarities and differences among them.

The United States has the biggest economy in the world, in terms of gross national product, and chapter 8, dealing with postwar fluctuations in the United States, is the longest in the book. We thought it wise to begin our discussions of economic fluctuations, trade-off curves, and cyclical loops with smaller and less complex economies, like Australia and Canada, before tackling the world's dominant economy. It is well that we did, because the behavior of the American economy proves to be even less orderly than the Australian or Canadian ones. True, apart from a brief spurt of inflation just after the war, as controls were lifted and pent-up demand for consumer and capital goods was unleashed, the 1950s and 1960s were decades of fairly steady and quite high growth. During the seventies inflation reappeared, this time accompanied by rising unemployment and falling GNP; the Keynesian system had broken down.

The scatter diagram of "discomfort points" for the United States, like the other national scatter diagrams, appears at first glance to be chaotic. However, when the points are joined by straight lines, in sequence, something like a pattern begins to emerge. It is possible to interpret the observations as a series of trade-off curves, moving northeast until 1983, then shifting southwest. It is also possible to interpret them as cyclical loops, although the pattern is less regular than the Canadian one. Much seems to depend on rational expectations concerning government policy, and the movements are increasingly unpredictable.

We then proceeded to an analysis of movements of discomfort points, trade-off curves, and cyclical loops for the various regions of the United States. Somewhat to our surprise, there are striking differences among American regions, in direction of movement, amplitude of fluctuations, timing of peaks and troughs, and indeed the general patterns of movements of unemployment and inflation. The American economy is not as well integrated as the American monetary authorities seem to regard it. In a way this discovery is good news; it means that much can be done to reduce both unemployment and inflation simultaneously by a fiscal policy that differentiates among regions, isolating the regions that are generating inflationary pressure and those where unemployment is concentrated, and designing a tailor-made fiscal policy for each.

In chapters 6 and 7 we play a game of "let's pretend." At the start, we pretend that we have never heard of Phillips curves, trade-off curves, or cyclical loops, and are trying to understand the apparent chaos of the postwar world. We focus attention particularly on unemployment and inflation, and the relationship between them, using two relatively small and simple economies, those of Australia and Canada, as examples. They prove to be big and complex enough to present some puzzles. We begin, naturally enough, by plotting time series for unemployment and inflation. We discover, to our astonishment, that the two series sometimes move in opposite directions, according to prewar rules, but that they sometimes move together, either up or down. We add the time series for Gross Domestic Product to the diagram, to see whether some regularity of movements in GDP to unemployment and inflation would explain the relationship between them. There is some tendency for unemployment and inflation to move up together during recessions, and to move down together during recoveries or booms, which only adds to the mystery; but even this relationship is not perfect.

Next it occurs to us to plot the figures for unemployment and inflation together, year by year. At first glance, the result seems like total chaos. But then we have the bright idea of joining the observations—"discomfort points"—by straight lines, so that we can more easily trace their movements through time. Now something more like a pattern appears for Canada; something closer to the order so dear to the scientist's heart begins to emerge. Clearly in the Canadian case, not so clearly in the Australian case, we could interpret the movements of discomfort points as cyclical loops. Are these the postwar transformation of the Juglar and Kitchin cycles we observed before the war? We could also interpret the movements as shifting trade-off curves. If so, are the cyclical loops formed by shifts in the TOCs?

At the beginning of part III, in chapter 5, because the concepts and tools of analysis will be unfamiliar to some readers, and because other writers have used them in different ways, we set forth some definitions and clarify some concepts as they will be used in this volume. In particular, the concepts of trade-off curves, shifts of these, and cyclical loops are explained in some detail.

Chapters 3 and 4 deal with the transition period in the history of thought concerning economic fluctuations, roughly from 1938 to 1955. This was the period when the first shock of "the Keynesian Revolution" was absorbed, and when interest shifted from business cycles to long waves, trends, secular stagnation, and to interactions among them. During this period there was a substantial increase in the degree of sophistication of both empirical and theoretical analysis, and a closer relationship between the two developed. The idea that "equilibrium" was the natural state of affairs in a "market economy" gradually retreated to the background, leaving the forefront to theories of cumulative causation and "the knife edge," with a tendency for cumulative movements *away* from equilibrium once that equilibrium is disturbed, and a strong likelihood of continual disturbances. We realized that there are many things that can cause an economy to fall off the "knife edge," either in the direction of unemployment or in the direction of inflation. During this period, however, there was little expectation that economies would fall into the abyss of unemployment and the inferno of inflation at the same time. Yet the increased knowledge gained in this transitional period was valuable. It prepared some of us, at least, for the shock that came after 1955: the discovery that we no longer lived in a world of alternating unemployment *or* inflation, but in a more complex world of simultaneously existing unemployment and inflation, with the co-existence capable of taking any form—rising together, falling together, or moving in opposite directions, with different patterns at different times and in different countries. It also made us understand that the prewar business cycle theories, which we tended to regard as *rival* theories, only one of which could be completely right, might in fact all contain some element of truth.

And so in chapter 2 we get back to our roots: the theories of business cycles, trade cycles, or economic fluctuations, produced between the wars. With the benefit of hindsight, we were able to find some truth, and a great deal of insight, in all these theories. Economists were confused at the time, and attributed the confusion to others, because most of us were passionate adherents to some school of thought, and believed that it, and it alone, had *the* explanation of the business cycle, and that all other schools were dangerously wrong. Now we know that each of them was to some degree right; all of these theories are worth studying, for the light they throw on the manner in which market economies function, and the ways in which they can go wrong. Some of the most powerful minds ever to be directed to the problem of unemployment, inflation, and economic fluctuations were active in this period, and there is still much to be learned from their findings and analysis.

In chapter 1, we described the evolution of economic reality, and attempts to explain it, from business cycles with alternating inflation and unemployment, through a transitional period of underemployment equilibrium, secular stagnation, and the "knife edge," to the strange new world of shifting trade-off curves and cyclical loops. Some economists find this new world so unfathomable and so uncomfortable for orthodox theorists that they take refuge in the concepts of "the natural rate of unemployment" or the "non-accelerating inflation rate of unemployment" (NAIRU). The implication is that whatever the rate of unemployment may be it is alright, since it is "natural" or "equilibrium," and all apparent unemployment is really voluntary anyhow, providing that inflation is zero, or at least is not increasing. Such a notion may be comforting to those who believe that a free market can do no wrong; but it is not comforting to a society experiencing double digit inflation with unemployment concentrated among the long-term unemployed and young school drop-outs who have never had a real job, leading to an extraordinarily high rate of youth suicide in countries like Australia, Canada, and the United States. In that chapter we signal one of our major theses: to have tolerable rates of unemployment and inflation we will need a fiscal policy that differentiates among regions in the country, according to the amount of inflation it generates and the extent to which unemployment is concentrated in it.

The chapter raises new questions that demand new treatment and new analyses, which the volume attempts to provide. Now that the book is finished, have we answered all the questions we raised? Not altogether. The simple truth is that we still don't know all there is to know about the Machine, the Structure, and the Game, in different countries, and in any one country at different times. By the same token, we still don't know everything about shifting trade-off curves and cyclical loops, at different times and in different countries. But we never knew all there was to know about business cycles either, when in 1950 they began to change, and in mysterious ways. But this book makes a start. It shows that we are confronted with new patterns of behavior of employment, unemployment, inflation, and gross national product; it describes the new patterns, tries to explain them, and suggests some possible explanations. I trust that it will at least provide food for thought, and thought about the world as it really is, and not about the world as it once was but is no longer, let alone an imaginary world as we would like it to be.

Index